1

MUSICOLOGY 2102:
A QUICK START GUIDE TO DIVERSE SYNERGIES

Editor: Anna R. Holloway, PhD

Library of Congress Cataloging-in-Publication Data
Jackson, L.A.

MUSICOLOGY 2102: A QUICK START GUIDE
TO DIVERSE SYNERGIES

Front Cover Artwork: Ras Leon "Imon" Mack, Jr.
Front Cover Photography: B.K. Jackson
Back Cover Artwork: Wil'Liam Louis Seidel
Photos: Rick Diamond, Ralph Gullatt, Cory L. Jackson
Project Manager: Cory L. Jackson

Editorial consultants: Gwendolyn Leverette, Jean Melilli, Tony Williams
Web & Design consultant: Eugene Morgan for Electronic Staff

To provide financial assistance for kids who lost their fathers—
beginning with Jariana Jackson, Holland and Heidi Pinkerton—
a substantial portion of sales will be donated to charitable organizations
like the R.A.M.S. Association and unique special interest groups.

This book is available at special discounts for bulk purchases,
sales, promotions, premiums, fund raising, or educational use.

Also available on MKM Entertainment, the accompanying music release *Exposer Series, Volume 4*. Features the Official Song of Musicology 2102, Marvin Gaye's classic *What's Goin' On?* by Baba Oje & The K.O.S.T.

Don't forget *Musicology 2101: A Quick Start Guide To Music "Biz" History* and its accompanying music release *Exposer Series, Volume 3*, featuring the Official Song of Musicology 2101, Kimosha LeToi - *Eyes Stuck On Me* plus great new music from out of this world!

MKM Publishing and MKM Entertainment are units of
MKM Multimedia Works
Atlanta, GA

ISBN: 978-0-578-15469-5

TABLE OF CONTENTS

ACKNOWLEDGEMENTS

God bless God, along with all family and friends
who have supported this project from start to finish.

A heartfelt RIP to recently fallen soldiers like my nephew Jarvis Jackson:
we never got to complete that book—but there's still a story to tell…
Nick Pinkerton—in a very short slice of borrowed time,
you became one of my best friends.
Also remembering my father's brother Uncle Roy Dennis,
Grammy-winning producer George Duke,
the proverbial Dr. Maya Angelou,
and my former CBS Records/Sony Music associates
Mike Bernardo, Don Miller, Tim Pritchett & Vernon Slaughter —
you are all sorely missed and won't be forgotten.

BIG THANKS to my lifelong mentor Bernard Percy
who has motivated me to write since the 5th grade in P.S. 289,
Public Relations Agent Lyn K. and Branding Specialist Afrika Jonee
for motivation after the deed was done. Tony Baraka—thanks for
believing in this project's *dream to reality*. Music veterans from way back:
my former CBS Records/Sony Music bosses
Roger Metting and Jimi Starks—looks like we're having fun again!

My friends at the Georgia Music Industry Association and NARIP:
"keeping people industry-educated,"
Peach City Records, Wade Jones, Kimosha LeToi and Onny—
here's to preparation meeting opportunity!
Michael Garret Jr. aka "DJ Mike Gee," Vernon "DJ 12" House and the
entire WRTR crew, I appreciate your support of the *L.A. Jackson Show* at
Raw Truth Radio (www.rawtruthradio.com & .net).

Chuck Taylor, your immaculate expertise with turning
the *L.A. Jackson Show* into video content is well appreciated.
My comrades B.K. Jackson, Ras Leon "Imon" Mack, Jr., Eugene Morgan,
Edsel Robinson and Gerald R. White,
thanks for your last-minute "artistic input" during busy times!

OVERVIEW

The purpose of this book series is to give a better understanding of music, so you can continue to enjoy listening to and playing this unique mode of communication. This goal will be accomplished by cutting down the intimidation you may encounter from attempts to learn something so different, personal and subjective as music. After taking on the Musicology series, I hope that you the reader, will continue your experience of music by reading more books, studying, and playing music as only you can do.

In the Musicology book series, we explore music's early beginnings, modern history, the birth of Rap and Hip-Hop, then break music down into its basic components. At that point, we'll analyze them piece by piece, part by part. Opportunities will be presented to dissect music, scrutinize it, and then reassemble it. By performing this process, you will learn the basic makeup of music composition, and how each part of music functions independently as well as in unison or contrast, with other parts of music.

During your adventure through the Musicology series, we will also take a look at music's effects, relationships, uses, and how people make money with it. You will see familiarities or differences in your own personal experiences and opinions with those of other people in the industry, and if you are not aware of how music is produced - live or in the recording studio, the section on music production should help you understand a little more about the process. Finally, we'll take a trip to the inside of a music city that evolved over time into a major music center. By the conclusion of the Musicology series, not only will you have learned quite a bit more about music, but you'll find that you've also learned more about one of the most important elements of music: YOU - for without you, music cannot exist; or even be understood.

This book series is not intended to cover every aspect of music, but to give a broad understanding about key fundamental topics of relevance on the subject. Additional publications, organizations and websites are listed at the end of each book for your convenience. During the data mining process, certain websites were accessed to gather historic facts, and information about the Spotlight Artists highlighted in this book. Scattered throughout are bits and pieces of data that's been gathered from sources such as libraries, bookstores, and search tools like www.wikipedia.org.

According to the site, "Wikipedia is a multilingual, Web-based, free-content encyclopedia project based on an openly editable model. The name "Wikipedia" is a portmanteau of the words *wiki* (a technology for creating collaborative websites, from the Hawaiian word *wiki*, meaning "quick") and *encyclopedia*. Wikipedia's articles provide links to guide the user to related pages with additional information. Wikipedia is written collaboratively; by largely anonymous Internet volunteers who write without pay. Anyone with Internet access can write and make changes to Wikipedia articles (except in certain cases where editing is restricted to prevent disruption or vandalism)."

In other words, Wikipedia may not be 100% accurate, but it certainly supplied some good information. Subsequently, I 'mixed-n-meshed' the results of this research with a colorful perspective to paint textual pictures of the topics discussed. To be clear cut, the focus of this book series is to unify explanations between historic subject matter, our Spotlight Artists and my professional experience in the music industry; as a bonus I threw in a few personal observations—this was done with the intent to weave all of the pieced data into a story about mankind's longtime relationship with music. Hopefully, you'll remember that this book is ultimately the result of contributions from many people, from just as many different places around the globe.

Also, please note that no attempt has been made to take credit for what others may have written about specific topics covered in this book, for they have all made valuable contributions to history, literature, technological innovation and my favorite subject matter: music. Without the efforts of dozens of dedicated folks, this book would be significantly different—so on that note, I'd like to acknowledge and thank the many unnamed writers and music lovers who contributed to source content, plus my editorial advisors. The efforts of many talented people helped to comprise the *Musicology* book series' foundation and for that, I offer eternal gratitude. This series is not intended to cover every aspect of music, but to give a broad understanding of key fundamental topics of relevance in the subject. Additional publications, organizations and websites will be listed at the end of each book for your convenience.

Who should read the Musicology series

Anyone—young or old with lots of, little, or no formal knowledge of music; teachers—as a guideline to introduce music to students; budding musicians, up-and-coming composers, producers or sound engineers who would like get a better fundamental understanding of music; music instructors seeking simple, alternate solutions to music education challenges with students; self-motivated beginning music students; people who previously had a hard time understanding music history or theory; people who would like to use music for specific tasks or objectives, artistic/creative people, non-artistic/non-creative people, shy people, cool people, nerds—ANYBODY that yearns to learn more about music! If you think you don't know a thing about music but would like to know a little more than you know right now, then this book is for you. Even if you think you know a lot about music—there is still something just for you hidden within these pages—hopefully, you'll find it!

How you should use Musicology

-as a resourceful guide you can reference back to
as you study music by playing or listening to it
- to identify and explore specific, basic elements of music
- to learn how to listen more closely to music form
- to identify specific music styles and traits
- to understand basic composition and music structure
- to learn and understand basic musical terms and usage
- as a tool to break down misconceptions about the complexity of music
- to gain insight into how you as an individual are connected to music
- to identify what about music that you - the reader, want or need to get a
   clearer understanding of (in music)
- to find something new and/or important to you
- to make goals of where you can go in your life after reading this book
- as a directory to find additional sources of information

How you will benefit from reading the Musicology series

You will:
- develop well-rounded music theory concepts
- develop the ability to improve your musical memory
- learn how to identify different types and styles of music
- find new thoughts and ideas to explore about music's vast history
- learn more about how you can get a career in the music industry
- have a quality source of information to go back to again and again
- understand how to analyze, compose, orchestrate, arrange, produce
- find new uses for time measurement, learn how to count bars/measures
- become musically confident, see/hear things you otherwise may not have
- gain understanding of creative processes, composing, recording of songs
- better understand, increase appreciation for this mode of communication
- increase knowledge and practical experience as an arranger, composer, programmer, DJ, engineer, musician, producer or technical professional
- better understand and identify *what* in your favorite tunes 'moves' you: it could be different parts of songs, rhythms, sounds, arrangements, etc.
- become a better, more intelligent listener - not only to music, but in essence, also to yourself and the world of sound around you
- better communicate with composers, musicians, arrangers, singers, and maybe even that cranky neighbor next door

Please note - some things may be repeated – there's a good reason why: Repetition is important in many aspects of not only music, but in life.

As you are reading serious information in-between my inserted dry wit, remember: this book was not written by some grim, stone-cold career intellectual trying to be funny, but moreso by a mild-mannered music lover with a unique sense of humor. Coming from 'around the way,' this music lover is simply trying to make a feeble attempt at being serious about something he's extremely passionate about. So at this time, please activate your antennas and order up a round of chuckles – there are certain sections that will require one or both, and hopefully everything's adjustable. Where possible, 'definitive definitions' will be provided along with professional and personal interjectional interpretations that hopefully will clarify the topic of discussion. In the rare occasion that you still have doubts, keep on reading – a friend once said, "even if you don't know where the ball is, just keep it moving!"

FOREWORD

Since the beginning of time, *change* has been inevitable. Empires have risen and fallen.... tectonic plates have shifted.... dinosaurs have become extinct.....

Why should the music industry be excluded from the chaos?

It's all very simple; in the music industry, if you don't change your tune, after a while you will inevitably find that no one is listening. In the not-so-distant past, hit records were bought and paid for by industry insiders. A record label would put out a CD by one of their artists – choosing a release date that would not conflict with the release of other major label acts. It was important to make sure that when you were in the process of "buying the charts" you didn't go head-to-head against a competing release on another label that could potentially afford to out-buy you.

You released a record or CD and then went down to the local record store where you and a couple of sales clerks spent Monday through Friday running record sales through Soundscan. The magic number was around $1.5 million in sales... and when the *Billboard* charts were next published, it would be no surprise to see your artist debuting at #1. On Sunday you went to church and prayed to God that your artist was good enough to sustain a *Billboard* ranking without the need of additional self-inflicted purchases. It was a quite effective strategy. The payola crackdown to radio stations had made it too difficult to continue buying off radio DJ's and program directors. So this was the logical progression for change.

Once you hit #1 on *Billboard* everyone wanted to buy your artists' record in order to find out what all the excitement was about. So you would simply take those $1.5 million of CD's and have them resold at a discount by the same backroom sales clerks who helped you initially run the Soundscam..... oooops, excuse me.... I meant Sound*Scan*, of course. In a good week at #1 on the charts, you could recoup about $1 million of your initial expenditure, and if your artist had any potential in the first place, you'd be able to make up the other $500,000 from new legitimate sales.

Change can sometimes be a very beautiful thing. As a result of the payola scandal, radio stations started becoming *automated*. They simply configured their playlists with the *Billboard* charts, believing that this is what the public wanted to hear. It became sadly laughable to see an independent artist walk into a radio station hoping that a station might play his/her brilliantly-produced record, only to be told by the program director that it was "not the radio station's job to break new records." Little did they know that they were breaking new records by rich record labels every single day. How many times have you heard a weak-sounding song on the radio and said to yourself: "How on earth is that song getting played...." I rest my case.

With Clear Channel and Cumulus Media owning a majority of the major radio stations throughout America.... and with most of those radio stations now being automated, hitting #1 on *Billboard* was all it took to have your artists' song getting played in the top rotation..... and nobody went to jail.

The record industry had become one the most powerful business empires on earth.

.... and then came the Mp3. Uh oh.....

The Mp3 was like a shift in the tectonic plates.... and the record industry was sitting on the fault line. There was a lot of public talk about the fact that you could not collect a royalty on an Mp3 (which of course is not true). The reality of the situation, however, was that the big record labels could no longer buy the charts in a cost-effective manner because once you purchased an Mp3 and ran up the Soundscan, you had nothing left to resell. If you paid the $1.5 million to chart at number 1 (which you had to do in order to get the radio airplay) then you would have to actually sell around 3 million units in order to recover your "promotional" costs. Suddenly artists were going platinum or double platinum and ending up broke.... and record labels were dropping artists and laying off their staffs at a *record* pace..... and at the same time file-sharing made it harder and harder to achieve platinum status at all.

In order to make ends meet, the record industry started imposing "360" deals upon their artists – taking away a percentage of their merchandising rights. Consequently, as the world continued to spin, the Indie market was necessarily born out of the rebellion. Finally, as the record industry lost its grip on the "distribution" of music, life as it once was in the music industry, suddenly imploded. Today, it's a much more level playing field out there. Anyone can become a star if they just apply a bit of ingenuity. I did it at Ruffhouse Records through street promotion optimization of acts like Kris Kross, Cypress Hill, The Fugees and Lauryn Hill—these are also acts that L.A. Jackson marketed while he worked at Sony Music.

Thank God for writers like L.A. Jackson. He's been there and done that… and he knows what's up. Through the MUSICOLOGY series, he's here to steer talented and deserving songwriters and performers in a positive direction. Will L.A. save the music industry next? Who knows, but I do know that he sheds great light on a topic he knows well. My guess is that your superior intellect may significantly go up after reading this book… and always remember: "Stay thirsty my friends—good music is alive and well." On behalf of myself and my new music group Anything But Monday's hit Dance song *99 Bottles of Beer*, "Drink—Don't Drive!"

Musically yours,

Stephen Stone

Branding/Marketing Wizard - Ruffhouse Records, The Fantanas, Anything But Monday, Mirosa Beer

MORE SPICES IN THE MIX

"He who unites the cultures speaks with wisdom and wins in the human race."

Another one of my Ancient Proverbs

For all returning music history adventurers, *Welcome Back* and to our new passengers, I hope you enjoy this part of our grand voyage. Some of you may remember that we wrapped up the previous book (*Musicology 2101*), after visiting Caribbean islands like Cuba and Puerto Rico. That mission has led us into this leg of our operation, codename *Musicology 2102*. Since everyone appears to be seated comfortably in the first-class cabin of our spacious and luxurious time machine, let's rev-up our minds for an in-depth look at more 'cultureful' music zones. We'll start this "Latin-Spanic" flavored portion of our trip into music *biz*tory by shifting our *mental vector alignment* (thought pattern frequency) to the land of Mexico—so here's a hearty *viva, viva, andale!* In English that means *come on, let's go!*

The Music of Mexico

Mexican music is a diverse genre originating from home-grown Indigenous and European styles. Popular songs include *La Bamba*; it became a major part of Mexican culture and was used countless times in scores of movies. In reality, there are many Mexican songs that have been popularized around the globe. Here's some background information to get you familiarized with Mexican music for further investigation, should you choose to accept the mission.

Mexico's music popularity in Latin America goes back for generations. In fact, the Mexican music market was known for catapulting lesser-known artists straight into the arms of America's Spanish *and* non-

Spanish speaking public. Artists like Selena, Julio Iglesias, Thalia, Paulina Rubio, Ricky Martin and Shakira all found fame and fortune by crossing over into the U.S. market through a well-developed Mexican fan base. Noticeable examples can be seen through the growing presence of Latin American artists on international music charts. According to *America Top 100*, Mexican acts had over 90 charted hits in Latin America during 2006, almost a third more than the U.S. did for the same period.

INFLUENCES

Let's connect a few dots: Mexico is close in proximity to the West Indies, so it easily could have been affected by Caribbean music. Some of Mexico's musical elements came from styles produced by South America's indigenous people, and many indigenous styles actually gained momentum by creating their own adaptations of Caribbean music. In turn, a few South American and Caribbean music styles include adaptations that came from influential rhythm creators across the waters—musicians of African heritage. Let's keep it moving.

On Mexico's East Coast, styles like *Son Jarocho* and *Son Huasteco* were largely influenced by Cuba's *Son Cubano*. Additionally, *Bolero*, *Chachacha*, *Danzon* and *Mambo* were popularized in Mexico, particularly in Mexico City and Veracruz. Many of our Mexican neighbors are descendants of indigenous Indians that mixed with Spanish settlers. The Aztecs were known for utilizing an assortment of handmade instruments, plus other Meso-American tribes like the Maya, Tarahumara, Tepehuanes and Yaqui also contributed to Mexico's music and dance styles. For more on the Mexican experience, please explore *Mesoamerica*; it's loaded with rich traditions of ancient Mexican art forms.

Mexican musicians use various instruments including percussive, string and wind devices similar to those used in popular American music. To add, a wide range of traditional Mexican instruments are still in use. Let's breeze through some of them:

- *Percussive* instruments include the ayotl, bubalek, regular and water gourds, huehuetl, maracas, musical bow, tenabaris and teponaxtle (also spelled teponaztle)

- *String* instruments include harps and guitars like the cuatro, guitarrón, huapanguera, jarana and vihuela. Other guitars include the fifth, sixth, and spike bass. The string family also includes the piano, psaltery, tawitols (triangular or hunting arch) and violin
- The *Wind* family of instruments feature the chichtli and singular or multi-chambered flutes made of bamboo, clay, or wood. Other wind instruments include the saxophone, tlapitzalli, trumpet and whistle
- Another popular instrument found in Mexican music is the accordian; it's often featured in styles like *Banda* and *Norteno*

Every instrument obviously can't be listed due to the technical aspects of space, so try to allocate some time down the line and compile more info on the vast amount of tools used for creating Mexican music.

MUSIC & DANCE

Many Mexican dances were altered by Spaniards who exerted much of their customs onto Mexican traditions. Among the many folk dances, two are the *Danza del Venado* (Dance of the Deer) and *Jarabe Tapato* (Mexican Hat Dance). Danza del Venado is symbolic of hunters and the hunted, while the *Jarabe Tapato* is performed by couples who express the story of love, as they dance. These dance styles and many more contributed greatly to Mexico's past and present culture. With advancements in technology and a global presence in the evolution of music, there's no telling what lies ahead for the future of Mexican music—but I see it growing.

Since more Mexican genres were uncovered than expected, a special forces agent will be brought in next; plus there'll be further elaboration on these styles in an upcoming book. Here's a list of some popular ones—you can expect to aquire more information on them soon:

Banda	Electronic music	Pop
Classical	Latin Alternative	Ranchero
Cumbia	Narcocorrido	Rock en Español
Danzon	Norteño	Rumba
Duranguense		Tejano/Tex Mex

SOUTH OF THE BORDER

As an aid in landing on the ground with spinning wheels waiting, I brought in an old friend from Mexico who's a special forces music operative—prepare to meet Carlos Tejeda, codename *Double A*: *Attorney Agent*. To kick things off, Carlos will highlight a popular style he likes called *Grupera*, then he'll give us a quick rundown on 'underworld music from the underground.' After that, we'll keep things moving into another popular style called Mariachi, then we'll turn the SPOTLIGHT ON a special singer whose mission was to bridge the gap between two neighboring countries as a homegrown, Mexican-American singing sensation. On that note, Agent Carlos Tejeda—come on down!

Thanks for having me aboard your international vessel of Superior Intellect, Señor L.A. I'm just wrapping things up at one of my favorite Atlanta-area eateries, where Mexican food is the main dish. I like to conduct secret operations by taste-testing new menu items (or some good old ones) at fast-food hotspots like Chipotles or Moes, and now I hear Taco Bell's serving breakfast… *really*? Plus, there's nothing like the dine-in comfort of my *Top Doce* (Popular 12) pit-stops:

On the Border	Frontera	La Prialla
Los Bravos	Los Reyes	El Taco Veloz
The Original El Taco	Jalisco	Mi Barrio
Uncle Julio's	El Torero	El Azteca

By the way, I know who that special Mexican-American *cantora* (singer) is, and folks you're going to raise some eyebrows on that one! Just to let you know a little bit about me, I come from Mexico City and as L.A. alluded to, one of my favorite music styles is *Grupera*, or to be more exact *Onda Grupera*. This type of Folk music fuses elements of *Cumbia*, *Norteño* and *Ranchero*, all of which L.A. Jackson tells me will be discussed in detail later, when he sheds more light on different aspects of music and gets how you say, "theoretically speaking." I can't let the whole cat out of the bag just yet—but I'd be happy to share some de-classified Mexican music information with you!

Our early Rock bands of the 60s did Spanish-flavored cover versions of hits from the States to attract the attention of local followers. Once a fan base was created, many acts went on to infuse homegrown styles like Cumbia, Norteño, Ranchero and slower tempo ballads into their

16

music. When the 70s rolled around, we had an increase in bands that converted slow ballads and Mariachi songs to the Grupera style; this brought even more listeners to the table… and to the dancefloor. Popular acts representing Grupera include:

Ana Bárbara	Los Humildes
Bronco	Los Muecas
La Migra	Los Temerariors
Limite	Joan Sebastian
Los Babys	Marco Antonio Solís
Los Caminantes	Myriam
Los Freddys	Yonics

As common practice, countries around the world mimic American music with their own adaptations and in Mexico, we are no different. Back in my 80s heydays, Grupera was the rave and everyone back home was listening to it, especially my rural amigos. Similar to American Rock, Grupera musicians converge into small squads with insruments like electric guitars, keyboards and drums. As the 90s came along, even more people began accepting Grupera, and it became more of a commercial asset. In fact, music-oriented shows like the *Latin Grammy Awards* and *Lo Nuestro* created categories that included Grupera.

Now here's my disclaimer: I'm doing a *favor especial* for Agent Superintendant L.A. Jackson but remember—what's coming up is *top secret* information. You're getting it because of my clandestine affiliation with Super Agent Jackson so in other words, *you didn't read this here!* Back home in Mexico, I would say this popular style was a 'music of the people,' but I'm not sure what they would call it if it came from America—maybe *Gangsta Rap*?

NARCOCORRIDO: Underworld Music

Narcocorrido translated to English is what we call a *Drug Ballad*. This type of Mexican music came out of the *Norteño Folk Corrido* pattern of music. It's listened to extensively on both sides of the border and there's an accordian-based Polka rhythm with a danceable foundation; but the lyrical content is what sets this music style apart from others.

Narcocorridos tells the story of working-class, poor, lost or forgotten people who struggle to survive everyday. To open the lens wider, let's call them "the hunted." Right behind them are "the hunters"— they're the ones who benefit from strategic tactics like politics or violence to capture power and control over the people, the land and its resources. The interesting thing about Narcocorridos is that many of our people listen to it, all from different regions of the Spanish-speaking Americas. While listeners represent a variety of ages and social classes, non-cartel/gang members make up a good part of the genre's audience. Our regional field operatives produced highly classified documents that reveal Narcocorrido is quickly becoming the new mainstream music in numerous lands like Bolivia, Colombia, Guatemala, Honduras and Peru.

As one can guess from its name, Narcocorridos makes light of criminal acts, from smuggling… to murder. And government corruption didn't help matters much. All these issues compounded to form political unrest; and protesting people. In case you didn't know, "narco" means "narcotics" and since the 30s, early corridos referenced drug smugglers. Non-narco corridos go back even further, to the Mexican Revolution of 1910. Story lines don't fall short, often keeping the dates and places somewhat factual. Although Narcocorridos are often based on actual events, some artists and composers might glorify controversial figures— many songs tell the stories of revolutionaries, while today's music watchdogs enunciate similarities between Narcocorridos and Gangtsa Rap. Either way, I still say Narcocorridos is the music of the people!

Drilling down a little deeper, we see musicians who contributed to growth of the Narcocorrido, like Los Alegres de Teran and Rosalino "Chalino" Sanchez. This important figure is known across Mexico as "El Pelavacas" or "the Cow Skin Peeler," in English. He also picked up multiple codenames like "El Indio" (The Indian) and "Mi Compa" (My Friend). As an immigrant from Mexico, he lived in Los Angeles and began distributing "mucho music" at an affordable price. Sanchez told stories comprised of love gone bad, revolution, and economics. Despite mass popularity, after a Culiacan concert in 1992, he was suddenly killed. This sent him into the pages of history as a legend—he went on to influence musicians from California to Mexico, and picked up one more name after his death: "El Rey del Corrido"—*King of the Corrido*. Throughout the remainder of the 90s, Narcocorrido songwriters, artists, bands and producers multiplied significantly:

18

Banda Nueva Clave de Oro
Emilio Carrillo
El As de la Sierra
El Compa Chuy
El Gavilancillo
El Halcon de la Sierra
El Komander
El Original de la Sierra
El Potro de Sinaloa
El Tigrillo Palma
Jorge Gamboa
Grupo Cartel
Grupo Exterminador
Grupo Patron
Larry Hernandez
La Nueva Rebellion
Los Alegres del Barranco
Los Amos de Nuevo León
Los Canelos de Durango

Los Cuates de Sinaloa
Los Huracanes del Norte
Los Dareyes de la Sierra
Los Inquietos del Norte
Los Incomparables de Tijuana
Los Morros del Norte
Los Nuevos Rebeldes
Los Originales de San Juan
Los Razos de Reynaldo
Los Titanes de Durango
Los Tucanes de Tijuana
Fuerza Norteña
Revolucion Norteña
Explosion Norteña
Colmillo Norteño
Arley Perez
Beto Quintanilla
Roberto Tapia
Leo Yoni

And here's one you may have to take a deep breath to say—*El Cuquio AKA Frankie Franco de Cuquio Jalisco Mexico*. Some of these musicians remained completely absorbed in the Narcocorrido style, while others were adept at many styles of music. Unfortunately, social disturbances led to companies, citizens and government agencies seeking to ban this genre. In Baja California, there was a voluntary radio station black-out so that, according to Representative Casio Carlos Narvaez, stations would not entice "people who break the laws of our country into heroes and examples." Even Mexican Presidente Vicente Fox was all for a ban on Narcocorridos. Music makes up a major part of the Narco culture and there are plenty anthems that have been banned from Mexican and U.S. airplay. However, pirate stations, streaming, downloading and other tricks like bootleg recordings sold in *tianguis* (outdoor markets) offered ways around "clashing civilities" and government bans.

Within a two-year period between 2006 and 2008, a dozen or more well-known Mexican musicians "met their makers." Many were most likely killed due to their proximity to Narcocorridos; and the Mexican drug war. In a similar manner to American gang bangers, very few arrests have been made after musicians like Valentin Elizalde and Sergio Gomez got killed. Memorially speaking, they were Grammy nominated in 2007 for their contributions to Banda. Sadly, there's a long list of musicians that have been killed over things like money, jealousy, love, romance and of course, who they knew. L.A. Jackson once told me his mother always used a saying when he was a kid: "show me your friends and I'll tell you who you are." *Aye Carumba!* My mother said the same thing, "dime con quien andas y te dire quien eres." In other words, choose your friends wisely, boys and girls.

Whether the media made a mountain out of a molehill is still up for grabs, but I'd say the dozens of lost musical lives speak for themselves—no one will ever hear the melodies of these music makers again. There were some people who might have been in the wrong place at the wrong time; they were subject to disfigurement and other forms of torture. These viscious acts have led some Corrido acts to put upcoming shows on standby, or cancel altogether. There was a huge fear of singing Narcocorridos in public, and vendors who sold CDs were literally caught in the crossfire of supporting certain drug traffickers over other ones.

In Mexico, we consider it important to pass on traditions to our children, so they can remember their past. Many cultures do this to instill a sense of identity in kids, because children are our future—but they are also the most vulnerable. With that being said my music amigos, I have to jump off board this incredible vessel of musical thought so I too, can shape and mold the thoughts of my little girl. She recently discovered her dancing abilities and is practicing to be a ballerina, so now I'm *DJ Daddy!* I appreciate the opportunity to share a part of my world with you so at this time, codename *Double A: Attorney Agent* is signing off. Hasta la vista, young Musicologists!

Mucho gracias goes out to Special Forces Agent Carlos Tejeda for sharing some Superior Intellect with us—no matter where it comes from, that's one thing we sure can't get enough of! Now let's grab a light snack at one of those *All-Am-Mexican* food establishments he mentioned earlier, then we'll look at another highly visible style that migrated from Mexico into the United States. Stateside, new fans were being reeled in daily: from local gatherings, to clubs, to corporate parties—even I'm a big fan! In the background, festive sounds are approaching. Hold everything: here comes a group of conventioneers, and they're all wearing sombreros and pinging at piñatas with little sticks…

VIVA MARIACHI!

Popularity of Mariachi bands has grown to extraordinary proportions, particularly in The U.S.A. Since the new millennium, I've personally seen more bands playing this music style than at any other time in my professional life. America is now more multicultural than ever, and our investigative analysts hint that the inclusion of more Mexican music and traditions into U.S. activities are signs of things to come. Based on that theory, we can count on seeing the country's cultural texture broaden its reach from urban cities into suburban and even rural localities, just like another cultural phenomenom did by the 90s—*Hip-Hop*.

Many of us probably think about Mariachi bands when Mexican music comes up for discussion, but there are actually lots of styles that crossed the border from this U.S. neighbor to the south. We'll explore some of them shortly, but at the moment you'll see an 'information shovel' has been placed in some sand. This is so we can dig a little deeper into Mariachi's origins. Not meaning to sound too much like Jimmie "JJ" Walker from *Good Times*, but this segment of Mexican music makes up a *Dyn-o-mite* aspect of sonic art from a cosmic zone I call *Musicolandia*!

Getting into the nuts and bolts of Mariachi, this is a style that originated from *Cocula*, in the state of Jalisco, Mexico. The average Mariachi band uses at least eight instruments: three violins, two trumpets, one Mexican guitar, a high-pitched, five-string guitar called a *vihuela,* and one *guitarrón*, or small-scaled acoustic bass. A Mexican band is officially deemed as "*Mariachi*" with the inclusion of the *guitarrón* and the *vihuela.* Band members usually perform dressed in silver studded charro outfits with wide-brimmed hats—I guess that explains the group of conventioneers I saw wearing sombreros and pinging at piñatas in the beginning of this section...

Since the late 1800s, Mariachi entertainment has expanded far beyond the site of its humble beginnings in Jalisco, a region that refers to its music as *Jalisciense*. Mariachi or more specifically, *Jalisciense music*, has been influenced by multiple cultures. Concert ensembles resembling European stylists often performed on Mexican haciendas (equivalent to ranches). The musicians usually played guitars, harps, violins and other instruments like jawharps. For those not aware, the jawharp has many names including the *Jew's harp,* although our operatives found no real connection to the Jewish culture. Other names include the *mouth harp,*

Ozark harp, trump and *juice harp*. Considered as one of the oldest musical instruments in the world, this lamellophone type of instrument is a part of the plucked idiophone family. It is made up of a frame with an attached metal or bamboo tongue or reed. Once it's inserted into a musician's mouth, fingers are used to pluck it and thus produce sound.

The jawharp has been associated with trances, magic and shamanic rituals, plus it can also be found in the Eastern hemisphere countries of Asia, China, Russia and Turkey. Looking at all this information, we can see that Mariachi music inherently connects with music from all over the world. From a distance, African music also had an influence on Mariachi. That's right—underground sources report there were coastal Folk music ensembles in place, and the African influence donated key rhythmic elements to many of them. Towards the end of the 19th century, the vihuela, two violins and the guitarrón (it replaced the harp) made up the arsenal of the Mariachi band. Topping things off, trumpets were added around the early 1920s; this was during the infancy of broadcast radio.

Once upon a time, original Mariachi performers were generically referred to as Mexican street musicians called *buskers*. These days, many Mariachi musicians get paid well to exhibit their craft inside plush venues but in the old days, many marched across unforgiving hot pavement to earn a half-decent living. Mariachi performers are great singers, and are often proficient with multiple instruments. Sometimes they back up talented singers like Luis Miguel and Juan Gabriel. Live performances have grown to be full-scaled productions—I had a great opportunity to see the magic of Mariachi on several occassions. You see, I was on the Atlanta production crew that 'rigged-n-ran' the sound reinforcement equipment for Juan Gabriel.

Opening the lens, Juan Gabriel's repertoire includes ballads, Pop, Rancheras, and songs backed up with the classic Mariachi sound. Around 2003, he gave an outstanding show at the Gwinnett Arena with an elaborate stage setup. Upon first glance, one would have thought the layout was for a small orchestra because each section of the stage had its own group of microphones and monitor speakers. But, the oddity of this event hit me when I was walking around onstage and noticed that although Juan Gabriel was set to perform with a full band, there was still a section reserved for Mariachi personnel. Even though I was a 'paid technical professional' that night, I was impressed to observe how much attention to detail was invested in this event.

In Mexico, Mariachi bands can be found serenading women on Mother's Day or for that matter, any day of the year. Mariachi bands have also manifested at *quinceañeras* (a girl's 15th birthday bash), weddings, formal occasions, large parties or at any other event. They've even been seen performing amidst American corporate functions in hotels I've done audiovisual work at. For some events, the A/V equipment was positioned to blend into Mexican themes which included colorful decorations, memorabilia, plenty Mexican food; and of course, *los Mariachis!*

There's nothing like watching a Mariachi band serenade the crowd, and the audiovisual profession afforded me that opportunity. Today, we can be assured of one thing: Mariachi bands and Jalisciense music are major forces in the world of corporate and social entertainment, as is another popular Mexican style—*Tejano*. Just in case you didn't know, Tejano music has a Queen… all hail as we *encender la luz*, or *flick on the light switch.*

SPOTLIGHT ON: SELENA

Billboard magazine's "Top Latin Artist of the 90s" and "Best Selling Latin Artist of the Decade" goes by the name of *Selena*. Making her mark as "*The Queen of Tejano music*," this highly talented singer-songwriter was born in 1971 to a Mexican father and a half-Cherokee mother—but was raised as a Jehovah's Witness. Culturally speaking, this combination makes for an interesting mix and was not uncommon to see; even the King of Pop, Michael Jackson, grew up as a Witness. However, I'm inclined to say that a rarer occurrence would be an American-born Tejano artist getting seven #1 hits and fourteen Top Ten singles on the "Top Latin Songs" chart!

Expecting a boy at birth, Selena Quintanilla's parents had another name in mind for their newborn baby–Marc Antony, not to be confused with Jennifer Lopez's *Marc Anthony*. By the time Selena was three, she began exercising her vocal chords in the singing realm. Six years later, she found herself in front of a sibling group called *Selena y Los Dinos*; they performed at the family restaurant, "Papa Gayo's." Moving from Lake Jackson, Texas to Corpus Christi, Selena's clan did shows at diverse places like fairs, weddings, and even on street corners.

When Selena was fourteen in 1985, she recorded an album for a local label, but it never made it to record stores; her father wound up buying them... all. Now that's what I'd call 'showing some love!' By the time Selena was in 8th grade, she was forced to abandon a normal way of life and furthered her education in-between shows, out on the road. Shortly after receiving her high school diploma, Selena's third album was released. When *Alpha* hit record stores, Selena's popularity soared even higher: she scooped up top honors for "Best Female Vocalist" at the 1987 Tejano Music Awards, a tradition she maintained for another seven years. Throughout the remainder of the 80s, Selena added to her numerous releases and developed a valuable catalog of hits. After she signed a recording contract with Capitol/EMI Records in the early 90s, just about every Spanish-speaking country was shouting out her name. Along the way, Selena opened doors for newcomers like Yolanda Saldivar, who stepped in and helped expand the empire by forming a fan club—Saldivar was named president of the organization.

Record labels knew that every so often, the music market munched on new offerings by young exceptional Pop/R&B female singers, considering the success of singers Whitney Houston, Mariah Carey and singer-musician Alicia Keys. Labels like Capitol/EMI compared Selena to Madonna and Gloria Estefan then they bought in; so did Coca-Cola by signing Selena up as their *"Texas Spokesgirl."* After that venture Selena's popularity ballooned again, so the sound of her backup band needed to match that growth and a guitar-playing hombre named Chris Perez was hired. In a flash, he was destined to be Selena's onstage and offstage cowboy... for life. Despite the odds, love at first sight still happened— FAST FORWARD to 1992 when the two exchanged nuptuals and Selena Quintanilla-Perez became a happily married wife, riding the waves of success. She was an artist who acquired accolades like gold Tejano records and a Grammy for "Best Mexican-American Album." The stars were all in alignment with Selena's impending "event horizon." Let's get some more snapshots:

- In 1994 Selena unbolted a pair of boutiques to carry her custom designs, complete with in-house beauty salons; she assigns Yolanda Saldivar as manager
- *Hispanic Business* reported income from Selena's ventures in the $5 million range, as the fruits of Selena's labor continued paying off with Billboard's *Premio Lo Nuestro* awarding her "Best Latin Artist and "Song of the Year"
- Coca-Cola commemorated a healthy, 5-year partnership by releasing a Coke bottle in Selena's honor
- After scoring a #1 song with the *Barrio Boyzz*, Selena embarked on a tour that took her from New York City, through Central-Latin-Caribbean-American countries like Argentina, Colombia, Panama, the Dominican Republic and Puerto Rico

In the fall of 1994, Selena wrapped up a busy year by releasing an album that went gold in Mexico. *Amor Prohibido* came armed with a show of four #1 Latin hits—this feat displaced Gloria Estefan, who previously owned the top chart position. Due to it selling over 400,000 copies in America, Selena was now performing for standing-room-only crowds. This extended tour affected her plans to record an English-language album—a project on hold since 1993. *Amor Prohibido* took the notch up a level in Selena's career, but a hectic schedule postponed recording of her English album until 1995. Was this a strange occurrence or destiny? You be the judge. The acting bug carried Selena to the camera later that year, through soap opera appearances next to the likes of Erik (CHiPs) Estrada, and film features with Marlon Brando, Johnny Depp and Faye Dunaway. Do you remember the Mexican music style we discussed in the previous section? That's right, folks: Selena "opened up" for A-Listers like BD&D (Brando, Depp and Dunaway), when she played a Mariachi singer role in the opening scene of the film, *Don Juan DeMarco*.

February 1995 saw Selena doing a performance for the *Houston Livestock Show and Rodeo* at the Houston Astrodome. Breaking the records of Country music stars like Vince Gill, Reba McIntyre and George Strait, the engagement drew in more than 65,000 fans. A month later, Selena headlined at Miami's *Calle Ocho Festival*, where the attendance records tipped the scales at over 100,000 loyal followers. Throughout the hoopla, Selena managed to stay grounded by donating her humanitarian efforts to organizations like D.A.R.E., the fight against AIDS, and promoting higher education. This musically reminds me of a quote my mother said that goes, *"Labor for learning before you grow old, for learning is better than silver and gold—silver and gold will vanish away, but a good education will never decay."* While Mom never made it to college, she made sure I did. As a staunch believer in education, Selena never forgot how important reading, writing and learning were for the future of our youth, or for her growth as a human being: not just as a star.

While I can't sing or dance a lick, I do know that education, supporting our youth and other humane causes are important, so for more 'Edu-Facts' about my other literary hobbies, excellent source material is available. They were all designed to enlighten folks about the art of supporting our youth: search for books like *How To Grow A Child: A Child's Advice to Parents*, *Recapturing Technology For Education*, *Moments of Astonishment*, *Help Your Child In School*, or *The Power of Creative Writing*. These "instruments of intellectual property" were written by another firm believer in youth education—my favorite fifth grade teacher, author and mentor Bernard Percy, who along with his singing wife Caralyn, has a trio of intellectually gifted daughters who are "well in tune" with the life of Selena.

As Selena's recognition increased through a growing fan base, plans were made for the release of her long-awaited English album in the summer of 1995. But before the album was released, there was a revelation that Yolanda Saldivar had been skimming money out of the fan club fund, growing steadily since the club was formed 5 years earlier. Faced with the threat of unemployment and jail, Yolanda agreed to meet Selena at a local hotel in Corpus Christi during March of 1995 to relinquish business paperwork. During this meeting, she experienced a momentary lapse of insanity—Saldivar wielded a gun and fired at Selena, striking her in the shoulder. Then Saldivar chased the singer as she fled in shock. Selena ran desperately for help until she eventually collapsed, due to the accelerated bleeding of a major artery. This dreadful incident took place barely two weeks before Selena's 24th birthday.

Yolanda Saldivar was convicted of murder and sentenced to life in prison, but was eligible for parole after thirty years. Her gun was destroyed and its remains were disposed into the Corpus Christi Bay. In the aftermath, broadcast networks terminated scheduled programming to report the bad news, while radio stations played her music nonstop. The *New York Times* had it as front page news for two days in a row, and *People* magazine printed a pair of commemorative issues—their combined sales totalled over a million copies. Requests for Selena memorabilia was in such high demand that *People* decided to publish *People en Español* (that's *People* in Spanish). Selena's funeral drew in mourners from all points of the globe and included celebrities like Celia Cruz, Julio Iglesias and Gloria Estefan. Even Madonna, who Selena's Tejano flair is often compared to, showed up. George W. Bush was Governor of Texas at the time—he declared Selena's April 16th birthday as "Selena Day" in the state, and she was inducted into the *Latin Music Hall of Fame*.

Some people may not be aware of a project Selena was working on before her untimely passing. It involved some childhood friends of mine from Brooklyn who grew up to become actors, artists, and a hit producing A-Team called *Full Force*. The group's Bowlegged Lou comments on an engagement where they collaborated with this monumental young artist:

"We were the last American producers to work with Selena. We remade an old song she did years ago called *Missing My Baby*. We recorded her new lead vocals and new music tracks; then she was supposed to come back to New York another day to complete the background vocals. Two days before Selena was supposed to come back to our New York studio, I remember my mom calling me and first, asking if I was sitting down. Then she told me that Selena was killed. *Maaan* what a sad day for us!

"We love Selena and her family; we always will. They ended up flying us down to Corpus Christi, Texas, and we ended up recording the background vocals to the song at her huge studio compound. It was a little sad and eerie to complete our music and vocals while listening to Selena's voice over the speakers. After we finished, her whole family came into the studio to hear what we did. The song title was ironic enough: *MISSING MY BABY*. After Selena's husband, Mom, Dad, her brother A.B. Quintanilla and the rest of her family listened to what we did, their father stood up and led the entire family in an appreciative applause of handclapping that we'll never forget.

"There's a *Missing My Baby* video uploaded by a You Tube fan, and I was surprised to find it. This song appears on her multi-million selling album called *DREAMING OF YOU* and we are proud to be a part of it. We did another song for the album too—a Spanish song called *Techno Cumbia*. Anyway, you can watch and listen as Selena's beautiful voice rings out, while our Full Force music and vocals soar behind her with memorable love. We love Selena so much—she will always be a great, talented, versatile young lady. REST IN PEACE SELENA."

Thanks to my good friend Bowlegged Lou for sharing that personal bit of history with us. To view the music video of *Missing My Baby* by Selena featuring Full Force, go to You Tube and do a search for the song, Selena, or Full Force. My search began with the one uploaded in October of 2008, when I went to www.youtube.com/watch?v=y_kxquWFMco#]Honors.

There are many worker angels that keep Selena's heavenly essence glowing for people on Earth to remember her by. A tourist attraction, music and video memorials, as well as assorted venues are all dedicated to keeping her name alive. Summer of 1995 finally saw the release of Selena's *Dreaming of You*, which combined Spanish songs with English ones. It debuted at #1 on the Billboard chart and made Selena the first Spanish speaking singer to do so. Her album was also the second highest debut—at the time, Michael Jackson's *HIStory* was number one. First day sales were over 175,000 units, making Selena the top selling female Pop singer to assume this position.

Within a year, *Dreaming of You* sold over two million copies, and it went on to top out at 3 times Platinum (3,000,000) by Recording Industry Association of America (RIAA) standards. Two songs, *Dreaming of You* and *I Could Fall in Love* crossed over at mainstream radio, pushing Selena into the Top 10 on Billboard's Hot 100 Airplay and Adult Contemporary charts. In Selena's wake stands Corpus Christi's *Mirador de la Flor*, a tourist attraction unveiled in her honor in 1997. A Hollywood movie about Selena had over 24,000 actresses competing for the starring role, and one called *J-Lo* (Jennifer Lopez) won out—her acting career blasted off from there and she was later nominated to receive a Golden Globe Award for "Best Actress in a Musical." Although J-Lo starred in a motion picture about Selena, overdubs of Selena's voice were used in the film's featured songs.

On April 7, 2005, Houston's Reliant Stadium held a tribute concert called *Selena ¡VIVE!* It occurred a week after the 10th anniversary of Selena's passing. Featuring acts from Pepe Aguilar to Gloria Estefan, Thalia and more, over 65,000 spectators came out to take in a good three hours' worth of Selena's song renditions, all performed by A-List artists. Capping off the list of entertainers was Selena's brother, A.B. Quintanilla, who performed with his band the *Kumbia Kings*. In the background of A.B.'s set, video footage ran; it featured none other than Selena herself, singing *Baila Esta Cumbia. Selena ¡VIVE!* was broadcast on the Univision network and became the highest-rated, most watched, Spanish-language show aired in American network TV history. Generating millions of dollars in revenue, Selena became an internationally attractive brand name that will always bear fruit and enshrine this captivating artist for future generations to behold. In concurrence, Corpus Christi's American Bank Center dedicated their 2,500-seat concert arena to be forever known as the "*Selena Auditorium*." You can get your very own Selena experience by going to sites like You Tube and listening to her music—over a dozen albums are floating around, plus you can visit her cyberworld at www.selenaforever.com.

MANAGING STATISTICS

Besides the popular Tejano style of Selena and the science of Jalisciense that our previously mentioned Mariachi bands bring to the table, Mexican variations in music include styles like Cumbia, Dance/Club, Pop, Hip-Hop, Reggaeton and Rock. Genres like these are influenced by music from Latin America, the Caribbean, Europe and Mexico's northern neighbor, America. These styles have all been increasing in popularity—particularly in Mexican youth culture, complete with its own set of issues that revolve around Mexico's social/political agenda. In summation, we can certainly expect to see and hear much more Mexican music take up residence in the *Land of the Free*; where even government bailouts come with huge price tags.

To help manage the deficit, be sure to bring "stacked" wallets with you when shopping stateside. Although the American dollar's disclaimer says "In God We Trust," us working-class folk may have to clammer for cold, hard cash in leiu of diminishing credit lines. And in an age where banks don't trust other banks any more, money's too tight to mention! A related slogan adapted from the Wu Tang Clan's song *C.R.E.A.M.* comes to mind: *cash rules everything around music*—no matter who makes it!

> **POLITICO FACTO:** America's Mexican neighbors share similar capitalistic and democratic governmental structures.

These days, modern technology gives us the capability to learn just about anything in a flash. While you surf the Web, be sure to check out a few of the many music styles that not only come from countries like Mexico, but also from places like South America. Discoveries made during this part of our journey include taking note of indigenous styles that exist in these areas; many of them had roots leading to far away places like Europe, Spain, Portugal and Africa.

Now here comes a little punch some may find a bit hard to swallow: unknown to many, a man of African-Indian lineage named Vicente Guerrero was at one time official 'Mexican government military issue.' Even as a man of darker color, Guerrero made a high climb to the rank of General in Mexico's war for independence from Spain. He later became President of Mexico (1829-1831), and abolished slavery there on September 15, 1829, over three decades prior to the United States taking positive action. Fast forwarding our time coefficients, we zoom in to see an African-American born in Hawaii named Barack Obama—he become the first U.S. President of color roughly 180 years after Vicente Guerrero escalated to Mexico's Presidential level.

Let's prepare to discover another country that developed its own distinctive sound, yet was still significantly touched by African music. Latin styles like Rumba, Mambo, Perreo, Salsa and forms of Mexican music were mentioned earlier, but now we'll bite into an entrée flavored with the meat and potatoes of South America's fabulous musical pastimes. One of them includes caliente codename *Samba*—as highlighted before, Samba is a variation of Cuba's *Son*. We'll discuss some exciting musicians, styles and dances, but there simply is not enough space to detail all of the musical entertainment that extends from U.S. borders southward. However, a lot of effort was made to describe as much as possible to get things started for your own adventure... or two.

In the quest to provide quality information to quality readers, declassified information about the 'musicultural' aspects of a targeted South American country on the eastern border will be expounded upon next. This chunk of real estate officially makes up the *Federative Republic of Brazil*, GPS CZC (Caliente Zone Codename): *Latitute 10 South - Longitude 55 West*. Visually speaking, "you'll just have to see it to believe it," so as the Behavorial Analysis Unit's Special Secret Agent Aaron Hotchner from TV's *Criminal Minds* would say, "Wheels up in thirty."

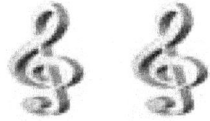

WHAT HAPPENS IN BRAZIL

Right now, you'll be asked to fire up your imagination to capture the full effect of our upcoming adventure, which takes us to the next stop on this peep through music *biz*tory. First, allow me to push PLAY on the intercom for a quick OAA (on-air announcement) from our Captain: "There's a surprise fiesta planned on our time-traveling vessel of thought so whenever you're ready, climb aboard!" The main galley of the *Salón de Fiestas* is now open, so we can all commence to the enjoyment of some HFLN (high-flight leisurely networking) and wait, there's more— (Dramatic PAUSE…)

The compass coordinates are set due south, and the GPS system is now out of PROGRAM mode. With the *next stop indicator* pointing to the geo-physic location of *Latin Music South*—BRAZIL—it's departure time. After we mix and mingle in the Salón de Fiestas, you may be tempted to hit REWIND; but we'll FAST FORWARD instead. This way, we can zoom in to see what one of our time-factored 'frequent flyer' Internet flights (and a few underground operatives) uncovered. RECORD this— your head might be spinning from all that imaginative mumbo-jumbo I just babbled, so you can take a contemplation break if you need one.

Let's switch scenes to the Salón de Fiestas, now filling up with chattering networkers. I've got some special guests to introduce, so be prepared to go on a few 'secret music missions' with real Brazilian Musicology agents! There's plenty of great sights to see in Brazil, but due to the time allotted on our itinerary, it looks like we'll have one key mission to accomplish. While passing through this particular time portal, we've been tasked to take a series of reconnaissance snapshots for later assessment. And then we'll plug them all into the big machine to examine the visual evidence that gets exposed. Once this literary investigation is complete, we should have a fairly accurate report on Brazil's exciting musical culture.

Right now, we're making our final approach into the airspace above *Latin Music South*, otherwise known as *Brazil*. Here's a special message to all stragglers: the Captain says "don't walk—*run* to the Salón de Fiestas in the main galley and enjoy our high flight fiesta of fun." As everyone networks, sips and nibbles, get ready for things to get spicier, because I'm about to pop a hot CD called *Odara* into the sound system! What makes the CD special is that it was written, performed and produced by my good friend, *Princess La Tremenda*. For those not in the know, let's cop a squat at a table near the speakers—as we nibble on finger munchies and sip some cool refreshments, I'll dispel the data...

According to her bio, Princess La Tremenda is *"Electrifying, Eclectic and Sexy."* But that's still not the half of it, because I had a chance to work with this all-around entertainer several times and they were all totally gratifying—let's hope there's enough space for me to expand on that later! Unlike many artists, Princess La Tremenda is committed to developing as a TOTAL INTERNATIONAL "A" CLASS artist and because of her goal, I was naturally drawn in. I mean, how many acts do YOU know who can seamlessly jump between English, Spanish and Portuguese lyrics? I rest my case. The Princess La Tremenda mantra: "Music is my way of communicating with the world." Blending traditional music styles with new world sonics to create a sophisticated, mature groove, Princess seems to have found a vehicle that will lead her to world domination in the near future. After seeing just one live performance, you'll get an eyefull—after listening to her CD, you'll get an earful. And after visiting her website, you'll get a brain full of PLT.

Acquiring plenty experience as a world traveler since she was a child, the singer has come into her own and now gracefully scopes out stages across the Caribbean, Europe, North and South America. In Brazil alone, she performed in front of over 500,000 people at the massive *Carnival* celebration. Folks, these numbers are nothing to sneeze at! And you sure can dance to the music—I even found my own Flatfoot Jack feet tapping to the beat while doing the sound at one of her shows with my partner in music-n-rhyme, Peach City Records founder Wade Jones III. I'll never forget it because she brought in a whole brass band (hold the bass player, add a tuba) to back her up. In addition to a drummer, there was also a percussionist and great harmony provided by Princess La Tremenda's background singers. In addition to Darryl Reeves (The Herbie Sessions) and The Atlanta Brass Connection, The Sound Table on Edgewood Avenue got blessed that evening by a talented singer who packed the house!

It's funny because when I met Wade Jones back around 2005, he was riding around with an R&B track by Princess La Tremenda called *You And I* that he produced prior our affiliation. I was taken aback when I finally met Princess, because she explained that she was *not* trying to position herself in the R&B space; she was after the international market. After the show, she gave me a CD but I didn't realize she had autographed it, too—a great personal touch. After listening to her *Odara* CD, I got her musical message; it was crystal clear!

Princess La Tremenda recorded all of *Odara* in Brazil to retain the Brazilian feel and it shines right through, thanks to the input of local musicians she had working with her. PLT's synergy of African, American and Latin sounds creates a sonic blend that she branded as "*Afro Latin Soul*" and again, I got the message crystal clear! While her music is accesible to just about any audience, I'm inclined to go out on a limb and say that Princess' music is for the *mature, grown, sexy—lovers and dancers*. Sade meets Gloria Estefan meets Maria Bethania? Take a listen for yourself and decide. In summation, Princess La Tremenda defies being boxed into one category and you don't have to take my word for it: go to princesslatremenda.com, reverbnation.com/princesslatremenda, facebook.com/tremendamusic, instagram/princesslatremenda#, or twitter.com/princesslat to form your own opinion.

We now switch scenes back to the Salón de Fiestas of our time traveling mod rod. In the background plays the title track of Princess La Tremenda's Brazilian-influenced CD, *Odara*. It's great music to travel with, and it's the perfect menu item to play at our Salón de Fiestas networking party during this intercontinental visit to Brazil. Here comes the Captain again, warning everyone to prepare as we conclude all networking, sipping and nibbling in the Salón de Fiestas and return to our first-class seats. Sounds like we're close to our destination, if you ask me.

TOUCHDOWN TIME

Aye Carumba! Similar to what Pop music star Carole King said in her 1971 hit *I Feel the Earth Move*, I feel some rapid deceleration occurring under my feet! Technically, there's a good reason the 'virtual phase shift' occurred: that time-portalled exit sequence from Mexico was *superfast*! So, like Soul II Soul said in their 1989 hit—we're going to *keep on movin'* to a location known in the Musicology world as, *Sambalandia*.

The flight crew hopes our readers had a chance to sample some tasty hors d'oeuvres and practice a little power networking at our 'feast of friendliness' in the Salón de Fiestas. Without falling into a *siesta of slights*, you should now feel our time craft descending into the GPS territory of 10 South 55 West, aka *Brazil*. This country's known for great weather and beautiful landscape, plus it harbors a harmonically balanced, multicultural mix of music and people. Within that mix, one can experience the rare essence of Brazil's infectious music, dance, cuisine, art and so much more.

There are certain rhythms that when combined, helped define Brazil's national dance, *Samba*. This genre ultimately became a dominant music force and one reason was because certain rhythms in Samba were at one time used to summon gods in ancient Africa. Like other styles previously mentioned, Brazil's offering of Samba turned into a cultural phenomenon. It opened the door for revolutionary new genres to step in and initiate overloads of foot stomping on beat-laden Brazilian dance floors. We'll take a more in-depth look at Samba a little later so for now, let's engage the sub-operations drive.

Brazil is a vast region that encompasses a diverse mixture of music, and its cultural makeup comprises indigenous Indians living in tandem with Portuguese, Iberian and other traditions. Among them are African styles, where Samba's derivative *Bossa Nova* was born. Looking at things in 20/20 vision, Brazil is the fifth largest country in the world, so it should be no surprise that music styles like Samba took shape here and since then has become nearly as popular in far away countries like Africa and Japan. Opening up the secret book of stats, no one steps to Brazil's dance music better than my good friend Regina Cnossen, codename *Agent Disco Queen*. As a resident of São Paulo, Regina knows all the great music and dance styles her country's chart-topping city has to offer, so she Has been assigned to guide us through this leg of '*Le Tour de Brazil*.'

Thanks, L.A., or as we say down here in my part of the southern hemisphere, *Obrigada*! I'm just getting here from the Salon de Fiestas because I couldn't get enough of that great music on your friend Princess La Tremenda's CD—I certainly hope to meet her and get my own copy before this excursion is over! Since L.A. let the cat out the bag and mentioned my attraction to music, I will share a little about my culture. The musical makeup of São Paulo is as diverse as in many other Brazilian cities. We'll go through a Top 10 list shortly but before that, allow me to introduce you to some of the music and artists that are popular in my country. Finding a home in São Paulo wasn't hard for the Classical music genre. This music form has been refined as well as redefined by modern composers like *Osvaldo Lacerda, Amaral Vieira* and *Edson Zampronha*, all proudly homegrown in São Paulo. Bringing the "state of symphonism" to an all-time high, we have what you call codename SPSS: the *São Paulo State Symphony*. They bring music offerings that are consumed by an international audience, from Latin and South America to North America, Europe and the rest of the world.

I must insert a noteworthy mention here of *Paulo Szot*—he helped bring new eyes and ears in to shore for 'incredible interpretations and renditions.' Dramatically speaking, audiences often got treated to the formula of *Sao Paulo* plus *Paulo Szot* equals *Sheer Perfection Squared*: in mathematical terms, that's *SP+PS=SP₂*. This dynamic entertainer gave Tony-nominated theatrical performances in 2008's rendition of the stage play, *South Pacific*. Throwing in his two cents, L.A. Jackson points out that he marketed the soundtrack album when he worked at Sony Music— we are so happy for him (wink). Like L.A. Jackson, many of our North American neighbors may have no clue of what Brazil's major cities are, so let's take a quick peek at our top cities as of 2010, along with the relative flags, capital states and populations each represent:

Rank	City	Flag	Capital	Population
1	São Paulo		São Paulo	11,244,369
2	Rio de Janeiro		Rio de Janeiro	6,323,037
3	Salvador		Bahia	2,676,606
4	Brasília		Distrito Federal	2,562,963
5	Fortaleza		Ceará	2,551,806
6	Belo Horizonte		Minas Gerais	2,375,444
7	Manaus		Amazonas	1,802,525
8	Curitiba		Paraná	1,746,896
9	Recife		Pernambuco	1,536,934
10	Porto Alegre		Rio Grande do Sul	1,409,939

Courtesy Wikipedia.org

Although I've visited many of these cities while L.A. Jackson hasn't yet (still making plans), he has seen pictures and can agree with me: they look as modern as any American city you can think of! Looking at the chart, you can see the population of these cities is nothing to "achoo" over: combined, these 10 cities make up an estimated 30 million people—that's roughly 10% of the U.S. population! To add to the equation, 20% of 30 million is 6 million, and Florida's prize city of Miami is home to almost that many people, with a healthy portion of Spanish-speaking Latin-Americans—some of which come from places like Brazil. I have an important Miami connection and will bring you more information about this connection 'a leettle later.' For now, we open up *secret* Samba files:

Born in 1912, *Adoniran Barbosa* found his place as a top Samba composer and singer who gained accessibility through São Paulo's early radio era. Expanding his cultural influence, Barbosa was highly received by Italian immigrants scattered around the Bela Vista vicinity. Touching the lives of lower echelon urbanites who teetered on a steep economic edge, Barbosa became a major draw local fans flocked to see perform. Similarly, acts like *Paulo Vanzoline* and *Demônios da Garoa* are noted for playing what I call *Old School Samba*.

Moving over into the Rock world, the group *Os Mutantes* made space at the front of new developments during the late 60s, as they infiltrated both inside and outside of Brazil's borders. This Psychedelic-rooted Rock band released five successful albums and stood tall among the leaders of São Paulo's avant-garde music movement. To show the time-insensitive massive appeal *Os Mutantes* had, their 2000 English album, *Tecnicolor*, featured songs originally recorded in the early 70s. My sources also reveal that it contained artwork designed by John Lennon's son, Sean. (For those asking "who is John and Sean?"—shame on you!)

As ripples of extreme 70s oil prices subsided, the 80s brought economic recession… and not-so-people-friendly military rule. After the government leadership changed hands, bands like *Ultrage a Rigor* (Elephant Intruder) jumped out from the underground, eager to unleash bold new sounds.   With strong overtones of being more people-friendly than the military, this Rock band openly voiced their opinions about the cultural evolution of São Paulo and Brazil in a post-military regime. As the 80s progressed, live entertainment began flourishing once again— Punk and Garage bands like *Inocentes*, *Ira!*, *Ratos de Porão* and *Titãs* fired up their amps. After the 90s rolled around, metal acts like *Angra*, *Dr. Sin*, *Korzus* and *Torture Squad* arrived on the scene.

Drum & Bass 'increased the beat' with acts like *DJ Marky*, *DJ Patife*, *Drumagick*, *Fernanda Porto* and *XRS*. Alternative flavors came from São Paolo's *Cansei de Ser Sexy* (codename *Cade SS*)—their name is Portuguese for "tired of being sexy." Before the old millennium's clock ran out of time in the late 1990s, a 'Type A' troop of *Tropicalia* musicians had expanded their reach to grasp the ears of countries like the U.S., Canada and more. For those not aware, *Tropicália* also goes by the name of *Tropicalismo*. To twist the theme more, let's add some wikidata that turned up in our search and happens to cover a thirty-year span: "*Tropicália* is a Brazilian art movement that arose in the late 1960s and encompassed theatre, poetry, and music, among other forms." For many, it was the first time they saw so many artistic creations; but it wouldn't be the last. Some of it turned up again in far away places like Miami, Florida.

According to the wikibanks, Miami is "the principal, central, and most populous city of the South Florida metropolitan area." I won't get into gazillions of motion pictures and TV shows like the classic *Scarface, Bad Boys, or Miami Vice* that have been shot there. Plus, dozens of the Sunshine State's best music artists and celebrities spell out this most southern U.S. city using four letters, H-O-M-E. Secretly speaking, the city of Miami also hosts secret dance parties for secret dance operatives like me—L.A. Jackson may not have gotten the memo, but Miami is another reason why I use *Disco* in my codename. Just thinking about Disco makes me want to dance right now…

Okay Agent Regina—let's get you booked on the next flight back to São Paulo, before you turn into 'Agent Too Much Information' on us! As an international *mulher* (lady) of mystery, our in-house Disco Queen's no stranger to styles like Salsa; or American sub-operative hubs like Atlanta and Miami. By the time I caught up with Regina on Facebook after missing her at the Atlanta office, she revealed the nature of a new secret mission she was on. Her reaction—"How do you feel after dancing Salsa with friends in Miami all night long? A-L-I-V-E!" All this author can say is: if there's some danceable sound to be found, our music-loving agent from São Paulo will *definitely* be around!

Thanks to Regina Cnossen aka Agent Disco Queen, for sharing her hometown with us and I'll remember to show some appreciation later on, at the after-party. Now let's bring up Regina's counterpart Silvia Camargo, codenamed *Agent Concert Connoisseur*—that's because every time I talk to her, she's either going to, or coming from a concert somewhere in the world!

That's right, L.A., I've been a big fan of live performers since my younger days, but I can't give out any dates—I'm an Agent on the clock but I still LOVE to rock! Getting down to business, let's pull out my trusted crystal ball. As we look into it, we see that basic compositional mechanisms of Brazilian music includes traditional string, wind and percussive instruments:

accordian	cavaquinho	pandeiro
acoustic	clavichord	piano
guitar	cuica	rattle
alfaia and	flute	shaker
snare drum	frying pan	tamborim
atabaque	gongue bell	tambourine
berimbau	guiitar	triangle
bow	horn	whistle
	Ilus	

L.A. Jackson promises to discuss instruments like these in an upcoming section of this book series, so keep on reading and you'll eventually get to it. Today, Brazilian music is embraced nearly everywhere it's played, but it had to get a start somewhere before arriving at its current platform in our high-tech, digitally inclined music world. Let's REWIND back in time to pick up a few 'musical nuggets' about my hometown, Brazil.

EARLY HISTORY

Brazil takes up a substantial portion of South America and has been a major influence on the music from this continent throughout history. As early as 1578, various writings described the music and dances of the Tupi and other native ethnic groups. By the end of the 1700s, a comedic dance known as *Bumba-Meu-Boi* gained recognition amongst Brazilians as a popular tale of a resurrected ox. The *Bumba-Meu-Boi* is led by a *chamador* who introduces each dancer before they make their appearance. This is but one of many stories which exemplify the influence that long-standing traditions had in Brazil during the shaping of its music. Staking claim on a new existence as the *Federative Republic of Brazil*, the country 'successfully seceded' from Portugal in 1822 and continued building its own identity.

One of our states, Minas Gerais, is the home of an important music collective called *Clube da Esquina* which in English means "Corner Club." There was also a recording of the same name—this double album came out on the EMI label in 1972 and its American release was pushed through by Brazilian musicians like Lô Borges and Milton Nascimento. There goes L.A. Jackson piping in to say that Milton is another CBS/Sony artist he marketed back in his younger days. I think we may have to use codename *Octopus* for L.A. if he keeps interrupting to tell us how many different artists he has worked with (get over it, L.A.). Getting back to business, the musical release of *Clube da Esquina* featured a young group of artists with plenty of potential. Lots of colorful sounds were embedded in the album's compelling compositions, and this project shined a light on the engaging power of Brazilian musicians. Earning instant recognition and global acclaim, the record became a contemporary music classic. 1978 saw a follow up release called *Clube da Esquina 2*; it featured new acts like Chico Buarque. Now here's a quick snapshot of influential contributors to the Clube da Esquina style:

14 Bus	Márcio Borges	Tavinho Moura
Nelson Ângelo	Fernando Brant	Wagner Tiso
Ronaldo Bastos	Beto Guedes	Milton Nascimento
Lô Borges	Toninho Horta	Flávio Venturini

Please note there are plenty of great musicians not listed here that deserve discovery, and I encourage you to do further research when you can. Zooming in, Clube da Esquina is a mixture of mainstream Rock blended with other styles like Progressive Rock, Bossa Nova, Jazz, Classical and Brazilian Country music. Believe it or not, diverse acts like The Beatles and The Platters have influenced the Clube da Esquina sound, too. Along with another style mentioned earlier called Tropicalia, Clube da Esquina initiated new music movements that gained momentum in the late 60s and early 70s. This was right around the time American music was heralding in major changes and new music styles, too—Brazilian music flourished everywhere and was embraced by a global audience.

Hailed as Godfathers of Clube da Esquina, Milton Nascimento and Márcio Borges crossed paths in the capital city of Belo Horizonte in the early 60s. This interception did not go unnoticed and the pair began collaborating, with Milton composing music and Márcio writing lyrics. Later, with Fernando Brant, Márcio Borges went on to play a key part in the genre's further evolution. Another important Brazilian act is a highly respected keyboardist named Michel Freidenson; let's get acquainted.

AN INSIDE VIEW: Michel Freidenson

Arranger, composer, producer and keyboard virtuoso Michel Freidenson was the genius behind an instrumental act known as Zona Azul—just don't be like L.A. Jackson and get the name confused with an act he once marketed for CBS Records, Austria's Joe Zawinul. At one time, Joe played keyboards with Weather Report and I'm sure there's more on him somewhere in this book series. Interestingly enough, I've just been notified it's in Book #3 at the Jazz-Fusion section; just look for a part called *Global Fusion*.

Michel Freidenson is one of my favorite music artists, but I still don't know how L.A. Jackson hears a similarity between Zona Azul and Joe Zawinul—do you? Well, I've got the baton in my hand now, so I'm going to keep on running with it! The first time I heard Michel Freidenson's music, I ran out and bought a Zona Azul record called *Zonazul*. Since Zona Azul got creative with the title of their first album, they took things up a level on another release by calling it *Luzanoz*—and yes, I would say there is a definite correlation between these album titles!

One good reason I enjoy listening to Michel Freidenson's music is because it's good for the heart, mind and soul. You see, I'm a well-trained music operative—in addition to analyzing the music of Brazil, I also intercept many sonic transmissions from America, Europe and other places to keep abreast of hits by groups like Chicago, Earth, Wind & Fire, Kool & The Gang, Led Zepellin, Pink Floyd, U2 and Van Halen. When I have the opportunity, I put on my party clothes and go out to see these groups perform my favorite songs: live onstage!

Comfortable on stages anywhere, Michel Friedenson performed for capacity crowds with other hot acts from my country:

Leny de Andrade	Dayse Cordeiro	Marcio Montarroyos
Badi Assad	Djavan	Duda Neves
Fafá de Belém	Jane Duboc	Hermeto Pascoal
Bocato	Léa Freire	Raul de Souza
Lô Borges	Ivan Lins	Tim Tires (Rolling
Ana Caram	Tim Maia	Stones)

And there are plenty others!

Michel Freidenson is a highly requested pianist who as Musicology codename *Professor Man*, is no stranger to making music for the big screen; so as far as teaching Music for Film at São Paulo's FAAP University, he can do that with the settings on 'auto-pilot.' From producing music to teaching it, Michel Freidenson has travelled the world over and was greeted with cheers everytime he made an appearance. Producing and arranging music on over 70 CDs is no easy task, but that's another thing Michel made seem easy. With shows coming to a town near you, don't miss the opportunity to check him out if he's on tour anywhere in the world. For more information on this dynamic musician, put www.michelfreidenson.com into the search box.

It's very exciting to go to the websites of artists I enjoy listening to, because there are all kinds of things to discover about them—especially new music. When I go to concerts, I am actually studying the music of acts like Chicago, Earth, Wind & Fire, Kool & The Gang, Van Halen and others, in the live environment. This helps me to understand the musicians much better and since I am from Brazil, it also helps me to get a clearer understanding of American culture. By the same token, I hope other cultures take interest and enjoy our Brazilian artists by listening to their music, visiting websites and of course, seeing them live. Here comes another act that made valuable contributions to the music of my country— hopefully you will see her significance to me as a fan, and will be inspired to learn more about how important she is to the Brazilian music and literary cultures.

THE MANY FACES OF: Maria Bethânia

An important Brazilian singer who was born in Bahia and refined in Rio de Janeiro is Maria Bethânia; we can add *Vianna Telles Veloso* to make up her full name. Flying high into the skies of an inherited musical kingdom, Maria began her television career in 1964 on a popular show called *Opiniao*. A year later, she released a single called *Carcara* and was launched into the upper stratosphere of Brazilian music *biz*tory. In short, Maria has a long line of album releases and was well-known for performing all around Brazil.

It may be hard to believe but as a child, Maria Bethânia wanted to be an actress. Due to her mother being a musician, she grew up in a house filled with music. Moving to Salvador, Bahia at the age of thirteen, Maria absorbed lots of intellectual entertainment offered by the city. Despite her musical abilities, she turned down an offer made by her brother Caetano Velosa—he was producing a film soundtrack and wanted her to sing on it. Even the film's director wanted her to perform in a musical he knew about. Eventually, Maria and her brother began working together as she linked up with a growing stable of talent like Gal Costa, Gilberto Gil and Tom Zé, who she performed with at the grand opening of the Vila Velha Theater. While performing one day, Bossa Nova music act Nara Leao asked if she'd be interested in replacing her in *Opiniao*. Her *Carcara* single followed next; it was a popular protest song, and a recording by her brother was also released around this time.

Maria Bethânia's next steps took her from Rio de Janeiro back to Bahia for a short pit stop between shows she was doing at nightclubs and other hotspots around Brazil. After RCA Records got wind of her song *Carcara* they pursued her; along with other labels that followed suit, eager to be the first one with this fresh "catch of the day." She became a highly sought-after artist and bounced between several labels during the 70s. Bethânia's 1973 release called *Drama, Luz Da Noite* was a fabulous display of traditional Brazilian compositions, enhanced by quotes from literary works. Her 1977 tour coincided with a gold album—they each shared the same name, *Pássaro da Manhã* and the following year, she released another gold album called *Alibi*. By the end of the 70s, Maria was evolving away from collaborations in the Tropicalismo music she was doing, and shifted into a more artistically refined mode.

The 80s and 90s found Maria the singer releasing music and touring to support it, with 1993's *As Canções Que Você Fez Para Mim* turning into the most successful album of the year. 2005 saw an album and group called *Música Popular Brasileira*, featuring four of Brazil's best: Maria Bethânia along with friends like Gal Costa, Gilberto Gil and Caetano Veloso. In 1977, Jom Tob Azulay directed a documentary about the group; another one followed about Maria Bethânia, directed by French filmmaker Georges Gachot. Just over 30 years later in 2008, Maria recorded with Cuban singer Omara Portuondo, and followed up with a live performance DVD. Tapping into the cyberworld, Maria got the green light from Brazil's Ministry of Culture to create a poetry blog, showing her continuing love for this special art form. I love watching how Maria sings and uses passages from literature, blending an incredible musical range with dramatic works. Here's a headstart on your Internet search:

www.mariabethania.com
www.youtube.com/watch?v=1SUci9X_4W8
www.last.fm/music/Maria+Beth%C3%A2nia
www.wikipedia.org/wiki/Maria_Beth%C3%A2nia
www.allmusic.com/artist/maria-beth%C3%A2nia-mn0000573410

Like Agent Superintendant L.A. Jackson, I spend a lot of time going undercover to analyze the psycho-effects music has on different cultures. However, my special area of expertise lies in the concert arena— my career objective is in going to concerts to see live performers. Who would want to stop enjoying that kind of job perk? As long as the office keeps transmitting my name to the secret booth at will call, I'll be there to pick up my tickets. Speaking of which, my Siri iPhone says a new concert just popped up on Brazil's *Citibank Music Hall* event listing. Allow me to introduce you to our next artist, while I make a VIP call to the will call—if I'm not back in time, Agent Superintendant L.A. Jackson will have to fill in on my behalf...

GETTING TO KNOW: Almir Sater

Born as Eduardo Melke Almir Sater, this composer, singer and guitarist also acted in telenovelas, the Brazilian version of American soap operas. Musically, he dabbles in experimental Folk stylings and strangely enough, he has a strong connection with groups of 10: he popularized the 10-string guitar, he released at least 10 solo albums, and he has three decades worth of hands-on experience playing music. Combining his style with Folk, Blues, Classical, Pop and Rock, he also features sounds of the accordian on albums like *Signs 7*.

Ever since he was young, Almir Sater gravitated towards the sounds of music and nature. After leaving his native Campo Grande in Mato Grosso do Sul for Rio de Janeiro at the age of twenty, Sater had his eyes set on studying law. As the force of music manifested itself within him, Almir flipped the script and jumped all the way into the study of music. Returning to Campo Grande, he started a group called *Lupo and Lantern*, with himself as Lupo. By 1979, Sater expanded his range and relocated to São Paulo to work with Tete Espindola and Diana Small.

The following year, his first album was recorded. Then he joined *Generation Silver House*, which helped expose music coming out of South Mato Grosso to a wider audience. Sater then immersed himself into 1986's secret operation *Hope Fellowship* with his unit; comprised of musicians, a journalist and a photographer, they set off on a mission to gather intelligence on a tropical wetland called the Pantanal. L.A. Jackson says it looks like Florida's Everglades to him, but you can compare for yourself. Travelling to remote locations, the resulting documentary gave an in-depth view of various sub-regional ecosystems, and the people that live there.

By the late 80s, Almir Sater was asked to be a special guest at the *Free Jazz Festival*, along with a host of well-known music artists. He even went to Nashville, home of Country music, and shared his Brazilian influences with the locals. During the 90s, Almir Sater picked up awards for his motivational Brazilian songs, followed by making his acting skills known. Almir starred in a telenovela and participated in the creation of a popular regional songbook with Renato Teixeira and Paulo Simões. Sater became famous for his experimental flair and for using various, lesser-known tunings of instruments like the 10-string viola, 12-string guitar and the charango, a small Andean guitar traditionally made from an armadillo shell back. Being influenced by a wide range of acts from The Beatles to Pink Floyd to Al Jarreau, Almir Sater had connections with fellow musicians from the Andes and from Paraguay.

Continuing to act in shows like *The Cattle King* and the *Rede Globo*, Almir Sater's acting stint was 'a wrap' in 2006 with a final appearance on the soap opera, *Bicho do Mato*, the *Bosco Brazil* and *Cristianne Fridman*. Paying legendary singer Roberto "King of Latin Music" Carlos tribute for a remarkable 50-year career, Almir Sater made a special appearance on a DVD called *Sertanejas Emotions*, which was highly acclaimed in Brazil. To sum things up, Almir Sater is memorialized in a number of shows through his acting, as well as musical abilities. Between 1981 and 2006, he played a handful of roles in front of the camera, and released ten albums along the way. He appeared on special music compilations and showed compassion for his peers by taking on philanthropic projects. It doesn't end here either, so you are encouraged to go online and look up the many accomplishments of Almir Sater at places like www.almirsaterbrasil.com.br, google and and of course, wikipedia.

A MEN "ACE" TO SOCIETY… AND A DAMSEL IN THE DRESS

Here's comes more brain food: another associate of mine uses the civilian name of Natan Reiter, but he also goes by Brazilian Agent codename *Dennis the Menace*. Natan got that name from all the pranks he played when he made pit stops at the U.S. operations office. There's no telling where Natan can pop up in Brazil, because he's an international man of mystery and has family spread out all over the place. For instance, Natan has a German last name, but his primary language is Portuguese. In fact, Natan's homeland has a strong concentration of German people, so when he pulled out a handheld device and dialed up his song menu for me, that's when a 'secret code' got clicked on (there's a message in the music). Natan boasts huge musical taste buds because he comes from a culture that appreciates a wide range of music genres—from Jazz to Pop, from Rock to Folk, from Electro-Acoustic to Experimental. This explains his cool, jazzy demeanor but don't get it twisted; as a Musicology agent in Club mode, Natan can be a wild and crazy guy, too!

Of many classified pieces of music data Natan updated me with, probably most indispensable was the recent spread of Rap and Hip-Hop into Brazil's culture. Like my associate agent from Colombia—Lorena (codename *Dancing Diva*), along with Brazil's Regina (*Disco Queen*) and Silvia (*Concert Connoisseur*), Natan gave me lots of legit Brazilian inside information and I'll share it with you when we get to what Agent Reiter calls 'the safe zone.' After hearing what these operatives told me, I plan on digging up my passport, antiglare sunglasses, palm tree shirts, khaki shorts and flip flops—then it's off for a visit to South America!

Now let's position our communications center to receive the latest updates from our next agent, Andrea Gomes, who's now chiming in. Then, we'll set up camp and visit more of Brazil's colorful music roots. Special *Triple A* Agent Andrea of the Americas codename *Diva La Model*, is another one of our 'confidential confidants.' I'm sure we'll have some interesting commentary about how her codename came about later, so let's look forward to it. Making her path from a place called *Rio de Janeiro*, Agent Andrea relays a declassified briefing about her home turf...

Obrigada (thank you) L.A., I'm so happy to be a special guest in your narrative encyclopedia. As I brush up on English as a second language, let me announce that "class is now in session" because back in 2012, I learned a lot playing *Word With Friends*! Everyone knows that "A" is for "Agent Andrea" but historically speaking, the Portuguese are known for putting the "R" in Rio. They discovered Rio de Janeiro on the east coast of South America during the 16th century, and its regional music has been evolving for over 500 years. As local plantations grew, so did the need for field labor. Sadly speaking, slaves were brought in from southwest Africa to work in the plantations of Bahia. African rhythms of slaves from the Congo, Yoruba and other West African nations quickly assimilated with the music of South American natives. The way I can best tell you what followed is that a circle of dominancy was completed when, as L.A. Jackson likes to say, "the music sub-divided into other stylings."

Please take note that many original and modified types of music have been embraced by my fellow Brazilians, including:

Axé	Forro
Bossa Nova	Frevo
Brazilian Rock	Musica Popular Brasileira
Brega	(also called MPB)
Choro	Rock
Classical	Samba
Drum & Bass	Sertanejo

Just a few quick pointers: Axé is popular in Salvador, a city located on the northeast coast of Brazil—Salvador is also the state of Bahia's capital. Bossa Nova is enjoyed by many Brazilians, thanks to contributions of musicians like Tom Jobim. He recorded a song called *Girl From Ipanema* in the late 60s; through versions by acts like Astrud Gilberto, João Gilberto and Jazz great Stan Getz, the song became a worldwide hit. My family has it in the record collection and surprisingly enough, L.A. Jackson told me he remembers hearing it played by his folks back in the day. As a matter of fact, we both still hear *Girl From Ipanema* in commercials, movies—and at top-secret black-tie affairs we inconspicuously pop up at, from time to time. Now to flip the script, let's get conspicuous with a top-notch musician who is full of Brazilian flair.

AN INSIDE VIEW: Tom Jobim

Tom Jobim is a well-known arranger, composer, singer and musician who became a key element in the popularization of Bossa Nova. His songs have been covered by numerous artists; from Brazil to points unknown. Born in Rio de Janeiro, Jobim was influenced by innovators like Pixinguinha, Lucia branco, Hans-Joachim Koellreutter, Claude Debussy, Mayrice Rave and Heitor Villa-Lobos. These composers played a major part in the development of Brazilian music, so please look them up when you have some spare time.

American Jazz also played a part in Tom Jobim's musical prescence. After collaborating with diplomatic poet Vinicius de Moraes in the mid-50s, they discovered a perfect fit and worked together on a variety of popular songs. Along the way, Jobim teamed up with Jazz saxman Stan Getz, João and Astrud Gilberto; two albums came out of his early 60s sessions. The first one, 1963's *Getz/Gilberto*, kicked off a Bossa Nova initiative and started a new trend in the U.S.—it quickly spread around the world. By the mid-60s the record was one of the best Jazz releases of all time, and it catapulted singer Astrud Gilberto to the top through songs like *Corcovado* and *The Girl From Ipanema*. While Norman Gimbel added English lyrics, by 1965 the *Getz/Gilberto* release scooped up a Grammy for "Album of the Year," "Best Jazz Instrumental Album" and "Best Engineered Album, Non-Classical."

Factually speaking, *The Girl From Ipanema* was written about a real girl named Heloisa Eneida Menezes Paes Pinto, who now goes by codename *Helo Pinheiro*. As the story goes, she was a resident of Ipanema, a small locality situated along the coast on Rio de Janeiro's south side. Supposedly when this pre-teen girl stopped by an area bar to purchase cigarettes for her mom, male patrons got loud and unruly—she often caused a ruckus on the way out. Even though it was the winter of 1962, things got a little "clima quente" (hot) in Ipanema's local bar one day: the song's composers sat having a drink and saw this tall, dark-haired brunette make an ebullient appearance. Then the female stunner left just as quickly as she had arrived, like a vision in the desert. Was this a mirage?

Looking at the big picture, there was *something* about this girl that inspired a worldwide hit to become 1965's "Record of the Year." Since then, it has been used in dozens of films and TV shows, and a Disco-Salsoul flavored cover was released in 1977 by Astrud Gilberto; it also got selected by the Library of Congress for inclusion into the National Recording Registry. As we can expect, Helo Pinheiro became a local star but in 2001 when she used the song title to name her new boutique *Garota de Ipanema*, the copyright heirs sued on behalf of their fathers. Fortunately for Helo, public opinion pushed the ruling in her favor—as the story goes, she lived happily ever after.

In a snapshot of things long before *The Girl From Ipanema* ever existed, we see Tom Jobim coming from a prominent middle-class family. He grew up around stately people like senators and other diplomats. In a case of bad luck, Tom's parents seperated and his father passed away in

1935. After receiving a piano from his new stepfather, Tom started playing in nightclubs and worked his way into becoming an arranger for a local record label. Getting married in 1949, Tom and his wife produced children with artistic talents of their own. While the kids and other musicians experienced plenty success, no one worked with as many artists as Tom did; for instance, the great Ella Fitzgerald and Frank Sinatra were among American acts who recorded his compositions on their releases, plus there were others like:

Tony Bennett
Rosemary Clooney
Natalie Cole
Chick Corea
Doris Day
Michael Franks
Art Garfunkel

Judy Garland
Herbie Hancock
Shirley Horn
Olivia Newton-John
George Michael
Oscar Peterson
Lee Ritenour

Carlos Santana
George Shearing
Sting
Barbra Streisand
Toots Thielemans
Julian Lloyd Webber
Andy Williams

On the Brazilian front, Tom Jobim's peers include top shelf artists like Chico Buarque, Gal Costa, Sergio Mendes, Flora Purim and Elis Regina. In addition, hit producer Eumir Deodato collaborated with conductor-composer Claus Ogerman to arrange a few of Tom's songs. Jobim recorded and toured all the way up until the 90s, when his new album *Antonio Brasileiro* was completed. Medically speaking, in 1994 problems of a urinary nature complicated things for Tom and after postponing surgery for spiritual healing instead, he finally consented to undergo an operation. Once completed, he experienced more problems and fell victim to a fatal cardiac arrest—just three days prior to his album release. In tribute to this great artist, a Rock group from Oregon called *Heatmiser* named one of their songs *Antonio Carlos Jobim*; it was off their *Cop and Speeder* album, released the same year Jobim passed away.

For the Red Hot Organization's *Red Hot + Rio* AIDS benefit album, a song called *How Insensitive* featured Jobim and former Police frontman, Sting. In 1999, the Rio de Janeiro International Airport was re-named *Galeão–Antonio Carlos Jobim International Airport*, showing his international appeal to the jetsetting airborn world at large. On the comical side, a Japanese anime show called *Cowboy Bebop* makes reference to all sorts of music and features three wise men: *Antonio, Carlos* and *Jobim*. To learn more about this fabulous icon of Brazilian music, go surfing online by using cybertools like Google, Wikipedia and You Tube.

PICKING UP THE PIECES

Like many places around L.A. Jackson's birthplace in the Caribbean and other parts of the world including South America, there are grand events called *Carnivals*. For instance, every year around June 25th in Portugal and Brazil, huge holiday-themed parties are thrown to honor *São João* (Saint John). No matter what secret operation I'm on around the world, I always try to make it home for these events. Most popular in northeast Brazil, there are plenty places that revolve around carnival-heavy celebration and the style known as *Forro*. A few interesting stories are told about this particular genre—one thought pattern points to the term being a derivatable of "for all."

There are also links stemming from early 1900s English engineers who worked on the Great Western Railway of Brazil in the vicinity of Recife. Now I don't know where the music fit in but on weekends, they threw balls and made some sort of game out of it. These ball games were for railroad staff only and were not deemed "for all" to participate in. This meant there were people playing; and people who watched. From this scenario, I'd be likely to assume a few musicians were on the sidelines tuning in, while tuning up ltheir instruments. In other words, Forro music was playing somewhere in the background...

Another view states that Forrobodo comes from the word *forbado*, which is a corrupted slang term for *fauxbourdon*. While its meaning points to *party* in Portuguese, some places relate to it as *boring*. Episode three of Forro's beginnings takes us to Hungary, where Forro means "burning hot." As Hungarians migrated during the 40s, thousands headed to South America, where the dance was named. Among carnival's many operational bases, São João and Forro are popular in *Caruaru* and *Campina Grande*. I lived in a place called *Recife*; it's the capital city in the state of *Pernambuco*. According to Agent Regina's Top 10 chart as of 2010, Recife was Brazil's seventh largest urban area with over 8 million people—this is where *Frevo* became a dominant force. For your information, we'll take a pit-stop right here so I can deploy what I call the:

> **ENORME FACT:** In Recife where Frevo is popular, a party called *Galo Da Madrugada* made it into the Guinness Book of World Records—for having the largest concentration of people. Guinness also declared the *Carnival of Rio de Janeiro* as "the biggest carnival in the world... and thus, the biggest party on the planet!"

As far as popular singers go, we'll close out our quick-start pointers with *Musica Popular Brasileira* or MPB, which boasts acts like *Gilberto Gil*, *Bebel Gilberto*, *Marisa Monte* and *Caetano Veloso*. Some of our best singers also include *Olodum*, *Timbalada* and *Ivete Sangalo*, who performs in major, Madonna-ish extravaganzas during tour time. Speaking of Madonna, I heard she may bring some of that new Mirosa Beer (www.birramirosa.com) along on her next tour. Personally, I like the Lemon flavor, and music *biz* superhero Stephen Stone's new group Anything But Monday says "*It's the Real Sensation!*" Since all this makes me think of the "lights, camera and action" of my younger days, I must get L.A. Jackson to pull out some of his audiovisual equipment to help me with the next part...

SHINING THE LIGHT ON: Ivete Sangalo

Entering the music world from Bahia, Ivete Maria Dias de Sangalo is a Latin Grammy winner popular in the *Axe* and *MPB* (Musica Popular Brasileira) arenas. Adding to her assets, Ivete expanded her visibility as an actress and TV host. This experienced singer comes armed and ready as codename *Best Seller*. Ivete released over a dozen albums; six with a group known as *Banda Eva*. Over four million copies of their music was sold and Ivete went on to release another seven albums as a solo artist. At the end of the day, Ivete Sangalo is recognized for selling over twelve million albums, with 14 Latin Grammy nominations, high energy shows, and popularity as far away as Portugal.

Like many of her Bahian neighbors, Ivete Sangalo has Spanish roots. In this case, it's on her father's side of the family. Ever since Ivete's youth, she was performing at various local events and special presentations at school. After winning the distinguished *Dorival Caymmi* trophy in 1992, her mind stayed focused on being in front of an audience. She signed on with Sony Music around 1993, and her former Axe group Banda Eva reunited for another run in the sun. A live album called *Banda Eva Ao Vivo* became a best-seller by topping the million unit mark.

By the late 1990s, Ivete Sangalo stepped up her game with a solo release full of Axe stylings and Bahian rhythms. The album went gold; and then went platinum. In 2000, she followed up with another release—it also went platinum. Ivete tapped into the vein of musical dexterity to deliver a widely accepted series of releases that continued to fill the pipeline after she went solo. Her *Festa* album shot her to the top of the "hot" list, and the *Festa* single became Brazil's most popular song in 2001. The video got tons of airplay and featured cameo appearances by almost two dozen Brazilian celebrities. In 2002, Ivete expanded her comfort zone with a new album. Special guest Brian McKnight (who I heard dramatically expanded his own comfort zone around 2011) performed a duet with her.

Many artists run a risk of losing their core audience by going outside of what the fans know and expect. Sometimes, they have to look at the big picture to create new markets for themselves and although it could be considered as risky business, a big payoff can supercede the danger of such an attempt. Over the years, Ivete Sangalo earned her fans' love, trust and respect—to that end, she has been inducted into the *True Brazilian Diva* club (I too am a member… and the President). With that induction, the star remains fault-free of any shortcomings and does no wrong in the eyes of her fans. In other words—even if Ivete fell short, she'd still have diplomatic immunity!

There's plenty more to learn about this gifted singer, so put your hands on a keyboard and mouse to allow your eyes a view of websites like www.ivetesangalo.com. This is where you can fill your musical menu with more tasty treats from yet another great artist from "beyond the border." There's one more great Brazilian singer I grew up listening to, named Djavan. Back in L.A. Jackson's younger days, he marketed and promoted a few records released by Djavan, like *Bird of Paradise* and *Puzzle of Hearts*. Let's see how this great artist yielded fruit to feed fans around the world, with plenty to spare.

ANOTHER BRAZILIAN VIEW: DJAVAN

Jumping right in, Djavan Caetano Viana was born in 1949 in Alagoas, near Brazil's northeast zone. Simply going by Djavan, this artist was a World music artist who had several releases going through the pipeline. In addition to combining traditional rhythms from Brazil with styles from Africa, Europe, North, Central and South America, Djavan musically depicts categories like Samba, Latin Dance and Brazilian Pop/Musica Popular Brasilerra (MPB).

Growing up without access to lots of stashed cash, Djavan still found a way to start a music group: *Luz, Som, Dimensão* or Light, Sound, Dimension—LSD. Psychedelically speaking, this group would probably have been placed under scrutiny of law officials if they were based in the States and used those initials. To thicken the plot, they performed a few Beatles songs; some of which were at one time considered "anti-establishment." As an example, some folks thought the Beatles hit, *Lucy in the Sky with Diamonds* referred to LSD—chemical codename, *Lysergic Acid Diethylamide*. Am I "daytripping," or should that be *LAD*?

Getting back to reality, Djavan moved to Rio de Janeiro in 1973 and gained access to more clubs to perform in. Within a matter of years, he had an album called *A Voz, o Violão e a Arte de Djavan*. The release spawned classics like *Flor de Lis*, a forerunner in a long stream of hits that followed. Djavan got so popular that R&B legend Stevie Wonder played harmonica on his record. To remain on the cutting-edge, Stevie often ventured off the mainstream path to experiment with other styles, like World music. Even martial arts giant Steven Seagal asked for Stevie's blessings on Seagal's musical offering, *Songs from the Crystal Cave*, around 2005. Here's a quick listing of a few hit songs composed by Djavan, maybe you've heard a few (or maybe you should):

Açaí	Oceano
Esquinas	Samurai
Faltando um	Se...
Pedaço	Serrado
Meu Bem Querer	Si

For those who don't know, the reason I mentioned you may have heard some of these songs is due to American artists like Al Jarreau, The Manhattan Transfer, Carmen McRae and Lee Ritenour; they've all recorded compositions made by Djavan. If that's not enough for validation, let me point out a long list of fellow countrymen who were influenced by this wide angled talent and recorded his tunes:

Gal Costa	João Bosco	Dominguinhos
Dori & Nana Caymmi	Chico Buarque	Caetano Veloso
Lenine	Daniela Mercury	Maria Bethânia
	Ney Matogrosso	

Djavan was marketed internationally by CBS Records and Sony Music, meaning that once again, L.A. Jackson recalls working on campaigns that included Djavan. Between 1984's release of *Lilás* and 1994's *Novena*, this Brazilian recording artist had over a half dozen major label releases. Staying abreast of world issues in 1998, Djavan donated the song *Dukeles* to the Red Hot Organization's AIDS benefit album, *Onda Sonora: Red Hot + Lisbon*. A 1999 double live album, *Ao Vivo*, topped the 1.2 million mark with the song *Acelerou*. It was embraced by Brazil as "Song of the Year" at 2000's *Latin Grammy Awards*.

Milagreiro was Djavan's final album with Sony Music, and his following releases came out on Luanda Records. Djavan has a track record that spans some forty years—I urge you to listen to the music of this 'el primo' artist, with or without your hand on the mouse. Just type his name in and click 'search,' or visit sites like www.djavan.com, You Tube and more. For our finale, here's some secret, classified info for your eyes only. Do you know what makes me happiest the most? It's an 'especial' style of music called *Samba*, which is very famous in my hometown of Rio De Janeiro—hopefully, you are yearning to learn more about it with Agent Superintendant, L.A. Jackson, because here he comes!

I appreciate you sharing a small part of your infinite yet top-secret wisdom with us, Agent Andrea. We'll discuss more about your favorite music style "in two and two," as Chuck Woolery says but here's some unrelated news: a little birdie tweeted us that you were a top model who often did what I like to call *the twist around walk*, on the runways of Rio de Janeiro. Was there ever any music in the background and can you expound on your experience a little bit for us?

Yes, L.A., I could explain more for you and your readers—my modeling career began at the age of thirteen and went until I was twenty. Doing fashion shows, commercials, billboards and layouts in popular magazines like *Veja* kept me busy in my younger days. At night, when I went out on promotional visits to clubs, the music kept me going. It was everywhere I went. Professionally speaking I loved it; and so did many supporters who came out to see me!

Unfortunately, my fan management system got out of control. After the security detail began asking me for autographs, I had to as you say, "pull the plug" and head north to America on sabatical. To coin a popular phrase I've picked up, "the rabbit hole runs deep." At this point,

L.A. Jackson advises me that whoever is not cleared to receive Musicology code TMI (*Too Much Information*) should make their way to the waiting room. In other news, let me do the "opt out," so I can brush up on more American buzz words and do like L.A. did—put a book out—one day, I will do the same thing. It has been wonderful to be a part of this marvelous adventure, but for now as we say in my South American homeland, "*tchau tchau!*"

Thanks Agent Andrea—I'll have to catch myself a flight for a 'visual visit' to your neck of the southern hemisphere one day, because South American lands like São Paulo, Rio de Janeiro and other parts of Brazil simply sound like cultural hotspots I need to plug into. Keeping things moving, the following is a briefing on *Samba*, which is recognized as Brazil's national music style. To get an inside view, we brought in more undercover help to open the lens on this popular music style. Since it also introduced a highly combustible dance, we'll go into stealth mode for the next leg of our adventure. According to declassified preliminary reports, Samba's history is a colorful one; let's open some files…

After Brazil seceded from Portugal in 1822, African *Lundu* began spreading from poor Black neighborhoods to affluent communities. In Brazil, this was the first type of music with sources pointing directly back to Africa. For many of the usual suspects (musicians), it was simply "business as usual." A number of sources point to different beginnings, so let's check a few of them out. First off, the word "Samba" is said to have originated from *Semba*, a Southern African, Congo-Angolan style of music and dance; the Congo region actually has a multilingual definition for the word Semba. Evolving from the word "Masemba" (a touch of the bellies), Semba alludes this dance is driven by a traditional form of music.

Semba has been popular for years before Angola pulled away and claimed independence from Portugal's system of colonialism in 1975. Many emotions get poured through this music style and that's one reason why it's so popular in Angolan life, from parties to funerals. If you remember, we've seen similar instances with other cultures. Affiliated Semba styles include a fast-tempo Techno-House style called *Kuduro*, plus others like *Kabetila*, *Kazukuta*, *Kizomba*, *Rebita* and of course, *Samba*. Some of these styles are influenced by Kongo line dances and Carnival music. The way I see it, Semba often describes life events with interesting morals to the story, while Samba simply makes you want to "get on down and partay." Let's dig a little deeper…

VIVA LA SAMBA!

In Brazil, new millennium Samba acts continually emerge to establish themselves and pay homage to greats who came before them. One famous act is Angolan artist Barceló de Carvalho, codename *Bonga*. He's partially responsible for exposing Samba to a World Music fan base, in which Brazilian music plays a major part. As lively Brazilian music plays in the background, dancers dance while non-dancers watch on with nodding heads and tapping feet, all moving in unison. Over at the bar sits our friend Natan Reiter, summoning us over to join him. Since back in the good old days, he's been rumoured to be a ladies man known as *Agent Dennis the Menace*. Natan takes a long slurp from his umbrella drink, then peers over the rims of his dark sunglasses to reveal some classified data:

Well L.A., during the early 1900s, Choro music gave way to Samba around the Rio de Janeiro area. Coming out of the city's urban areas, descendants of slaves kept their traditions alive and passed the music down through generations. As Samba became more internationally known, another style called *Samba de Enredo* centered around the region's Carnival celebration. Throughout the remainder of the 20th century, other Samba styles appeared: *Samba de Breque* has a choppy, Reggae flavor, while *Samba-Cancao* is featured at a variety of nightclubs. *Samba Pagode* is another modern form found in this popular music genre.

I've also unearthed a protocol and dance technique called *Folk Samba*, and I wish I could take credit for developing this people-friendly style. It features songs made for couples who enjoy dancing closely. Recently acquired counter-intelligence reveals this modern Samba style literally changed the face of dance but remember, many modern styles are really just improved versions of older ones. Samba became the new and improved version of Choro. I could tell you more, but I see a counter-intelligence disposal squad looming around—I suggest we break camp with the safety crew and reconvene later. See you in three clicks at our pre-assigned alternate location!

Unravelling a secret communiqué Agent Reiter slipped me upon our retreat, the rest of this mission unveils itself. Folks, it looks like we are about to go deeper into the heart of Samba and its related styles—this is a part of Natan's standard mode of operation called *The Samba Experience*. As evidenced earlier, Samba gained popularity around the beginning of the 20th century. This was largely through efforts of influential Blacks from the Brazilian state of Bahia, near Rio de Janeiro. At that time Bahia was the capital but by the 60s, entertainment slowed in Brazil due to the untimely arrival of dictatorship. When the 70s rolled around, Samba reappeared in clubs and over the airwaves, with attention-grabbing songs for listeners to enjoy.

Composers and singers like Beth Carvalho, Clara Nunes, Martinho da Vila and Paulinho da Viola were cast into the forefront of Brazil's music scene, and the rest is history. At the end of 'el dia' (the day), mainstream Samba charted its own course and took on wider forms than in the elemental days of Folk Samba. That was when music-promoting operatives like Agent Reiter were secretly coaxing couples to dance closer; this explains a huge population explosion since those good old, Folk Samba days. Speaking for many, a big "thanks" could go out to Agent Reiter's coaxing initiatives—what they've led to is more people than ever dancing to all kinds of Samba music! The security alert just went off so once again, let's catch up with our secret source, Agent Reiter aka *Dennis the Menace*; he relocated to a new rendezvous point three clicks east to avoid counter-intelligence detection. Before any media sources intercept classified data and go public, we'll gather more information from Natan, so we can gain a better grip on the Samba situation down here in Brazil territory. Are we "code green" yet, Agent Reiter?

Yes, and it's good to be back L.A.—sometimes you never know whose eyes are watching, out here in the bunkers of this thick Brazilian music jungle. Let me toss you another piece of the puzzle: after being eclipsed by genres like Disco and Brazilian Rock in the 70s and early 80s, the mid-to-late 80s marked Samba's radical resurgance. This time, its metamorphosis occurred in the suburbs of Rio de Janeiro through a style called *Pagode*. The renewed version of Samba came armed with instruments like banjos and tan-tans. This style became a cultural phenomenon that opened doors for other genres and newly-concocted phrases, plus slang terms known as *Gíria*. Brazilians also began embracing more Rock, Rap and Reggae; thus my conclusion suggests that when a popular music style like Samba becomes dominant, it subdivides into fusions like *Samba-Rock*, Samba-*Rap* and *Samba*-Reggae. To add, *Samba-Reggae* components of the 80s were brought in from places like Pelourinho, Brazil. The blending of these two popular genres enabled bands like *Olodum* to spread earlier social messages of musical activists like *Ile Aiye*.

Domestically speaking, White and upper-class Brazilians initially associated Samba with their poor, darker-skinned countrymen because of its West African lineage. Based on this perception, we can assume that like in America, racism reached a certain degree before attempting to re-face the musical culture of Brazil (at least to some extent). Was this merely a perception for some, or more of a grim reality? What's your opinion? Along with me and Agent Superintendent L.A. Jackson, inquiring minds would like to know... With the exception of a few, American slave-owners were adamant about curtailing slaves' access to traditional instruments—it was feared they were used for secret communication purposes. But here in Brazil, I'm happy to report that our plantation owners rarely impeded slaves from practicing customs like drum-playing. This particular privilege constitutes some of the reasons why certain forms of Brazilian Samba by composers such as Antonio Carlos Jobim, can sound so similar to American Jazz from music mazes like Louisiana.

Culturally speaking, Samba not only entertained, it united people across the Americas through socially expressive music, clothes that displayed fashion bravado, and bodily movements that were full of what I call 'panache.' Like American Hip-Hop, Samba-Rap and its related styles had lyrics that stimulated pride and human rights awareness, coupled with underlying chants for civil freedom. Sportswise, in 1994 Samba played an important role at an international sporting event called the FIFA World Cup soccer tournament, which had its own Samba song called *Copa 94.* Speaking of the World Cup, I have coincidentally been summoned to a high-level planning meeting for the next World Cup game. This one's a must-attend, so I must bid you all a hearty see you later, or *até logo!*

Thanks for your input Natan and folks, it's no secret that Agent *Dennis the Menace* is a key operative in events like the World Cup—but I must say one thing about those so-called "planning meetings." I've often seen Natan bring up planning meetings before going to his favorite sporting event (*the big game*) and subsequently accumulating gobs of gambling ticket stubs. Natan plugs his earbuds up to the iPod, iPad, iPhone or whatever it is, while dialing up a secret playlist. Then he dons a cherry red Ferrari cap, jacket and matching car—with that said, let's make a quick pit stop to pick up a sharp point.

One reason why Natan's so proud of the Brazil's soccer event is because it held the distinguished record of having the largest attendance in World Cup history. Another reason is because they let him drive his exotic car right up to the stands, where he parks close to his seat. Comically speaking, I've just been handed an envelope and upon opening it, a satellite photo reveals 'a key Musicology operative' cruising slowly through a crowd near an arena. Unsurprisingly, it's *Agent Dennis the Menace* aka Natan Reiter—in his bright red Ferrari, matching cap, jacket, 'iThing,' gambling tickets and all. So our quick point is, that sure was some kind of "planning meeting." Regardless, we appreciate Natan sharing time with us and if you're ever in Brazil, please look him up in the "Secret Agent" Yellow Pages!

Upon conclusion of our Brazilian intelligence gathering mission, please note that data acquired from Special Agents Regina, Silvia, Andrea and Natan helped shine light to teach a few important lessons: one is how diverse the country of Brazil can be. Also, Samba as a genre unified people through sonic exchanges between musicians, listeners, dancers… and outspoken artists with social commentary to offer. In many circles, interactions like these permitted artists to exhibit their distinct music styles, and these interactions were not uncommon. No matter what one's social or ethnic background is, many of these exchanges fused strong relationships. Plenty of styles were popularized by various cultures— Samba was one that contained the glue of unification for a once severely-fragmented country. Thanks to our special Musicology agents, the country of Brazil remains safe: as one of the world's top music producers. There's one more project for us to do prior to heading back to the Northern Hemisphere: let's grab a few 'synergy snapshots' that show the all-encompassing diversity of Brazilian music. With that said, it's time to get an INSIDE VIEW of styles flourishing within the range of sounds that blended into Brazil's African communities.

AFRO-BRAZILIAN MUSIC

- **Afoxe** - A style with Candomble roots pointing back to religious music. Associations have been made with regards to Black social activism in Brazil and the Indian independence movement of Mahatma Gandhi. Groups like The Filhos de Gandhi (Sons of Gandhi) tipped the racial scales by appearing at Salvador's Carnaval event, previously heavily attended by light-skinned Brazilians
- **Capoeira** - Considered as a call-and-response version of Folk music, this style focuses around the popular sport known as Capoeira. This type of music features instruments like the *atabaque*, *berimbau* and the *pandeiro*. Improvised or popular songs composed by experienced *mestres* tell stories of Capoeira's past history
- **Maracatu** - found in the general Olinda/Recife areas and is often heard at Carnival events. This style of music plays alongside parade groups representing traditional ceremonies from the colonial era that honored the Kings of Congo. These African slaves assumed key leadership roles in the slave community. Musicians played percussion instruments including alfaia drums, metal gongue bells, shakers and snare drums

BRAZILIAN FUSION STYLES

- *Samba–exaltação* or exaltation Samba – a subgenre inspired by Ary Barroso's popular song *Aquarela do Brasil*
- *Bossa Nova* (New Beat) – a type of Samba often played with Jazz instruments and sung with softer voices than more popular versions of the genre
- *Samba de Roda* – a ritual dance style preserved in some Bahian towns, this type of Samba is performed in a *capoeira roda*. Roda refers to *capoeiristas* (capoeira players positioned in circular form)
- Other Fusion styles include Neo-pagode, Samba de breque, Samba-canção, Samba-enredo and Samba de Gafieira

By 2001, a new Samba form from Bahia made its appearance, fully equipped with rhythms influenced by Reggaeton, Calypso and Latin melodies. Next, a huge undercurrent of acts stepped forward with politically themed lyrics embedded in their music. Although we've navigated through a few of Brazil's popular styles, please remember there is still much to be discovered about Samba-Reggae and Afro-Brazilian music. Before we jet out of here, the Captain says that according to the coordinates displayed in our time-plotting visionscope, we can sample more music genres coming out of Brazil in an upcoming installment of the Musicology series.

Remember, we've barely scratched the surface of Brazilian music, but plenty of information exists on music from this exciting region of South America—and we still have tons of snapshots to review. While more "truth is out there," the sheer purpose of our subvertive operation was to inform and encourage inquisitive minds that "yearn to learn." Translated, take the ball and run with it. You should run out and investigate more styles of music from Brazil and the sprawling South American continent—what you discover may just ignite your inner cranial cavity and set forth a course of neuro-cosmic ascension to level SIS: *Superior Intellectual Status*. For extra credit, I encouraged you to discover a style that suits your musical tastes… and share it with a friend or two!

Well folks, the Captain suggests we resume our networking party in the main galley's Salón de Fiestas, because it's time to head on back to the States. I don't know about you, but I sure could use a nice, thick Cajun burger right about now! As long as it's seasoned right and comes with a nice beat behind it, we're in good shape. For those of you readers with sensitive taste buds, feel free to season your next serving to taste with…

A TOUCH OF SPICE

As our intercontinental soirée unfolds, we find ourselves leaving the Southern Hemisphere and shooting across the Caribbean region—looking down, we see tons of tiny islands. One of them stands out to me because that's where I was born: on the island of Jamaica. Let's kick some quick Caribbean stats as we do a fly-by. On August 27th 2006, an article in Jamaican newspaper The Gleaner (www.jamaica-gleaner.com), reported that over the course of 182 years (1820 and 2002), 68 million people from the Caribbean had migrated to the United States. That's enough people to rival the state of California's population—twice!

Minus the slaves kept to work on Caribbean plantations, most Africans were separated and classified in this zone before being shipped off to the U.S. and elsewhere. The article also showed approximately 2.6 million Caribbean natives called America home at that time. That's like the city of Chicago or the state of Nevada full of Jamaicans. To bluntly clarify what I'm saying, this meant the Caribbean region harbored the largest group of Black people that were reeled in as a direct result of the slave trade era. During the 1800's, the Caribbean region became highly sought after due to its trade routes, strategic point of defense and mainland proximity, so in time the U.S. acquired more commodities from the area.

By the 20th century, Puerto Rico was a U.S. territory, and Puerto Ricans later began filling labor positions in America's North, South, and as far west as Hawaii. Even though Puerto Ricans were free laborers, racism caused some to be treated like the indentured servants of yesteryear. Around 1920, large numbers of Caribbean laborers were migrating to the U.S. and establishing their own communities in major cities. This transition was like a spin-off of early European explorers who left their countries to colonize newly discovered lands abroad.

The 1st World War led to high demand for local labor, as America tightened restrictions on European immigration. Over 100,000 Caribbean travelers passed through the U.S. looking for work: at one point there were more Caribbean people living and traveling to the U.S., than were in their own respective homelands. It didn't take long for Cuban, Puerto Rican and other Caribbean visitors to land in New York, Chicago, and Miami (90 miles from Cuba) to share abundant musical heritages. Some also showed up in a city with a moniker that turned two words into one: *"Nawlins."* Around this time, America quickly became a sonic melting pot that stewed with tasty new musical flavors in areas previously dominated by the Blues and Gospel. This is prevalent in the fusion of African, Blues, Caribbean, Latin and European music. Early *Jazz* was born, along with sub-culture styles (*Cajun* and *Zydeco*) in the New Orleans region. Since my craving for a Cajun burger is now reaching outrageous proportions, our Captain tweets that coordinates have been set for this time-traveling vessel to touch down immediately in *"Nawlins"* (New Orleans) next—please fasten those seat belts as we put the wheels down and decelerate...

Landing back on solid ground, let's drill a little deeper into the past by making note that the culture of Louisiana was heavily influenced by the descendants of African, Caribbean and French people (Creoles). It's also said the Cajun-Creole culture is related to an ethnic group called Acadians—around 1755, England expelled them from the Canadian Maritime near Nova Scotia. In addition to the homegrown influence Acadians brought to Louisiana, they also partook in the music of their newfound countrymen. The fusion of these cultures can be heard in the percussive resonance of Zydeco, which comes loaded with the attributes of Native American, African, British, Caribbean, French and German cultures. Through musical osmosis, emergent styles like African, Blues, Cajun, Caribbean, Gospel and wide variety of Jazz engulfed the entire New Orleans vicinity. This is the short version, but www.democraticunderground.com has more to be explored in this saga.

Woefully speaking, New Orleans' fun-loving people experienced their own share of racial encounters, dividing the social barriers between Whites and non-Whites. These divisions were often compounded by internal strife between relatives baring differing skin tones—mainstream society usually favored light-skinned people over darker ones. When this domestic condition was mixed in with the socio-economic positions of Whites, Negroes and others, it then becomes clear how this recipe could easily cook up what I'd call a "deadly communicable concoction" known as racial violence. On the other hand, New Orleans is undoubtedly one of few places where diverse racial groups like the "Afro-Franco" (Black and French), and "Afro-Indian" (Black and Native American) continue to reside. Today, there are healthy homegrown cultural factions and an international populace:

Afro-American	French	Italian
Afro-Caribbean	German	Jewish
Canadian	Greek	Scottish
English	Indian	Scandinavian
	Irish	

These cultures and more still convene in the Louisiana Bayou for special events like:

Essence Music Festival	Satchmo SummerFest
French Quarter Festival	Shrimp Festival
Jazz and Heritage Festival	New Orleans Wine &
Mardi Gras	Food Experience
Ponchatoula Strawberry Festival	

Sans le beaux beaux (without messing things up), here's a little *lagniappe* (freebie) to keep things moving—two thumbs go up for the previously discussed *Second Line*, and those Saints winning the Super Bowl back in February of 2010. That accomplishment set off a huge celebration, as the words "*Who Dat*" echoed from fans in a '*gumbo ya-ya*' sort of way across the Bayou. Now that's how you pass a good time in the stands—or out on the field in the middle of the muck, because it can get *beaucoup crasseux*, and I do mean *dirty dirty*!

Before we move ahead to more featured guests from our forum of stars, let's zoom around New Orleans to take targeted snapshots for later analysis. Appropriately labeled as "The City That Care Forgot," the 2005 disaster of Hurricane Katrina turned *The Big Easy* into a city struggling to regain its place as one of the country's most viable hotspots. News of the Katrina crisis rang throughout the world—even Jamaica's *Weekly Gleaner* newspaper in their August 2006 issue stated, "Louisiana became a failed state. Neither the State nor the Federal government was able to protect the lives of its citizens." There was also "Spike Lee's documentary *When the Levees Broke*, follows the theme that the largely Black state of Louisiana failed because of the mixture of politics, bureaucracy and racism." But were there other variables that contributed to the degradation of New Orleans' keeping up with the times? Looking on from the sidelines, we'll wait and see if Congress gets any new batteries installed in their *citizens care clock*. Our Captain says it's now time to board a designated shuttle and head to the city of Shreveport for a few inside views from my slightly action-packed, superhero-like past.

In writing about "The City That Care Forgot," I would be remiss not to reflect upon one of Louisiana's "Clocks of the New Day." He's a muscle-bound guy that runs like the Energizer Bunny named Robert "*Superman*" Blount. My professional association with him is heading on 25 years now, sans *one* unpleasant experience in that time span—that's more than I can say for a lot of folks! A Shreveport, Louisiana resident who I've known for a minute, Superman the "*Muscle Rev*" heads up a ministry called *Fit For Life Inc*. This real-life hero tapped into close friends like eight-time *Mr. Olympian* champ Lee Haney to become a "beacon deacon," as he keeps a quartz-like watch on the state of health in Louisiana. Working in tandem with the President's Council on Fitness, Superman's *Fit for Life Day* helps to increase awareness of the dangers of childhood obesity. Superman planned on taking this event, complete with bodybuilding shows, on tour throughout the state of Louisiana and if you're lucky, it might come to a city near you!

Through support from the Senate, in October of 2008 Superman was appointed to head the Commission on Men's Health and Wellness by the Governor of Louisiana, Bobby Jindal. Now Superman was overseeing data evaluations and making recommendations on the improvement of men's health initiatives in Louisiana. With thirteen important members on the board including the Chief Health Officer of the state's Department of Health and Hospitals, we can expect this supercharged, ordained minister to continue spreading a positive message to all the people he reaches. Among clients who have been fortunate enough to work with him are NBA All Star and Hall of Famers like Dominique Wilkins and Head Coach Glenn "Doc" Rivers, movie actor Tiny "Dee Bo" Lister, CEO and President of Fruit-of-the-Loom Bob Farle and U.S. Gold Medalist swimmer, Steve Lunquist.

I first met Superman during the late 80s while out in the field, marketing CBS Records product in Atlanta. This meeting took place at a local record store on the south side of town, near Old National Highway in College Park. Running into him at a record store let me know that bodybuilders like to "pump up" to the beat of engaging music. We immediately hit it off and hadn't skipped a beat since recently reuniting, thanks to the magic of an Internet search. Way back before the World Wide Web was being accessed by the masses, Superman was popular around Atlanta as a media-friendly bodybuilder, gracing town among the likes of nationally known bodybuilding celebrities like Tony Atlas, Tony Pearson and Lee Haney.

Moving to Atlanta from Shreveport to play football for Morris Brown College during the mid-70s, Superman Blount made appearances and wrote articles in nutritional/health publications throughout the world, including *Muscle & Fitness*, *Flex* and *Iron Man* magazines. By 1980, Superman was under the professional training of World Class Power Lifter, U.S.A. Bodybuilding Champion and Pro-Wrestler, Tony Atlas. After a year of working together, Superman began training with Mr. America, Mr. Universe and Mr. World, Tony Pearson.

FAST FORWARD: Beginning in 1984, Superman professionally trained, coached and motivated Lee Haney for seven years to win seven consecutive Mr. Olympia Championships. RECORD: This tremendous feat surpassed the record set by another famous bodybuilder, spokesperson and actor, codename *Gov Pump-You-Up*, Arnold Schwarzenegger. Since I've known Superman, he has always been one of those people that would PAUSE to hold an extended arm out for those in need, and as I PLAY the tape to look at things these days, he's only gotten busier. Becoming smitten with The Holy Spirit, Superman hit REWIND and made a trip back to his hometown in the late 90s. You see, he had been given a vision from God that no orders had been issued for him to STOP; other plans were in store for him.

Learning to use his body as a temple of the Lord, Superman began synergizing physical fitness and nutrition with a little uplifting music, thus mixing together his own ministry. This is the guy I'm going to talk to about becoming a music evangelist! But seriously speaking, Superman cites a connection between the Bible and being fit: "Besides the assistance of larger animals, Christ and his disciples walked or ran to their destinations… they had to row boats to get across the seas; man, they had to be healthy." And I'd be willing to bet they traveled with singers and musicians for 'mobile' sound. Even with a lack of the sophisticated powered motors of today, Superman modulates that ancient man traveled vast distances across land and sea, spreading The Word. And spread it they did; with the sun, wind and stars guiding them along the way. As it grew one region at a time, cultures around the world eventually recognized Christianity to coexist in the spiritual realm with African and other, even older religions.

Partnering with radio stations like KRMD, KMJJ, Magic 102.9, MixFM 97.3 and Supertalk 1340, Superman's message becomes larger than life. Down-playing the magnitude of his grand efforts, he remains humbled by the widespread devastation caused by Hurricane Katrina. In conjunction with ongoing initiatives to rebuild New Orleans, Superman plans to fulfill his mission by also improving the health systems in places like Shreveport. This high-powered precision "Clock of the New Day" astutely believes "God can use anybody." How's that for never forgetting? Can you spell I-N-S-P-I-R-A-T-I-O-N-A-L! Hopefully, you'll be inspired enough to check out Superman's *Fit For Life Weekend Challenge* held annually around the end of May. And folks, please don't forget to visit his website at www.bfitforlife.org–stop by sometime to pick up your very own, super-charged blessing. Now let's hop onboard the super-shuttle and head back to New Orleans, where we'll get refreshed with a little more 4-1-1 on Jazz and 'pop the cork' to get a fluid look at this section's special treat, codename *Bubbles*.

The United States became a major supplier of world entertainment through cities like New York, Los Angeles and Chicago taking the lead as major hubs. New Orleans was always an iconic symbol of American history too, until Hurricane Katrina devastated the city in 2005: this gave things a whole new meaning. However, prior to that deadly tempest, New Orleans regularly hosted food, sporting, music and other events that attracted people from around the globe. Locally speaking, the age-old tradition of *Super Sundays* made New Orleans look like a huge "Crescent City juke joint," as young city dwellers relieved their daily stresses. They did this at hotspots like Orleans and Rampart by enjoying the cool vibes of music, dancing and weekend-styled partying. Here's a quick heads up—similar social activities also bonded people during the Blues, Jazz and other important eras of history.

Jazz soared from New Orleans, Louisiana to uncharted heights as a new staple of sound. Like in New Orleans, the genre was absorbed throughout the Mississippi Delta region and was performed by musicians who often played styles like the Blues. The descriptive musical stories of trials and tribulations made Blues music extremely popular in the Delta. Additionally, many people supported acts that sang and tap-danced a way into their hearts; we'll highlight one of these acts next.

Although various musical elements were documented in the 19th century, one can only imagine how well the business of entertaining patrons functioned in the early years. I point this out just for the record, because the inception of a capitalistic approach to supply the demands of customers is what spawned the American music industry. Our upcoming itinerary was designed to help you 'see with your own eyes' and visualize how the music *biz* evolved from its early beginnings. Those who were watching at the time saw a major musical feat that took place along the way. The process of capturing sound as *recordings* led to the captivation of music-hungry listeners; this in turn initiated lucrative opportunities for those who manufactured and sold little vinyl discs called *records*.

During the early days of show business from the 1880s to 1930s, American *Vaudeville* and *French Cabaret* reigned supreme. Cabaret consisted of comedy, song, dance and theatrical performances in restaurants, or on nightclub stages. They were often hosted by what is called a *Master of Ceremony*, or MC. Some Cabaret performers went as far as expressing political viewpoints... or even showing up in drag. Vaudeville was also popular; these variety shows featured an assortment of live acts, acrobats, animals, celebrities, comedians, impersonators, magicians and of course poets, singers and musicians. Let's flash the SPOTLIGHT ON an incredible Vaudeville singer/dancer/all-around entertainer with the name of *John W. Bubbles*; this legendary performer was admired much by icons like Michael Jackson. In fact, the "King of Pop" himself studied John's moves and even named his pet chimp after him. Don't get it twisted though: Bubbles the chimpanzee never got his dancing chops up to par with John Bubbles—was it because the chimp loved to eat never-ending bananas at Neverland? And were banana splits also on the menu? With that little humor check completed, we'll get on with the show...

BUBBLES UP!

Born in Louisburg, Kentucky circa 1902, John William Sublett changed his stage name to *John W. Bubbles, tap dancer*. Migrating to the Midwest, he landed in Indianapolis and teamed up with a singing piano player named Ford L. "Buck" Washington. By 1919, they became known as *"Buck and Bubbles."* As Buck sang and played his Ragtime piano, Bubbles tap-danced for enthralled onlookers. By 1931, they were the first Black entertainers to appear at Radio City Music Hall in the *Ziegfeld Follies*. Five years later, the pair accomplished another feat: they graced the first, then known as "high-definition" TV program in England and were thus dubbed as the first Blacks to perform on the "tele-tube." Back in those days, high-definition was characterized as 240 lines of resolution on a TV set. Today, that's as low on the totem pole as you can get because hi-def has been totally redefined and televisions are now pushing upwards of a whopping 1920 lines!

Fred Astaire adored the flair of John Bubbles to the point that John gave him personal tap dancing lessons, early on in his career. George Gershwin's 1935 opera *Porgy and Bess* exposed Mr. Bubbles' talent to the masses, as the character "Sportin' Life"—he went on to make periodic appearances in the Gershwin oeuvre for the following twenty years. From the late-30s and into the 40s, John appeared in motion pictures and television shows, displaying his flair in front of the camera for reeled-in gazers to behold. As the 'Father of Super-Rhythmic Tap,' Bubbles supercharged the standard form of toe tapping as personified by contemporaries like Bill "Bojangles" Robinson. Bubbles' highly percussive tap dances were performed atop Jazz improv; this ultimately altered and cemented-in the renewed art of tap-dancing... permanently setting him deep inside the pages of history books.

Paying homage to soldiers in the Vietnam War of the 60s, John Bubbles supported the troops by joining up with the USO for a tour of the war zone. The 70s saw him adding public speaking to his 'many special gifts' list, through seminars on Vaudeville at places like Los Angeles' Variety Arts Theatre. With a humble attitude, he often cited that Fred Astaire was a great dancer "because Bubbles taught him well." By the 80s, John Bubbles topped off his many accolades with the American Guild of Variety Artists 1980 "Life Achievement Award." His final stop before going off to the realm of eternal music in 1986 was a place where some would say is the live theatre and entertainment capital of the world, New York City. To capitalize your knowledge of John W. Bubbles, hit the search button to pull up dozens of pages that will help you tap into a wealth of information on this tier one entertainer: you can even "Like" him on Facebook!

As this part of our adventure comes to a close, please remember that much of music's story can be told through the lives of those who thrived in *the life*. Many of these artists brought truly unique offerings to the table, enabling the music industry to expand its reach upon the listening audience. While we can't see or touch music, it certainly has touched the lives of many people, whether they were Black, Brown, Red, White, Yellow; or any color in-between. With that said, we will now shove off into a new portal and take a spin on a style I'm sure many people were not aware even existed. Let's discover some new musical terrain by heading to higher elevation…

MUSIC UP IN YON HILLS!

An interesting thing happened to me during the early part of writing this book: one day while channel-surfing the airwaves, I came to a screeching halt on *PBS* upon hearing the words "Negro," "Nashville" and "Grand Ole Opry" in the same sentence. After the opening captions scrolled by, a picture of a Black musician appeared. This looked like it was worth watching, so my remote was immediately put down as I cued in to the program and munched on some butter-flavored "O.R.," codename *Orville Redenbacher*. Okay, let's REWIND and get the story popping!

SPOTLIGHT UP ON: DeFord Bailey

A musician credited with helping to bring Country music more up front and center is DeFord Bailey. Born in 1899 in Smith County near Nashville, Tennessee, DeFord defied the odds of racism to become the first Black musician featured at a White-only Country music venue. DeFord was raised by an aunt after his mother died when he was two years old. His determination showed up early in life by overcoming a battle with polio at age three. Rumor has it that after his aunt gave him a harmonica, he was never seen without it again. During the early 1900s, he played what is known as *Black Hillbilly* music: or to be politically correct, *Mountain* music. Bailey went on to break the color barrier at Nashville's Grand Ole Opry by performing with his harmonica, codename *mouth organ*. Although he appeared at the Opry nearly twice as much as any other musician, our analysts report that socio-economics, stacked with racism, was what discouraged him from pursuing his true passion—performing live.

As a young man, DeFord Bailey bounced around Tennessee for a while living with relatives, until he finally landed a job as a houseboy with a prominent White family. Bailey took pride in everything he did, like when he promptly nursed his employer's family back to health after they contracted the flu. Musically speaking, DeFord's caretaking duties took a back seat after the employer discovered his musical dexterity—since then, it was imminent that harmonic expressions of sound would become DeFord's primary job. DeFord Bailey hailed from a family of musicians: his grandfather was an unequaled fiddler (violinist) who played Mountain music and passed 'tricks of the trade' on to DeFord. In addition to violins, the type of Folk music they played was performed with banjos, drums, guitars, harmonicas, harps and mandolins. If the Baileys were still around today, they would be walking contradictions of modern-day Country music artists. Because of that perception, more light must shed on what was discovered about this now-faded genre.

REWIND: Musicians were highly valued during the days of slavery—some slave-owners sent their slaves to New Orleans for fiddle lessons, so they could entertain plantation guests. After the emancipation of slavery, many Black fiddlers kept their instruments and improved their craft; DeFord's grandfather Lewis Bailey was one of them. As stated earlier, DeFord learned much of his repertoire from his grandad, a veteran fiddler who at the time was considered to be *"the best in Smith County."* Now, let's take a closer look at this entity called *Black Hillbilly* music.

Hailing from various parts of Kentucky, Tennessee, Virginia, North and South Carolina, this music style thrived amongst Blacks and Whites. Its influences included other forms of Folk music such as Bluegrass, Country and Blues—if you look hard enough, you might even find a touch of Gospel in some forms of Mountain music. Just to be clear, genres such as Bluegrass, Blues, Country, Folk, Gospel and Mountain music have been commonly enjoyed by Blacks and Whites side by side. Events like community barn dances were very popular in certain areas; folks prepared for barn dances by first clearing the ground of debris. Then, they'd drop sawdust down to cushion the dance surface so they could maneuver in sync with the sounds local musicians created on their instruments. FAST FORWARD to the new millennium, where DJ's showed up with laptops, CDs and MP3s to 'rock the house'—often atop interlocked, drop-down dance floors which are connected piece by piece (similar to what's used for basketball court flooring). But back in the old days when acts like DeFord Bailey showed up, people from all walks of life flocked towards these dances for good, clean fun *together*. Eventually, record companies reflected a sign of the times when they stepped in and *seperated* the music by color, to make *a whole lotta green*.

Besides DeFord Bailey and his family, another anomaly found in 20th century Black Mountain/Bluegrass music was a diverse group of fiddle and banjo players called the *Carolina Chocolate Drops*. Not all of the Chocolate Drops came from the Carolinas; some came from as far away as Arizona, in America's great southwest. Although the origins of group members varied, their musical heritage pointed to the foothills of the Carolinas' Piedmont mountain region. At that time, musicians like the Baileys and the Carolina Chocolate Drops represented a long-standing tradition of string music styles that had been popular with Blacks and Whites since the 19th century. Now let's switch back to DeFord Bailey where unfortunately, the death of his father in 1918 prompted DeFord to move back to Nashville and live with relatives; but more hard times forced some of them to head to Detroit for work at the Ford Motor Plant.

DeFord opted to stay in the south, eventually getting his break in 1925 after performing at a formal dinner party. His talent led to a fellow musician insisting that he join him for a live radio broadcast of *The Barn Dance* show at a local station, WDAD. Without as much as an audition, DeFord Bailey signed on as a regular harmonica player on The Barn Dance show, later renamed as *The Grand Ole Opry* in 1927. Many White listeners didn't know Bailey's ethnicity, but Black people and the insurance company that sold lots of policies to WDAD's listeners knew. For over a year *The Barn Dance* was Bailey's on-air stage to keep people tuned in, while the insurance company happily paid to sponsor his show.

By 1928's end, DeFord Bailey relocated to Knoxville's WNOX radio for more money, but returned to Nashville the following year after negotiating a better Opry deal. After his return to Nashville, DeFord got married but not long after, the Great Depression of the 1930s barreled in to shake up economic stability. Looking ahead, Bailey spread his interests and became a multifaceted entrepreneur by opening a barbecue stand, shoeshine stand and a rooming house. Business was good in Tennessee, but it took more than good business to keep Mr. Bailey content.

By 1933, DeFord Bailey began touring with other Opry performers who wanted him in their shows. Touring meant prejudice lurked wherever he performed, so simple things like eating or relaxing in public places frequented by Whites could have been hazardous for Deford's health! Other critical face slaps occurred when DeFord's radio show was acquired by a national network and reprogrammed. Insiders believe certain record labels continued receiving airplay during this reprogramming period, because the labels aligned themselves with radio's professional 'clearing-house' protocol. In fact, many labels established relationships with radio stations. To attract the ad dollars of local, regional or national advertisers, programmers used new music from record promoters to fill song slots on the airplay list. Record companies also aligned with formidable music licensing agencies. Unions like these gave agencies authority to charge fees for using affiliated and licensed compositions. Secret contracts were rumored to have been negotiated between record labels, radio stations and license organizations, through back-door politics like handshake deals.

Matters worsened for DeFord Bailey when the performing rights agency (ASCAP) imposed higher fees on its members—this alienated radio stations across the country. A storm was brewing between certain radio stations and ASCAP as opposing forces in broadcast radio and music licensing engaged: one side pushed forward and the other side pushed back. Radio stations nationwide refused to surrender and eventually, many of them were forced to ban the airing of ASCAP-licensed material… or risk losing their jobs. As bad luck had it, the ban was supported by DeFord Bailey's station, WDAD. This meant DeFord's ASCAP music repertoire would have to be replaced with newly licensed songs, in order for him to be heard on his own radio show.

Industry problems quantified when back-door politics formulated into a system that arranged music according to color: this is what I call "musician classification." This system developed into *race records* and was based on the notion that music made by White musicians was primarily bought by Whites (Country/Pop/Christian), and music made by Black musicians was purchased by Blacks (Blues/Gospel/Jazz). Race records posed another threat to the future of DeFord Bailey and other minorities who played this genre, because this practice enabled record labels to negotiate or deed artist percentages of record sales according to their artists' race. DeFord Bailey became a casualty in a war that would spurn industry-wide scrutiny. This whole fiasco reminds me of an 18th century debacle that had early American colonists screaming bloody murder at the British *faux pas* of "taxation without representation."

As with most monolithic growth processes, the broadcast mediums united once again and formed a performing rights agency named *Broadcast Music Incorporated*, or BMI. BMI's shareholders were mostly radio stations, so this constituted their ownership of a music catalog. Once BMI got a catalog established, the need for radio stations to pay ASCAP for "rental" of their music was eliminated. The concept was like, "why rent–when you can own?" The only people that BMI would now have to pay were the copyright owners of a catalog *they* administered. DeFord Bailey knew the Opry's management wouldn't pay the higher fees for his ASCAP-administered music after the Opry became members of BMI. Bailey's station pressured him to compose new songs for BMI, but Deford was reluctant because the older releases were what he and his fans preferred. So in effect, he ended up in a lower-rated portion of the program. When the dust finally cleared, DeFord Bailey found himself cut out of the loop. Due to his unwillingness to conform to the station's ban on ASCAP-administered music, he was released in 1941. As this tug of war caused seismic ripples across the musical playing field, America was reinvesting into another global menace: *World War II*.

After the final tally was done on his career, Deford Bailey's weekly Grand Ole Opry performances cemented him as the man who appeared on the Opry twice as much as any other act. Signing on in 1927, DeFord Bailey spent close to 15 years with the Opry. After leaving in 1941, Bailey declined new offers to perform, but did make a last visit to Opryland on his 75th birthday in 1974. Despite clouds of economic and racial injustice, I'd say DeFord's quiet passing in 1982 "sealed the deal" with regard to his music industry contributions… and as a most influential Southern-bred talent.

MIRROR IMAGES

While many White Mountain musicians recorded and released commercial records, only a handful of Black musicians did this during the 1920s and 30s. One lucky group, *The Mississippi Sheiks*, traveled around the South and recorded dozens of releases for OKeh Records. Their song *Lazy Lazy River* offers a good illustration of the band's traditional Folk style. Although the Mississippi Sheiks made some early monumental recordings, many Black string musicians in the surrounding area quickly learned they had to play other styles like the Blues: if they wanted to get recorded. Unfortunately, the 20s marked the beginning of the end for Black Mountain music, after urban-based record labels decided to head south to record traditional rural music—and a lot of it was the Blues.

Black string bands eventually faded away, but hopefully the music made by these dedicated musicians won't be lost or forgotten. In its wake, Black Mountain music did its part to influence Country music, but many decades of blatant disregard by record companies essentially caused the

PAUSE button to be pressed on this genre. In the midst of expanding its development, this music style got shifted into the rear hallways of music *biz*tory's memory banks, as styles like Blues, Country and Bluegrass expanded their reach to new heights.

To some observers, Bluegrass might be conveyed as a sound delivered through America's Southern musical influences but in actuality, this style also has ties to Irish and Scottish Folk music. Others may think it sounds like a stripped down form of *Soul* music, except Bluegrass depends on instruments like banjos, mandolins and dulcimers for its authentic sound. Not many people know the banjo's origins trace back to Africa, so should it be any surprise that Country music is popular in Africa, too? Yet, while many American Blacks remain adverse to this genre, we can still find many fans of Bluegrass, Country or better put, *Folk* music scattered across America, Africa and other lands. In some places, modern Bluegrass and Country flavored acts like Dolly Parton, Willie Nelson or Emmylou Harris could be found on the same listening plate as the Folk-Pop of Tracy Chapman and Funk legends Parliament-Funkadelic.

Fiddle-banjo music was popular in the Kentucky, Tennessee, Virginia, North and South Carolina areas of the U.S., but is believed to have come from the connecting southern Appalachian Mountain region. For a more in-depth view, let's zoom in to Piedmont Stringband music. This style often focuses on the banjo as the lead instrument of a composition. In Black ensembles of this era, the banjo tended to set the rhythmic pace, while the violin or fiddle served as an accompanying instrument. This was a common collaboration in the creation of Piedmont Stringband music. Slide guitars and mandolins were not unheard of, either. In certain ways, folks can find the melodies, harmonies, and string choruses of Black Mountain music compares to traditional African music.

Country music stars such as the Carter Family with Leslie Riddle, Bill Monroe with Arnold Shultz and Hank Williams with Rufus "Tee-Tot" Payne were influenced by the sound of Black string players. For their assorted contributions, notable mention goes out to Black string musicians that include Libba Cotten, Dink Roberts, John Snipes, Emp White, Joe, Odell and Nate Thompson. This style can also be heard through the sounds of other string musicians like John Jackson, fiddler Howard Armstrong, the great Taj Mahal, and of course our SPOTLIGHT artist, DeFord Bailey.

That brings us to the question: How will the legacy of DeFord Bailey's induction into the Country Music Hall of Fame in November of 2005 affect future generations? You can try comparing it to Elvis Presley's induction into the Gospel Music Hall of Fame in November of 2001 to get some ideas. That's right folks, the *King of Rock-n-Roll's* early association with God and Gospel music back in Mississippi got him recognized and forever immortalized as pure Gospel treasure. Pushing his envelope further, Presley clinched the title for most songs charting on *Billboard*'s *Top 40* (104) and *Top 100* (151). And here's the icing on the cake: Elvis is irrefutably recognized as the "King of Rock-n-Roll," yet he never won *the big one*—a Grammy Award—for it. On a side note, the King did scoop up *three big ones*, for his Sacred and Inspirational recorded performances between 1967 and 1974.

FAST FORWARD: In 2005 when DeFord Bailey was inducted into the Country Music Hall of Fame, an associate from the audiovisual industry called and informed me about it. PLAY: During the call, Eric Miller, who at one time worked at the Grand Ole Opry, also informed me about the inductions of the group Alabama, and Glen Campbell codename "Rhinestone Cowboy." PAUSE: It was nice to hear, but I was perplexed about DeFord Bailey, because it took twenty-three years after the passing of this distinguished musician's musician for a tribute to finally take place. RECORD: To me, it's a shame because seventy-five years had gone by since Bailey walked in and became one of the Opry's top radio draws.

REWIND: Had things changed much by the time of Bailey's 1982 passing? Will more Folk-focused organizations step in to take up the slack? And who will ensure that the memories of greats like DeFord Bailey, guitar master Robert Johnson, the iconic Billie Holiday and Blues matriarch Ma Rainey remain intact for future generations? I've got few peers who are doing their part: Tom Davis at www.dr-love.com, Rogene Bailey at WALR-FM, Charles Mitchell at www.jusblues.org, Keith Gantt and Frank Lovejoy at www.thehistoryofjazzmusic.com are just a few of the proud who are plugged into '*the music preservation mission*.'

Here's a final thought to reflect upon: in 1994, the U.S. Post Office issued a 29-cent stamp to commemorate Ma Rainey, who went 'homeward bound' in 1939. Let's do the math here—fifty-five years had gone by since *her* passing. So in contrast to the timetable of postal stamps, we hope that more artists will be recognized not only as proof of stamps sold through postal economics, but also for their lifelong contributions—while they are still breathing air.

Some of us are looking out for a DeFord Bailey stamp, but everyone knows that financial woes have recently ravaged the postal system. With that said, we'll wait to see what happens as their top officials sing the Blues and U.S.P.S. troubles soar to an all-time high, like other parts of the government. The postal system has experienced major budget cuts; I'm sure employees have wondered if it would all end after bankruptcy, closure or perhaps even... new ownership? Inc. magazine did a reader probe in its October 2009 issue to answer the question, *"How Would You Fix the Post Office?"* While some good suggestions poured in, my proposal is to offer more stamps of music artists—like DeFord Bailey. And not just every now and then, okay? If you've got answers to this or any other questions posed, just "holla back!"

A permanent record documenting the lifework of DeFord Bailey was created by his good friend and author, David C. Morton. With some help from writer Charles K. Wolfe, Morton wrote an autobiography entitled *DeFord Bailey: A Black Star in Early Country Music*. David Morton also presented Bailey's only public recordings during the mid 70s. In this author's eyes, DeFord Bailey is part of an elite breed of unsung Black Mountain music heroes. You can find lots of facts about African-American music *biz*tory at www.blackbanjo.com and at all the usual sources. While you're at it, take a peek at Bluegrass, Hillbilly/Mountain and Country music in Charles K. Wolfe's *Hillbilly Fever: The Lost Tradition of Black String Bands*. And in case you need more info on DeFord Bailey, please log onto sites like www.pbs.org to read more.

The section above was designed to assist in filling a few gaps with regard to musicians like DeFord Bailey, as well as other artists from that era of musical transmutations. You can also visit my #2 and #3 favorite books about music history, *The Music of Black Americans* by Eileen Southern and *Martin Scorsese Presents The Blues*. These books provide additional information on Folk artists like DeFord Bailey, our next subject Leadbelly, and more. Select sources were scoured through for historic facts in order to compile the data found here in the music *biz*story chronicles, otherwise called the *Musicology* series. Hopefully, it will become your favorite book series too!

In passing notes, DeFord Bailey's son, DeFord Bailey, Jr., also turned up in Nashville's Black music scene. It was around the same period of the 60s when Rock god Jimi Hendrix was in the area awaiting the arrival of a bass playing Army buddy... and honing his chops. Jimi kept sharp by playing with R&B groups like The Imperials and The King Casuals, before fate led him to the West Coast to write his own chapter of music *biz*tory.

> **MUSIC FACT:** Today's Nashville is dominated with White Country music artists, but it was much different in the 1960s. Nashville also had a healthy Black population and Soul music scene that spread like wildfire back then.

Before Nashville was overtaken by Country music, it was also a town for R&B/Soul artists, independent record labels and nightclubs that supported Black music. The top radio station WSM and its rival WLAC both played R&B and Soul to attract Black listeners. But how strange would a Black musician who sang Country music that catered to mostly White audiences have sounded back then? One more interesting anomaly during the 60s and 70s was a Black Country music singer who dominated his segment of the market with 4% of Country music sales. Charlie Pride's music was respected and purchased by Blacks and Whites across America: in other words, he was the #1 Black Country music act.

Country music had been popular for decades and by the 50s, Nashvilles's Country music population was skyrocketing. Out of the blue, an unexplainable chain of events caused more and more Country-based musicians and publishing houses to head Nashville-bound to Music Row, with hopes of hopping on the swiftly moving Country music train.

CLASSIC FOLK COUNTRY

In Mississippi, Folk styles like Country derived from Blues. Leadbelly was a Black musician whose appeal to White audiences stemmed from his unique blend of Folk and Blues. Much like other struggling musicians of his era, Leadbelly's road to stardom wasn't straight and narrow; but his charisma was second to none. This was demonstrated during his incarceration in Louisiana—he miraculously got released after writing a song about the state's Governor. Leadbelly later moved to New York where he expanded his musical options, establishing a Black and White following that embraced his style with open arms.

Other Folk styles such as Country-Western, Hillbilly and Bluegrass also used elements of the Blues to attract a large White audience. But the industry at large classified music performed by White artists like Jimmie Rogers as Country, even though those songs had obvious Blues elements. White Blues performers were often referred to as "Country & Western" artists; despite the fact that many of their songs included the *"B"* word ("Blues"). As some folks started using the "Americana" music tag, the popularity of Country & Western grew and subdivided into Country-Folk, Country-Pop, Honky-Tonk, Country-Rock, Rockabilly, Progressive and Traditional. All of these styles were becoming legitimate music forms in their own right. As if it hadn't been said before, one telltale sign that a music genre is here to stay appears when the music subdivides into smaller factions.

During the 50s and 60s, a huge conglomerate of White Country singers, musicians and integrated resources migrated to Tennessee for its hot music scene and turned Music Row, the Grand Ole Opry and most of Nashville into Country music's headquarters. At the end of the day, Country & Western artists like Bill Monroe, Leslie Riddle, Arnold Schultz and Hank Williams inherited much of the Black Hillbilly sound. This music form also influenced artists who performed other styles, like multi-instrumentalist Taj Mahal—a robust player of African, Bluegrass, Cajun, Caribbean, Gospel, Hawaiian, Reggae and of course, Blues. Let's shine some light to illuminate the world of a sensational, multi-genre-ational instrumentalist.

SPOTLIGHT ON: Taj Mahal

Without a doubt, Taj Mahal is an artist who laid out the blueprint for his own path to success. He won critical acclaim as a solo act, and his collaborations with other musicians netted valuable fruit, as well. Even with little support from the mainstream world, Taj Mahal developed his own fan base and amassed huge accolades along the way:

- Designated as the Official Blues artist of Massachusetts
- Awarded an honorary Doctor of Humanities degree from South Carolina's Wofford College and does a three-song performance
- Received 9 nominations and 2 Grammy Awards—for *Señor Blues* (1997) and *Shoutin' in Key* (2000)
- Scooped up Blues Music Award for Historical Album of the Year—*The Essential Taj Mahal*

With at least 50 albums to his credit, Taj Mahal developed a Blues picking style of his own—he played lead lines with a pick just as easily as he finger-picked rhythmic riff lines. Before Taj Mahal arrived at this destination however, he traveled many roads that took him from Harlem to

Massachusetts, from California to Hawaii; and our agents are still trying to confirm if he ever made it to the historic mausoleum in India that his name alludes to. While we await the results, let's get more acquainted with this eclectic musician—for instance, he was born in Harlem as *Henry Saint Clair Fredericks* in the year 1942. This self-taught, Grammy-winning Blues musician and film composer uses the stage moniker of *Taj Mahal* because, according to data sources, the not-so-secret codename arrived through a dream "about Gandhi, India, and social tolerance." He began using the name around the late 50s to early 60s, while attending the University of Massachusetts.

REWIND: Growing up in Springfield, Massachusetts, Taj Mahal had a musical family—his mom sang in a local Gospel choir, while his dad played piano and did Jazz arrangements. PAUSE: As a child, he had access to something his friends didn't have, a short-wave radio. RECORD: This electronic component picked up broadcasts from all over and it eventually filled his mind with World music. PLAY: He began taking note of similarities and differences of popular music, and the music his family played at home. FAST FORWARD: When the Jazz bug hit, Taj Mahal couldn't ignore it—he took in sounds created by greats like Milt Jackson, Charles Mingus and Thelonious Monk, while tuning in to folks like:

Toumani Diabate	Sleepy John Estes	Howlin' Wolf
Mississippi John Hurt	Jimmy Reed	Son House
Big Mama Thornton		Sonny Terry

Taj Mahal's parents instilled a sense of self-worth in their children by telling them about the Harlem Renaissance of the 1920s and 1930s; like history-laden griots, they also passed on traditional African and West Indian stories. Well-respected in the music industry, Taj Mahal's father was at one time given codename *The Genius*, by Ella Fitzgerald. With a musician for a dad, Taj Mahal's home became a stomping ground for local, national and international artists from Africa and the Caribbean. Having so many musicians around gave a young Taj Mahal more options than his peers, and he later took to studying African music. Although he started off playing piano, it wasn't hard for him to pick up the clarinet, harmonica or trombone—at the end of the day he had mastered other instruments, like the banjo and guitar.

Fatally speaking, Taj Mahal experienced a devastating loss at the age of eleven, when a tractor tumbled over and crushed his father accidentally. His mother remarried shortly thereafter, and her new husband was a guitar man with a good guitar—he let Taj take lessons and practice with it. Mahal was lucky because his teacher Lynwood Perry was roughly the same age and played Blues guitar fluently—as a matter of fact, his uncle was a popular Bluesman named Arthur "Big Boy" Crudip. During high school, Taj Mahal continued practicing music on instruments he came across; he also began singing in a local Doo-Wop group. While music wasn't bringing in cash to pay for food, farming did. Taj started at the bottom working at a dairy farm at the age of 16 and by the time he was 19, his title had changed to 'Foreman.' He oversaw the facility's maintenance, milking of cows, plus he grew herbs and vegetables like alfalfa, clover and corn.

Taj Mahal was a naturalist who believed everyone should grow their own food. Because of his position on the subject, Taj turned into a regular performer at the *Farm Aid* benefit concerts. Luckily for the music world, he changed his mind about farming and decided to pursue music instead. This was after he spent time taking agricultural classes, agronomy, animal husbandry (breeding), veterinary science and studied the practice of using plants to sustain life through food, fuel and fiber production. Keeping his 'playing chops' up to speed during college, Taj Mahal fronted a Rhythm and Blues band, *Taj Mahal & The Elektras*.

By 1964, Taj Mahal pointed his compass to the west coast and Santa Monica, California, where he was called out to begin a new chapter of life with *Rising Sons*. This group was made up of music pals like Ry Cooder and Jessie Lee Kincaid. A Columbia Records deal soon followed but because the group was multiracial, their single was poorly promoted—a tragic sign of the times. Some thirty years later in 1993, Legacy Records put out earlier recorded material under the title of *The Rising Sons Featuring Taj Mahal and Ry Cooder*. In his early days, Taj Mahal collaborated with the likes of Sleepy John Estes, Buddy Guy, Lightnin' Hopkins, Howlin' Wolf, Muddy Waters and Junior Wells. Although his group Rising Sons opened for lots of top touring acts of the 60s (like Otis Redding and the Temptations), an album was never released and they eventually disbanded.

After the breakup of Rising Sons, Taj Mahal remained with Columbia Records and released new material during the late 60s. Between this time and the 70s, he recorded a dozen albums for Columbia. Maintaining his affiliation with Ry Cooder, the pair performed with The Rolling Stones and he landed in a film called *The Rolling Stones Rock and Roll Circus*. As the 70s progressed, Taj Mahal worked on the movie score for *Sounder*, starring Cicely Tyson—I remember watching this movie back in elementary school at Brooklyn's P.S. 289 when it first came out. Around this time, Taj Mahal began integrating other genres like Jazz, Reggae and Caribbean-West Indian sounds into his music. Leaving Columbia for Warner Brothers in 1976, Taj Mahal released three albums under that arrangement; one of them was the motion picture soundtrack for 1977's *Brothers*.

The mid-70s was a time when Hard Rock and Disco moved to the forefront of the industry, pushing everything else to the curb. With a stalled career, Taj Mahal kept the compass pointed west and headed to Kauai, Hawaii by the early 80s. While there, he started *The Hula Blues Band*; they could be found performing… in-between fishing sessions. Throughout the 80s, Taj Mahal watched many peaceful Pacific sunsets; but he wasn't meant for early retirement just yet and the dawn of a new day finally arrived:

- Around 1988, he signed with Gramavision and had a new album called *Taj* in the works
- The 90s took him to Private Music; Blues, Pop, Rock and R&B albums led to work with acts like Etta James and Eric Clapton
- Taj Mahal performed on an Antonin Dvořák tribute—out of this effort, the Americana album, *Largo* was released
- The 1998 album includes production by Rick Chertoff with songwriter David Forman, and collaborating acts include Rick's longtime poster child for fun, Cyndi Lauper; plus others like Levon Helm of The Band, The Chieftains, Garth Hudson, Rob Hyman, Willie Nile and Joan Osborne
- In 1997, Taj Mahal won "Best Contemporary Blues Album" Grammy for *Señor Blues*
- By 2002, Taj Mahal took home a Grammy for *Shoutin' In Key*

Taj Mahal was also featured on a 2002 compilation album from the Red Hot Organization called *Red Hot and Riot*, which was dedicated to a famous Afropop musician, Nigeria's Fela Kuti. Proceeds from this project went to support AIDS charities and for interested parties, there was also a critically acclaimed, self-titled stage play dedicated to the memory of this great African musician. Taj Mahal found that being in the vicinity of hotspots like Club 47 and Ash Grove in Massachusetts and Los Angeles (respectively) was a tremendous aid in developing his sound. Being a Blues scholar, Taj Mahal's study of ethnomusicology brought him front and center to the Folk styles of Caribbean and West African music, which were incorporated into his songs. He now pulled from an expanded list of sources that included Calypso, Country Blues, Jazz, Gospel, Reggae, R&B and Zydeco. Utilizing these styles easily qualified him as a well-branded World Music artist.

The late 90s saw Taj Mahal recording with Africans who left him with a sense of musical empowerment, because he was now a conduit between African and African-American music appreciation endeavors. Recalling the experience, he once commented, "if I don't play guitar for the rest of my life, that's fine with me…" A definitive moment came with the 1999 release of his *Kulanjan* album. Among the embedded special treats, Taj Mahal collaborated with Toumani Diabate, a Kora master of the Malis Griot tradition. Once Mahal reconnected with musicians from the motherland, it stimulated a name change once again: he would thereafter bear the codename of *Dadi Kouyate*.

Taj Mahal's preference to perform mostly in outdoor environments stemmed from his desire to see audiences move to his music and respond to his vocalizations. In contrast, he had difficulties performing in front of people who looked like they were sitting there, watching television. Despite a highly successful career, Taj Mahal reiterated what folks like famed Bluesman B.B. King has verbalized on numerous occasions: although mostly White audiences show up to take in their music, there's still an overall lack of interest in Blues by African American audiences. Depending on where you look, that same theory also holds true for styles like Jazz and Reggae.

Finally, my 'tally it up' question is, what happens when the true innovators of this important music pass on to Blues Heaven? It readily strikes me as odd, because Blues was created by Black musicians and is a legitimate music genre but these days, it seems as if less and less Black folks are listening to the music, playing the instruments, or simply passing it on. In all actuality, Blues, Jazz, Reggae and Rap have all been fully absorbed into mainstream America, but it appears that Whites have proven to buy more of this music than the very people who created it—Taj Mahal was quoted busting some stats: "Eighty-one percent of the kids listening to Rap were not Black kids."

Regarding the connotation that Blues (and Rap, for that matter) reflects negative thoughts and despair, Taj Mahal offers a stark disclaimer—"you don't ever hear me moaning and crying about how bad you done treated me." And he has plenty more to say, so take some time and look Taj Mahal up at places like www.tajblues.com and www.pinecone.org to learn great facts about this worldly musician, philosopher, humanitarian and philanthropist. Since Taj Mahal points out that the most important color today is GREEN, enjoy some of his music while deciding for yourself whether he means money… or the environment. Taj Mahal was a true musician in every sense of the word, because he covered all the bases when it came to being a multi-genre-ational sensation. Yet, there were still other genres that needed exploration; several key talents stood up to accept the challenge…

TRUE BLUE CLASSICS

Classical composers, poets and writers like Ralph Ellison, Zora Neale Hurston and Langston Hughes often mentioned the Blues in their poems; even the Library of Congress embraced the sound of Blues and incorporated it into their growing repositories of musical compositions. George Gershwin (1898-1937), mixed Jazz rhythms, melodies and harmonies with Classical form in his extremely popular piano concerto, "Rhapsody in Blue." George Gershwin also composed the still-popular opera *Porgy and Bess*, which is an amalgamation of African American and European music. At one point in time, shows were performed regularly: by both Blacks and Whites. Aaron Copland (1900–1990) incorporated various styles like Jazz and Blues, as evident with his *Clarinet Concerto* commissioned by Jazz clarinetist Benny Goodman. Charles Ives (1874–1951) also included Black music in his compositions, along with marches, dances and spirituals, which were sometimes simultaneously combined and performed in venues across the land.

The cross-fertilization between Classical and African American music didn't begin in the 20th century. One close source pointed out that the Czech composer Antonin Dvorak (1841-1904) spent several years in the United States around the 1890s. Dvorak was struck by similarities between the Negro Spirituals he heard, and the Folk music of his native Bohemia: his *New World Symphony* includes many tunes sounding like Spirituals and Czech music. The mournful feeling of the second movement played by a solo English horn later had lyrics added, and was renamed *Goin' Home*—it was popularized by a performer with a solid foothold in both the European and African music worlds, Paul Robeson.

Paul Robeson inspired and influenced almost anyone who listened to him, from avid fans to flamboyant performers like a singer-pianist known as *Screamin' Jay Hawkins*—Hawkins was a highly visible act that helped shape the evolution of Rock-n-Roll. Our agents will expose how he did it when we tune the frequency in to an infamous radio Disc Jockey named Alan Freed. Here's a data update: our Captain says that's all coming up in a voyage he's mapping out for us at this very moment. You'll need to get your animal skins, flaming skulls and red leather outfits on deck, because you're going to need them when the time comes!

Right now, the *Superior Intellect Shuttle* is waiting to ferry us through a few dangerous wormholes, so the "Fasten Seat Belt" sign has been turned back on. Pick your favorite colored spectroshades and we'll profile some "unsubs" who performed special *operational ops* around the earlier decades of the 20th century, during the music industry's infancy. This was a period when record labels primarily marketed music to their mostly White customers who purchased Classical, Opera, Christian hymns, Folk and Country & Western music—labels also marketed the soulful sounds of Gospel, Jazz and the Blues. A bombshell dropped however, when record companies noticed that White fans across all economic platforms were purchasing Black music, which meant new policies had to be put in effect.

Many American cities were populated with sophisticated classes of rich people, as well as people who did the day-to-day struggle. Upper classers often enjoyed the pleasant experience of elaborate European operas and symphonic compositions. Historically speaking, music from the Classical, Baroque and more recent Renaissance eras cultivated audiences that often formed tight-knit social circles. Composers of this genre generally created Classical, Opera and related styles with long, drawn out performances (movements) that required lots of 'listening energy.' Some composers wrote short (a few minutes long) pieces, including dances, marches, overtures and other forms that massively speaking, are still under-performed. Like other traditional homegrown styles such as Blues, Country, Folk, Gospel and Jazz, the Classical realm and its associated literature may seem gargantuan to some. However, next to the more mainstream Pop, Rock, Dance, R&B and Hip-Hop genres of today, the previously mentioned styles all dwarf in comparison; but thanks to legions of talented artists, they continue gaining new audiences…

There was one common element that always seemed to raise its head, even in genres as *upscale-ificantly diverse* as Classical and Opera. No matter what style of music Blacks in America performed, it was still difficult for many to escape the double-edged racism card, and problems probably compounded in the area of female singers. So not only from a historic point of view but from a few others too, we tip our hats to groundbreaking Classical and Opera singers like:

Roberta Alexander	Wilhelminia Fernandez
Marian Anderson	Barbara Hendricks
Carmen Balthrop	Isola Jones
Kathleen Battle	Marvis Martin
Harolyn Blackwell	Leona Mitchell
Gwendolyn Bradley	Jessye Norman
Grace Bumbry	Leontyne Price
Cynthia Clarey	Florence Quivar
Clamma Dale	Shirley Verrett

With this many great singers, you'd be reading about their ascension up 'music mountain' for days if you got started right now. In order to get a better view of this high caliber of artists, I picked one that still rings a bell in my head. I remember learning about this legendary singer back in grade school, at Brooklyn, New York's P.S. 289.

SPOTLIGHT ON: Marian Anderson

A contralto singer known all over the world, Marian Anderson 'cleared a clear path' from early on in her career. This was the result of overcoming challenges like performing in front of 75,000 people—and millions more via radio broadcast from the steps of Washington D.C.'s Lincoln Memorial, way back in 1939. With unexpected feats like these

86

under her belt, Marian went on to break through abundant obstacles, claiming fame in 1955 as the first Black artist to perform at New York's Metropolitan Opera.

Although an organization known as the Daughters of the American Revolution denied Marian from performing for an integrated audience at Constitution Hall, VIPs like President Franklin D. Roosevelt and his First Lady stepped in to help the singer grace an even larger crowd—at the Lincoln Memorial. This is a perfect example of how one door closes… but another one opens. Between 1925 and 1965, Marian Anderson gave numerous critically acclaimed performances at top venues with A-List orchestras across America and Europe. With a repertoire consisting of concert themes, Lieder (German art songs), Opera, Traditional and Spiritual songs, Anderson emerged as a unanimous vocal victor of the masses, both on records and on stage.

Besides Marian Anderson's many accomplishments BEFORE the 1960s, she went on to become a symbol of peace DURING the turbulent civil rights movement by singing at 1963's *March on Washington for Jobs and Freedom*. AFTER earning high accolades with the United Nation's Human Rights Committee, the U.S. Department of State tapped her to become a "goodwill ambassadress." Marian Anderson's name will be remembered well into the FUTURE, due to her many acts of compassion. Through the music she delivered, Marian received her just rewards:

1963 – Presidential Medal of Freedom
1972 – United Nations Peace Prize
1977 – Congressional Gold Medal
1978 – Kennedy Center Honors
1980 – ½ ounce gold medal (coined by the U.S. Treasury)
1984 – Eleanor Roosevelt Human Rights Award of the City of New York
1986 – National Medal of Arts
1990 – Silver Buffalo Award (highest Boy Scouts of America honor)
1991 – Grammy Lifetime Achievement

As a topper-off of Marian Anderson's dollar value to the United States, her picture can be found on Post Office stamps and on the Treasury's $5,000 Series I Savings Bond. So friends, we hope you can see that although Marian retired from singing way back in 1965, the momentum she developed in her early years created an unstoppable juggernaut that didn't just knock on the doors of racial inequities, it kicked them wide open. Marian Anderson's name can always be found floating around the top; she's ranked in *100 Greatest African Americans*, by noted scholar Molefi Kete Asante. Continuing to push this iconic lady's legacy forward are websites like www.mariananderson.org—to see what other doors await, just open up a few Internet windows.

There are also a few males that experienced nominal success in the Classical and Opera arena, like Simon Estes, William Estes, Paul Robeson, George Shirley and William Warfield. You can still find more gold nuggets than these at sites like http://wiki.answers.com, and during your search, maybe you'll get lucky: you could even score your own double-headed nugget, like I did. On one side, these singers went against the grain and followed their own voice to wherever it led—on the other side, content providers on sites like those listed above made fabulous multimedia contributions for you to see and hear. Together, they deserve a double thumbs-up, coupled with a closer look and listen. In addition to the history of a few select dominant male singers, you might just be surprised at how much music *'biz' her-story* you'll find, too!

As stated earlier, these great voices and more had to overcome their own bumpy ride through various degrees of prejudice—a few broke through the barriers, while others remained somehow tangled up in a web that snagged even the best of the best. In fact, a critically acclaimed, classically trained, multi-lingual vocalist could travel the world over and receive high international accolades; he could even earn in excess of $100,000 per year as World Wars drained the economies of major countries: but still come back home to segregation. Georgia's Roland Hayes was one of these people. Let's fire up the big lamp for a brief moment in Hayes time…

SPOTLIGHT ON: Roland Hayes

In the year nineteen hundred and forty-two, Roland Hayes' color balance flickered from black to white to red. This was after his wife and daughter sat under a fan in the "Whites Only" section of a shoe store just south of Curryville in Rome, Georgia… and were promptly kicked out. When Hayes addressed the merchant about it, the police entered the picture, beat him and his wife and then arrested the world-renowned tenor singer. Instances such as these were contributing factors in Roland Hayes' decision to exit Georgia and get America's fourth state *off* his mind. And for those who may have missed the cyphered briefing, this Southern haven of greenery has a capital city called Atlanta—21st Century codename: *City Not Too Busy To Care, formerly City Too Busy To Hate.*

Musically speaking, I'd say that Roland Hayes was best summed up back in the 70s, when a writer named Marva Griffen Carter wrote for the *Black Perspective in Music:* "Hayes's life of almost ninety years reveals a remarkable story of a man who went from the plantation to the palace, performing before kings and queens, with the finest international and American orchestras, in segregated communities before Blacks and Whites alike.... When he sang, art became more than polished excellence. It appealed to something beyond the intellect, something one could call the soul." Well, what can be said after that but words from the man himself? In a 1947 *Christian Science Monitor* interview, Roland Hayes spoke about the universality of his work: "When I began my career I realized that if I would speak to all men, I must learn the language and the ways of thought of all men..."

Pulling out the microscope, we see a baby Roland Hayes born to former slaves in 1887, just north of Atlanta in Curryville. Going back a few generations, the view opens to show ancestry pointing at African chiefs, while other reports point to a touch of Cherokee Indian in his blood, too. With those pieces of evidence presented, I'd be willing to say some important 'evolutional elements' went inside this musical virtuoso to 'set his sonics' at such a high level! Whatever it was, it mixed in well and gave his vocal chords an extra capacity to sing heartfelt songs. Hayes pushed the limits of performance by singing songs in French, German and Italian. Hayes also goes by Musicology codename *Major First*, because he achieved critical acclaim worldwide as the first African American male concert vocalist—in other words, before him there was no other!

After training under respectables like Arthur Calhoun and at Fisk University in 1911, Roland Hayes began his tour de force with the *Fisk University Singers*. Speaking of the Fisk University Singers, here's a quick shoutout to Linda King and Stephanie Wanza of the *Atlanta Fisk Club* (www.atlantafiskclub.org). With the participation of leading men like actor Mel Jackson, they host star-studded events like the "Annual Fisk Winter Scholarship Extravaganza Gala" and the Annual "Legacy of Song" program at places like Atlanta's King Center, where I was the Keynote Speaker at their September 2013 "Legacy of Song" event. Working in tandem with Fisk University, Linda and Stephanie help to provide elementary through high school students with trips to tour the college campus. This is just what kids need, so 'big ups' to the Atlanta Fisk Club and their ongoing efforts to present students with tools for a solid educational future. Scoring extra points on the big board, students are introduced to a reputable institution of higher learning. On a historic note, the Fisk University Singers began touring in 1871; they also made a landmark recording back in 1909 called *Swing Low, Sweet Chariot*, so just imagine how they sound today...

Touring with the Fisk University Singers expanded Roland Hayes' skill set considerably and led to even greater opportunities for him. He paved a way from his hometown of Curryville to Chattanooga then Nashville, and his next stop was Boston. Here, he perked up more superior intellect with a great 'enabler,' Arthur Hubbard. Next came London, where he trained with knowledgeables like George Henschel and Amanda Ira Aldridge. Taking the best of the best from his coaches, Hayes went on to perform huge feats in a career that spanned over thirty years. Here are some highlights:

- 1916 – Hayes put together recitals and national tours; over the course of three years, he touches down at places like New York, Boston, Philadelphia, Washington, D.C. and Atlanta
- 1917 – launches tour as The Hayes Trio, with William Richardson and William Lawrence
- 1920 – London debut, with pianist Lawrence Brown; soon after, Hayes was popping up in major European cities
- 1923 – Hayes returns home to America to find that nothing much has changed with regards to race relations
- 1924 – Receives various honors and finds things starting to change; just not fast enough

In 1925, Roland Hayes gave a command performance for Queen Mother Maria Christian of Spain. That same year, he was awarded the Spingarn Medal, given annually by the NAACP for "Most Outstanding Achievement Among Colored People." Over the next few years, Hayes traveled to Italy and the Soviet Union; then humbly accepted 8 honorary degrees, including a Music Doctorate from Fisk University in 1932. Despite all his accolades for outstanding performances over the next 10 years, he permanently moved away from Georgia after the 1942 shoe store incident in Rome. By 1948, Hayes authored *My Songs: Aframerican Religious Folk Songs Arranged and Interpreted by Roland Hayes*.

Roland Hayes started teaching at Boston University in 1950 and also obtained professional management from Boston's Symphony Orchestra Concert Company—while a lot of people were feeling the pinch of bad economics, Hayes' earnings were in the $100,000 per year bracket. Passing on his experience to those who "yearned to learn," Hayes added *vocal coach* to his magic bag of treats and kept it moving by showing the ropes to Canadian soprano singer, Frances James. By 1954 he was touring again as a top draw in places like England, Holland and Denmark. Even at the age of 70, enthusiastic reviews came in from columnists like the Boston Herald's Rudolph Elie who wrote, "What Mr. Hayes does is live each song he sings…" In 1962, Hayes performed a farewell concert at Carnegie Hall; it was his 75th birthday. Record labels he recorded for include American Columbia, Vanguard, Veritas and Vocalion but unfortunately, our agents report his records are hard to find. In light of falling on the 'endangered recordings' list, 1990 saw the Smithsonian Institution releasing a compilation of his performances between 1939 and 1965, *The Art of Roland Hayes*.

Once Roland Hayes walked through the secret door, he laid the foundation for other Black acts to build upon; many followed his marker and proceeded through to great success. Keeping the musical train of thought ever-moving, Hayes offered profound advise to those coming after him in a documentary called, *The Musical Legacy of Roland Hayes*: "I started all this.... Now, you can't stop where I stopped; you've got to go on." It's been said that great acts have other great acts behind them— Roland Hayes worked with a multitude of greats like Lawrence Brown, Arthur Calhoun, George Henschel, Arthur Hubbard, William Lawrence, Frances James, William Richardson plus many others. And folks, we shouldn't forget that there are great discoveries to behold outside of the more dominant styles of Pop, Rock, Dance, R&B and Hip-Hop. Upon launching your own search, you'll uncover many musical treasures from the slightly smaller worlds of Classical; as well as Blues, Country, Folk, Gospel, Jazz and Opera.

Although Roland Hayes left us in 1977, he did his best to navigate through the realities of the early 1900s music business by remaining true to his art form, and staying close to educational institutions. Even though it must have been a chore to wiggle between the tight lines of segregation, Hayes navigated a path that took him from racism in his hometown to countries some folks can't even pronounce. To memorialize this affluently gifted vocalist who once had a bad customer service experience while shopping for shoes, there are now tributary structures that stand tall and keep Hayes' name in plain view: Calhoun, Georgia has its very own *Roland Hayes Music Guild and Museum*, while the University of Tennessee has a Roland Hayes concert hall. And as far as Higgins Shoes in Rome, Georgia, recent reports indicate they can still be found selling shoes on Shorter Avenue. For more Roland Hayes info, just check the Net.

This brings us to the final 'topper-offer' for this chapter and I must admit, the buildup has been incredible! Our next stop takes us to St. Louis, Missouri, where a young lady entered the world and proceeded to change it *singlewomanly*. If you haven't been inspired by the artists mentioned above by now, I believe you will be after reading what our undercover operatives found on one *Dr. Maya Angelou*, who goes by the Musicology codename of *Good Human Doctor*. Truth be told, she inspired me to develop a special 3-part section coming up called, *Singers Who Could Act... Or Actresses That Could Sing?* That's all coming up shortly but for now, put on your sunglasses—we're about to turn the...

SPOTLIGHT UP!

One day in March 2014, I was minding my own business setting up some audiovisual equipment at the Marriott Marquis in downtown Atlanta. Sometimes working hard (or hardly working sometimes), you have to take a break from time to time, and I had been noticing more and more women filling the atrium level of the hotel. Finally, my inquisitivity got the best of me and I had to see what was bringing in all those women—was it me in my "show blacks?" Stepping off the escalator, I was confronted by a lifesize standup of the one and only, Dr. Maya Angelou. The sight of this cardboard figure almost knocked me back onto the escalator, because here was a 20-something year old Diva in a figure-enhanced dress... standing next to an African congo drum!

Regaining my equilibrium, I decided to zoom in to what was going on and realized this A-List celebrity was in the building. Making my way through the crowd, I saw another standup of present-day Dr. Angelou. This time I took note of signage saying she was there to speak at a "Woman 2 Woman" conference. I said to myself, "Self, you obviously got booked on the wrong AV gig!" I knew Dr. Angelou was an actress, author and poet, but gazing at the beautiful young woman with a gap in her teeth standing next to an African drum told me something: I missed the memos about her being a recording artist; or friends with Billie Holiday. I had to call in the *Musicology Special Operations Team* for more intel, and this is what I got...

Opening up her bio at www.mayaangelou.com, it says "Dr. Maya Angelou is one of the most renowned and influential voices of our time" and she is "Hailed as a global renaissance woman." I just call her *The Good Human Doctor* because over the past 50 years, this celebrated philanthropist wore many hats: actress, civil rights activist, dramatist, educator, filmmaker, historian, memoirist, novelist, poet, producer, and who knows what else we don't know about. Sounds to me like she may have some Jamaican DNA in her blood with all those jobs, mon!

As a matter of fact, before being blessed with worldly status, back in the day a young Maya Angelou earned her living as a professional dancer in clubs around San Francisco. One of them was *The Purple Onion* and Maya wound up recording her first album, *Miss Calypso*, as a result of her act at the Onion. That's funny, because one of the first clubs I checked out after moving to Atlanta in the early 80s was called the Purple Onion—but they didn't play Calypso music in *this* joint. As my good friend and founder of *Raw Truth Radio* Michael Garrett Jr. codename DJ Mike GEE says, "*SMH, SMH*"—that means *shaking my head*. An honorable shoutout goes to my music information hometeamers at www.rawtruthradio.net: Vernon "DJ 12" House, Jacob W. Anderson II aka Jacob Tunes, DJ Novi, Shank Boogs, DJ Yung Cell and DJ Boozie. Tune in 24/7/365 at "the Internet's Home of Good Music" and uncut "raw truth!"

Now, let's open up the books on our Good Doctor Maya Angelou. Being the second child of Bailey and Vivian Johnson, April 4th proved to be a monumental day for the child born as Marguerite Ann Johnson. While most people think about their arrival date with happy thoughts, this day brought with it mixed feelings after her 40th birthday. Besides a global tragedy that took place on April 4, 1968 (take a guess), this young lady endured her first 40 years walking a line that often got blurred, due to a variety of dishes served to her by life. As we delve deeper, more light will be shed to unveil secrets of our mysterious saga.

Taking the timeline back a few generations, the pointer shows Dr. Angelou as a descendant of West Africa's Mende clan. Her great-grandmother Mary Lee was emancipated after the Civil War. Not uncommon back in those days, Mary's slave master John Savin impregnated her and allegedly forced her to sign papers that said another man did the deed. Even though Mary Lee's master was indicted for forcing her to commit an act of perjury, he was found 'not guilty' by a jury of his peers. Despite being the father of her child, he got off with a slap on the wrist, while she was shipped off to Missouri's Clinton County poorhouse with her baby girl. Our undercover operatives are still clueless as to how Mary Lee's baby was named Marguerite Baxter, when her real parents were named Savin and Lee—evidence suggests that the falsely accused father's name may have stuck. Be that as it may, Marguerite Baxter's family line extended itself through time and ultimately bloodlines blended, making her out to be Dr. Maya Angelou's grandmother.

After her birth in 1928, Maya Angelou and her older brother Bailey Jr. grew up in St. Louis then moved to Stamps, Arkansas. Due to her parents breaking up when she was three, young Maya and Bailey Jr. were sent to Stamps to live with their father's mother. Our wiki agents point to her brother being the one who bestowed Marguerite with the name "Maya"—it was reportedly a chopped down version of "My" or "Mya Sister." Since I can't remember a thing about my own life when I was three, hopefully young Maya didn't recollect the terror of being shipped off with her brother all by themselves on a train to Stamps. Although many people both Black and White were poor because of the Great Depression and World War II, some folks prospered. One of them was Maya's grandmother. Around 1935, she owned a general store that sold basic commodities which were always needed; she also made a few good investments. Living in Stamps with her grandmother, Dr. Angelou walked through a deep gash cut by a double-edged sword: brutal racial discrimination, coupled with "the unshakable faith and values of traditional African-American family, community, and culture." If that doesn't build character, I don't know what else could!

Four years after being sent to live with their grandmother, "dear old dad" re-emerged unannounced to send the kids back to their mom. Returning to St. Louis, Maya Angelou was now eight years old and just starting to take in the world around her. But the ever-troublesome Messenger of Misery arrived to thicken the plot. In a tragic scenario that unfortunately still plagues families today, the child was preyed upon by a sexual predator—her mother's boyfriend. After being attacked, the helpless victim reported the incident to her brother and he did what any good family member would do—he informed the rest of the family. Jailed for just a day, the perpetrator was released. But after four days, "street justice" got served up in full: he was found murdered, end of story. This tragedy left poor young Maya mute, not speaking for nearly 5 years after the occurrence. Somehow, she believed telling on her mother's boyfriend got him killed; she thought she'd never speak again through a fear of killing someone else!

While Dr. Angelou suffered in silence as a girl, she somehow learned to memorize large chunks of data; from literature to spoken word to different parts of her surrounding world. After the tragic incident, Maya and Bailer Jr. returned to Stamps, Arkansas to live with their grandmother again. A family friend who was also an educator eventually steered Maya back into the realm of speaking by opening the worlds of art and literature to her. This was done through artists like Frances Harper, Anne Spencer and Jessie Fauset; as well as authors Charles Dickens, Douglas Johnson, James Weldon Johnson, Edgar Allan Poe and William Shakespeare. These crafty individuals all made a significant impact on the young lady's personal and professional life. By the time Maya Angelou was 14, she and her brother were going back to live with their mother. On this go-round, they headed west to Northern California to give life in Oakland a try.

A deep affinity for the arts earned a youthful Dr. Angelou her scholorship in dance and drama at the Labor School in San Francisco, however she dropped out and jumped on another train to pursue dreams that festered inside. At the age of 14, she assumed the title of "cable car conductor"—San Francisco's first lady of color in that position! Even with a steady job, Maya Angelou knew she had to finish high school and just after graduating, gave birth to her first child. To keep food on the table, the young mother worked assorted jobs in the food industry… and outside of it. Eventually, Maya's love of artistic expression overcame the desire to expand culinary and the other skill sets she acquired; it was time for her to pursue the entertainment *biz…* on a large scale.

The 50s came along and matrimony soon followed—Maya Angelou married a Greek man named Tosh Angelos, who had been an electrician, sailor and budding musician. But her interracial marriage was frowned upon by society; particularly her mother. Never allowing this to hinder her, Dr. Angelou studied Modern Dance, which led to working with dancer-choreographers such as Alvin Ailey and Ruth Beckford. It didn't take long for Angelou and Ailey to form a dance duo called "Al and Rita"—they performed Modern Dance routines for Black fraternities around the San Francisco region.

After her marriage ran its course in 1954, Maya Angelou danced professionally in clubs around San Francisco. With sights set on Europe by the mid-50s, Angelou joined a production of *Porgy and Bess*, touring with the cutting-edge opera for several years. Soon, she deployed a protocol of learning the language of countries she toured. Initiating plans to expand her superior intellect in Modern Dance, she joined forces with people like Martha Graham. This leg of her artistic adventure took her through television and nightclubs like *The Purple Onion* in San Francisco. During this time, she officially changed her stage name to *Maya Angelou*, which sounded like a "distinctive name" that would set her apart from the crowd. That name captured the essence of her Calypso dance performances and by 1957, she recorded a debut album called *Calypso Lady*. There was also an associated film, 1957's *Calypso Heat Wave*.

Exiting San Francisco, Maya Angelou headed to New York City in 1958 and connected with the Harlem Writers Guild. This was followed by an acting opportunity in the critically acclaimed Off-Broadway stage play of *The Blacks*. The 1961 play also featured Roscoe Lee Brown, Godfrey Cambridge, Louis Gossett Jr., James Earl Jones, Abbey Lincoln and Cicely Tyson. After her acting stint in this Jean Genet production, Dr. Angelou went on to write and perform in the landmark *Cabaret for Freedom*. Her stage play inspired the film *Calypso Heat Wave*, which allowed Angelou to sing and perform her own, self-penned compositions. In New York, the entertainer studied African dance with Trinidadian dancer Pearl Primus. A year later, destiny returned her to San Francisco.

In 1960, Maya Angelou decided to 'go global' once again: this time, she moved to Cairo, Egypt and become the editor of an English language weekly called *The Arab Observer*. As an education doctor, Maya Angelou's international superior intellect had kicked in—for 1962 Maya took the ball and ran with it to Ghana, doing what Damian Marley and Nas said in the song *As We Enter*: she "switched up the language" and became a professor at the University of Ghana's School of Music and Drama. While living in Accra, Ghana, her son had plans to attend college, but was hurt in a serious car crash. So "Mother Dearest" aka The Good Human Doctor remained in Accra for his recovery and wound up staying there until 1965.

To augment her intellectual experience around the decolonization period, Dr. Maya Angelou took on jobs as features editor for *The Africa Review* and also wrote in Ghana's version of the *New York Times*, called *The Ghanaian Times*. She wrote and broadcast for Radio Ghana, formed an alliance with Ghana's National Theatre and performed in a revival of *The Blacks* in Berlin, Germany and Geneva, Switzerland. By now, the literary bug had manifested itself throughout Dr. Angelou's very being as she absorbed more international languages including Arabic, French,

Italian, Spanish and the West African dialect of Fanti. During her stay in Accra, Ghana, Dr. Angelou met famed Civil Rights activist Malcolm X and this opened a new chapter in her life. By 1964, Angelou was back in the States, helping Malcolm lay out the infrastructure for his latest project, the *Organization of African American Unity*. As we all should know, the Messenger of Misery hates to see positive people moving ahead in life—shortly after this project began, Malcom X was gunned down and the organization never materialized into the dream Malcolm X and Maya Angelou had envisioned.

The negative forces deployed by Mr. Misery still had some learning to do: you can take away a leader, but the dream was still alive and in motion! Joining her brother in Hawaii, Dr. Angelou resumed singing. This was followed by a move to Los Angeles, where she focused on developing her writing skills. She worked in Watts around 1965 doing market research, witnessing volatile riots that summer. Acting and writing plays, she made a return engagement to New York in 1967, where she met close friend Rosa Guy. Rekindling her alliance with James Baldwin, Maya Angelou would soon benefit greatly from his compassionate efforts on her behalf; they had met in Paris during the 50s.

The momentum was gaining for Civil Rights reform and by now, at the request of Dr. Martin Luther King, Jr., Dr. Maya Angelou became the Northern Coordinator at the Southern Christian Leadership Conference, codename *SCLC*. At the beginning of this briefing, I mentioned how Maya Angelou had mixed feelings after her 40th birthday—that's because Dr. King was assasinated on her birthday in 1968. Not only did this send shock waves around the world, it deeply derailed Dr. Angelou. To overcome her trauma, an old associate encouraged her to start working on a book. That associate was heralded novelist James Baldwin and Maya's book came to be known as *I Know Why the Caged Bird Sings*. Other people who initially cheered her on include cartoonist Jules Feiffer, his wife, and Random House editor Robert Loomis. Published to global acclaim around 1970, this book led to dozens of literary bestsellers in poetry, fiction and non-fiction. According to the wikipedia data banks, biography author Marcia Ann Gillespie stated, "If 1968 was a year of great pain, loss, and sadness, it was also the year when America first witnessed the breadth and depth of Maya Angelou's spirit and creative genius." Fitting words for such a pivotal point in America's colorful history.

Even with little experience, Dr. Maya Angelou wrote, produced and narrated *Blacks, Blues, Black!* This ten-part series of documentaries for *National Educational Television*, (precursor of PBS) expounded on the connection between Blues music, American-African heritage, and traits the Good Doctor addressed as "Africanisms still current in the U.S." Dr. Maya Angelou's second autobiography, *Gather Together in My Name*, describes her late teenage years. The book illustrates her life from the age of 17 through 19 and "depicts a single mother's slide down the social ladder into poverty and crime." Dr. Angelou's third autobiography, *Singin' and Swingin' and Gettin' Merry Like Christmas* was a milestone—this book set her on a new plateau, as it signified the first time a Black author had written a trio of autobiographies.

Dr. Angelou's writing skills enveloped the world of literature, then she expanded her reach into the film and TV universe through screenplays and original compositions. As an example, the author wrote 1972's *Georgia, Georgia*, the first script by an African-American female to get filmed; and she scored it, too. While Dr. Angelou wrote the screenplay for this movie, it was produced by a Swedish film company and filmed in Sweden, reeling in a Pulitzer Prize nomination for the celebrated author. Around 1973, Dr. Angelou tied the knot in San Francisco with Welsh carpenter Paul du Feu. Continuing forward on her meteoric career climb, she was cast in *Look Away*, which racked up a Tony Award nomination for the "reluctant actor." Biographer Marcia Ann Gillespie was quoted saying that over the next ten years, "She had accomplished more than many artists hope to achieve in a lifetime."

As I stated earlier, Dr. Angelou *singlewomanly* changed the world by expanding borders of the entertainment industry. Her contributions to the music world were astronomic—in addition to composing and performing songs used in her own nightclub act and in motion pictures, she wrote tunes for legendary recording artist Roberta Flack. Roberta made great hits I remember from the 70s, 80s, 90s and beyond. I even had a chance to shoot Roberta (with a spotlight) at a concert she gave at the Georgia International Convention Center around 2005: my good friend and former Epic records labelmate Tony Terry assisted on background vocals. A few Roberta Flack songs that I still enjoy listening to off her Greatest Hits CD include *The First Time Ever I Saw Your Face, Killing Me Softly* (remade by The Fugees' Lauryn Hill), *You Are My Heaven* and another personal favorite, *Back Together Again*—these last two songs were recorded with a legend who left us far too soon, *Donnie Hathaway*.

Getting back to *her*story, Dr. Angelou's circle of friends had the immense power of a black hole; it drew in folks who went on to achieve galactical greatness in the entertainment universe, like Oprah Winfrey. During the late 70s when Oprah was a TV anchorwoman in Baltimore, Maryland, her trajectory was intercepted by The Good Human Doctor. Through the osmosis of cosmic synergy, the two became good friends and a mentorship process was initiated. Well, we all know what happened to Oprah after her affiliation with Dr. Angelou began—she became talk show TV's Queen Bee! During this time, there was no stopping the juggernaut created by Dr. Maya Angelou's use of superior intellect:

- 1977 – appearead in TV adaptation of Alex Haley's Roots
- In 1981, Angelou and then-husband Paul du Feu broke up; she then settled in the southern region of the United States
- 1993 – featured appearance in John Singleton's Hip-Hop flavored film *Poetic Justice* amidst Tupac Shakur, Janet Jackson and other A-List cast members. That same year, composes and reads a "Presidential Poem" for Bill Clinton's inauguration—it was broadcast live around the world "On Pulse of the Morning" show
- This recitation garnered instant fame and earlier works picked up tons of recognition. Dr. Angelou's appeal was now broadened "across racial, economic, and educational boundaries"—she picked up a Grammy Award for this effort

Sources reveal that after Dr. Angelou's 1993 recitation, her paperback book and poetry sales skyrocketed by 300–600%. If you do the math, you'll know that's a pretty big jump in activity! Random House published the poem later that year, but they scrambled to reprint 400,000 more copies of her books just to keep up with demand. Reports say Dr. Angelou had more of her books sold in January of 1993 than in the whole year of 1992, amounting to an impressive 1200% increase. Dr. Angelou's autobiographies raised the bar for female authors of African heritage, causing an overall surge in literary offerings by African-American writers.

June 1995 saw Dr. Angelou deliver a package Richard Long noted as her "second 'public' poem," *A Brave and Startling Truth*. It commemorated the 50th anniversary of the United Nations, transcending the celebrity into a global philanthropist. In 1996, Dr. Angelou achieved a goal of directing her first feature film, *Down in the Delta*. The movie featured top actors like Alfre Woodard and Wesley Snipes; through this effort, she became the first African-American woman to direct a major motion picture. In 2000, she created a line of profitable products for the Hallmark greeting card company, and added a distinguished line of decorative household items to her dossier. Topping off 2000, the Good Human Doctor received the Presidential Medal of Arts.

Since the 1990s Dr. Angelou has "toured the town" in a custom-fitted bus, making roughly 80 stops a year on the lecture circuit: this was an activity she practiced well into her eighties. In over thirty years since first writing her life story, a sixth autobiography, *A Song Flung Up to Heaven*, was completed in 2002. She also whipped up her cooking and writing skills in a 2004 book called *Hallelujah! The Welcome Table*. The book featured 73 recipes she learned from her mom and grandmother.

By 2008, Dr. Maya Angelou owned a pair of homes in Winston-Salem, North Carolina, along with a huge Harlem brownstone. This spacious abode housed a library full of books she amassed along her path of life, along with artwork she collected over a wide span of decades. There are also a number of African wall hangings and a collection of paintings, including Jazz musicians and a watercolor of famed civil rights activist, Rosa Parks. 2008 also saw Dr. Angelou reel in the distinguished Lincoln Medal. She then composed poetry and narrated for an award-winning documentary called *The Black Candle*, directed by M.K. Asante. As a political activist, Dr. Angelou campaigned for Senator Hillary Clinton in the Democratic Party's 2008 presidential primaries. After Clinton's campaign ran its course, Dr. Angelou supported a pre-President Barack Obama and later spoke at a rally for the newly-inaugurated President. America's first Black family then moved in to further colorize the White House, formerly known as the *Executive Mansion*.

Our White House correspondents report Dr. Angelou may have wanted to help out the Presidential chefs with her second cookbook, *Great Food, All Day Long: Cook Splendidly, Eat Smart*. It was published in 2010 and focused on developing good, healthy Presidential-level eating habits. That same year, the famed writer donated personal papers and career memorabilia to Harlem's *Schomburg Center for Research in Black Culture*. Angelou's care pack consisted of almost 350 boxes of documents featuring handwritten notes on yellow legal pads for *I Know Why the Caged Bird Sings*. The donation also included a 1982 telegram from Martin Luther's wife Coretta Scott King, plus fan mail and correspondence from industry peers like editor Robert Loomis. In 2011, President Barack Obama presented Dr. Angelou with the Presidential Medal of Freedom.

By 2013 at 85 years young, Dr. Maya Angelou published the seventh autobiography in her series, *Mom & Me & Mom*; this one examined her mother-daughter relationship. Using the same editor (Robert Loomis) all through her long-lasting writing career, he became known as "one of publishing's hall of fame editors." Loomis was an executive editor at Random House who retired in 2011. Practicing her own "writing ritual," the Good Doctor was spotted waking up early to check into her lab (a hotel room), where she laid on the operating table (the bed) and used legal pads to write on—by early afternoon, she vacated the building. Writing an average of about a dozen pages a day, she would edit them down to three or four pages by evening time.

Confirming her inclination to fill paper with words, Maya Angelou once said "I make writing as much a part of my life as I do eating or listening to music." To that end, she has written seven autobiographies. These autobiographies all focus on her childhood and early adult experiences. Our wiki sources say "Dr. Angelou's depictions of her experiences of racism has forced White readers to explore their feelings about race and their own privileged status." Adding to her oversized bucket of autobiographies, the Doctor wrote three essay books; and several more of poetry. Sticking with writing about what she knew best, her subject matter addressed family, racism, self-identity and travel. However, in writing about what she knew, efforts were made to ban her books from some U.S. libraries; Dr. Angelou's realities have been so intense that some schools thought they were too graphic for younger students. Still, her body of work is heavily referenced in schools and universities around the world.

Serving on 2 presidential commitees, Dr. Maya Angelou became a true icon for mainstream America. Not only that, she remains at the forefront as a major celebrity representing females and African-Americans of traditional and even Hip-Hop pursuations. With 3 Grammy Awards and over 50 honorary degrees under her belt, since 1981 Dr. Angelou has been a Reynolds Professor of American Studies at Wake Forest University in North Carolina. She taught various subjects that reflected personal interests like ethics, philosophy, science, theater, theology and writing.

It is thus fitting to concur and quote a section from The Good Human Doctor's online bio at www.mayaangelou.com: her *"words and actions continue to stir our souls, energize our bodies, liberate our minds, and heal our hearts."* Sadly, on May 28, 2014, Dr. Maya Angelou passed on to the great spiritual realm in the sky. To me, this was an extremely depressing time because I recently sent her my first book, *Musicology 2101: A Quick Start Guide to Music "Biz" History*, along with the profile you just read about her. She requested a copy of Book 2—which now needs to get mailed to Heaven, where Dr. Angelou has joined God and His singing angels. In the interim, let's remember that the story of music is not just one of how an enchanting idea turned into a business that turned into a major industry—it's one that tells a story about *people* and *relationships* they've forged together, over time.

Dr. Maya Angelou contributed to the music industry's growth in a big way, by recording an album to support her nightclub act. Plus, she composed and performed music for films. To add, she recorded poetry to CDs that sold well enough to reel in multiple Grammy awards. Personally speaking, I've heard about Dr. Maya Angelou's many accomplishments throughout my life; and still do to this day. Last but not least, I certainly hope that you too, are inspired to learn more about this fantastic lady who fans everywhere flock to get a glimpse of, wherever she appears…

-4-
HIGHER GROUND

In my book, it's a no-no to conveniently ignore genres like those mentioned above, due to a lack of significant radio airplay. With the further advancement of technology through cellphones, the Internet and satellite radio, there's already a plethora of programmable, commercial-free music stations for people to enjoy. Incidentally, styles like Folk and Popular music existed for centuries alongside Classical music; in fact, many Classical forms evolved from Folk variations. To me, this means Classical composers obviously had no qualms about using Folk and Popular music elements. As an example, the "Ode to Joy" theme is labeled as "Folk Song" in the score. Being music *biz* nature, there's no constant like change—new trends would constantly arise to send people running in a new direction. Opening up the lens further, we see that like Classical, Folk and Pop, newer styles like Hip-Hop and Reggaeton have gone as far as borrowing elements from other styles, too.

Between the 1800s and 1900s, condensed two to four minute compositions in Folk and Popular (Pop) music became the standard format, while Christian/Gospel, Classical/Symphonic, Blues, Jazz, Country & Western continued to capture a growing fan base. Around the Appalachian mountain region, Bluegrass spread its wings. Popular American music became more refined by borrowing the textured, lush sounds in European music for its compact structure, as love songs became known as *ballads*. While people tended to dance slowly to ballads, the pendulum picked up speed for other styles and eventually, faster beats pushed music's momentum to an even higher plateau. Dancers often worked themselves into adrenaline-filled frenzies to diligently keep pace and in the meantime, tempos rose to all-time highs.

During the early 19th century, Americans were regularly taken aback by amazing new trends in music, like women who could sing as well as act; in the meantime, shows and events were built around exposing them to the masses. Starting off in Cabaret or Vaudeville, many of these ladies worked their way up the male-dominated "showbiz" ladder of success. These days, we can rewind the tape to see that some made it all the way to Hollywood—through motion pictures, television appearances and theatrical productions. As usual, there simply is not enough space to mention every iconic lady of talent here, but we'll zoom in to highlight three important divas that have always tweaked my interest:

Pearl Bailey, Lena Horne and Dorothy Dandridge were all icons that did more than just a little stage commandeering, both during and after the Cabaret-Vaudeville era. Hopefully, the upcoming segments will encourage you to sing the Gospel of countless females who made a mark in the male-heavy entertainment *biz* during its infancy. So at this point, we'll take a "pause for the cause" to absorb some singing/acting morsels—in the next instant, prepare for a portion called:

Singers Who Could Act… Or Actresses That Could Sing? *Part I*

In Virginia, a highly awarded diva named Pearly Mae Bailey was born in 1918 and before her sweet sixteenth birthday, she was on stage singing! That must have been a tricky feat to accomplish, since her father was a minister and she grew up in a "Holy Roller" evangelical church where people were known for speaking in different tongues… and for dropping onto the floor to roll around "in the Spirit."

By the 30s, Pearl Bailey went secular and began winning amateur contests, as well as performing in Philadelphia nightclubs like the Pearl Theater and Harlem's Apollo Theater. After that exposure, she gave the entertainment *biz* a run for the money through countless recordings as a singer, Vaudeville performer, Broadway actress, and Hollywood movie star. Settling down in New York, Pearl continued performing in nightclubs, and the company she kept included the likes of Cab Calloway. Then she began a targeted assault on America's East Coast! During the early 40s, Pearl also supported the World War II troops by touring with the USO, like the aforesaid John Bubbles did. Many famous celebrities took time out of their busy schedules to entertain and hang out with America's "Dogs of War."

By the end of the 40s, Pearl Bailey was performing on Broadway and criss-crossing the country on tour, all as she made new recordings and films. She managed her stage and film schedule well into the 50s and 60s, with roles in films based mostly on successful plays. She also acted alongside entertainment icons like Nat "King" Cole, Dorothy Dandridge,

Mahalia Jackson, Eartha Kitt and Sidney Poitier. Pearl Bailey gave a new twist to the production of *Hello Dolly!* in an all-Black cast rendition of the popular musical. Her honors cover the entire spectrum of entertainment; even touching sports fans by singing the national anthem at New York's Shea Stadium during the 1969 World Series. The following year, she was appointed to the role of U.S. "Ambassador of Love" by President Richard Nixon. The 1970s marked another pivotal period for Pearl Bailey—she became a household name with her own TV show, was a spokeswoman for Duncan Hines, and was also a voice-over actress for animated movies. During Bailey's "Golden Years" of the 70s, she assumed leading roles in theatrical productions, and even sounded off as a campaign supporter for President Gerald Ford. Not bad for an entertainer in her late fifties!

In 1985 at the ripe young age of 67, Pearl Bailey added a Bachelor's degree in Theology to her list of accomplishments. By 1988, she was honored with a Presidential Medal of Freedom. Less than two years later, she made her home-going trek to music heaven to sing for the "Most High." Pearl will always be remembered for her unparalleled commitment to showbiz, and the dedicated service she selflessly gave to her country. There were plenty of talented entertainers in the 30s and 40s, but Pearl Bailey was blessed with the rare ability to sing, act and dance, in a God-given sort of way. In performance mode, she turned into a dynamic talent that blessed the folks who came out to see her.

Speaking of blessings, let's say that the balance of this book would be grossly tilted if an honorable mention didn't go out to Gospel and Spiritual music—these particular genres co-existed with secular music since the very beginning. Theologically speaking, although Pearl Bailey left the church to sing secular music, she still shone on stage by never losing faith in the divine purpose she was born for: to bestow her abundant talent upon millions of listeners. Need more anointing? Just hit the search button for additional info on this rare Pearl. We'll now *opt in* to more greatness, by taking a pause for the cause to discuss another great gem that came out of the Gospel world—to be honest, I can't think of Pearl Bailey without thinking of our next legendary icon. Looking back to my younger days, their records could have been close together in the family's album collection, but for whatever the reason, this singer became one of the most polished gems in the field of God's music—or any music style for that matter, when you really think about it…

THE GREATEST

Grammy Award-winning singer Mahalia Jackson is known to most as the first "Queen of Gospel Music." Highly regarded around the globe, she recorded somewhere in the neighborhood of thirty albums for Columbia Records alone. In-between the albums, she amassed a dozen million-selling gold singles. Let's go in for a closer look at this exceptional wonder of the Gospel music world.

Born in New Orleans in 1911, a young Mahalia Jackson grew up in a packed house with strict rules, but she made it through and later took on a leading role in "family management." Growing up singing spirituals with her mom, Mahalia grew to become a featured performer at festivals around America and Europe. Hitting the road during the Great Migration, Jackson landed in Chicago circa 1927 at the age of sixteen. In almost no time, she was singing with professional Gospel groups all over town!

By 1929, Mahalia Jackson had an encounter with the "Father of Gospel Music," composer Thomas A. Dorsey. They later entered into a collaborative performance arrangement, which produced a long-term relationship that netted standards like *Take My Hand, Precious Lord*. Around this time, her five-year marriage was complicated by pressure from her husband to sing secular music. Mahalia swore she'd never sing secular: it was a promise she never broke, either. During the mid 40s, she was well on her way to racking up greater fame, ending up with a huge hit—1948's *Move On Up A Little Higher*. Constantly selling out in record stores, this song capped out around the eight million units mark; fifty years later, the song won a Grammy Hall of Fame Award.

Mahalia Jackson took her performances from churches to concert venues, while shifting her sound accompaniment from piano and organ, to fully orchestrated extravaganzas. Word of Mahalia Jackson was spreading all around the world, and she began picking up accolades in places like Denmark, France and Norway. From the mid 40s through the mid 50s, songs like *Amazing Grace, Go Tell It On the Mountain* and *His Eye Is On the Sparrow* topped global music charts to become instant classics. The 50s brought with it new feats, like being the first Gospel act to do a live performance at Carnegie Hall in New York. At this point, she was selling out to raving audiences everywhere. Next was a radio show on CBS and being signed to their record label, Columbia Records. Halfway through the decade, Mahalia Jackson was hailed by many as "The World's Greatest

Gospel Singer;" even recording an album in 1955 bearing the same name. Around the time Mahalia went mainstream, some supporters of the traditional Gospel sound argued that she toned down her intense performances to appeal to a wider audience.

In the late 50s, Mahalia Jackson became the first Gospel artist to make ascension into Hollywood, and she performed at the 1957, '58 and '59 Newport Jazz Festivals. Mahalia was so popular that she got invited to sing at the 1961 inauguration of President John F. Kennedy. A year later, her first Christmas album was recorded. Even across the waters in England, Mahalia Jackson became a regular face on British television; her fan base grew from lots of media popularity. Mahalia bestowed her special gift in front of domestic audiences at places like New York World's Fair and internationally in Africa, India and Japan—not many places were left unblessed by Jackson. At the famed 1963 *March on Washington* where the Rev. Dr. Martin Luther King Jr. dutifully delivered his "I Have A Dream" speech, over 250,000 saw Mahalia Jackson perform. Even in the wake of Dr. King's death Mahalia was right there, sending him home with her heavenly voice.

By the 70s, Mahalia Jackson recorded her final album, did her last show in Germany, and also made a special appearance on *The Flip Wilson Show*. During her professional career, Mahalia touched the lives of many people through her numerous performances and acts of good will. In her trail was college foundations and other honors, such as the Silver Dove Award. At her 1972 funeral, notables like Coretta Scott-King, Ella Fitzgerald and Sammy Davis Jr. were present to pay their respects. When the "Queen of Soul" Aretha Franklin sent her mentor, the "Queen of Gospel" on her homecoming, it was with an emotionally charged version of *Take My Hand, Precious Lord*. The city of New Orleans will always be proud of its daughter Mahalia Jackson—a true singer's singer that you can get more info on at www.mahaliajackson.us.

While it literally would take an act of God to bring forth another singer as memorable as Mahalia Jackson, there are many more great artists who brought their talent to the forefront of the industry. Even though religious music rarely hits the mainstream, its artists still must demonstrate lots of discipline when recording tracks or performing live in front of an audience. With wide options available to them, religious acts can perform original songs, remake compositions that were previously covered by artists like Mahalia Jackson, or add a new twist like Kirk Franklin did in the early 90's. Collaboratively speaking, projects like these were all done in a manner that's similar to their secular counterparts. This leads me to conclude that like any other music artist who's serious about achieving success, Spiritual artists deserve much honor and respect for what they do. As we draw towards the next phase of our trip into everlasting musical sanctity, let's get the inside scoop on what some of our good neighbors are listening to, at church.

HOLY HOLSTON!

Personally speaking, one of the reasons I consider myself blessed is because I can walk just across the driveway to seek spiritual guidance and get in a good dose of The Word—thanks to our friendly neighbor, Pastor Manuel Holston and his beloved family. For the past few decades, Pastor Holston has led services at the City of Atlanta's Martin Street Church of God and from what I've seen over the years, he's done a magnificent job!

I recall watching the congregation grow from being sequestered in a smaller-sized House of Worship right behind I-20 near downtown. Then they moved down the street into a brand new facility that takes a full-sized staff to manage. Around the new millennium, a distinguished guest and commencement speaker at the grand opening services for the larger facility was none other than Atlanta's then-Mayor, Bill Campbell. That wasn't the only time I crossed paths with Bill either; I rubbed elbows with him again at a *Bridging the Digital Divide* luncheon at City Hall. It was for the Mayor's Council on Youth Education—the guest speaker was author, educator, my 5th grade teacher and mentor, Bernard Percy.

Doing sound or video for different churches at various points in my career enabled me to "see and hear the light" by working with audio consoles, video cameras, plus gadgets like remote controls, signal switchers and distribution amps. As a multi-faceted audiovisual vicar of technology in Atlanta, I've worked with Pastor Holston's son and "Minister of A/V Theology" Marcus; he's a key figure of the church's in-house sound and video unit, *Grace Productions*. Over the years, Grace Productions stepped up their game by upgrading the broadcast quality gear they had… to a higher level. Remaining at the cusp of technology, this church utilizes hi-tech tools like wireless microphones, digital mixing boards, LCD projectors; even a robot-like video camera to record live footage. With innovations like these, gone are the days of me (or someone else) floating around the pulpit in full view during a packed sermon, loaded down with a big bulky camera on the shoulder. From the podium to the screen, Martin Street's Grace Productions team works behind the scenes to help spread God's message. Let's get a big *Amen* in for that!

Among many services offered by the Martin Street Church of God, there are spiritual awareness tools—like a nice monthly newsletter from celebrity Kirk Cameron. They also utilize interactive mediums including a website, social networking pages, a phone-in prayer line, and church staffers even call to check on members who may be 'missing in action.' As an integral part of this family-oriented church, the Children's Council is made up of parents who meet regularly for planning, input and support. The Children's Minister keeps exciting things planned, and the Teen Ministry known as J.A.M. (Jesus And Me) allows teenagers to express themselves while sharing The Word. I've seen them tear the roof off the church on many occasions with great songs they sing. I believe the proof is right there in the "pudding of prophecy"—these fine young disciples deliver a message worthy of hearing!

Surprisingly enough, Pastor Holston is a serious music lover who makes sure that uplifting songs are an important part of the program—to make it happen, music minister Brother Dennis is always on hand. So whose music do praise leaders listen to for inspiration? One day when I directed this question to Pastor Holston, the first name that came out of his mouth was Mahalia Jackson, who we just gave praises to as *The Greatest*. Now let's close this section out with a trip to the center stage of Martin Street's Church of God, where the SPOTLIGHT now hits the J.A.M. Ministry. Check out more glorious news about family-based Martin Street Church of God at www.mstcog.org, as this anointing youth group prepares to exercise their vocal chords. We're about to go "down to the river" in an energetic, fun-filled praise session. *Amen, Amen…* and *Amen*!

As mentioned before, the Gospel and Spiritual music world is growing exponentially, by keeping up with the same technological advances found in secular music. It's easy to find tons of Gospel and other Spiritual music on the Internet, as well as on dozens of sites featuring the Bible and other information relative to Christianity. Additionally, there are loads of libraries and retailers that offer more documentation and supporting products to help spread the "Good News"—all you have to do is hit the search button. Here's a short list of notable acts you can find making important contributions to the world of Gospel/Spiritual music:

Yolanda Adams
Helen Baylor
James Blackwood, Sr.
The Blind Boys of
Alabama
Rev. Shirley Caesar
Terri Carroll
Ricky Dillard
Georgia Tom Dorsey
O'Landa Draper &
The Associates
Kirk Franklin
Al Green

Mark Hubbard
Canton Jones
John P. Kee
Mary Mary
Babbie Mason
Mighty Clouds of Joy
Smokey Norful
Albertina Walker
Hezekiah Walker
Ethel Waters
The Williams Brothers
The Winans
Thomas Winfield

The Jackson Southernaires

Don't forget, there are plenty others! On a side note, offshoot acts like Bebe & Cece Winans of The Winans family veered into a new lane on the track by producing songs with a unique combination of inspirational lyrics and R&B overtones. This technique burgeoned itself into a crossover marketing protocol, attracting a broader fan base through airplay on R&B (codename *Churban*: *C*ontemporary *H*it *Urban*) formatted radio stations. This approach seemed one-sided for a while, meaning transitions for religious acts into the secular market could be much more forgiving than the other way around.

Possibly as a result of campaigns to increase their appeal, popular R&B or Hip-Hop acts moving into the spiritually-connected Gospel music market still happened. Our next artist is one who successfully made that switch; for those who may still be in the dark, there's a little more light left to shed on this trendy combination. With our beacon aiming towards Michigan, let's meet a singer who stepped out of the background in the R&B/Funk world, directly to front and center of her own spiritually uplifting world.

SPOTLIGHT ON: Alicia Myers

Every now and then, an R&B artist is saluted for singing "The Word," like in the case of Detroit native Alicia Myers. As we know, a lot of good music came out of Detroit and as an original member of Al Hudson's Soul Partners, Alicia's responsible for a small chunk of it. Being born in a musical family and the success of her older brother Jackie gave Alicia an edge—he was in an act called *The Chairmen Of The Board*. They tallied up a huge 1970 hit called *Give Me Just A Little More Time* and I just heard that song in a commercial, so that means it's still generating publishing income for someone.

After Alicia Myers co-wrote and recorded lead vocals on the Soul Partners' 1979 hit *You Can Do It*, they shifted over from ABC Records to MCA. Then the group got a name change and transformed into R&B/Funk supergroup *One Way featuring Al Hudson*. the band mushroomed into a 'big fish in a little sea' and moved from Detroit to Los Angeles to become a 'big fish in a bigger sea.' This followed the escape route of another Motortown native to the west coast (last name Gordy). As *One Way*, hits like *Push*, *Music* and one of my faves, *Cutie Pie*, began flying out the door and right up Billboard's charts.

Sometimes, a harried band life leads to members leaving the pack with their own aspiring hopes of finding fame and fortune and eventually, Alicia Myers sparked up a solo career with MCA—the same label One Way was signed to. Alicia released several albums and although much of the mainstream knew her from prior One Way releases, one song in particular called *I Want to Thank You* can still be heard on the radio today. This song gave her career a spiritually lifted boost up the R&B and Gospel charts in 1981. Thirty years later, Alicia continues performing on the road and can also be found on TV at places like *The Mo'Nique Show*, singing her classic hit and telling her story. These days, you can get your Alicia Myers looks, listens and likes on by visiting online portals like You Tube, bet.com/video/.../monique2150-alicia-s1.html, myspace.com/aliciamyers07 and of course, at www.facebook.com/AliciaMyersFanPage?sk=info: she might even "thank you" for stopping by!

"Singers Who Could Act... Or Actresses That Could Sing? *Part II*

Here's a "forever young" lady whose story was so compelling, it got made into a movie starring Halle Berry. Dorothy Dandridge entered the world in 'go mode,' because when she was born in 1932, her mother was already in the game as a seasoned entertainer. Dorothy and her sister Vivian were exposed to life on the road at an early age; this gave them the experience they needed to succeed down the line. Before you could say *go*, "The Wonder Children" were performing around the South. They were no strangers to the "Chitlin' Circuit" but during the Great Depression, phones stopped ringing for many performers...

Heading to Hollywood, Dorothy Dandridge made her debut playing small roles in motion pictures and on the radio. By 1935, she had taken root and later appeared in a Marx Brothers film, *A Day At the Races.* Like Lena Horne, she was captivating to look at—but was still given stereotypical acting roles to portray. Again like Lena, Dorothy overcame obstacles by exposing another side of her many talents to nightclubs across the country. Next to her good looks, Dorothy's stage presence and natural singing ability kept things rolling throughout the 40s and 50s. By the mid-50s, she was sharing the screen with the likes of Pearl Bailey, Harry Belafonte and Diahann Carroll in a production called *Carmen Jones*. Dorothy was later nominated for an Academy Award, and thus became the third Black person nominated for an award of this stature: the first two were Hattie McDaniel and Ethel Waters.

Although her professional career was shiny and bright, Dorothy Dandridge's private life had murky periods including a pair of bumpy marriages and a sickly baby. Dandridge was later forced to come to terms with herself for institutionalizing her child due to brain damage. Add to that mix bad money management and ergo, you get a recipe for unavoidable personal disaster. Selling her house to settle up taxes with Uncle Sam led to a lonely Dorothy Dandridge's encounter with a nervous breakdown. With new-fangled plans underway by the mid-60s, she prepared for new engagements beginning in New York. Depressingly speaking, she wound up not making it to her own show—Dorothy's manager found her lifeless body in a room. An autopsy determined that she probably suffered an accidental overdose of anti-depressants but inharmoniously thinking, it's doubtful that anyone really knows. This sort of reminds me of the sad circumstances surrounding the death of an actress called Marilyn Monroe.

Honorably speaking, let's just let the record show that Dorothy Dandridge finally got her true accolades in the 1980s, through fellow actresses like Angela Bassett, Janet Jackson, Jada Pinkett, Cicely Tyson and Halle Berry. Their acknowledgment of Dandridge's efforts was displayed in various film renditions of her works. Exhibit A: Profiling this quintessential group of fine ladies, we find Halle Berry's tribute to Dorothy was highly visible—her portrayal of Dandridge in a biographical film won tributes like the Emmy, Golden Globe and Screen Actors Guild awards. In the end, Dorothy Dandridge received mass recognition for her many contributions to the then-small world of Blacks in film. Closing arguments show she even got her very own star on the Hollywood Walk of Fame to commemorate ascension as a true groundbreaker in the *showbiz chronicles*. As we wait for a final verdict, feel free to hit the search button for more online exhibits on the one and only, Dorothy Dandridge.

WORD'S UP!

A music artist's success or flaws are deeply enhanced by the people's perception, in tandem with the endeavors of whatever label they're signed to. Over the course of music *biz*tory, a number of Gospel labels like Benson, Canaan, DaySpring, Home Sweet Home, Light, Myrrh, Rejoice, Reunion, Star Song, Word and others had achieved some level of charted success. Some Gospel labels made distribution deals directly with major record companies, while others remained independent. And then there was the 'both-siders,' who did a little of each by partnering with a major label while distributing smaller Gospel labels.

When I rewind back to my 'not so top-secret' top list of CBS/Sony distributed labels, I recall one with a sizeable crop of spiritual acts that I had the pleasure to market and promote. By 1990, I was looking at my sixth year of employment with CBS Records, which had recently been purchased by Sony and subsequently renamed Sony Music Entertainment. Around this time, Sony signed a significant deal—its Epic label was designated to distribute the music of a Gospel label called Word Records. Now if I can "get a witness," let's get the word on Word.

The year 1951 saw Word Records founded in Waco, Texas as a label with an emphasis on spoken word recordings, before branching out to the Christian and Gospel circuit. By 1954, Word assumed the duties of being a record label and a publishing house. Early employees of Word included major players in the Gospel music game like Kurt Kaiser and

Ralph Carmichael; these gents kept it moving to achieve grand slams in Gospel. Over a matter of years, Word amassed a pipeline that included Canaan Records in the 60s, Myrrh, DaySpring and Light Records in the 70s, with Rejoice Records getting added to Word's portfolio in the 80s.

REBORN FACT: Two of the above labels still exist as of this writing, but in a restructured form: the Myrrh Label reincarnated itself in 2005 as a Praise and Worship label called Myrrh Worship, while Canaan Records was resurrected in 2007.

Economic tides often tend to engulf those in its vicinity: since Gospel music labels coexisted with labels representing all genres, they were not privy to escape when seas got rough in the industry. As financial storms developed, many unprepared labels got drowned, sold or otherwise swallowed up. In-between these storms brewing and subsiding, new developments occured:

- In 1976, owner Jarrell McCracken sold a share of Word to the American Broadcasting Company (ABC)
- Within 10 years, ABC merged with Capitol Cities, Inc. and McCracken was then commanded to "exit the building"
- By 1983, Home Sweet Home Records made their move from Benson Records to distribution by Word
- Even though Word was turning into a music powerhouse, the major labels still yielded a bigger stick in the industry; Word devises a plan to "make it to the majors"
- To get closer to the big machine between 1984 and 1990, Word engaged in a distribution deal with A&M Records, a part of the RCA conglomerate

At one time, RCA was a stable American-owned company that distributed labels like Clive Davis' Arista Records, and Herb Alpert's A&M Records. Back around 1984 when Word jumped into the larger music pipeline with A&M, I happened to begin my major league career with CBS Records. Prior to one of our competitors (RCA Records) getting absorbed by the German-owned Bertelsmann Music Group (BMG), RCA was known for their affiliation with the Victor brand. Victor's logo depicted a small pooch (le doggie) with his ear perched next to a turntable horn—I still think that's one of the cutest logos around.

When Word's distribution pipeline switched over to Sony's Epic Records in the 90s, their affiliation remained intact until 2002. I remember how Sony made a big effort to establish Word in its system, and that's not just because a 'most important' market for Gospel was where I lived—in the Southeast (the Bible belt). To be honest, there was a whole lot riding on this deal! As previously mentioned, Word distributed Light Records in the 1970s; during the 80s, Ralph Carmichael purchased Light after he left Word. Star Song was another affiliate distributed by Word but by the 80s, they decided to "let go and let God guide the ship."

Before long, Word was signing Reunion Records to compensate for losing labels like Light and Star Song—Reunion remained a Word affiliate until the 90s. As you'll see, Word Records grew into a dominant force because in addition to a first class artist roster, they orchestrated distribution deals with numerous labels during the 70s, 80s, 90s and beyond. This label's incremental rise to the top of the Gospel music industry came through strategic advertising, distribution, promotions, and housing a who's who stable of talented Christian and Gospel music acts. Here's the short list:

The Archers	The Imperials
Steve Archer	Love Song
Helen Baylor	Kenny Marks
Brooklyn Tabernacle Choir	Babbie Mason
Rev. Milton Brunson	Rich Mullins
Carman	The Nelons
O'Landa Draper	Sandi Patty
Florida Boys	Petra
Bill Gaither Trio	Point of Grace
Gaither Vocal Band	Michael W. Smith
Happy Goodman Family	Paul Smith
Rusty Goodman	Sweet Comfort Band
Amy Grant	Russ Taff
Al Green	Wayne Watson
Guardian	White Heart

There are hordes of other great acts, but we've only got so much space on the pallette! The following is a briefing on Word Records' roller coaster ride through the throngs of its corporate lifecycle, and then we'll flip the page to view a few snapshots that are still in focus within my mind's eye...

In 1992, Word was purchased by Thomas Nelson, Incorporated. It went through Capital Cities ABC in a deal that closed for $72 million. After taking ownership, Nelson tinkered with its new toy by making a few changes: they developed a new logo for their book division and unveiled it in 1995. They also moved the corporate headquarters from Waco to Nashville. During the 70s, Donny and Marie Osmond mixed *a little Country with a little Rock-n-Roll*, but thanks to Word the landscape was changing to look and sound a lot like Country, with a hint of Christian music too! Bringing a new image and logo into a fresh neighborhood to "share The Word," tinkering time with Word music was not over—by now the industry had already bowed in recognition of the label.

By 1996, Thomas Nelson divvied up Word Records' music label from its book publishing division and eventually sold the label to Gaylord Entertainment. Six years later in 2002, the Word Entertainment group was sold to AOL Time Warner. After former Atlantic Records Christian division manager Barry Landis came aboard, Word was restructured and their Los Angeles music publishing office was closed. Then, Myrrh Records, Squint Entertainment and Everland Entertainment were absorbed into the Word Label Group, leading to a reduced personnel list. Later, Curb Records bought a few shares in Word; by 2004 the label was resold as a compliance policy of the deregulation divestiture Time Warner completed earlier that year. When the clouds cleared, businessman Edgar Bronfman and his group of investors had formed a bigger, more powerful entity, the Warner Music Group. Due to the constant variable of change, there's no telling who owns Word as of now—but we can best believe it will continue to attract promising new spiritually-based groups, as they continue to harbor established acts and other great Gospel record labels.

Now, we'll breeze through those snapshots of my mind's eye, all captured and prepared for viewing. As a result of Sony's 1990 affiliation with Word Records, a chunk of their artist roster came to us through Epic Records. This included Reverend Milton Brunson, O'Landa Draper, The Brooklyn Tabernacle Choir, Al Green, Helen Baylor, Babbie Mason, Reverend Shirley Caesar and a long list of others. Since this was my first experience marketing Christian and Gospel music artists, let's REWIND the clock so I can divulge a little info about some of the artists I was blessed to market and promote back in the day.

Plenty of great singers analogous to Sam Cooke 'genre-jumped' from Gospel into R&B, Soul and Pop while navigating forward to claim their fame. On the other hand, songstresses like Alicia Myers, Helen Baylor and Terri Carroll jumped into Gospel from genres like R&B and Jazz. Then, there are the artists that seamlessly flowed from one style to the next without regard, like a fabulous talent I had the pleasure of marketing for Columbia Records, Regina Belle (I recently saw her acting in a movie). And we can't forget those artists whose Hip-Hop upbringing influenced religious lyrics, like DC Talk and Kirk Franklin. On another platform, the inspirational Bebe & Cece Winans were among numerous others who sprinkled their own R&B flavored, Spirit-filled blessings into the master mix. Finally, there's the one and only Al Green, who started off in Gospel, jumped into secular, and returned to Gospel—before ultimately combining a spiritually driven delivery with R&B, Soul and Pop elements.

In summation, the above-mentioned acts plugged into a higher power and tapped into an unlimited source of energy, all from the Big Guy's Big Plan to deliver *sound* souls! Along the road to enlightenment, many artists encounter life-changing experiences. Today, some can be found sharing vivid stories about how God's blessings got integrated into their quest to transform into *supreme singing spiritualists*. Now let's 'get prayed up,' as we redirect our focus to a previously mentioned artist who weathered the storms over decades of evolution in the music business.

Al Green

For the few who've never heard of Al Green, this could be your lucky day—he's just another one of the music world's great wonders and here comes some great info on him. This includes the inside scoop on a few prodigious Green events I partook in, while helping to support his new Word Records release. To give you the code Green on Rev Al, he's logged in at #65 on Rolling Stone's "100 Greatest Artists of All Time" and is a certified *Rock and Roll Hall of Famer*, with over 20 million records sold... and counting.

Al Green came a long way since his early years in 50s-era Forrest City, Arkansas. When he was ten, Al performed in his family's Gospel quartet, the Greene Brothers. The family group often found itself acting like a mobile unit as they moved from Forrest City to places like Grand Rapids, Michigan. Al performed and traveled often to spread The Word with his family; but the family lived their lives as devout Christians, while Al had bigger plans on the secular platform...

> **GREEN FACT:** Al Green got fired by his father; for listening to secular sounds of singers like James Brown, Sam Cooke, Wilson Pickett and Jackie Wilson. Retrospectively speaking, Al once revealed he hoped to record with the often-introspective visionary, Marvin Gaye.

Al Greene & the Creations was formed in the 60s when Al was still in high school. This led Curtis Rogers and Palmer James of the Creations to start an independent label, the *Hot Line Music Journal*. Scoring a string of moderate regional hits, Al's group later changed their name to *Al Greene & the Soul Mates*. Even without racking up a major national hit, young Al was determined to make it big—although idols like Sam Cooke and Marvin Gaye added an "e" to their last name, Al went contrary and dropped his "e." By 1969, he linked up with producer Willie Mitchell and never looked back.

Through what we'll dub as "Expedition Green-Mitchell," the duo went on a sonic voyage with an action-packed trek across the music skyline. In doing so, they painted a glistening trajectory for the entertainment universe's cosmic canvas to behold. Al Green's distinctive sound of success had gone terrestrial. With co-pilot Willie Mitchell on the faders, Green crooned in coordinates to a far away destination that distanced them from all other 'contenders for the crown.' Along the way, their multi-staged climb included 7 back-to-back Gold singles. Al's Green-Mitchell ferry was fully deployed with a touch of the fingertip and by the 70s, Green was piloting his very own meteoric ascension to destination *Da-topada-charts*!

Overcoming a number of 'gritty' obstacles in his personal life, Al Green found himself on a new mission: as codename *Soul Survivor*. In this new position, he began serving the Lord—as an ordained pastor. Since 1976, Rev. Green spread The Word at Memphis' *Full Gospel Tabernacle*, right down the street from Elvis Presley's *Graceland*. The remainder of the 70s saw Al Green doing more performances in the Gospel vernacular, but when the 80s drew around he not only had a documentary made about him, but also teamed up with Patti Labelle. Along with other notables, Al set off to perform in theatric musicals through a series of 'stage missions' called *Your Arms Too Short to Box with God*. These missions featured onstage collaborations of Al with Patti the Diva and her blessed voice.

The Lord guided Al Green's ship into more bright lights during the 80s, reuniting him with his old hit-making production mate, Willie Mitchell—this fruitful partnership yeilded 8 Grammy Awards for *Best Soul Gospel Performance*. The latter 80s kept Green moving through fertile pasture with The Eurhythmics' Annie Lennox; they performed on the soundtrack for Bill Murray's big-budget 1988 movie, *Scrooged*. Al Green also paired up with super-producer Arthur Baker and a long list of brilliant music-makers who'll be revealed momentarily.

By the 90s, Al Green moved over to Word/Epic and released a compilation called *One In a Million*. This album was a collection of fine songs from his Gospel albums of the 80s, and it just happened to hit the streets somewhere around the time I was either promoting Public Enemy's 1990 *Fear of a Black Planet*, or pre-promoting 1991's *Apocalypse 91... The Enemy Strikes Black...* Although colorized images in my old RAM memory are slowly turning gray, I can still remember this period: it was the same time a major image change took place for me. I had gotten myself a "jheri curl" back in 1980 and by 1990, was ready for a new look. I decided it was curl-cut time, so operation *Going Back to Black* was put in full effect. Strangely enough, after I chopped the curl, I still look around and see that it still remains popular for a select few...

In addition to the rest of the free world rejoicing that I had finally applied '*death to the 'doo*,' Sony Music celebrated Al Green's new release by throwing an exclusive listening party at the Peachtree Plaza hotel in Atlanta. We invited everyone from the southern Gospel music community—retail, radio and other media personnel came out in full force. To me, it didn't matter what kind of music Al was making because a bunch of people still flew in or drove a great distance to see him. There had to be a good reason for this, and I later discovered what it was. You see, Al was not only blessed with a silky voice—he also had a heavenly sense of humor. As guests dined and took celebrity snapshots, he too got busy: Al had people cracking up with jokes and humorous stories he told!

GOING FOR GREEN - AT THE MALL WEST END

To support Al Green's latest album, Sony Atlanta set up an in-store appearance at Peppermint Records' West End location. I always took the time to show my stuff at artist in-stores, because this was when I secured the best locations to plaster merchandising materials like posters up on walls, around the bins, and in other key areas. For major releases, the front window was often 'that place,' followed by the space just behind it, as well as near the cash register. As protocol, I checked with our in-house sales reps to ensure that enough Al Green's music would be on hand for sale. Just as important as any other component in the plan, ads promoting the event were placed on the radio and with local papers.

In-store appearances accomplished several things, like putting the artist directly in front of fans, but in an off-stage environment. Secondly, they opened doors for more music sales: fans gained close access their idols and bought autographed music products. As a by-product, supplemental merchandise is often purchased, and we can't discount the amount of traffic that's generated at the event location! These days, it's even easier to get overwhelmed, thanks to technological innovations like texting and tweeting. Social networking tools like these make me wonder how an already full-to-capacity crowd at Greenbriar Mall would have looked when we did an early 1990s Xscape in-store at Peppermint's other in-town location. Similar to what I did for Al Green at the West End store, I made a huge window display to get the message out, and it pulled music buyers right in. After I concluded videotaping highlights of the Xscape in-store, I recorded footage of us running with the girls out of Peppermint's, through a long back hallway and into the waiting limo. I'll review my footage and compound the data—"more news at 11…"

In all honesty, the Al Green in-store event at Peppermint's West End location was just as exciting as any other in-store I was involved in. A secret sign was given at day's end, when the "final tally" was being calculated: we sold out of everything! It was a great experience to watch the action unfold before my own eyes—from setting up the store displays, to seeing the store pack up with fans, to hearing the cash register sound of "chi-ching" with each purchase of an album, cassette or CD of the very man these customers fought their way to get next to. As a sidenote for those who weren't aware, Al Green did a great job in 1970 with a song that made it to #1 by The Temptations, 1969's *I Can't Get Next To You*. Al had a knack for composing soulful songs, but he was good at covering other tunes too—like the Bee Gees' first #1 American hit in 1971, *How Can You Mend a Broken Heart*. Al Green recorded a cover version of the song in 1972; it later landed in motion pictures like 1999's *Notting Hill* and 2010's *The Book of Eli*.

Disdainfully speaking, my job's success curtailed on two simple measurements: the quantity of *customers* that showed up, plus the amount of *cash* exchanging hands and landing into the register. Luckily, my memories of this Al Green event are locked away in a photo I took with him while behind the counter helping to sell his music. That in-store event wasn't just a success because we sold tons of product—it was also successful because Al Green 'initiated positive interactions' while signing autographs for a store full of his fans. And just like at our Al Green party in Atlanta's Peachtree Plaza hotel, his healthy sense of humor and infectious disposition resurfaced as he told hilarious stories, while cracking some funny jokes! In summation, I'm willing to say the Al Green in-store at West End Mall helped to bring a little "*Love and Happiness*" into the 'hood, if only for one day.

A few memorable in-store events include the one above with Al Green, Tony "She's Fly" Terry, and Xscape at Peppermint's Greenbriar Mall location. There was also the trendy Rap/Hip-Hop duo Kris Kross at Turtle's Records on Memorial Drive and I-285, herbified MCs Cypress Hill down the street at Sound Warehouse in Stone Mountain, and Rock legend Ozzy Osbourne at Record Bar's Town Center Mall location in Marietta. (And no, I didn't see any bats or blood… that day!)

Getting back to the evolution of Al Green, by the 90s he returned to his Soul/R&B roots and expanded his boundaries by working once again with Arthur Baker. He also collaborated with a group called the Fine Young Cannibals, thus producing more Green-flavored hits. Al also got into doing music for TV shows and working with artists in a variety of genres, like Country's Lyle Lovett—and more Grammies followed. Al's 1992 *Love Is Reality* came next; the album was produced by Tim Miner, who at one time was a Motown recording artist. Tim gave Al fresh productions loaded with bright touches, and arrangements sprinkled with hints of other *flavas of the era*; like *New Jack Swing*.

A secular album was released in 1995, and the *Rock and Roll Hall of Fame* made Al Green a made man. Continuing to do well with live shows, Pastor Al rode the 90s right into the new millennium by publishing a semi-biography entitled *Take Me to the River*; this enlightening dossier sheds a lot of light on his landmark career. Green's success entails *Grammy Lifetime Achievemen*t awards, movie soundtracks, and classic albums with music pal Willie Mitchell. It was certainly clear to see that Al Green's momentum was locked in "pinging the perigee" mode—yet he had been dutifully cleared for a nonstop mission to hit the apogee!

Coordinates along Al Green's voyage through "New Millenni Way" included musical pitstops with Queen Latifah, Questlove of The Roots, John Legend, Anthony Hamilton and other notable notemakers. In 2008, Green's *Lay It Down* album cracked the Top Ten on Billboard and became his most successful release in over 30 years. Green closed out the decade by participating in assorted music projects including *Oh Happy Day: An All-Star Music Celebration*, plus he made special appearances and received more honors. All I can say is, it's nice to have crossed paths with this phenomenal music magnet—Al Green both transmitted and attracted a certain flow of energy with his enthralling vocal tones, while touching just about every soundscape spectrum on the map of musical aptitude. If you want to "Go Green" on the web, visit www.algreenmusic.com but for now, let's drop a little deeper into the well of musical mystery to find out more about a former labelmate of Al Green's, Helen Baylor.

Helen Baylor

For as long as I can remember, Helen Baylor has been proven to be one of Gospel's leading ladies. She impressed this upon me by receiving not one or two, but three Gospel Music Association *Dove Awards*, four *Stellar Awards* and one Soul Train *Lady of Soul* Award. This proves that Helen Baylor's not only a contender; she's a winner against all odds.

But before the big win, Helen Baylor had to overcome her share of personal/professional obstacles, just like some other artists featured in this section: Alicia Myers, Al Green and Terri Carroll, who you'll get acquainted with shortly. Although Helen currently anoints listeners with her touching Gospel songs, she didn't start her career off doing it that way. Born in Tulsa, Oklahoma, she was brought up in the City of the Angels (Los Angeles) and as a starry-eyed teenager, did shows in nightclubs. This was only the beginning; it quickly led to gigs opening up for headliners like Aretha Franklin, Stevie Wonder and B.B. King. Helen even performed in the musical extravaganza, *Hair*.

During the 70s, Helen Baylor continued working in musicals and sang with Pop stars like The Captain & Tennille and R&B/Funk's Chaka Khan. Similar to many others in the music *biz*, drugs infiltrated her mix during the 1980s—it should be no surprise that her career began to tarnish at about the same time. Helen sobered up after strengthening her Christian faith and launched a new career, in Gospel music. Around 1990, her first new musical effort was released on Word Records. By 1993, the song *Sold Out* (from her *Start All Over* album) earned Helen distinguished recognition as "Contemporary Gospel Recorded Song of the Year" at the Gospel Music Association's 24th Dove Awards.

Let's dwell in the river right here to 'witness' another spiritual event that took place in 1993: Helen Baylor was ordained by her pastor, Dr. Frederick Price, at his *Crenshaw Christian Center*. This was pretty interesting, because when I think back to my post-high school life in 1980, I was living on Crenshaw Boulevard near Manchester Boulevard in Inglewood, California—right across the street from the Crenshaw Christian Center! A well-known celebrity often seen when visiting CCC was football great Rosey Grier. Rosey was blessed to be an actor, singer and minister, on top of the fantastic feats he performed as an original *"Fearsome Foursome"* of the Los Angeles Rams. Before the Rams, Grier was a New York Giant and a Pennsylvania State University sports star: he even earned a spot in the NCAA's 100th anniversary list of 100 most influential student athletes.

FAST FORWARD: All five of Rosey Grier's fellow parishioner Helen Baylor's albums pinged the Top Ten of Billboard's Top Gospel Albums chart. One of her more successful albums is 1994's *The Live Experience*—it hit #1 on the chart. In 1995, Baylor received an Honorary Doctorate Degree in Sacred Music from Friends International Christian University. RECORD: With over a half-dozen fruitful albums in her garden of Gospel music, *My Everything* became Helen's first studio project in five years.

Combining the pipelines of Provident Music Distribution with BMG to push her music to Christian retailers, the album was marketed through a joint venture between sister labels Verity Records and Diadem Music. With the attention of four music companies focused on Helen Baylor, there was no disputing her arrival as a leading Gospel artist. PLAY: Helen's seventh Gospel album offered up a duet with none other than Pastor Marvin Winans of the faith-inspiring Winans Family—Baylor and Winans deliver a touching version of *Lord You're Holy*. And in a manner similar to the music of siblings Bebe & Cece Winans, *My Everything* renders a hybrid mix of modern R&B and traditional-sounding Gospel harmonies.

To pick up more clues about Helen Baylor, you owe it to yourself to 'take a PAUSE for the cause' and check out her sugar-coated cover version of Marvin Gaye's *How Sweet It Is* (*To Be Loved by You*). Another notable on the album is Bill Maxwell, who produced music for Gospel greats like Andre Crouch, Bebe, Cece and the rest of The Winans. Helen Baylor teamed up to be an exclusive member of old friend Babbie Mason's *Inner Circle* (coming up next). Helen will also have you hitting STOP and REWIND on the controls as she shares important insight, channeled through her gift of connecting the dots with fans everywhere! You too can connect with her, at www.helenbaylor.com.

Babbie Mason

Let's continue our 'wordy' discussion by looking at another Word artist I had the opportunity to work with. Babbie Mason not only sings praises to the Lord and writes great songs, she has a lengthy listing of prestigious honors and awards too. Among Babbie's highest accomplishments are high-level security clearances on the Presidential list: Ford, Carter and Bush can all 'bear witness' to her inimitable abilities. Babbie is also a decorated winner of the Dove and Stellar Awards, as well as a key participant in the *Women of Faith* tour. With a resume like this, Babbie Mason is literally a walking plethora of superior intellect for women around the country, if not the world, to emulate.

Moving to Atlanta from Jackson, Michigan, Babbie Mason has long been festering God's power. You see, her dad was a founding pastor at a church where she grew up as a piano-playing music minister. Although it seems as if Babbie enjoys singing more, it's clear to see her greatest love is for God, her family, and the modern-day church. Babbie's music can be found in hymnals and is featured around the world on popular Gospel radio and television shows. As a music composer, producer and publisher, Babbie's songs have been recorded by A-class notables; like her colleague and former Word Records labelmate, Helen Baylor. Additionally, Babbie's vast repertoire has been covered or recorded by acts like the Brooklyn Tabernacle Choir, Larnelle Harris and Cece Winans. Check this one out—Babbie Mason's *All Rise* has risen to become one of the most recorded songs in Christian music history! Here's a short list with some of her popular tunes:

All In Favor	Pray On
All Rise	Standing In The Gap
Each One Reach One	Trust His Heart
Hallowed Be Thy Name	With All My Heart
Jesus The One And Only	Yours For Always

Babbie Mason's many attributes carried her into high-profile opportunities like authorship, as well as being a professor of songwriting at Atlanta Christian College and Lee University. On top of that, she recently became a TV talk-show host. When we last spoke, she told me she's booked several years in advance for a slew of events, which leads me to ask the question: *how's that for being in high demand?* Sometimes it's hard to believe my association with Babbie Mason has actually outlasted my 10-year stint at the label where we met—the brunt of my marketing of Babbie's music transpired in the early 90s at Sony Music's Atlanta branch. Our professional affiliation officially kicked off at a show she did in Marietta, Georgia, at the largest church I had ever seen at the time. Babbie gave a magical performance, and I believe the angels touched down to see that show!

I met Babbie's husband Charles at this performance and afterwards, I began stopping by their office on Powers Ferry Road in Marietta, just northwest of Atlanta. Apart from our Word Records affiliation, my friendship with Babbie and Charles grew strong enough to be like that theme song on "Cheers," *Where Everybody Knows Your Name.* One time, we all had lunch at a nearby Chinese restaurant—on the menu was Peking Roast Duck, complete with fried rice, steamed veggies and egg drop soup. The food was so good I forgot to ask whether the egg drop soup was duck… or chicken! Nevertheless, I was impressed from the get-go; everyone at the restaurant knew Babbie and Charles by name.

While we're on the subject of food, operation *food for the soul* is a Babbie-Charles specialty. Their kitchen knack is in your face like a drop-down menu—the couple serves up satisfying dishes by sprinkling just the right amount of spiritual spices for hungry fans. All plates come guaranteed to improve inspirational vision, and are professionally preheated… by the grace of God. Babbie and Charles took things further by cooking up a little music with laughter on DVD, through a video called *Chuck Roast.* After you entertain yourself with that entree, embrace some desert why don't you? Babbie's latest CD *Embrace* was whipped up to wrap itself into *and* around listeners. Many people know that God sometimes uses the kitchen as a homebase for spreading His Word but in reality, a Heavenly *connection of unification* between the Shepherd and the Sheep can "go live" anywhere.

This brings us to a remarkable day of divinity—it was quickly cooked up at Centennial Park for the victims of 9/11/01, and hosted by an organization called *Atlanta Unites*. My credo is based on the concept that in less than three weeks after the 9/11 tragedy, Atlanta Unites produced a sizeable benefit concert to honor victims of the disaster. Moreso, it featured a bundle of Atlanta-based acts, including Babbie Mason and Arrested Development. In another strange occurrence, I had just met the Grammy-winning Hip-Hop group a matter of days before this event… and just happened to be tagging along with them at show time. To show the group's long-time drawing power, they did not one, but *two* sets!

Humorously speaking, I got good at executing *Operation Tag Along* because deep down inside, it felt like I was practicing for a role as "The Tour Crasher." Let me add that as a result of tagging along with Arrested Development, I witnessed their 2002 Hollywood Bowl show with Isaac Hayes and Maceo Parker—it drew in over 18,000 fans. After a club appearance with an exciting group called Maktub, we flew up to San Francisco. Along with Africa's Matollhalla Queens, A.D. entertained fans at the Stern Grove Festival—that one brought in over 12,000 pairs of eyes and ears. We ran into Maktub again while performing later that night at a local club—I *still* don't know how that one happened. Back on the East Coast, Atlanta Unites was a biggie: over 75,000 people came out to support the event. It was covered by news agencies across the country and as an added bonus I recorded some video footage from the inside out. No pun intended, but onstage with Arrested Development looking towards the audience, all I could see was a sea of people that filled Centennial Park!

Regardless of what my camera captured, I was humbled to rub elbows with distinguished gents like Georgia Governor Roy Barnes, Senator Max Cleland, talk show host Montel Williams and former U.S. Ambassador/Atlanta Mayor, Andrew Young. I've heard the Lord works in mysterious ways—I witnessed it onstage and backstage, where I bumped into none other than the *anointed apostle* herself, Babbie Mason! Needless to say, after Arrested Development's performance I stayed for Babbie's show, picked up a double blessing… and kept it moving. In a weird sort of way, could all of this have been a strange occurrence, or destiny?

To shed additional light on this dilemma, let's open the lens a little more: I ran into Arrested Development's spiritual advisor Baba Oje earlier in 2001—it was right after the infamous "*Derwin Brown Affair*" which you may have read about in Book #1. I just completed work on the *Atlanta Artists Against Gun Violence* project for the Million Mom March Foundation. As the stars would have it, my meeting Baba Oje was prior to his group's performance at the Music Midtown Festival that summer— they shared the stage with other fan magnets, like Erykah Badu and Talib Kweli. Getting back to the story, I was doing a little work to get some things going for Baba, and had just formed *The B.O.M.B.* (Baba Oje Management Board) to oversee his affairs. Thanks to the lovely and talented Barbara Bersell, a GAP commercial popped up and we flew out to Hollywood for the shoot. We returned to Atlanta with tons of GAP gear, so thumbs up to Miss Barbara (www. bersellcasting.com) for that one; and to quote songwriter supreme Randy Newman, "I love L.A.!!"

On the flight back, Baba Oje and I shared cabin space with members of Parliament-Funkadelic spinoff group, *The Original P*. They were returning to Atlanta from the sports-heavy ESPY Awards. Singer J Love impressed me so much I asked her to collaborate on an all-star remake of Marvin Gaye's *What's Going On* that I was planning to do with Baba Oje, Alexander O'Neal and a few more notables. A few weeks after touching down at Atlanta's Hartsfield Airport, Baba and I were flying right back out to Los Angeles; this time, the entourage included Speech and Arrested Development; we were also armed with the legendary DJ Machete X. As mentioned before, the group pulled off an awesome pair of shows in Los Angeles and San Francisco. I didn't know it then, but it would be another ten years before I'd run into the phenomenal DJ Machete X again, at 2012's Riverdale Seafood and Beer Festival—he performed with Klymaxx and cut records onstage like a butcher cut meat (thus his name)! To save space in this section, there will be a full report on the Riverdale event and DJ Machete X coming up later on…

Even though it had a whirlwind effect, I was blessed to witness how inner-workings that keep the show moving actually work—through experience. From flying in turbulence, to bumpy landings; from lost luggage to late limos; from sound check to radio interviews. Looking back at the one-of-a-kind Atlanta Unites event, I believe God was showing me how He also uses the stage for 'His Work' during quandaries.

I sometimes wonder if it was a strange occurrence or destiny when Babbie Mason and Arrested Development were called to help out because without batting an eye, they were right there!

A recent project Babbie Mason took on was the musical, *Right Where You Are*. Reflecting a true passion for daily worship, she encouraged God's sheep to *walk in faith and joy only attainable through Christ*. As I expected, she wrote songs and collaborated through her inner circle; including producer Cheryl Rogers and Babbie's youngest son, Chaz. The song *Yours For Always* is a duet with Chaz that teamed them up for a rendition calling to mind Gospel greats like Bebe & Cece Winans. Chaz put in work growing up on the road with his mom; he picked up skill sets like singing, songwriting and performing. All I can say is between Babbie, her husband Charles, her preaching father and her talented son, I see a bright future ahead for this Heavenly-bound, creative clan.

Wait folks, there's more! You can be a part of Babbie's spiritual team by joining her organization called *Babbie Mason's Inner Circle*. I kid you not; this Friday to Saturday weekend retreat is filled with life-changing information—all within an intimate setting. Attendees get up-close and personal with Babbie Mason, Christian songwriters and Babbie's closest industry confidants, such as the aforementioned Helen Baylor. There's also a chance to 'gossip the Gospel' with inspirational leaders like Morris Chapman, or hear Carol Cymbala, Director of the Brooklyn Tabernacle Choir. So if you've ever dreamed of finding someone to help you excel in your gifts and talents, are searching for a mentor, or need someone with the tools and techniques to manage a successful music ministry, LOOK NO FURTHER!

Babbie Mason's *Inner Circle* is an intensive workshop designed to do all that and more. Come on out to find your own personal mentor, with their own personal touch of Superior Intellect. You'll receive much needed inspiration, information, encouragement and networking opportunities, too. This where you can begin a career in music ministry, jump-start creativity by sharpening your songwriting skills, learn how to book, manage and promote your ministry online, understand how to make a master CD on a budget; and much more! So you're officially invited to share this exciting experience and meet other people who want to rise above: they are the few and the proud—the new pulse of Gospel music.

Wrapping things up, it's re-emphasized: feed your "faith buds" a little by nibbling on Babbie Mason's *Chuck Roast* DVD, and don't forget to serve up some spiritually flavored desert with her latest CD, *Embrace*. You can also feed your faith by picking up Babbie Mason's latest book *Faith Lift*... as one who knows, I affirm that you too can grow your superior faith and intellect through Babbie's heavenly voice, songs, talk show, teaching and moderating skills. To get things started just visit her website, and don't miss logging in for additional personal development at www.babbie.com/inner_circle.htm.

For the purpose of this voyage, please buckle up: we're making our final approach to the landing strip of musical sanctity. As we get closer to touchdown, I'll share a story about our final Word Records artist—I was blessed by working with her in the early 90s and she came to be known as *"The First Lady of Gospel."* Shortly after visiting our quaint city of Atlanta, I heard she added the title of "Reverend" to her name. Let's get the Gospel rundown on yet another of God's dynamic creations...

Shirley Caesar

Hailing from Durham, North Carolina, Shirley Caesar was born in 1938 and developed into a universal artist with a musical timeline that spans some six decades. She has tributaries including dozens of Grammies, Dove, Stellar, Essence and NAACP awards. True dedication always pays off and Shirley would come to be known as a focused disciple of God's Word who lives completely in God's world. She picked up the "Black Gospel Album of the Year" award for her work on a number of releases, including *Live at the G.M.W.A.*, *Celebration*, *Christmasing*, *Sailin,' Live... In Chicago*, *Go* and *Rejoice*. Let's hit REWIND to get a clearer view of this phenomenal lady, through our trusty Gospelscope of people, places and time.

Great things often come in small packages—since first walking into a recording studio in 1949 when she was just eleven, Shirley graced the masses with over forty albums, sixteen compilations and three Gospel-based musicals interwoven through the *Mama I Want to Sing* conceptual theory. As an inductee into the Gospel Music Hall of Fame, Shirley Caesar sold millions of albums and performed on Disney World's *Night of Joy*, *The Gospel According to VH1*; she even blessed the George Bush White House, prior to its transformation into the Obama House. Shirley went on to grace the microphone with popular acts like Inez Andrews, James

Cleveland, Dorothy Norwood, Delores Washington and a long list of others. Not only did Shirley reach out to grab hold of Gospel artists and fans, she also garnered attention from the corporate world through a series of commercials for MCI. Even my good friend David Cato heard about it, because he produced tons of MCI commercials back in the day.

Bursting with Superior Christian Intellect, Shirley Caesar is no stranger to the institution of education, either. They know her name well at places like Duke, Shaw and Southeastern Universities. Shirley followed a musical path from singing for family and friends, to performing with the reigning Queen of Gospel, Albertina Walker and one of Gospel's most popular all-female 50s acts, The Caravans—Shirley recorded and toured with them from 1958 to 1966. After migrating away from the Caravans, Shirley went solo and spent the tail end of the 60s traveling on a journey across the Gospel circuit. Guided with wisdom from above, she followed a custom-made map across a well-lit trail of exposure through popular TV programs, among them being the Bobby Jones Gospel show.

The year 1971 brought in Shirley Caesar's first Grammy Award—it was a sign of what was yet to come; and the first Grammy for a Black female Gospel singer since Mahalia Jackson made the cut years earlier. The remainder of the 70s kept Shirley recording classic songs and performing in shows to sellout crowds, leading to advances up the Grammy ladder in 1980, 1984, 1985, 1992 and 1994; during this period, Shirley brought home a total of seven Grammy Awards. Looking at her musical 'afterqueue,' some could say Shirley Caesar successfully navigated across the dawn of new decades. At the same time, she kept her ship tight on a well-guided course across waters deep enough to swallow up most who dared to voyage across its uncertain currents.

Back on land at her North Carolina home, 1987 saw Shirley Caesar making a run for public office, winning an election to the Durham City Council. In her new post, she focused on providing seniors and the needy with housing and special assistance. A 'highly revered' singer whose voice is well expounded into the secular world, Shirley Caesar found herself collaborating not only with industry peers like Kim Burrell, Arnold Houston, John P. Kee, Dorothy Norwood, Dottie Peoples, Tonex and Tye Tribbett, but also with more mainstream acts like Faith Evans, Whitney Houston and Patti LaBelle. To me, this just goes to show that big things can still come out of small packages!

Here's an inside view of my professional promotional life in the Gospel music lane: like we did with Al Green, a special invitation-only reception took place in Atlanta's Peachtree Plaza hotel. This time, it happened when Shirley Caesar came to town in support of her 1991 release, *He's Working It Out For You*. To take full advantage of her time in town, the itinerary had me down to accompany her to a few retailers in downtown Atlanta's Five Points district. As with normal marketing protocol, I made sure the retailers knew she was coming to town in advance and although her album was selling well at the time, I suggested stocking up on a few extra copies. Working with a major label had embedded perks that allowed me to secure the best spot in record stores for posters to go up. No matter what the event was, I always made sure my store managers got pictures taken with the artist, because it often caused a trickle-down effect. What I mean is, a few impressive pictures hanging on the wall can perk up store managers and employees when a customer comes looking for new music. A well-placed celebrity shot can sometimes excite retailers and customers who might have a personal connection with the people in the picture—resulting in extra ALE.

On being a professional solo artist in the Gospel music *biz* "*After 40 Years... Shirley's Still Sweeping Through The City.*" Her similarly titled 2007 album was recorded live at her home base in North Carolina, Mount Cavalry Word of Faith Church. In addition to her unending duties as a preaching performer (or is it *performing preacher*?), Shirley Caesar co-pastors this Raleigh church and since 1983, has been married to Bishop Harold Williams, keeping God's love totally "in-house." Spreading her unbridled love around God's house, Shirley channels a percentage of concert revenues to her Outreach Ministries. This is where she blesses the congregation with weekly sermons and a yearly convention designed to inspire, motivate and educate attendees.

With a hint of Blues tucked in the mix, Shirley Caesar's *After 40 Years... Still Sweeping Through The City* CD comes loaded with over an hour's worth of inspirational songs. According to her website, it's a "floor-stomping, hand-clapper, choral sing-off, storyteller" collection of compositions, all on one disc. So should you hear the calling to pick up a few copies of Pastor Caesar's 'testament of truth to the people,' your cup will runneth over after visiting www.shirleycaesar.com... you can 'Like' her and while you're at it, go ahead and join the Pastor's Facebook group!

Just like there are many major label record releases, there are just as many (if not more) releases on the independent side of the game. But where the major label artists often have the luxury of substantial budgets behind them, many independent artists are fighting for the same piece of pie—with little or no budget to perpetuate their music further into the market. Our next recording artist has weathered many storms as an indie act, but still manages to shine like a phoenix with each of her new releases. One of them, *Happy*, is featured on the *Exposer 3* CD. That's the accompanying CD to my first book, *Musicology 2101: A Quick Start Guide To Music "Biz" History*. All I can say is, "God Bless the artist who delivers His message!"

Terri Carroll

It's time to give an honorary mention to a two-time Stellar nominated, Atlanta-based singer named Terri Carroll: she's a longtime, local friend that in my eyes, has stood the test of modern times. Around the late 90s, I met Terri through an even longer longtime friend, Norm Banton, who's a top sound engineer and video editor. Besides working with A-listers from DJ Easy Lee of Kool Moe Dee fame to the Blackeye Peas' Will.i.am, Norm helped me upgrade and maintain my recording studio from the 90s forward, and his circle of friends bled into mine upon introducing me to *Apostle Carroll*.

Studiowise, during the late 90s, Norm was my "neighbor in the yellow house"–our studios were next door to each other, back at Edsel Robinson's studio compound on M.L.K. Jr. Drive near Hightower on the west side. In 2013 while reminiscing on old times, another friend I discovered we all shared turned out to be Haywood Tucker; Haywood was my studio mentor in the early 80s when I first moved to Atlanta. And what do you know—it turns out Haywood does a lot of Gospel music these days, too! You'll get to know more about Norm, Ed and Haywood later in the Musicology series but for now, let's jump into Terri's corner and see what she's been sweeping up!

Terri Carroll is no stranger to the Gospel music world. She started singing in church at the age of three, and went on to win a slew of talent shows, contests and pageants growing up in Gary, Indiana. Terri's voice was popular in certain locales; as a youngster she wrote and sung commercial jingles that aired on Chicago area radio stations. Completing her circle of youth, Terri entered college, the army, marriage, and experienced the greatest blessing of all: motherhood. Unfortunately, the challenges of life led to a break-up in her marriage, with three young mouths that required constant feeding. To keep food on the table, Sister Carroll went on to front a top Atlanta Jazz band, which led to leading her own band during the early 90s.

As they often tend to do, drugs and alcohol creep around people's lives, and Terri's Carroll's supernatural world was not immune. When the mischief known as addiction signed its lease to occupy, Terri's life was difficult to manage until 1996, when an old high school friend (Terry Garmon) resurfaced to help save the lost soul. Terri shared with me, "God works in mysterious ways, because Terry had become a producer; more importantly, he was also a pastor." It didn't take long for Terry and Terri aka codename *TNT* to hook up and RECORD a self-titled debut Gospel album, *Terri Carroll*, in 1998. Even though she received two nominations at the *14th Annual Stellar Awards* the following year, her label CGI Records went bankrupt in 2000 and she was abruptly "cut out of the loop."

When faced with the task of what her next move would be, Terri Carroll hit PAUSE and went deep into prayer after realizing the people who supposedly "had her back" didn't return her calls at a time of dire need. PLAY: Obviously God had Terri's back throughout her ordeal, and she aptly reflects, "I was at an impasse." Despite the hurdles, Terri switched to FAST FORWARD mode and began the task of reclaiming her place, front and center, in the Gospel music uplights. By 2005, she linked up with friend and producer Paul Persley, releasing an EP (extended play) project entitled *Holding Out 4 God*. Terri hits the REWIND button and says, "We didn't have a budget, but what we did have was a faith in God that said as long as we took one step, He would take two." In my book, that's a perfect example of "walking by faith and not by sight!"

Terri kept busy by performing in several Gospel stage plays, capturing leading roles in *Listen to the Spirit*, *True Love* and *Can a Hoochie Become a First Lady*, featuring R&B star Keith Sweat. In 2007 Terri penned a personal testimony, *This Is Not Your Destination*. February of 2009 saw Terri wrapping up filming of the script, delivered in the form of her first movie short. Because of that endeavor, Terri now adds independent filmmaker, writer, producer, co-director, prop-mistress, caterer and technical consultant to her skillset dossier. As of this writing, Terri was putting the finishing touches on her second script, *Secrets*.

On top of being a singer and filmmaker, Terri Carroll has also been a good friend to me by always extending an open hand. And besides owing Norm Banton for helping me *plug up the power* throughout the different incarnations of my own studio, I owe him "e*NORM*ously" for introducing me to this gifted Gospel singer. On the mainstream tip, Terri Carroll still hasn't received the true recognition she deserves: but in my eyes she has already earned it, and I plan on being there when the big ship casts a line in!

Musically speaking, Terri Carroll's collaborations exude a cutting-edge mix of urban R&B, Hip-Hop and Jazz—through lyrics about life's trials and tribulations. The singer told me, "*Holding Out 4 God* is delivered in accordance with scripture straight out of the Bible." Personally speaking, what I like is how the songs are enunciated—in a way that only Terri can do it! The title track, *Holding Out 4 God*, plus other praise songs like *The Master* are as good as it gets so all I can say is—based on the signs, I foresee God continuing to keep anointing Terri in preparation for "the big one." Terri Carroll leaves learning readers who yearn to be all they can be with sound advice: "Whatever God has for you, He has equipped you fully for it. And that's whether you realize it or not. Trust Him; continue seeking His face and doing His will for your life. The race is not given to the swift or to the strong, but to the one who endures until the end. NEVER QUIT!"

You can trust your senses to feel, taste, see and hear even more from Terri's world by checking her out at www.reverbnation.com/terricarroll, http://www.facebook.com/terricaroll1, or simply by contacting her at widowsmiteent@gmail.com. To reel in Terri's musical blessings for your own personal enjoyment, pick up a few tracks at Amazon, iTunes, Napster and Rhapsody. And don't forget, you can find Terri's hot track, *Happy*, on all her links as well as on the accompanying Exposer 3 CD from my first book, *Musicology 2101: A Quick Start Guide To Music "Biz" History*. Just FYI, the bosses have just approved a *Musicology 2102 Exposer* CD!

Before we launch into the next snapshot, it's time to administer some closing comments relative to this section. There are plenty of talented recording artists who travel across the Gospel, Christian, Inspirational and Spiritual music realms, so feel free to check deep into the informational vaults for data on them. Here's a little known secret—you can also pick up extra blessings by listening to their music. Better yet, go ahead: invest in some of their music and watch your collection grow spiritually! And folks please remember, true devoutness is often measured by the amount of lives you actually *touch*, not just by how many people you talk to. In other words, talk is cheap without affirmative interaction with your fellow man… or woman.

One more thing: there are enough problems in today's gadget-based world and with the adjunct of the Internet with radio, TV and satellite, more folks than ever have an unlimited virtual archive into the goods and bads of mankind. All of these electronic mediums have crossed cultures, generations and the legal parameters of human rights to get the public broadcasting industry where it is now and please believe me, it's far from over! So if you really want to be remembered in the physical world, just "reach out and touch somebody" in a meaningful way, because nowadays, there are multiple platforms to use as communication tools. While we keep things moving through people, places and time, let's make another *pit stop at a sweet spot*, as you are presented with the final portion of our tribute to:

"Singers Who Could Act… or Actresses That Could Sing?" Part III

As we focus the camera on singer-actress #3 in our special SPOTLIGHT series, we'll get to know a talented neighborhood girl who evolved to be seated among the best of the best, at the top of the entertainment *biz* food chain. Lena Horne hailed from an upper-middle class neighborhood in Brooklyn's Bedford-Stuyvesant area. In fact, it wasn't too far from where yours truly grew up. I'm in awe of this celebrity not only because she was a local gemstone, but also due to her being an enigmatic figure who left an imprint that forever changed the industry.

Not to take anything away from "full-blooded" cultures, but some of the most popular multiethnic performers from back in the day retained inimitable characteristics that helped to propel them through the entertainment industry. In the case of Lena Horne, her African-American, Caucasian and Native American ethnicity yielded an extremely photogenic entertainer and extraordinary singer. Like other minorities, Lena also experienced blatant discrimination, yet she broke down color barriers without working up much of a sweat: in a sense, the minority would hold great influence over the majority. Some might say it was Lena's striking good looks that guided her through show business. She went from the chorus line of New York's famous Cotton Club, to being a featured performer in the Cotton Club Parade. After Lena's Cotton Club appearances in the early to mid-30s, she began singing with orchestras and big bands. But traveling didn't appeal to Lena, so she settled for work in and around New York City.

During the early 40s in New York, Lena Horne replaced Dinah Shore as the featured vocalist for NBC radio, and soon began recording for the RCA Victor label. After a while, she conquered her fears and set sights on the movie world by heading west. Miraculously, Horne landed a long-term deal with MGM, becoming the first Black person to gain full access to the A-list Hollywood world. She appeared in a string of musicals and motion pictures but unfortunately, was never awarded a leading role. In fact, she was sometimes re-edited in films because certain states had restrictions on Blacks being seen in movies. Looking back now and given the magnitude of racism; particularly in entertainment up to the 60s, it would seem farfetched that Lena Horne's celebrity flair grew. But it did, and exponentially expanded through 70s and 80s TV programs like *The Flip Wilson Show*, *Sanford & Son*, *Good Times*, *The Jeffersons*, *The Fresh Prince of Bel Air* and special appearances in blockbuster movies.

Comparing the entertainment mentalities of days past to the present, we can see change has occurred in many facets of motion picture production. For instance, now a viewer can turn on the 'telly' (TV) and see more diversity; depending on where you live, you might get lucky and see the execution of "multicultural interoperability." Black actors may be doing better these days but prior to the 60s, Lena Horne exercised her rights and voiced her political views at a time when the powers-that-be didn't want to listen. When Lena stepped up, Hollywood suddenly stepped back, and its single-eyed camera lost its luster upon her—soon, the mutual magnetism between Miss Horne and Tinsel Town subsided.

After getting blacklisted from the silver screen, Lena Horne didn't make a return until the late 60s. Not one to be shunned from Hollywood's spotlight, Lena then cast her eyes on doing more nightclub engagements and immediately regained her forum as a premier nightclub performer. Lena went on to scale to the top of the free world's "most requested entertainer's list." She even recorded a live album that became the top-selling record by a female singer in RCA-Victor's history. Despite her hiatus from the movie industry, Miss Horne was well-loved on American, Canadian and British television during the 50s, 60s and 70s. Lena shared the TV screen with stars like Harry Belafonte, Tony Bennett, Perry Como,

Vic Damone, Judy Garland, Peggy Lee, Dean Martin, Ed Sullivan and Andy Williams. She even appeared on *The Cosby Show* and its spin-off, *A Different World*, in the 80s and 90s.

Continuing to record and perform well into her 80s, Lena Horne's trail is filled with Tonys, Grammies and dozens of classic recordings. It's sad to say, but this iconic singer passed away on May 9, 2010 in New York—she'll always be remembered for her stunning fountain-of-youth looks and major contributions to yesterday's, today's *and* tomorrow's entertainment. For those interested in hearing the cyber-toot of Lena's horn, check out www.lena-horne.com. This concludes our in-depth look at fabulous singers who could act, or is it... actresses that could sing?

With a timely appearance, the explosion of two wildly popular styles, Rhythm & Blues and Rock-n-Roll, catapulted the not-so-quiet birth and ensuing evolution of the record industry to all-new heights. Capitalistic society's "love-child" (the music business) encountered a few growing pains along its path (racial discrimination and unstable economics), before running into its biggest free enterprise challenge to date—a digital beast called the Internet. Who could have predicted how this entity would penetrate every part of the world? With universally accepted communication platforms like wireless, ringtones, MP3, video downloading, newsfeeds and streaming plus other forms of file sharing, the global spread of many music genres got uploaded: and incrementally unfolded what would be a winning hand.

Developments like the Internet led to an influx of players in a new multimedia entertainment environment that churned out musical icons, or 'e-cons' as I sometimes call them. Some shone in the spotlight, while others broke molds behind the scenes; many mushroomed into larger-than-life action figures. Brashly speaking, a few came 'fully loaded' with assorted trophies and momentos bearing their likeness, displayed on office walls and fireplace mantles. However, one thing was definite: to survive in the digital age, industry leaders would have to compete with tons of flashy multimedia content that all came alive, in the cyberworld.

Before we cruise into the next leg of our musical episode, please try to remember that the timelines for many entertainers and music styles often overlapped or ran concurrently. Sometimes it's a very difficult task to talk about one particular artist, music or dance style without mentioning a related entity; hopefully, you've taken notice of this trend during our adventure. We will now prepare to embark onto new ground in our quest for greater knowledge about music *biz*tory. With that said, let the music play as we look at other aspects of this sonic force of human expressionism. To keep things moving forward and "into the future" like Steve Miller said in his 70s hit *Fly Like An Eagle*, we must now take off on another tangent of our magical, mystical, musical odyssey. In the facilitation of that order, I present you with The Letter "M" Dream Team: "*Music, Money, Madness*, and more…"

-5-
FROM AN INVENTION COMES A MONOLITH
The Birth of the Record Industry

The recording industry was formed from unprecedented technological events that stemmed from what I'd call a 'crucible of evolutionary revolution.' As music and technology harmoniously intertwined from the growth of 19th century wax cylinders, America's music incubation period dawned with a new day. The age of high-tech electronics had arrived, with single-track *mono*, then *stereo* vinyl recordings. Multitrack, tape-based analog formats followed, before the inevitable switch to digital devices of every kind forever intertwined the 20th and 21st centuries. But had it not been for certain 19th century developments, the timetable may have been significantly delayed.

Everyone knows about his contributions to the light bulb, but in 1877 Thomas Edison spawned some of recorded music's earliest endeavors when he invented and thus industrialized the wax cylinder phonograph. By age thirty, he was praised after making one of the world's first recordings on a sheet of tinfoil: it was a song called *Mary Had A Little Lamb*. Edison was a distinguished inventor and businessman who marketed and mass-produced his discoveries. Among the principals of his new phonograph business was the father-in-law of telephone inventor Alexander Graham Bell. Incandescently speaking, since Edison's music machine needed additional improvements at first, he decided to devote most of his time to perfecting the light bulb; the rest is *his-story*. In a way, we can surmise that forward-thinking figures like Thomas Edison enabled people to "shake their boodies" to freshly recorded music, under the glow of his newly created incandescent lights.

Although well known for his inventions, Thomas Edison wasn't the only talented genius to make great strides during the early years of recorded music. From 1890 to 1895, the amount of wax cylinders our next 'i-sub' (identified subject) reportedly sold was between 25,000 and 50,000. By 1895, codename *President Phonograph* was a guy known as George Washington... Johnson. He had a pair of songs called *The*

Whistling Coon and *The Laughing Song*: they became the best selling recordings in the U.S. at that time. Just-in reports from the field confirm Johnson unanimously won the vote and was elected as the first African-American recording star of the phonograph machine. However, here's something that many people don't know: during the formative years, wax cylinders and early records were in all actuality individual master recordings. Thus, we could hypothetically say that each recording sold by George Washington Johnson had its own distinctive 'Presidential touch.'

DUPE THIS!

PLAY: These days, the recording and manufacturing process is a lot different than in earlier times, due to certain evolutions of technology. The digital domain opened up new platforms that provide avenues of getting music out to the people faster than ever before, and details of that incredible story are coming up. REWIND: As we look at days gone by, there was a much slower manufacturing process in place at the time. RECORD: Singers, particularly those with resilient voices, made several recordings via multiple recording machines that simultaneously registered their performances.

Back then, it wasn't uncommon for a robust singer to record tracks some fifty or more times a day in the studio to amass the quantities of recordings that eventually went out for sale. PAUSE: This was a primitive form of duplication, but it worked. In a matter of years, the record manufacturing process would be totally automated. FAST FORWARD: Since the 80s, this entire system was automated through a network of integrated computers, black boxes and cables that push data through CD/DVD burners, satellites, routers, cellular and wireless networks.

There are quite a few artists, songs and instances that sources like CNET UK's *Crave* says made big impressions using technology and music to create long-lasting legacies. Look out for a heavy-hitting *Chart of Firsts* along your voyage through this book series—it was created to show a variety of technological *firsts* pumped through the music *biz* pipeline of history. As an example, through an extensive TWITTER TWEET we find: Around March 2008, the first voice recording was allegedly unearthed in Paris, France… it was estimated at being some 20 years older than Thomas Edison's first phonograph recordings! The find was discovered by a group of American audio historians and supposedly has undergone intensive sonic testing, with revealing results.

In a RE-TWEET, on-site correspondents suggest the 10-second *phonautograph* sample was made on April 9, 1860. The French folk song *Au Clair de la Lune* was made by an unknown male singer. This alleged recording was said to have been produced by yet another unidentified subject or *unsub*—however, varying reports reveal each *unsub* could in fact be the same person. Bringing you additional information, our on-site correspondents are presently engaged in *"TWEETING for a TWACK"* but to keep your brain cells from boiling and getting even more confused, let's just FAST FORWARD from all this babbling about TWEETS, RE-TWEETS and TWITTER TWACKS.

FRENCH FACT: *Au Clair de la Lune* was made on a special phonograph called a *phonautograph*. This device was designed to record by notating sound markings visually on paper: but it had no capability of playing them back.

In response to the uncanny fact above, a quality control team of correspondents (headed up by my pals Stephan Minyono and Julien Cahen) are en route to France in hopes of asking the engineers: *"Je suis perdu—combien une de ces machines aurait coûté?* (I'm lost—how much would a machine like this have cost?) The FRENCH FACT above mentions that these early phonautographs initially had no playback capability—but later, a small improvement made phonautographs playback capable. This was accomplished by converting the markings on the paper to make actual sound, and the recordings were called *phonautograms*. I'll go out on a limb here and hint that sales of these devices picked up afterwards, but we'll play it safe and wait on the final word from our quality control experts...

Okay, the time has come to get back on track now because upon initial thought, it sure would be hard to play a song that was 'creatively recorded' using early phonautographs! A special head nod goes to the superior intellect exercised by scientists at the Lawrence Berkeley National Laboratory in Berkeley, California. These guys spearheaded a great act of technical wizardry—hopefully they all got bonuses, promotions (or both) for that one... On a serious note, California became the home of Silicon Valley, where massive quantities of electronic components are produced—many of which are destined for digital devices that include tools of technology like: computers, music instruments, sound recording and video equipment.

Picking up our story from 1877, Thomas Edison debuted the phonograph and that same year, a gentleman by the name of Emile Berliner got a patent for his *gramophone*. Unlike the phonograph that recorded to a vertical cylinder, this device recorded sounds to a horizontal disc. Within twenty-five years of the phonograph's debut, the 19th century closed out; but through the minds of visionaries like Edison and Berliner, commercial vinyl discs soon began entering the industry. Emile Berliner was a pioneer who went on to form his own record company but later decided to sell it—the *Deutsche Grammophon* label was ultimately absorbed by PolyGram Records. As a label, PolyGram was well known for making history by touting one of the world's top music catalogs; by the late 70s the label built the first CD-pressing factory. Initially, PolyGram signed and produced Classical/Opera acts, then followed up by promoting their recorded vinyl media. This was often in the form of live shows and other records that catered to the upper-class society which record labels often targeted during the early 20th century.

On a different plane, working-class Americans began embracing affordable entertainment they could listen and dance to, like Popular/Folk music. Upper echelon Classical music and Opera fans tended to enjoy being catered to—this was often the case for those who lived lavish lifestyles. And then there were people who enjoyed the best of both worlds; they shamelessly enjoyed Popular/Folk, as well as Classical/Opera without worrying about being looked at sideways by other classes of people. Folk-Dance music of by-gone eras include *Danse*, *Gavotte*, *Gigue*, *Waltz* and more. Because of what I'd call "musical evolution," some would argue that certain styles lacked contemporary rhythms and were eventually "tuned up." They became shorter, catchier, high-revving styles that didn't require long, drawn out movements, wealth, V.I.P. invitations, or allotted time to get decked out in tuxedos or gowns. Let's 'ad-dress' some fast stats:

- The early 1900s saw the Victor Company entering the marketplace with their version of the modern phonograph machine
- Although Popular/Folk and Classical/Opera were in the mainstream, around 1917 Jazz recordings jumped into the market; once record companies tapped into and released additional genres, the industry experienced dramatic growth
- Two record labels, Victor and Columbia, vied for the top position in the market; by the 1920s, more than 100 million records were produced

- Commercially introduced in the early 20s, radio broadcasting rapidly grew in popularity
- By the end of the 1920s, America's stock market crashed and the Great Depression went into full effect—no one was safe through these turbulent times, not even record labels
- As per data in an RIAA industry report, some companies saw their sales drop as much as 90%

Let's tune in for a more granular look at what was going on back then: Before the Depression hit around 1927, the Jukebox made a humble appearance. After an amplified speaker became a permanent addition, interest in this device grew. Circa 1929, record sales reached a high of 75 million per year, a direct result of the newfound magnetism of the Jukebox. By 1933, the Depression caused sales to drop down to lows of 5 million a year. While the record industry struggled to overcome its less-than-favorable economic position, the Jukebox gained popularity and helped improve record sales. By the mid-30s, Jukebox operators were ordering over 10 million records a year to satisfy consumer demand and by 1938, sales hit a high of 25 million a year. Taking things further, a new configuration called the 78-rpm (revolutions per minute) disc was introduced—resulting in almost 20 million sold by the end of the decade.

By 1940, America had some 400,000 Jukeboxes in use—to boost record sales, phonograph dealers sold record players, often in department stores, at bargain prices. With 2 speeds (for 45s and 78s), they sold well. Unsurprisingly, record manufacturers took note of an emerging trend and designed their distribution operations to fill the needs of a growing supply chain. Record companies initially sold through the dealers, but their businesses expanded when department stores increased space for music by adding sections that sold records and players. Throughout the 1940s, record releases skyrocketed from a low of 10-20, and leveled off at a high of almost 100 per week on average.

When problems surrounding World War II poured into corporate America, they overflowed right into the music industry. While the world was at war for a second time, a strike by the American Federation of Musicians (AFM) set the industry back from 1942 to 1945. The strike caused a whopping decline in sales and airplay, partially due to large bands demanding an increase in royalties. This action was countered by the record companies' decision to pay fewer personnel, in lieu of paying sizeable groups of radio staff, or higher royalties to musicians. This meant record companies would focus on utilizing downsized musical ensembles typically composed of a lead singer, drummer, bassist, guitarist, keyboards, background vocals and occasional percussion, horns or strings.

To FAST FORWARD through the royalty turmoil, broadcasters were still playing big band records over the airwaves, but people became enticed to new music forms—heard through jukeboxes and turntables. Another random act of music *biz* action occurred as Black music (race records) and Country music (Country & Western) became as famous as Pop music. Around this time, the music industry launched "the next big thing" via 7-inch, 45 rpm vinyl discs. Driving even more record sales, "one-stop" distributors were structured to carry multiple product lines from multiple record labels.

PAUSE: Since wholesalers were already selling music product to record stores and jukebox owners, everyone reaped short-term rewards. As individual entities, large volume record labels manufactured and sold product with their own name stamped on it. They also charged smaller 'low volumers' for the service—in the end, someone had to pay the cost to be the boss. Although they were smaller, independent retailers often paid higher base prices than national chain retailers did, but the small retailer could buy music from different labels, all in 'one stop.'

Alternatively, major record labels benefited by selling music from their stable of artists to multiple one-stop wholesalers—without having to deal with hordes of 'onesie-twosie' low revenue producers; like the independent retailer. RECORD: Not long after the majors started reeling in hordes of cash from one-stop distributors, local independent labels caught on to this money making approach and in addition to selling records out of car trunks, they started selling music product to one-stops, too. Because of their ability to react to new trends faster, independent record labels eventually dominated the Black and Country music markets, as one-stops spread from major markets into smaller ones. All of the key players were fully set up for high-volume record *biz* traffic in their respective territories.

ON CUE: Network giant CBS Inc's Columbia Records appeared on the scene as "Big Red" in the late 40s with its newest configuration, a 33 1/3-rpm monophonic (one channel) disc that sold for less than $6.00. Unlike the maker of the early *phonautograph* that couldn't play back what it recorded, Columbia Records paid really nice salaries (and probably also great bonuses) to a staff of creative technical engineers. Big Red maintained a packed pipeline, full of funds for their scientists to tap into. With virtually unlimited funding, the lab guys executed their superior intellect and technical wizardry, ensuring that Columbia stayed out front and ahead of the curve with regards to keeping fine-tuned with the latest turntable technology. CBS Records' *technical whitecoats* probably worked in 24-hour high security shifts, constantly making improvements to the company's high-level production and manufacturing process, with a keen focus on their vinyl records' playback capabilities.

> **FRANK FACT:** The first commercially released, single-disc, long-playing album (LP) was released by Columbia in 1948 with Frank Sinatra's 10-inch LP, *The Voice of Frank Sinatra.*

The 10-inch Frank Sinatra album was later followed by the release of the first 12-inch LP, Mendelssohn's *Concerto In E Minor*, by Nathan Milstein and the Philharmonic-Symphony Orchestra. Technological improvements eventually led to the introduction of stereophonic (two channel/left & right audio) recordings. Back in the early days two-track stereo was big news, so when the availability of three, four and eight tape tracks occurred, it caused a major change in the ability to manipulate the sound quality of music. Adult Contemporary (AC), Easy Listening, Soft Rock or Middle-of-the-Road (MOR) genres later became modern popular music and would henceforth be referred to as "Pop" music. Around this time, many studio sessions were recorded in one take, leaving little room for error; this meant master recordings had to be near-perfect.

Exceptional singers and musicians became a necessity for professional level recordings—they were of paramount importance to record labels. Back then, the only way to get a different mix of the same song was to record a completely different take; nowadays, a few clicks of the *ProTools* mouse could unlock new perspectives in song composition, musical arrangements and alternate takes. Thanks to compilation/mix CDs and the Internet, different versions of classic songs are re-emerging in the marketplace, especially online. But before CDs and the Internet ever existed, there were key operatives executing technical tasks that took the recording industry to a whole new level. In addition to several major players previously mentioned, there were a few more true innovators who revolutionized the recording and reproduction process to turn the meter up by several decibels—get ready to meet one of them next.

Question: Is it possible to go from bomb making, to making bomb recordings?

Answer: It's entirely possible, if your name was Thomas J. Dowd!

THE DOWD BOMBER

My good friend Wade Jones hipped me to a well-known fact: Thomas Dowd helped shape the sound of the 50s, 60s, 70s, 80s, 90s and beyond in a big way. Throughout the latter portion of this elongated time period, professional mixing consoles came with 8, 12, 16, 24, 48, 96 or more channels. After receiving 'a message from beyond,' Tom foretold the popularity of multi-track recording systems for use in the commercial music world. The use of stereophonic sound reproduction began in the 30s and 40s; but Tom was first to use stereo in the recording process. During the 50s and 60s, he opened up new lanes on the sonic highway by popularizing 2-track stereo sound as an important production protocol.

NEWSFLASH: In a detailed report from Criteria Studios Manager Trevor Fletcher at www.criteriastudios.com, a technological chain of events revealed that after mono and stereo sound proved to be a success, multi-track recording was born in 1958 with 3-track recording. This must have been a pretty big deal, because it took six years for the next phase to kick in. By 1964, 8-channel 'live' mixing consoles were making their way to the forefront, while 1966 saw 4-track 'recording' consoles become the new standard. Studios like Criteria in South Florida were among the first in the Southern neighborhood to 'house the hardware,' along with technical developments like a *live stereo chamber*. Those achievements were nominal, but Tom Dowd had more than that up his sleeves; one of them permanently changed the face of mixing consoles. To get a better understanding of what I'm hinting at, let's run the tape from the top.

Born in 1925, Tom Dowd was the son of a certified concertmaster and an Opera-singing mother, so it's not surprising to see a young Tom inheriting musical abilities on the piano, string bass, tuba and violin. With his parents' blessings, Tom went on to excel in music, math, science… and physics. Eventually Tom became a music conductor, but a once in a lifetime opportunity turned into a true miracle for him at the age of sixteen. In the year 1942, Tom found himself studying physics—and doing top-secret work at New York's Columbia University: this endeavor came to be known as the *Manhattan Project*. Getting drafted into the Army when he was 18, Tom Dowd, codename *Special Scientific Issue*, went on to perform tests on various components found on the Periodic Table of Elements. The thing that made Tom's tests a bit different from other Army units is, he was deployed at the Neutron Beam Spectography division. Working with notables like Nobel Prize winner James Rainwater, Tom was destined for greatness by using his military wisdom to apply towards the electronics of music making.

By completion time for the Manhattan Project, Tom Dowd was a hefty 22 years old; he subsequently became a sergeant in the Army Corp of Engineers and supervised a unit of radiation detection specialists. With a job like that, let's just say Sergeant Dowd had some "juice." Although Tom's secret nuclear projects began in 1942, the world would not get "blown away" with the superior intellect of scientists until 1945, when the U.S. dropped an atomic bomb on Hiroshima. By 1946, Tom returned to civilian life but found he couldn't receive college credit for the top-secret work he supposedly 'didn't do' as a 'secret science student' at Columbia University in Manhattan. Outgrowing any further possibilities of being educated there, Tom kept things moving into the next segment of his life.

Tom Dowd's timing was impeccable because as one door closed, another one opened—after he landed a job at a recording studio, the musician's union began talks of a strike. This caused business to shift to the recording sector of the *biz*. By the end of the 40s, Tom had his hands full of projects to 'elementally electrify.' In 1950, he recorded an artist named Eileen Barton during a three-hour session and in his words, "never saw the girl again." Needless to say, he was shocked to learn that one of the tracks they recorded, *If I Knew You Were Comin' I'd've Baked a Cake*, got into the hands of radio broadcasters and became a huge hit. Tom Dowd went on to push the limits of sound and created an onslaught of technical innovations. He was the first one to individually assign a microphone for each recorded instrument, and was a key proponent of direct-to-disc recording. Visiting www.criteriastudios.com and www.thelanguageofmusic.com, I made a few discoveries; among them was how Tom masterminded the fabrication of new rooms at Miami's Criteria Recording Studios in early 1970—and then he relocated to Florida to run the operation.

After his arrival at Criteria Studios, Tom Dowd imported the *Dixie Flyers* rhythm section from Memphis. With a permanent house band to lay the foundation for tons of new recordings, the birth of 'Atlantic Records South' was imminent. An early project Tom took on in the sound lab was Duane Allman, a Florida-based guitarist he encountered while doing work in Muscle Shoals, Alabama. Duane brought his organ-playing brother Gregg down to Criteria to cut some tracks, establishing The Allman Brothers Band in the process. Through 'goods and bads of life,' the relationship nurtured itself into one that stood the test of time—Tom went on to record the band for over 30 years. Next thing you know, Tom Dowd had friends all over the place—from musicians to tech-heads. Tom's power to manipulate sonic energy into hit records came second to none: tons of people standing in line to work with him was all the proof needed.

> **A-B FACT:** Tom Dowd was the one who came up with the idea to split a long recording of Ray Charles' *What'd I Say* into A and B sides of the hit record.

The projects on back-order quickly multiplied as electronics wizard Tom Dowd became "the guy to work with" for A-Listers. To reiterate a saying I've coined: *Eagles don't dilly-dally on the ground with turkeys, they soar the skies—with other eagles.* Spanning a test of time from the 1940s to early 2000s, Tom Dowd produced and engineered a list of legends from The Allman Brothers Band to Aretha Franklin, from Charles Mingus to Wishbone Ash.

Earlier I mentioned Tom Dowd helped shape sound and music from the 50s to the new millennium but in actuality, his fingers continually pulsated with what was yet to be. Looking back, his early use of multi-track recording systems pioneered new options in the commercial world; he went on to even greater accomplishments like tweaking out mixing consoles. Before computers came along, recording studios used mixing consoles to combine sounds flowing through the system. As stated earlier, 70s-era professional mixing consoles often came with 8, 12, 16, 24, 48, 96 or more channels—but Tom spent tedious time 'expanding the system' further. Rewinding the tape, we find that this is the man who introduced linear (straight) channel faders, which permanently replaced the outdated look of rotary knobs on mixing consoles.

Keeping things real as an audio engineer myself, one of the main reasons I was drawn to the recording environment was because I wanted to slide faders up and down. Now it's done with a click on the mouse—to be blunt, nothing is constant like change! I'm sure I speak for many by saying THANKS to Tom Dowd's miraculous alteration to the look of oh-so-important studio hardware, like mixing consoles! Putting 'whipped cream on the cake,' Tom also pioneered the process of sonic alteration—better known as *sound reinforcement*. This is when aspects of the sound are changed after the primary recording was made. Tom was influential enough to have his character featured in 2004's big hit *Ray* so if you missed it, here's a great opportunity to learn about more things music. Even though Tom lost a battle with emphysema in October of 2002, many of his gifts have been left behind for mankind to contemplate forevermore.

A true-life story, *Tom Dowd and the Language of Music*, was featured at the 2003 *Sundance Film Festival*, and there's tons of content available for immediate interaction at www.tomdowd.com. Thanks to Tom, the archaic look of round black knobs got a facelift—to the sleeker looking, sliding linear fader; then they automated all the motion and give it recallable memory! To me, Tom Dowd was an original, sound-designing, multi-tracking, ahead-of-his-time guru who set the standard that great recordings are measured against. Putting on my radiation suit to take intensive readings, I calculate it's safe to say Tom Dowd easily qualified as a human atomic bomb who made serious music *biz*tory blow up and send shock waves around the world!

WHO'S WATCHING THE ACTION?

In the early days, Classical music and Broadway show tunes were only available in the 10- and 12-inch vinyl formats, but after Popular (Pop) music became a dominant force through the 7-inch 45, 10-inch records lost their appeal and faded away. The 12-inch album quickly evolved into a novelty because many music fans were enamored with unique artwork and liner notes on the front cover, the inside sleeve, and on the back cover—these attributes presented interesting graphics and acknowledgement of contributors to the project. As the Pop music culture took root, record label revenues fed a growing taste for new product configurations and the next debut was a 12-inch, double-album: Bob Dylan's 1966 *Blonde on Blonde*. Best-selling recordings like these became certified million and multi-million sellers. Now let's take a moment to get acquainted with the people who certified best-selling songs and albums.

In 1952, a non-profit trade organization called the Recording Industry Association of America (RIAA) was born. Representing members of the record industry—mostly record labels—the RIAA stepped up with key objectives in mind. They included acting as a voice for the industry and promoting the mutual interests of record companies, with regard to addressing consumer needs and changing technologies. Put another way, the RIAA was an intermediary between record companies and the consumer market. If you consider yourself to be an artist, writer or producer, it behooves you to know the ins and outs of the "music *biz*" as much as possible, starting with its supporting organizations. You should be well-aware of how the music industry machine works; and how people can rip you off, too! These and other factors can better prepare you for calculations, when figuring out where your money's coming from; and/or going. The RIAA helps to address issues like these by working on record companies' behalf to eradicate bad industry practices, so everyone gets compensated for their efforts "legitimately."

Today, the RIAA continues fighting to reduce inconsistencies within the industry, like unauthorized recordings—better known as piracy, bootlegging and counterfeiting. These practices cut into the revenue generated by legitimate music sales, meaning that record labels, publishers and artists lose money for their efforts. To offset this practice, the RIAA retains attorneys and investigators who work with federal, state and local law enforcement to identify, apprehend, and prosecute violators. In truth, the educated consumer is the key weapon in combating music thieves who prefer to eat the fruits of others' labor. No matter what the product's configuration was, shady people have always found ways to acquire, bootleg, counterfeit or pirate audio and video recordings. It happened on the Internet through 'file sharing' MP3s, with CDs of the 80s, 90s and beyond, with cassette tapes of the 70s and 80s, and vinyl of earlier days too. This is far from being a domestic U.S situation—it's a global pain that warrants holistic analytics, so let's look at the worldwide statistics for 2000 to get a measurement on where some of these problems incubate.

Major music piracy countries in 2000:		
Country	Level of piracy Value ($USm.)	Proportion of units sold (%)
China	600	90
Russia	240	65
Mexico	220	65
Brazil	200	50
Italy	180	25
Paraguay	110	95
Taiwan	100	45
Indonesia	65	55
Malaysia	40	65
Greece	40	50

Source: IFPI

Now here's a homework assignment: If *you* were running the RIAA, what would you do to help reduce unauthorized recordings? Allow me to turn on the telly-tube (TV) while awaiting your response... As the camera lens widens, we see America rolling through the 1950s with its consumers becoming mesmerized by a new apparatus called *television*. Corporate America scrambled to place commercials onto this new medium, so they took advertising money from their radio station budgets to make it happen. In order to accommodate this lost revenue, radio stations shifted their focus from broadcasting live and recorded music, to primarily playing records. For the most part, record companies were satisfied with this programming change, until they realized more people were staying home watching TV than were running out to buy records. This growing trend would forever change the music industry's *modus operandi*—method of operation.

During the 40s and 50s, radio programs consisted of news, time and weather, plus live and recorded shows. Most stations played music at some point between their regular programming; they also featured mysteries and narratives, which were predecessors of the modern-day TV soap opera. During programs, the radio announcer or actors were usually handed a script they'd often read from, word for word. With the advent of radio's nemesis—television—program directors and station owners were willing to take a chance on broadcasting almost anything to reclaim their lost audiences… and revenue streams. A new broadcasting protocol, "personality radio," was hovering somewhere over the terrestrial horizon. There will be a more in-depth briefing delivered about radio, after we take a look at a musical instrument radio stations have broadcasted over the airwaves for roughly a hundred years now…

-6-
RISE OF THE MODERN AXE

Back in *Musicology 2101*, we discussed how different phases of the Blues evolved from the acoustic guitar. Now, we'll address a radical instrument called *the electric guitar*, which led to a radical evolution in popular music taste. Concurrently, Easy Listening and Middle-of-the-Road artists of the 40s and 50s began taking a back seat to Rock-n-Roll's brisk new sound, renowned in some dance spots where it got served up as 'the flavor of the month.' Among the first electrically charged, amplified guitars was a Hawaiian-sounding instrument coined in 1931 as the *Frying Pan*. It was designed by an innovative thinker named George Beauchamp and built by Adolph Rickenbacker.

While doing research at places like www.crave.cnet.com.uk for music and technological breakthroughs, it was noted that in 1932 bandleader Gage Brewer gave the first performance on an electric guitar. It didn't take long for the fuse to trigger more action out on the playing field. Even though other musicians from the 30s and 40s Blues and Jazz worlds had utilized the new electric guitar sound, its popularity didn't fully bloom until musicians like Chet Atkins, Chuck Berry, B.B. King, and Les Paul performed with it. While there isn't enough space to illuminate every guitarist of significance, I am going to make 'one heck-uv-an attempt' to provide you with some good data on the above-mentioned musicians who have been dubbed codename MGPs: *Master Guitar Pickers*.

SPOTLIGHT ON: Chet Atkins

How does fourteen Grammy Awards, a Grammy Lifetime Achievement Award, nine Country Music Association's Instrumentalist of the Year awards and an induction into the Country Music Hall of Fame grab your attention? While most people know Chet Atkins as a "Certified Guitar Player," he was actually a well-rounded musician who worked at radio stations, plus he served as an A&R man, record producer and head of RCA Records' Nashville division.

Chet Atkins is probably best known for accrediting a smooth Country style coined *"The Nashville Sound"* What made it so appealing was that it broadened Country music's reach into the Pop and Jazz arenas. Even guitar heroes had their heroes—Chet was influenced by greats like George Barnes, Les Paul, Django Reinhardt and Merle Travis, so that's where I'd recommend you start any secondary investigations from. Atkins' skills reeled in legions of fans in a way previously unheard of: through regular Country music listeners and many listeners of genres from outside the United States. Just the mere fact that he produced records for Elvis (King of Rock-n-Roll), says it all, and for added credentials Chet produced acts like:

The Browns	The Everly Brothers
Porter Wagoner	Eddy Arnold
Norma Jean	Jim Reeves
Dolly Parton	Jerry Reed
Dottie West	Skeeter Davis
Perry Como	Waylon Jennings

Born in Tennessee, a young Chet Atkins began his guitar adventure on the ukelele, moved on to the fiddle and then the guitar, all by the time he was nine. Extracting all the joy he could from his music, in his 1974 biography Chet recalls being so poor that his family had no idea there was a Depression until the 1940s! That period was detrimental enough to keep Chet out of the poor house later in life, because his guitar picking was unmatched by anyone; and it put him in high demand. But before the good times arrived for good, Chet had to make it through a severe asthma condition that forced him to sleep in a chair, just to breathe easily. For therapy, his guitar was never far away and he often played it until he dozed off. Chet was the type of guy who probably continued strumming the strings, in his dreams.

By the time he was in high school, the "certified" title started becoming a distant possibility. It was later in life however, that Chet Atkins was bestowed with the honorary degree of *Certified Guitar Player*. This reference lent its availability to a few selected others like Tommy Emmanuel, John Knowles, Jerry Reed and Steve Wariner. After tagging her sideman Paul Yandell with the credentials in 2011, Chet's daughter Merle Atkins Russell pulled the plug and retired the CGP acronym. Going back to 1939 in Georgia, a younger Chet Atkins heard Merle Travis on WLW radio—it was then that he knew the musical direction he'd take. By 1942, Chet had dropped out of high school to work at Knoxville's

WNOX-AM. Backing up singers like Bill Carlisle and comedian Archie Campbell, Chet went on to work at stations like WLW in Cincinnati, and then he was off to Raleigh, North Carolina and Richmond, Virginia.

Chet Atkins' laid back style and intricate picking sometimes left station managers wondering how 'Country' Chet really was; a few managers couldn't see or hear it, and this doubt led to him being let go from a few stations. Fortunately, he was able to land other gigs. Atkins kept things moving through Chicago, Springfield, Missouri and Denver before he came to the attention of RCA's A&R man, Steve Sholes. By 1947, Chet was cutting tracks for RCA Records in Chicago. They didn't immediately put him into the fast lane, so he rolled on to Knoxville and joined *Mother Maybelle and the Carter Sisters*. This group got reeled in to the Grand Ole Opry; by 1950, the act made Nashville their new home base, and Chet kept the sound tight enough to keep folks interested. Chet's ship finally sailed in with his first hit, 1955's *Mr. Sandman*. These days, the song is still generating cash—I recently heard it in a Kia car commercial featuring Rock troopers, *Motley Crue*.

No stranger to the recording studio, Chet Atkins began organizing sessions in his growing capacity with RCA Records. Once the TV medium got a hold of Chet's music, it was a done deal. His tunes gained traction, with the camera opening up on *The Eddy Arnold Show* in 1956; then came the *Country Music Jubilee* in 1957 and *Jubilee U.S.A.* in 1958. By now, Chet had the attention of guitar manufacturer Gretsch and was brought in as a design consultant, leading to a whole line of guitars with his name on them—Chet enjoyed this relationship for 25 years, from 1955 to 1980. It's safe to say that by now, Chet was speeding in the fast lane—he became the manager of RCA's Nashville studio. As a studio manager, Chet got so advanced with the technology that he used his superior intellect to oversee the deployment of RCA's *Studio B*. This famous sound lab was built for the sole purpose of serving Nashville's *Music Row* clients.

The entrance of Rock-n-Roll in the late 50s saw a shift from not only Easy Listening and similar genres, but from Country music as well. Riding high on the waves was RCA Records producer Steve Sholes, who just delivered Elvis to the masses. Steve passed responsibility of RCA's Nashville division over to Chet Atkins, who promptly found a solution to declining sales due to that 'rowdy Rock-n-Roll sound.' Atkins followed suit with Owen Bradley by phasing out fiddles, steel guitars with other 'Country-centric' elements to appeal to the mainstream audience, and presto—*The Nashville Sound* was born!

Once a rare occurrence, more and more Country acts started 'genre-jumping' their way onto the Pop charts. All the pieces finally fit into place for Chet Atkins, whose style of playing fused elements of Country, Jazz, Classical and Pop. The hard times of years gone by were now forgotten—Chet had the flexibility to start a recording at RCA's main studio, and then take the tracks to his home studio to sonically decorate them. Paying attention to detail, Chet's standards included extraordinary playing and openness to experimentation by modifying certain aspects of the sound. Even though he picked up codenames like *Mr. Guitar*, Atkins was much more than a guitar player in the studio; he was also arranger, engineer and producer.

During the late 50s, Chet Atkins recorded and released an album that paid homage to his *Mister Guitar* moniker. Sitting in on engineering chores were chief engineer Bob Ferris and Bill Porter, who later replaced Bob at RCA's Nashville studios. Chet Atkins even reflected how 'in-tune' Porter was with Studio B. Commenting on when Porter left in 1964, "the sound was never the same, never as great." Chet remained to play his part at the studio, so in a sense it wasn't a total setback for RCA. Atkins was such an asset that he became a regular performer at the White House. In the 60s, Atkins was so influential that his magnetism snagged in top acts for RCA; there were Dolly Parton and others like:

Bobby Bare	Willie Nelson
John Hartford	Jerry Reed
Waylon Jennings	Connie Smith

The vast amount of musicians he influenced goes from Eddy Arnold to Earl Klugh, to Mark Knopler and Marty Stuart. Please believe there are many others, but just not enough space to list them all here.

Chet Atkins even walked a thin line with his superiors during the mid-60s Civil Rights Movement by signing Charlie Pride, the first Black Country singer to achieve real crossover success. The 60s also saw a big hit single for Chet, *Yakety Axe*, adapted from colleague Boots Randolph's version called *Yakety Sax*. As the 70s rolled in, Chet Atkins got sucked deeper into administrative label duties as a division head. Yet, he maintained 'guitar pickin' time' with good friends like Jerry Reed. Jerry was a popular actor who burned up the streets and silver screen with Burt Reynolds and Jackie Gleason in the *Smokey and the Bandit* series of films. But word has it Jerry Reed was a great guitarist *before* the acting bug hit.

The latter 70s saw Chet Atkins going light with producing, but he remained heavy in performance mode. He even teamed up with another guitar hero named Les Paul, releasing records like *Chester and Lester* and *Guitar Monsters*. More changes came about—Chet switched his support of Gretsch guitars and went with Gibson, then he jumped ship from RCA to Columbia. While at Columbia, he released an album that featured Jazz stylings he longed to create for listeners. I remember his 1985 *Stay Tuned* album well, because it was released just after I started working for CBS Records (Columbia's distributor). I even 'managed to merchandise' a few *Stay Tuned* displays in record stores, using *point-of-purchase* materials like posters, album cover flats and CD header cards.

Flashing back for a moment, I was watching TV one day in 2012 and saw a video of Chet performing a song called *Yankee Doodle Dixie*. As I tuned in, my ears picked up the distinct melodies of two different songs—Chet was playing *Yankee Doodle Dandy* and *Dixie* at the same time! This was incredible and caught me by surprise because the way I saw it, he made a statement by intertwining favorite songs of the North and South into one creative, musical message. It was actually the first time I saw this done by a musician, although I surmised it was do-able; if you could play by ear, improvise, read music and play Country, Jazz and Classical… like Chet Atkins could.

To me, that's the wonder of being a top-notch musician—a few others who made the grade include Jamaican musicians Sly & Robbie and the bass player from R&B/Funk group ConFunkShun. Opening the lens wider to show view #1, at the end of a Black Uhuru set I saw footage of drummer Sly Dunbar take his sticks and beat the strings of Robbie Shakespeare's bass guitar—they simultaneously played a riff on Robbie's bass. In view # 2, ConFunkShun's bass player had a few moments of mistaken identity as I saw him act like a DJ and "cut" through a medley of songs with the swiftness of a Ninja sword master. I'll try to expand the view on those stories and slate them for a later time.

Getting back to Chet Atkins, he started doing a wider variety of collaborations, picking up honors like 14 Grammy Awards, including the Grammy *Lifetime Achievement Award*, plus nine Country Music Association *Instrumentalist of the Year* awards and Billboard's *Century Award*. Although he left us in 2001 for Guitar Heaven, Chet Atkins inspired string pickers all over the world, due to the multiple styles he played. The contributions of Chet Atkins, codename *Certified Guitar*

Player, will stand on their own forever; his 2002 induction into the *Rock and Roll Hall of Fame* is all the proof you need. To make your own assessment, please visit sites like www.misterguitar.us and other online information silos. Keeping the guitar string plucking, let's take a look at another guitar hero who claims his own share of fame, through many musical contributions.

LES IS MORE

Les Paul was mentioned earlier as a key proponent of the guitar's popularity. Not only was Les a virtuoso in his own right, but he also designed and built one of the first ever solid-body guitars. Among his numerous technical achievements, Les Paul was also a major supporter of the newly discovered multitrack recording process. An early recording experiment yielded the 1948 release of *Lover (When You're Near Me)*. As an inventor of landmark sonic devices, Les Paul built the first multitrack recorder by adding extra tape heads to an Ampex Model 200 tape recorder Bing Crosby gave him. Les funded Ampex engineer Ross Snyder in development of 1955's first 8-track, Selective Synchronous (Sel-Sync) recorder. As can be expected, the new technology was expensive but by the early 60s, Pop stars like The Beatles and The Beach Boys used the multi-track recording process extensively. Before the decade's end, multi-tracking became the rule and was no longer considered an exception.

> **LES PAUL FACT:** During construction of the Capitol Records building in Hollywood, Les Paul designed custom echo chamber rooms with speakers on one side and microphones on the other. The rooms were built thirty feet under the ground floor.

It quickly became status quo for an artist to be seen with a guitar strapped to his or her body. This instrument became a catalyst for Rock music and the musicians who played it. By the time the 50s begin gaining traction in history books, it seemed as if every young male had gotten himself "plugged in" to someone's circuit. Many guitar players became obsessed with cranking up the volume until the sound was so loud that their speakers simply couldn't handle it. Thus was born 'distortion' and needless to say, the audio equipment repair business boomed after this. Dirtying up the sound with *distortion* and *overdrive* set historical new plateaus for the previously 'clean' acoustics of the guitar.

One more aspect of guitar recording came through the innovation of *sound effects* that augmented the sonic quality of guitars and other instruments. These little "black boxes" amassed plenty of mileage from being used by nearly every electric guitar player on the planet. Among the more popular effects are the previously mentioned distortion and overdrive; as well as chorus, delays, detuners, echo, filters, flange, fuzz tone, phase shifters, slapback, sweepers, tremelo, wah-wah and more. Effects units will be discussed in more detail another time but for now, you can check out some popular songs found listed at Pandora (blog.pandora.com) that utilized these devices:

EFFECT: *Song* – Artist
- **CHORUS**: *Pictures of You* - The Cure, *The Shango, Pt. III* - Charlie Hunter, *Hungry For You (J'Aurais Toujours Faim De Toi)* - The Police, *Heaven Knows I'm Miserable Now* - The Smiths
- **DELAY**: *Three Days* – Jane's Addiction, *Run Like Hell* - Pink Floyd, *Permanent Daylight* - Radiohead, *Pride (in the Name of Love)* - U2
- **DISTORTION**: *Rock And Roll Ain't Noise Pollution* - AC/DC, *Mr. Brownstone* - Guns 'n Roses, *You Really Got Me* - The Kinks, *The Ocean* - Led Zeppelin
- **TREMELO**: *Human Fly* - The Cramps, *Tidal Wave* - Dick Dale, *24 Hrs.* - Man or Astroman?, *The Sheriff of Noddingham* - David Marks & the Marksmen
- **WAH-WAH**: *Tales of Brave Ulysses* - Cream, *Theme from Shaft* - Isaac Hayes, *Up From the Skies* - Jimi Hendrix, *Voodoo Chile (Slight Return)* - Stevie Ray Vaughan & Double Trouble

This is just a random sampling, but there are many songs in many styles that feature effects like these, used by themselves or in even more complex combinations. Since its very beginning, Rock-n-Roll was rowdy, and "the establishment" didn't like it one bit! Elvis Presley, Chuck Berry, Jerry Lee Lewis and Little Richard motivated kids to get up, get loose, and dance to the music. The "raunchy dancing" this genre induced through youth was forbidden by much of the older generation. As bad luck would have it, many members of that stern, stricter society tried putting a halt to it early; but this growing phenomenon was just the tip of the iceberg.

Believe it or not, Rock paved the way for another rebellious style called Rap to come through, in quite an unscrupulous manner. By the 80s, break-dancing, Rap and the entire Hip-Hop culture contributed to a brand new music revolution—we'll get more into this event upon arrival at a future Musicology endeavor codenamed *Hiphopology*. By 2005, *Rolling Stone* magazine's Top 10 All-time Great Guitarists included:

Rank	Artist	Popular Style(s)	Affiliated band(s)
1	Jimi Hendrix	Blues, R&B, Rock	The Jimi Hendrix Experience Band of Gypsies
2	Duane Allman	Blues, Rock	The Allman Brothers
3	B.B. King	Blues	The Beale Streeters
4	Eric Clapton	Blues, Folk, Rock	Cream, The Yardbirds Derek & The Dominos
5	Robert Johnson	Country Blues	N/A
6	Chuck Berry	Blues, R&B, Rock	Sir John's Trio
7	Stevie Ray Vaughan	Blues	Double Trouble
8	Ry Cooder	Blues, Folk, Rock	The Rising Sons
9	Jimmy Page	Blues, Rock	Led Zeppelin
10	Keith Richards	Blues, Rock	The Rolling Stones

An honorable mention goes out to Roy Clark, a phenomenal Country & Western guitarist whose talents included playing the banjo and classic 12-string guitar. In addition to staking claim to dozens of albums and awards, Clark had plenty of charisma. I remember as a child in the 70s, using my *manual remote* (changing channels by hand) to watch him on television's first Country music variety show, *Hee Haw*, which aired from 1969 to 1992. This musical comedy show featured the hottest Country, Western and Bluegrass performers along with Clark, who mastered the art of *singin' 'n smilin'* while playing a banjo or guitar.

Somehow, one of Roy Clark's songs from Dot Records (a division of film giant Paramount), ended up in my parents' record collection. In the 70s, Clark's song "*Yesterday, When I Was Young*" had a special Elvis/Tom Jones type of appeal to me. This song blended in perfectly with the various genres in my parents' collection and the music I took in from weekly TV programs like *Hee Haw, American Bandstand, Ed Sullivan, Don Kirschner's Rock Concert, Saturday Night Live, Soul Train* and *The Midnight Special*. Even at that age, I was jotting down the guitar's role as a featured instrument on many of these shows.

160

Well into the 70s, the electric guitar's appeal still had bands cranking up their amps, just like it did during the 50s and 60s. FAST FORWARD to the 21st century, where guitar manufacturers Fender, Gibson, and Ibanez led the way in mass-production of electric guitars. Guitar sales totaled over 5 million in 2004, with a near-equal split between acoustic and electric guitars. Like treasured jewels, American-made guitars have increased in value, with some collectors paying thousands for much sought after models, like the *Les Paul*. The guitar era had come of age and now stood on its own accord, becoming as American as apple pie.

LET'S "TUNE IN" TO …

A guitarist some considered to be more obscure than most was Johnny "Guitar" Watson, who was born in Houston, Texas in 1935. In addition to the guitar, this multi-instrumentalist learned to play piano, bass and drums. The guitar was an instrument that Watson's father was also well "in tune" with. Allegedly speaking, upon receiving a guitar from his preacher-grandfather one day, Johnny promised never to play Blues on it—a promise he reneged on, shortly thereafter.

As a teenager Johnny played with Blues masters Albert Collins and Johnny Copeland, before heading west to Los Angeles. Watson wound up mastering the Blues, Jazz and R&B… he also told great stories while poking fun at life's more pressing issues. Songs like 1977's *A Real Mother For Ya* came out during that era's gas crisis. (Was it a real crisis–compared to today's insane prices?) The song cleverly used humor to describe the woes of inflation: when fuel was less than a buck a gallon.

> **SONIC FACT**: Johnny "Guitar" Watson was experimenting with reverb and feedback during the 50s, way ahead of many other musicians at that time.

Throughout the 50s, 60s and 70s, Johnny "Guitar" Watson recorded and released many songs with cutting-edge musicians like Frank Zappa, who turned Jimi Hendrix on to "the pedal" (wah-wah, that is). Watson continued making songs into the 80s and 90s, even having his music sampled by Dr. Dre and Snoop Dogg. This Hip-Hop duo was also known for their samples of another important musician who will forever be remembered: Roger Troutman of the Funk band, Zapp. Watson closed out his career on stage in Yokohama, Japan by passing into the next phase as he performed at a Blues café in May of 1996. Watson used spoken word, slang and melodic phrases in his music and this contributed to making him a phenomenal orator and true talent. One final note: Johnny "Guitar" Watson created memorable, "down home" songs to establish his own legacy that lives on—whether through fans' music players or on the Internet, this is one string picker who delivered many soulful messages packed with social awareness.

Another hot guitarist took showmanship to a whole new level—guitarist extraordinaire Chuck Berry was born in St. Louis, Missouri. This incredibly talented musician made his live performances sizzle by taking mental notes on what excited people at shows. He studied mystifying performers like Nat "King" Cole and Muddy Waters. By combining other styles with innovative techniques, Berry developed his own niche that kept him in the limelight for decades. Chuck is credited as being the "best of the best" with a tenure that began around 1953 with *Sir John's Trio*. He went on to form his own Black-Hillbilly-Blues-early Rock group called *The Chuck Berry Combo*. Berry's extensive discography spans some fifty years and covers dozens of releases, including big hits like *Johnny B. Goode*, *Maybellene*, and the incomparable *My Ding-A-Ling*. Although this was Chuck Berry's only #1 Billboard hit, he wasn't the tune's original writer: keep on reading for more details.

In the beginning it wasn't so easy for Chuck Berry—he ran from station to station promoting his songs to get radio airplay. Making right connections along the way, Berry amassed lots of airplay and it all converted to sales of his music. He had the magic formula all laid out: radio airplay meant record sales, publishing and tour income. Chuck knew there were labels eager to sign him and push his career through the express lane. However, he settled on just one to make it happen during the early days of Rock-n-Roll: Chess Records. Please believe it when I say Chess Records and artists like Chuck Berry took the "modern axe" sound to a whole new plateau in music performance and publishing.

Berry's sound was influential enough for writers to work his flamboyant character into films like *Back to the Future* and *Cadillac Records*. Chuck Berry and his famous "duck walk" helped labels like Chess get on the map; fans reached out for personal enjoyment, time and time again. I mentioned earlier in Musicology 2101's *The Electric Blues* section about divulging more information on Chess Records' many contributions to the music world, so here it comes...

THE CHESS GAME

Chicago-based Chess Records specialized in Blues, Gospel, Jazz, R&B and Soul. The label is probably remembered best for their chart-topping, early Rock-n-Roll releases. When we discussed Blues and Electric Blues earlier, there was mention of an eminent relationship between Blues and Rock-n-Roll. Early Rock music was essentially sped up Blues, so before Rock staked its claim to fame, a preferred style for many Chicagoans was Blues. The Chess Records pipeline made wondrous advancements in music and led the way to those good old, 'golden days' of Chicago Blues.

Two brothers, Leonard and Phil Chess, set up and managed "the Chess board." During the evolution of Chess, the brothers produced a long streak of hit music from different field bases around Chicago. As the label moved into adolescence, several key figures used their superior intellect to make strategic music moves in-between the sound room and the boardroom for Chess. Some of these figures include Willie Dixon, Ralph Bass and Roquel "Billy" Davis, who chalked up experience working with Berry Gordy during the early Motown days.

In the process of their meteoric ascension, Chess Records was referenced on the Rolling Stones track, 2120 South Michigan Avenue. Back in 1964, the Stones recorded at this studio location during their maiden voyage from England to the U.S. But one visit wasn't enough— The Stones came back for more, as did other trend-setting artists who called the Chicago studio "home." Within Chess' studio, an all-star cast of house musicians included Earth, Wind & Fire's founder, Maurice White. He laid down the contagious drum sounds that kept many beats going for Chess and its royal subjects. Now let's open the lens up on a Chess artist who went from zero to a hundred, by *Wang Dang Doodling* her way to a million records sold.

AN INSIDE VIEW: KOKO TAYLOR

Koko Taylor went from the lower end of society to the highest ranks of the industry, where she performed in dozens of concerts each year and influenced artists like Janis Joplin, Bonnie Raitt and Susan Tedeschi. Born as Cora Walton in Tennessee, Koko Taylor took root in Chicago singing Blues; and blossomed into the only singer to win a whopping *25* W.C. Handy Awards. Koko's traditionally rough vocalizations and expressive performances helped her land a properly fitting title, "Queen of the Blues." Like another edgy singer named Millie Jackson (profile coming soon), Koko was the daughter of a sharecropper; but she didn't let that stop her from pursuing childhood dreams. In Koko's case, she left Shelly County, Tennessee for Memphis and by the early 50s, Chicago was calling. Making an executive decision, Koko took off with her truck-driving husband Robert "Pops" Taylor—the trip north opened doors that would have remained closed had she stayed south.

By the late 50s, Koko Taylor began popping up in local Blues clubs and became an ISO: *Identified Singing Object*. Capturing the attention of Chicago music man Willie Dixon in 1962, her live show itinerary quickly filled up with new dates… and she clinched a recording contract with Chess Records. Koko suddenly went from *0 to 100* with her first million-seller, a song by Willie Dixon that was previously recorded by Howlin' Wolf: *Wang Dang Doodle*. Among Koko's career trademarks are various renderings of this song—like a live version recorded at 1967's American Folk Blues Festival with harmonica blower Little Walter and guitar wizard 'Hound Dog' Taylor. Around the mid-60s, Chess Records relocated to a larger spot at 320 E. 21st. Street. As a testament to many years of creative songwriting input for Chess, *Willie Dixon's Blues Heaven Foundation* now sits on the South Michigan Avenue property.

The late 60s and early 70s saw Koko Taylor picking up new fans while touring and then in 1975, she signed on with Alligator Records. While styles like Funk and Disco clearly overshadowed Blues during this period, 8 out of 9 albums she recorded got Grammy nominated and pushed her further up the music *biz* totem pole. In the female Blues singing category, it was quickly becoming a difficult task to out-do Koko Taylor. As Koko's headlights shined straight ahead, she swooped into the fast lane—with no flashing blinkers. As luck would have it around 1989, the Messenger of Misery made a guest appearance in her car: we almost lost her in a near-fatal crash. After a lengthy recovery, Koko popped up in motion pictures like *Blues Brothers 2000* and *Wild at Heart*.

By 1994, Koko Taylor opened a Chicago Blues club; it did well for a number of years, and then moved to another location before shutting down permanently in 2000. Taylor lived in an affluent part of the city, and losses such as these weren't taken lightly. Her finances didn't improve much with the IRS stepping in next, claiming she owed back taxes from the late 90s. Things got more dismal for Koko after giving a performance at the *Blues Music Awards* in May of 2009—sadly speaking, she suffered from internal bleeding, then passed away a month later in June. Koko Taylor leaves behind a legacy that's definitely worthy of a closer look in bookstores, libraries or online at places like www.kokotaylor.com. Now let's get back to her old label Chess Records, to see how the label's moves were made on the game board of music *biz*tory.

Like many record companies, Chess also operated through aliases like *Checker*, *Marterry*, *Argo* and *Cadet* to achieve maximum airplay for their artists. A series of other label affiliations sprouted up during its 70s heydays and by the early 80s, *All Platinum Records* owners Joe and Sylvia Robinson possessed much of the Chess catalog. As the lens closes, we see that bad management in the planned 'golden years' for All Platinum got things a tad rusty, and the Robinsons moved on to achieve other milestones. One of them was Sugar Hill Records and yes, we'll get to that story down the line. As music *biz* process goes, the Chess master tapes from All Platinum turned up at MCA Records, before landing at Geffen Records under the giant Universal Music umbrella. The Chess catalog accounts for huge amounts of publishing income, plus many hits of the 50s, 60s and 70s. Chess headliners include Koko Taylor, Willie Dixon, Muddy Waters, Etta James, Bo Diddley, Chuck Berry, and Howlin' Wolf. Other names that made it at one time or another to the roster include:

Big Bill Broonzy	Denise LaSalle
Gene Chandler	Memphis Slim
The Dells	Little Milton
The Flamingos	Little Walter
Benny Goodman	The Moonglows
Buddy Guy	The Ramsey Lewis Trio
John Lee Hooker	Sonny Stitt

Chess Records became the focus of films like 2008's *Cadillac Records*, starring a talented Diva known as Beyonce—she played the impassioned Etta James, Musicology codename *Song Seamstress*. The reason she's tagged with that name is entangled in a web she spun that encompassed multiple music styles like Blues, Gospel, Jazz, R&B, Rock and Soul. Let's put some illumination on this multi-genre-ational singer.

SPOTLIGHT ON: Etta James

Making her landing in the *biz* during the mid-50s, Etta James released a slew of hit recordings, among them being *Dance With Me, Henry, I'd Rather Go Blind, Tell Mama* and another favorite, *At Last*. Despite personal issues that surfaced in the 70s, Etta rebounded by the late 80s with a new album that once again put all eyes on her. A 'short list' of artists influenced by Etta includes:

Adele	Christina Aguilera
Beyonce	Elkie Brooks
Shemekia Copeland	Paloma Faith
Janis Joplin	Bonnie Raitt
The Rolling Stones	Diana Ross
Rod Stewart	Joss Stone
Hayley Williams of Paramore	Amy Winehouse

Opening our lens further, we see a singer born in 1938 as Jamesetta Hawkins, beginning her vocal training at the age of five. Moving from Los Angeles to San Francisco, she later started a Doo Wop girl group called *The Creolettes*. Musician Johnny Otis helped them get a record deal with Modern Records, and their name was changed to *The Peaches*. Jamesetta transformed into *Etta James* and by 1955, the group released an answer record to Hank Ballard's *Work With Me, Annie* called *Dance With Me, Henry*—it hit the #1 spot on Billboard's R&B chart.

Along the peachy female group's trek to the top, Little Richard had them as his opening act on a national tour. While they were on the road, Pop artist Georgia Gibbs did what became common practice in the industry—she recorded a cover version of Etta James' song. *The Wallflower* had modified lyrics but anyone who heard Etta's version knew it was really her *Dance With Me, Henry*. Gibbs' version quickly crossed over to Billboard's Pop side on the Hot 100—before James' original tune did. Brutally speaking, stories like this are not uncommon in the music *biz*.

The following years saw Etta James scoring other hits, but by 1960 she left Modern Records and signed with Chess. This period signified a new direction for her and in time, Etta found herself in a collaborative engagement with Harvey Fuqua—he had a group called *The Moonglows*. Recording a series of hit singles together, the pair grew a steady following before Etta released a solo hit, *All I Could Do Was Cry*. The success of this R&B song gave label owner Leonard Chess thoughts of shaping Etta into a crossover act, complete with violins and other symphonic instruments. As Etta's new sound developed, she kept a high profile by adding vocals to songs like *Back In the USA*, by labelmate Chuck Berry.

Many would agree that Etta James' single and album called *At Last* etched her into the music *biz*tory books due to several outstanding, multi-genre-ational productions. The single shot up Billboard's charts and became Etta's signature song. There are dozens of different versions out there but to me, Etta's still stands out above the rest. For the next few years, Etta released widely acclaimed albums that pushed the limits of that time by incorporating Gospel arrangements into some songs. It didn't take long for a live album to be recorded, and by 1963 it was released. Although Etta stayed in the game, things cooled off by the mid-60s; but she made a strong comeback in 1967 through an R&B tune called *Tell Mama*—it was penned with *Master Music Man*, Clarence Carter.

Showcasing her gutsy command of Blues, *I'd Rather Go Blind* became the B-side of *Tell Mama* and was covered by many acts. From hit recordings to sold-out shows to an autobiography, Etta James revealed many different perspectives to the public during her years with Chess Records. Etta continued recording and performing well into the 70s, dabbling with Rock and Funk to add into her mix. Beefing up her repertoire with new songs, the mid-to-late 70s found Etta on the road opening up for acts like the Rolling Stones; she also gave a critically acclaimed performance at the Montreal Jazz Festival. Eventually departing from Chess, things slowed down for Etta afterwards, and then dastardly drug demons made a steady approach to further antagonize her. But drugs weren't enough to derail the Etta James train.

The late-80s saw increased visibility for Etta James after she appeared in a documentary and released a new album through Island Records called *Seven Year Itch*. Making a number of recordings at Florence, Alabama's legendary FAME Studios, Etta's guns were fully loaded again… and the safety was off. In 1989, she mixed her Jazz vocals with the Hip-Hop of Def Jeff on his *Just A Poet With Soul* release. Etta James was immortalized in 1993 when she got inducted into the *Rock and Roll Hall of Fame*. Other huge feats include recording a Billie Holiday tribute album, winning Grammys, and even recording a Christmas album. She also got inducted into the *Blues Hall of Fame*, the *Rockabilly Hall of Fame* and in 2004, was voted in as #62 on Rolling Stones' *100 Greatest*

Artists of All Time. A few reasons she made the cut includes those hit releases on Chess Records—but Etta wasn't the only lucky lady to find success at Chess. We will soon head into the *Land of Funny* to meet a lady who laughed her way straight to the bank, while unleashing her own brand of comedy on Chess. Before we head out to the Funny Farm, here are a few final pointers on Etta James:

- 2009 – does her final TV appearance, wins Soul/Blues Female Artist of the Year from the Blues Foundation: for the 9th time
- 2010 – hits the road on tour but cancels due to a decline in health
- 2011 – final album *The Dreamer* is released, rapper Flo Rida samples Etta's 1962 *Something's Got A Hold of Me* for his *Good Feeling* single
- 2012 - recording act Avicii hits #1 with *Levels*—it had a sample of Etta James' *Something's Got A Hold of Me*

As a musical chameleon, Etta James jumped in the game and evolved through Blues, Doo Wop, Pop, Jazz, Gospel and Soul. A reason she was voted as one of the "Best Singers On Earth" by the *Encyclopedia of Popular Music* is because she did a 'definitive dot-connect' between R&B and Rock-n-Roll. Along the way, she influenced dozens of artists—from Diana Ross to The Rolling Stones. Fighting illness and addiction, Etta traveled a long road to stardom, then slipped away to make yet another return: thus satisfying a worldwide fan base hungry for her music. Although she left us on January 20, 2012, the Internet has plenty of music, pictures, video footage, writings and more on this fabulous singer's singer.

When I think of Etta James, I think of a young singer my Virginia-based friend DJ K-Ski introduced me to, one day in early 2012. Here's a quick point: It's indeed a rare occasion that I listen to people sing on the phone, due to the terrible sound quality. It's also rare for me to run across an artist who belts out an Etta James tune the way *Amber Yholeata* does. DJ K-Ski gave me her links (www.amberyholeata.com, www.youtube.com/watch?v=pYJqqbZY1j0) and when I went online, not only did I find her performing *At Last* live, but I also discovered there was a bunch of other content by this up-and-coming performer. In defining this envelope-pushing singer, DJ K-Ski said "Amber's version of *At Last* is so good—if it were my call, I would have included her in the *Cadillac Records* movie." Even though the casting director went with Beyonce, something tells me it's not over yet for Amber Yholeata, either…

In addition to casting Beyonce as Etta James, the *Cadillac Records* film featured another music giant, Hip-Hop actor-slash-MC Mos Def, who played the guitar-toting Chuck Berry. If you remember, we discussed Chuck prior to zooming in on the 'Chess Records game.' *Cadillac Records* also included celebrities like *Adrien Brody*, *Cedric the Entertainer*, *Q-Tip* of *A Tribe Called Quest* and *Jeffrey Wright*, whose performance as guitar great Muddy Waters was unsurpassed. While we're on the subject of Hollywood renditions of *fast life* and *rough times* in the music industry, you can also check out 2006's *Dreamgirls*, if you haven't done so yet. Stars like *Beyonce*, *Jamie Foxx*, *Jennifer Hudson*, *Danny Glover*, *Anika Noni Rose* and *Eddie Murphy* served up stellar performances on the silver screen. Due to my personal interest in these types of films, you can quote me here: *Cadillac Records* and *Dreamgirls* each get "two thumbs up!"

-7-
CHESS & THE FUNNY FARM

Along with singers and musicians, many comedians made it big by releasing records and doing live shows. At one time, funny lady *Jackie "Moms" Mabley* had an association with Chess Records. Billed as "The Funniest Woman in the World" from 1919 to 1939, Moms was one of the top comedians of her era who performed "un-politically correct" stand-up routines. Mabley's film career spanned from 1933 to 1974, in a number of credible acting roles. Performing with the likes of Paul Robeson in motion pictures such as *Emperor Jones,* Moms carved out a path in entertainment big enough for the world to fit in. Between 1961 and 2004 over twenty recordings were released, including a 1964 Chess album called *The Funny Sides of Moms Mabley*. A fit forerunner from the Vaudeville days, Moms was no stranger to the *Chitlin' Circuit* mentioned in earlier sections of this book series. Because she was like a mom to fellow comedians during her reign of 50s and 60s tours, Mabley tacked the matriarchal reference onto her stage name and the rest was *herstory*.

Influencing upcoming jokesters like Bill Cosby, Phyllis Diller, Whoopi Goldberg, Bernie Mac and Richard Pryor, Moms Mabley was often seen wearing non-gendered clothing during her 20s and 30s performances. Around the age of 27, Moms professed her alternative lifestyle and even recorded a few lesbian stand-up routines: this was long before "coming out of the closet" became fashionable. Ironically, her confession opened the closet door wider—she became one of the first comedians to earn the rating of "XXX." For Moms, doing a "racy" show live in front of a crowd was just as easy as acting in a G-rated film and she generated figures like $10,000 a week performing at places like the Apollo Theater in Harlem.

Moms Mabley expanded her audience during the 60s by performing at venues like Carnegie Hall, and appearing on television shows like CBS TV's #1 rated *Smothers Brothers Comedy Hour*. In the summer of 1969, she demonstrated how a satire song could blend with her jokes: by releasing a rendition of Dick Holler's tune, *Abraham, Martin and John*. Although covers were previously recorded by artists like Dion, Smokey Robinson & the Miracles, Marvin Gaye and Harry Belafonte,

Mabley's version still hit #35 on Billboard's charts of the late 60s. At 75 years young, Moms Mabley became the oldest celebrity to earn a Top 40 hit. Racking up a star spangled career, Moms appeared in movies, on television and in clubs everywhere. Her final performance was at the *Michigan Women's Festival* in 1975. Shortly thereafter, she left fans with a permanent smile across her face and departed to the comedy afterlife, at the robust age of 81.

Compared to today, entertainment of the 60s and 70s was somewhat limited, but for some reason the music, movies and television programs back then just felt different. Of course my handy-dandy manual remote (changing channels by hand) was always in use but too often on TV night with the family, my 'inferior intellect' got the best of me... was I hearing voices calling out to me from between record jackets in the music collection? It seemed like the music from my parent's record collection regularly filled our living room with soul; and found me in a tranced state as I dug through all kinds of records to play on our German-import Grundig component system. The practice of peeking through my folks' record collection helped me figure out the musical tastes they had, so I could figure out mine.

One day, I was left scratching my head after finding a Moms Mabley album. Naturally, I was curious about what this comically clad woman was 'singing' about. When I played the album later, I got schooled. (She wasn't doing any singing, either.) I knew my folks had a wide-ranging music menu but after I asked, no one volunteered to give me the 4-1-1 on how *that* one made it to the collection. Mom and dad deemed my kiddy interrogation and subsequent oral turbulence wasn't scratching any surfaces, and remained silent. But the constant questioning and pleads for answers ensued them like machine gun fire until finally one day, all I heard was *"bwoy, tun up di sound 'pon dot TV—Sanford an' Son ah come on."* In our family, no one talked when shows like *Sanford and Son* or *Flip Wilson* aired; we were too busy laughing!

One of the many featured guest stars on *Sanford and Son* was also a Chess Records act named Slappy White. Like Moms Mabley, White was fortunate and marked his own comedic path to success by working with old friends like Redd Foxx during the 50s and 60s days of stand-up comedy, while cruising through the *Chitlin' Circuit*. White was also blessed to have acted in motion pictures like *Mr. Saturday Night* and *Amazon Women on the Moon,* and made cameos on TV shows like *That's*

My Mama, *Blossom* and *Cybill*. Again like Moms Mabley, Slappy helped open the doors for a slew of Black comedians who came after him. It's been said that as a child, Slappy White "ran away to join the circus." That rumor hasn't been confirmed yet, but proof has shown that Slappy was always one of the best 'clowns' at Friar's Club Roasts for legends like Milton Berle. This is where Slappy's infamous, quick-witted humor became popular for getting a faltering "roast session" back into the funny lane, if another comic failed to tickle the audience's funny bone.

Flipping the script of his normal comedic works, Slappy White wrote and performed a memorable routine about racial equality during the civil rights movement. Applauded by President John F. Kennedy, the routine consisted of a poem recital: using a black glove on one hand, and a white one on the other. Because of cutting-edge performances like these, it's no wonder why labels like Chess Records sought to make him one of their main acts. Slappy White passed away in 1995 but thanks to a few "bootleg" Friars Club Roast recordings, Slappy's popularity resurged and his comedy record sales increased. Consistent royalties are what every act in the industry dreams about, but they need to get those royalties… while they're still alive!

Some space was allocated to squeeze in some heavy-hitters, but please note there are *plenty* of funny guys 'n gals who get the proverbial 'old school thumbs up'—and many had lucrative deals with record labels:

Franklyn Ajaye	Dick Gregory	Rosey O'Donnell
Roseanne Barr	Eddie Griffin	Lawanda Page
George Carlin	Kathy Griffin	Pig Meat Markham
Chevy Chase	Arsenio Hall	Richard Pryor
Cheech & Chong	Robin Harris	Don Rickles
Margaret Cho	Shirley Hemphill	Chris Rock
Andrew Dice Clay	Benny Hill	Nipsey Russell
Billy Crystal	Bob Hope	Pauly Shore
DC Curry	Sam Kinison	Sinbad
Mark Curry	Jerry Lewis	Skillet & Leroy
Rodney Dangerfield	Dean Martin	Lily Tomlin
Sammy Davis, Jr.	Steve Martin	Jimmie Walker
Phyllis Diller	Paul Mooney	George Wallace
Redd Foxx	Rudy Ray Moore	The Wayans family
Whoopi Goldberg	aka Dolemite	Robin Williams
Bobcat Goldthwait		Flip Wilson

While our next comic wasn't signed to Chess Records, he sure did take comedy in a new direction by shoving in an overload of what we can call 'laughter steroids.' As a true all-around comedian signed to Columbia Records he not only cracked jokes; but could sing, dance and act, too.

SMILES + MURPHY = SMURPHY

An act that continues to take full advantage of getting paid while he still breathes is my fellow Brooklynite Eddie Murphy, codename *Certified Comedian*. Back in the 80s, Eddie Murphy took FUNNY to a whole new level by pouring lyrical adrenalin into the comedy of influences like Richard Pryor, Redd Foxx and Bill Cosby. Eddie Murphy went on to become the *second* highest grossing actor in America. For those with curious minds, 60-something year-old Samuel L. Jackson comes in at #1, with 100 plus films that grossed almost $7.5 billion domestically. To get worldwide gross tallies, just double the domestic sales! Eddie logs in at just under half the amount of films that Sam Jackson made (50), with just about half the gross of Sam Jackson ($3.8 billion)—all I can say is: *Hey 'possibly' Uncle Sam, I'm shaking the family tree so if you happen to be my long-lost uncle, let's link up…*

While his mom was a phone operator, Eddie Murphy's father was a transit police officer by day… but at night, he became codename *Actor-Comedian Dad*. Although he passed away while Eddie and his brother Charlie were still young, at the end of the day it's easy to see how DNA was pushed through the two brothers, who in fact 'both turned out to be a bit touched.' Over time, Charlie Murphy popped up just about anywhere and for the most part, that's just what he did as an actor, writer, voiceover talent; and Rap/Hip-Hop artist. That's right folks; for a hot minute in the late 1980s he signed up as a member of the *K-9 Posse* and was regularly featured on *Yo! MTV Raps*. One place he actually stuck around was on Dave Chappelle's show, from 2003 to 2006. As a key figure in the infamous comedy show, Charlie picked up prime time exposure as a writer-actor, scooping up new fans along the way. Talking about Charlie's extra face time, between 1989 and the present, he starred in over two dozen films—to shed some light, here are just a few big ones:

1989-Harlem Nights
1990-Mo' Better Blues
1991-Jungle Fever
1993-CB4
1998-The Players Club
1999-Unconditional Love
2003-Death of a Dynasty
2005-King's Ransom

2006-Night at the Museum
2007-Norbit
2008-The Hustle
2009-Frankenhood
2010-Freaknik: The Musical
2011-The Cookout 2
2011-Tower Heist

He also wrote for 1985's *Vampire in Brooklyn* and 2002's *Paper Soldiers*—on the boob tube, Charlie was just as effective:

Saturday Night Live
Martin
One on One
Denis Leary's Merry F#%$in' Christmas
The Boondocks
Thugaboo: Sneaker Madness
Wild 'n Out
We Got to Do Better
Natural Born Komics
Charlie Murphy: I Will Not Apologize
Are We There Yet?
1000 Ways to Die

Charlie Murphy even made appearances in video games like *Grand Theft Auto: San Andreas* and *Getting Up: Contents Under Pressure*. As he continues working his way from the silver screen to beyond, we'll see more raw Murphy talent shine, because it's obvious that the same dose of talent got passed on from Daddy Murphy to Charlie and his younger brother. The only difference is back in the early 1980s, Eddie's dose pushed him straight to front and center in a hurry. All I can say is, Charlie still made it to the finish line and the rest is "all gravy."

As a teenager, Charlie Murphy's kid brother Eddie was like a horse out the gate when it came to creating tons of over-the-top comedy sketches. Lots of hard work finally paid off as a cast member of the long-running *Saturday Night Live*, codename SNL; he did skits depicting icons like *Gumby*, *James Brown* and *Michael Jackson*. Taking over operations of the *TTB* (Talented Token Black) position from funnyman Garrett "Still In The Game" Morris, Eddie Murphy appeared from 1980 to 1984—due to my age at the time, I think I saw every episode. Murphy's standup comedy took his persona to another level, one that I saw become a dominating platform that developed from his "wild and crazy" skits among folks like Dan Akroyd, Steve Martin and Joe Piscopo.

At the beginning of this section, you were presented with a textual equation (SMILES + MURPHY = SMURPHY)—well here's a more complex one: Outrageous mind + XXX mouth + live microphone = Eddie Murphy's self-titled debut album on Columbia Records. Recorded in 1982 at New York's *Comic Strip*, he covered clichéd topics like Black movie theaters and alternative lifestyles; it even had a song called *Boogie in Your Butt* stuck up in the mix. That album was so popular that there were still copies of it in the promo bins when I started interning at CBS Records' Atlanta branch in 1984. There were also copies of Eddie's second album, 1983's *Comedian*. If Murphy's first album was a jaw breaking side-splitter, then his second effort was a 'massive triple bypass,' in medical terms. This release reeled in a Grammy Award at 1984's ceremonies, and the concert was released as an HBO special, *Delirious*: a fitting title, indeed!

With a budding movie career in the works and two successful albums under his leather belt (he probably had at least a dozen belts—with matching outfits), Eddie Murphy flipped the script by pulling out a suit and tie to produce 1985's *How Could It Be*. This album featured more singing than wisecracking and Eddie actually got a Top 10 hit out of it, *Party All The Time*, produced by close friend Rick James. Rick was still riding his reign of the late 70s to mid-80s as the *King of Punk Funk*. He also had his hands into producing acts like Eddie Murphy, the sultry Mary Jane Girls; and another act I promoted during my time at CBS Records, *Process and the Doo Rags*. This reminds me to 'point out a proverb'—*the top 5% of hit music supports the weight of the remaining 95% of non-hit music*. Although Process and the Doo Rags was produced by Rick James and the record had good songs on it, Columbia threw it out there without the super glue that was used for acts like Eddie Murphy. You've seen what happens when a liquid is thrown against the wall—it doesn't stick, but slides right off. In other words: if you release a single, EP or album, it behooves you to PROMOTE IT PROPERLY!!

175

One perk of being a successful movie star was making records in-between movies. Getting Rick James to produce *Party All The Time*, Eddie had thoughts of being taken more seriously on his music releases. He followed that hit up with a ballad: the title track *How Could It Be* was produced by Aquil Fudge. As part of their routine, comics often mimicked singers—with that said, it was already a given that Eddie's rendition of singers like James Brown and Michael Jackson prepared him for this moment. And like Eddie, my lifelong love of music prepared me to work for a major record label.

The year 1987 was most interesting for me because I finally graduated from Georgia State University that year; more importantly, I was offered a full-time job at CBS Records as an Account Service Representative or street name, *merchandiser*. Since I had been doing parts of this job for a few years as a College Rep, I already considered myself trained to perform in this position. I didn't know it at the time, but a year later I would marry another CBS Records employee; she worked in the sales office at our manufacturing plant in Carrollton, Georgia. There's more commentary located elsewhere in this book series (by the story's end we broke up, the industry imploded, and the plant closed down). But when I was working for CBS Records before all the drama, I often got passes to movie screenings that Columbia or Epic released accompanying soundtracks to. During my courtship, I scooped up some passes to see Eddie Murphy's *Raw*, his 1987 stand-up comedy offering. Eddie filmed it at New York's Felt Forum, located in the Madison Square Garden entertainment complex. I figured if my girl could make it through the first thirty minutes of Eddie's laugh-inducing antics, she'd be able to handle mine; boy was I wrong!

Eddie Murphy's *Raw* was directed by Robert Townsend, who had his hands in plenty of projects around this time—as a home video, this release became an instant hit. We now have 'raw' data coming in from our street operatives about Eddie's use of the "F" word: our *word-counters* lost track after 200 times, while the critics fell off after 210… unconfirmed reports have it at 223. Profanitively speaking, by this point Eddie had broken the film industry's record for most uses of the word. In layman's terms, this means *Raw* "out-F'd" *Scarface*, the previous record holder. It would be three years before Eddie's title was shattered: the new record breaker was 1990's *Goodfellas*—ain't that a b@#$%!

176

By 1989, Eddie Murphy had already implanted his funny bone into films like *Beverly Hills Cop I & II*, *48 Hrs.*, *Trading Places*, *The Golden Child*, *Best Defense*, *Harlem Nights* and *Coming to America*, but it was four years since his last album release. Eddie decided that it was once again time to put out a music album and his second one, *So Happy*, was it. He now had two comedy albums and two music albums; this record featured production by Murphy, along with a pre-Mariah Carey Walter Afanasieff. There was also Cameo's Larry Blackmon, Chic's Nile Rodgers and Narada Michael Walden, who had success with Whitney Houston through assorted music releases... like *The Bodyguard* soundtrack. Keeping humor in his new project, Eddie Murphy's first single was *Put Your Mouth On Me*—it made it to #2 on the R&B charts, while *Till the Money's Gone* made it to #75; each song was produced by an old favorite from the 70s, Narada Michael Walden.

When I was discussing Eddie Murphy's *Delirious* release earlier, I couldn't help thinking of a group that toured with him after his blockbuster 1982 movie, *48 Hrs.* The Bus Boys were also featured in this film. You know how the last song in a movie is the one you remember best? *The Boys Are Back In Town* was the song that ran with the closing credits of *48 Hrs.* The Bus Boys hit the road with Eddie on his *Delirious* standup comedy tour, and were in an HBO special as well. With perfect timing, they were the musical guests on a January 1983 episode of *Saturday Night Live*, hosted by none other than Eddie Murphy. The Bus Boys are a great example of what a Rock-n-Roll Boogie Woogie bar band sounds like—to me, they're reminiscent of Jake and Elwood's band, *The Blues Brothers*. That said, let's open the lens...

Formed in the late 70s, The Bus Boys rolled out of Los Angeles across the superhighways of mainstream America. With their appearance in *48 Hrs.* and *Delirious* tour with Eddie Murphy, The Bus Boys segued into their next pit stop, 1984's *Ghostbusters* film soundtrack; it was nominated for a Grammy. Releasing music on Clive Davis' Arista Records, their 1988 album featured the track *Never Giving Up*. Making sure he was prominently placed in the chorus, we find one Eddie Murphy, now a certified SAC (Singer-Actor-Comedian). Murphy also made an appearance in the accompanying music video—was this payback for Eddie's earlier help? Was Eddie's ego on the loose? Or was Eddie just being Eddie? Someone said we should look at Sean "P. Diddy" Combs for answers.

177

No strangers to life on the road, The Bus Boys might have changed members from time to time, but they never lost the sound that attracted fans from all over. Throughout the 80s and 90s, they played in concerts with top acts like Linda Ronstadt, Brian Setzer and The Stray Cats and ZZ Top. The lens opened even wider for them on TV shows like *American Bandstand*, *Don Kirshner's Rock Concert* and *Soul Train*. By 2000, a new album featured re-worked versions of their songs from *48 Hrs.*, now almost 20 years old.

Getting a good run from media exposure, The Bus Boys generated publishing revenue by having their music played in TV Sports programs. Among them were the NBA and Fox Sports Network's theme music for Major League Baseball, plus some music for the NFL. By 2005, the band adopted a new name, *Brian O'Neal and The Bus Boys*, before they performed for the *Capital One Bowl* on New Year's Day. Making a digital splash in 2006, a new album called *Sex, Love and Rock & Roll* was released for download—the CD version wasn't planned for release until a year later. With a documentary film in the works, the group kept the wheels spinning through good and bad times.

FINANCIALIZING

Eddie Murphy and The Bus Boys successfully navigated between television, film and music. During the process, their music generated lots of radio and club airplay, with huge ticket sales at the box office. Please do a search online for more info on these acts; in the meantime, here comes a financial breakdown of the types of numbers that Hollywood films, particularly Eddie Murphy films, can generate. Just to give you a rough idea of what Eddie's taking home to the mansion, his salary for *Tower Heist* as listed in the Hollywood Reporter on 11/18/2011 was a mere $7,500,000…

Year	Movie	Role	1st weekend	US Gross	Worldwide Gross
2012	A Thousand Words	Jack McCall	$6,176,280	$16,597,840	$16,597,840
2011	Beverly Hills Cop IV	Axel Foley (No additional data)	(N.A.)	(N.A.)	(N.A.)
2011	Tower Heist	Slide	$24,025,190	$78,046,570	$148,746,570
2010	Shrek Forever After	Donkey (Voice)	$70,838,207	$238,736,787	$752,600,867
2009	The Incredible Shrinking Man	(N.A.)	(N.A.)	(N.A.)	(N.A.)
2009	Imagine That	Evan Danielson	$5,503,519	$16,123,323	$16,123,323
2008	Meet Dave	Dave	$5,251,918	$11,803,254	$50,648,806
2007	Shrek the Third	Donkey (Voice)	$121,629,270	$322,719,944	$798,958,162
2007	Norbit	Norbit/Rasputia/ Mr. Wong	$34,195,434	$95,673,607	$158,973,607
2006	Dreamgirls	James 'Thunder' Early	$378,950	$103,365,956	$154,965,956
2004	Shrek 2	Donkey (Voice)	$108,037,878	$441,226,247	$919,838,758
2003	The Haunted Mansion	Jim Evers	$24,278,410	$75,817,994	$155,750,628
2003	Daddy Day Care	Charlie Hinton	$27,623,580	$104,148,781	$164,285,587
2002	I Spy	Kelly Robinson	$12,752,803	$33,561,137	$60,279,822
2002	The Adventures of Pluto Nash	Pluto Nash	$2,182,900	$4,411,102	$7,094,995
2002	Showtime	Trey	$15,011,430	$37,948,765	$78,948,765
2001	Doctor Dolittle 2	Dr. John Dolittle	$25,037,039	$112,950,721	$176,101,721
2001	Shrek	The Donkey (Voice)	$42,347,760	$267,655,011	$484,399,218

Year	Movie	Role	1st weekend	US Gross	Worldwide Gross
2000	Nutty Professor II: The Klumps	Sherman Klump/ Buddy Love/Mama Klump/Papa Klump	$42,518,830	$123,307,945	$166,307,945
1999	Bowfinger	Kit Ramsey	$18,062,550	$66,458,769	$98,699,769
1999	Life	Ray	$20,414,775	$64,062,587	$73,521,587
1998	Holy Man	G	$5,106,919	$12,069,719	$12,069,719
1998	Doctor Dolittle	Dr. John Dolittle	$29,014,324	$144,156,605	$294,156,605
1998	Mulan	Mushu (voice) (Voice)	$22,745,143	$120,620,254	$303,500,000
1997	Metro	Scott Roper	$11,411,107	$32,017,895	$32,017,895
1996	The Nutty Professor	Sherman Klump/Buddy Love/Lance Perkins/Papa Klump	$25,411,725	$128,814,019	$273,814,019
1995	Vampire in Brooklyn	Maximillian/Preacher Pauly/Guido	$7,045,379	$19,637,147	$19,637,147
1994	Beverly Hills Cop III	Axel Foley	$15,276,224	$42,586,861	$119,180,938
1992	The Distinguished Gentleman	Thomas Jefferson Johnson	$10,611,040	$46,434,570	$46,434,570
1992	Boomerang	Marcus	$13,640,706	$70,052,444	$131,052,444
1990	Another 48 Hrs.	Reggie Hammond	$19,470,596	$80,818,974	$153,518,974

Year	Movie	Role	1st weekend	US Gross	Worldwide Gross
1989	Harlem Nights	Quick	$16,096,808	$60,857,262	$95,857,262
1988	Coming to America	Clarence/Prince Akeem/Randy Watson/Saul	$21,404,420	$128,152,301	$288,800,000
1987	Eddie Murphy Raw	Himself	$9,077,324	$50,504,655	$50,504,655
1987	Beverly Hills Cop II	Axel Foley	$26,348,555	$153,665,036	$276,665,036
1986	The Golden Child	Chandler Jarrell	$11,549,711	$79,817,937	$79,817,937
1984	Beverly Hills Cop	Axel Foley	$15,214,805	$234,760,478	$316,300,000
1984	Best Defense	Lieutenant T.M. Landry	$7,872,297	$19,265,302	$19,265,302
1983	Trading Places	Billy Ray Valentine	$7,348,200	$90,400,000	$90,400,000
1983	Eddie Murphy Delirious	Himself	(N.A.)	(N.A.)	(N.A.)
1982	48 Hrs.	Reggie Hammond	$4,369,868	$75,936,265	$75,936,265
		Total Grosses		$3,805,184,064	$7,161,772,694
		Average Gross		$100,136,423	
	Average Opening Weekend		$23,296,891		

Source: *Nash Information Services, LLC*, © *1997-2012*

Record labels might be known for distributing records and net royalty payments, but television and motion pictures are also two entities I consider as formidable instruments that help generate publishing income too: just ask Eddie Murphy—he knows! Songwriters can develop television and motion picture royalty revenue through *synchronization rights*, which enable writers and publishers to realize payment options from songs they own copyrights to. There will be more on publishing as you make your way through this book series.

In summation, the revenue generated by comedians could be quite staggering, as Moms Mabley, Slappy White, the Murphy brothers and the chart above reveals. While music artists generate a bulk of sales for record labels, comedians clearly contribute more than just jokes to the big picture, too. And because many comedians wrote their own material, they happily partook in lucrative sales, publishing and touring income. We will now keep it moving as the guitar strums to the beat, but while you're busy cracking up to the comical pun of your favorite jokester, remember there's also a $ERIOU$ side to the Funny Farm, in the music *biz*.

-8-
GUITAR-HEAD GIVES
AN INSIDE VIEW

I'd like to thank my Head of Agent Operations, good friend and modern guitar 'afficianado' *Slick* Nick Pinkerton for unearthing classified data on a musician named *Irving Lee Dorsey*. Like me, Nick was an old-school music agent and a heavy user of technology in regards to his music experience—he went everywhere with his personal music player. It was configured to play music *and* receive transmissions from Sirius satellite radio: now that's what I call taking your music seriously. As a special treat, Team MKM's Super Agent Nick P. will jump in and share some classified info he disclosed to me, just before a major first for him—the birth of his beautiful baby girl… and now he has two!

Thanks, L.A.—between my growing family and a guest spot in your informational warehouse of music *biz* data, allow me to start off by saying, *these are special times*. To kick things off and lighten the load, Irving Lee Dorsey shaved off his first name to go public, then went on to become an important component in music's evolution during the 60s and 70s. Lee Dorsey's legend started with songs that were also covered or re-made by artists like Petula Clark. Her "Ya Ya Twist" in 1962 was a French version of Dorsey's popular "Ya Ya," which got revived in the process. I'll have more to mention about that song in a minute, but here's some little-known information I pulled from my "Slick Nick Pink" files to share: the successful Techno-Pop group *Devo* released their version of "Working In The Coal Mine" to welcoming fans, and the *Beastie Boys* made a connection with Dorsey through a reference in the song "Sure Shot" — "*Everything I do is funky like Lee Dorsey*." From this short list of multi-genre-ational acts, you should get a good sense of Dorsey's appeal to the music industry.

Similar to several musicians discussed earlier by L.A., Lee Dorsey was born in New Orleans, Louisiana and later moved to Portland, Oregon where he served in the Navy. With his "eye on the prize," Dorsey then focused on a boxing career: he was a successful light-heavyweight fighter around the early 50s and they called him "Kid Chocolate." FAST

FORWARD to the early 1960s: Dorsey's career aimlessly threw blank punches, until he jabbed songwriter-producer Allen Toussaint—this eventually led to Lee getting signed to the Fury record label. Inspired by a group of children chanting nursery rhymes, the song "Ya Ya" sparked Lee Dorsey's ascent to stardom; in 1961 it rocketed to #7 on the Billboard Hot 100. Unfortunately, after other songs failed to produce meaningful fruits for Fury, the label folded and Dorsey returned to punching the clock at a car repair business he wisely started years earlier.

Allen Toussaint later emerged on the Amy label and began his work with Dorsey again. During the mid to late 60s, Dorsey landed seven songs onto the Hot 100, with the most successful one being 1966's *Working In The Coal Mine*. And featured in the musical arrangement was the classic, "All-American" sound of the electric guitar. Although this is still one of my favorite guitar songs, the tune became Lee's final Top Ten hit. By 1970, Dorsey and Toussaint collaborated on an album called *Yes We Can*. The title song of this album became Dorsey's concluding stamp on Billboard's Pop Singles chart. Incidentally, this anthem later became a big hit for the Pointer Sisters, re-titled *Yes We Can Can*.

During the final stages of Lee Dorsey's career, he remained active by appearing on an album with New Jersey's Southside Johnny and the Asbury Jukes. This led to several more recordings with ABC Records around the late 1970s. Scanning that decade, we see the state of New Jersey yielded another famous music icon: longtime Columbia Records act *Bruce Springsteen*, who L.A. Jackson promoted years later at CBS/Sony, the distributor of Columbia. Springsteen, codename *The Boss*, burst onto the music scene from a nearby area—Asbury Park. Another Asbury Park connection, codename *Hurricane*, is also a part of L.A. Jackson's inner circle at the Georgia Music Industry Association (www.gmia.org). Guitar virtuoso Roger "Hurricane" Wilson sits on the board with L.A., but more importantly, he plays a *mean* Blues guitar—check out his CD with Willie "Big Eyes" Smith for a taste of history (www.hurricanewilson.com). If anyone knows the stormy story of Blues, that'd be the Hurricane!

Hurricane Wilson, Southside Johnny and Bruce Springsteen each enjoyed a nominal amount of success from the 70s moving forward. Asbury Park would later become known as the home of New Jersey's *Music Hall of Fame,* a place where I'm sure Lee Dorsey has some allocated space. By 1980, Dorsey was in his mid-50s, opening up shows for popular British Punk Rockers like the Clash. As a sad song played in the background, Lee Dorsey contracted emphysema and in 1986, succumbed to the illness in his hometown of New Orleans at the age of 61. There's good news though—all kinds of content on him exists in bookstores, libraries and online.

Although our following artist didn't make it past his twenties, Lee Dorsey survived the often-turbulent highs and lows of the music industry for over a quarter century; personally, I'll always remember him for lots of influential contributions. Before I head out, let me just say his style was covered by too few but enjoyed by many; myself included. Lee Dorsey's music generated lots of radio airplay and publishing income from acts that remade his tunes. As L.A. mentioned earlier, the standard formula of accumulating radio airplay in multiple markets meant record, tape and CD sales, plus tour and merchandising income.

When this happens, publishing revenue is also generated for the copyright owner or owners. I'm not an expert, but there's a good bet royalty rates have been updated to address online airplay and purchasing, which continues growing. L.A. recently told me about something called "360 Deals," so I'm sure he'll have more to say about that elsewhere in his book series. Allow me to reveal one more dose of ubiquitous music info to you intellect-seeking readers. See if you can digest what I call *Agent Slick Nick's Superior Intellect Pop Quiz*!

QUIZ QUESTION: Robert Johnson, Brian Jones (Rolling Stones), Jimi Hendrix, Janis Joplin, Jim Morrison (The Doors), Kurt Cobain (Nirvana) and Amy Winehouse are all unique members of *The 27 Club*. Can you guess why, and what pocket-sized item has supposedly been found in their possession after some of them died? The answer's coming up after we review some intelligence on arguably one of the best-known electric guitarists in history, and a "message from our sponsors." Happy reading— it's time to have tea with my two little angels, then it's off to perform a multi-platform, "psycho-deployment" from the data center!

I'd like to thank my old pal, Agent "Slick" Nick Pinkerton for file-sharing his Superior Intellect (SI) with us—"see you on the other side." Now without further delay, here's some interesting music history notes on an all-time favorite of ours. Although my old Sony Music boss spelled his first name the same way as our next artist, *starkly speaking* I never saw him play guitar like this guy. Allow me to introduce the introverted-yet-extroverted yet often misunderstood guitar virtuoso known throughout the "galactic guitarsphere" by his first name, last name, or both.

GUITAR CRUNCHING 101: with Jimi Hendrix

While some people may know much of the history behind guitar legend Jimi Hendrix, many are not aware that he spent some lean times in various cities before moving on to fame and fortune in Seattle, Washington. When he first returned stateside from serving in the Army in the early 60s, Jimi lived in Clarksville, Tennessee. While waiting for his Army pal and bass player Billy Cox, Jimi did small gigs around town. Billy and Jimi had previously played music on the base and around Clarksville in a group called *The Casuals*—they later changed the name to *The King Casuals*.

Billy and Jimi played in other bands but were never able to "stack the dough" they desired, so it wasn't uncommon for them to be seen "grinding on their knuckles" from time to time. Opening the lens wider for full expoure, in 1962 Jimi entered a talent contest at New York's legendary Apollo Theater: he won a whopping *$25.00*. After a 'spending spree' that must have lasted a few weeks, Jimi headed back to Clarksville, literally starving for action … and some food. Reforming his old group The King Casuals, he continued performing wherever he could, for whatever the gig paid. By late '62 Jimi headed west to Vancouver, where he stayed with his grandmother and joined an R&B group called *Bobbie Taylor and the Vancouvers*.

> **FUNNY FACT**: From Cheech & Chong fame, Tommy Chong's name came up as a singer in *Bobbie Taylor and the Vancouvers*—there are many comedians who develop a knack for being good singers too so for extra credit, round up a few friends and find out who some of them are!

By 1963, Jimi found himself in the heart of Bluesville: Mississippi. He got his first taste of the *Chitlin' Circuit* as a band member playing with Slim Harpo and Tommy Tucker. Jimi went on to play with a wide variety of groups like *Bob Fisher and the Barnesvilles, The Imperials, Ironing Board Sam, Nappy Brown, The Marvelettes,* Curtis Mayfield's group *The Impressions,* and *The Isley Brothers*. Around this time, Jimi embarked on a tour that took him through Southern venues for the following two years. The Black patrons of these venues were known to be hard on performers who failed to impress them.

Sarcastically speaking, the agency that booked acts in these venues was the *Theater Owners Booking Association*, but their TOBA acronym was twisted around to form "Tough On Black Asses." Many Black performers looked at the venues as proving grounds before breaking big: it enabled them to hone their skills, as well as eat and sleep. One last nugget—the Southern venues Jimi Hendrix, Sam Cooke, Jackie Wilson and a whole grid of other Black musicians played in became places where their performance capabilities got tuned up, in preparation for the big time.

Now in supercharged mode, Jimi Hendrix quickly outgrew the Chitlin' Circuit... and taking orders from folks like bandleaders and booking agents. That's pretty much the same attitude his Army superiors saw; before kicking him out of the 101st Airborne Division in 1962 at age 19. By 1964, the frustrated guitarist moved to Harlem and regrouped. As he got familiar with the area club scene, Jimi started playing in groups. Picking up new friends—and girlfriends, he was supplied with food, shelter and a pair of backup singers called the *Ghetto Fighters*. Within a month of living in New York, Jimi entered the Apollo Theater amateur contest that won him the whopping $25 first prize. And then in the blink of an eye, he landed a new gig: playing guitar for *The Isley Brothers*.

As 1964 rolled by, Jimi Hendrix prepared to get unleashed in a new environment—the recording studio. He recorded and toured with The Isleys, then quit to work in Nashville with tour MC George Odell, codename *Gorgeous George*. I was fortunate to work with George back in the 80s. This was when acts like Isley Jasper Isley and James Brown made pit stops in Atlanta, and moving forward, I still ran into him from time to time. Speaking of codenames, Jimi increased his use of them and was going by the handle of *Maurice James*—he hooked up with Little Richard and learned to mimic the singer's voice with his guitar. Jimi toured all over with Little Richard, even recording with him in the studio. Working for Little Richard, Jimi performed in shows with the likes of Ike and Tina Turner; but the only problem was that Jimi didn't always take orders well. In 1965, Jimi left Little Richard and regrouped with The Isley Brothers.

In 1965, Jimi Hendrix hooked up with New York's *Curtis Knight and the Squires* due to being neighbors at Times Square's *Hotel America*. Hendrix recorded and performed with Knight for about eight months—by the fall of 1965, he was ready to take things to the next level. Besides Curtis Knight, Jimi Hendrix recorded and performed with King Curtis, Ray Sharpe, Lonnie Youngblood and Jimmy Norman. Along the way, many of Jimi's backing tracks and unused takes got overdubbed, chopped and spliced to make "new" recordings; even tracks that he wasn't a part of surfaced as Hendrix recordings. For a while, it seemed as if everyone had an unreleased track with Jimi on it—tragically speaking, throughout Jimi's career many people took advantage of him.

As the 60s rolled on, Jimi Hendrix went by codename *Jimmy James* and put together a band called *The Blue Flame*. Sources can't confirm whether he intended for the names to rhyme, but it sure did work out well for him. One day while playing around New York City, Hendrix met the girlfriend of Rolling Stones guitarist Keith Richards. Linda Keith helped provide freeway access by telling influential people like Andrew Long and Seymour Stein about Jimi. Eventually, bassist Chas Chandler of The Animals took a chance and "went in." He flew Jimi to London, signed a few contracts and changed *Jimmy* to *Jimi*. After pulling in fellow Brits Noel Redding and Mitch Mitchell, *The Jimi Hendrix Experience* was born.

Chas Chandler took Jimi around the circuit, introducing him to cool cats like Brian Auger (Oblivion Express), Eric Burdon (WAR), Pete Townshend (The Who) and Eric Clapton, who just formed Cream. After the Jimi Hendrix Experiencce was formed they did a whirlwind tour, beginning with a Johnny Hallyday show in France. From there, they jammed with Cream, hit hot clubs, and appeared on UK TV. As a result of hastily signing a bad three-year recording contract with businessman Ed Chaplin, Jimi was obligated to record an album not affiliated with *The Experience*; as a perk, Chaplin reeled in 2% of U.S. sales from Jimi's catalog. Incoming updates reveal the contract was disputed because after Jimi got popular, some old recordings with Curtis Knight were released as Jimi Hendrix recordings.

Strangely speaking, the contract Jimi signed remained in force, even after Jimi broke the relationship off and wound up getting a 1% royalty: young artists new to the game were and still are privy to getting scammed. These days, there are "360 degree" contracts, where an act gives up a piece of *all* income, no matter where it comes from. In 2007, Ed Chaplin's bubble burst after he failed to abide by the contract and pay Hendrix' estate court-ordered royalties—he was charged almost a million bucks. Getting back to Jimi in late '66, word had spread across London to locals like The Beatles, Jeff Beck, Brian Jones and The Who. Jimi signed on with Track Records—after songs like *Hey Joe* and *Stone Free*, 1967's *Purple Haze* and *The Wind Cries Mary* put him in the UK's Top 10.

HAZEY FACT: Jimi Hendrix' classic *Purple Haze* is said to have been conceptualized through a chemical induced dream—he was strolling underwater, surrounded by hazy shades of purple, codename *Purpuration H. Purple Haze* may have gotten lost in the sauce by peaking at #65 on the U.S. charts, but this second hit for him was later found lodged in the Top 3 position on the UK charts.

As Jimi Hendrix became more popular across Australia, Europe, Japan and New Zealand, America for the most part, remained standoffish. This would change as he continued his offensive by doing cover versions of songs by Howlin' Wolf and B.B. King. When the Jimi Hendrix Experience released *Are You Experienced* in 1967, it shot to the top of the UK charts; but was prevented from hitting #1 by The Beatles' *Sgt. Pepper's Lonely Hearts Club Band*. Recorded on four tracks, *Are You Experienced* showed what could be achieved on a guitar by using fuzz pedals and other effects. Jimi's stage presence now covered attention-grabbing antics, like setting guitars on fire. One of these guitars was found and restored by one Frank Zappa. It was Frank who turned Jimi on to "the joy of wah-wah" after meeting him in July of 1967; Zappa's band *Mothers of Invention* happened to be playing in New York City at the time.

When Jimi Hendrix ran into Frank Zappa and saw Frank's new wah-wah pedal, he ran out and got one to use in future recordings and shows—then started smashing guitars onstage. Frank used Jimi's restored guitar to record a 1971 album called *Zoot Allures*. Twenty years later in the 90s, Zappa's son Dweezil inherited the legendary instrument. Rewinding the tape, we see a now-popular Jimi Hendrix ramping up for a frontal assault on the U.S. music scene; but he wasn't finished with the British yet. Hendrix played Beatles tunes in Beatles territory and the crowd loved it—so did Sir Paul McCartney. (Between McCartney being a *Beatle* and a *Sir*, this expressive songwrting bassist soared with *Wings*!)

In 1967, Jimi Hendrix appeared on Dutch TV and toured Stockholm, Sweden. He struck up a relationship that produced a son who adopted his father's first name and his mother's last name: James Daniel Sundquist. Unable to settle down, Jimi kept his show going on the road and in recording studios. Jimi had become a hot item in Europe, but was still working on finalizing his mainstream access in America because his first single *Hey Joe* didn't even make it to the Billboard charts. Since Paul McCartney was already a fan, he suggested to the powers that be for Jimi and his group to perform at the Monterey International Jazz Festival. An event like this drew a large crowd and would be 'followed in full scale' by the media. The exposure would put Jimi at front-and-center, plus a film was also in the works: it would immortalize Jimi Hendrix burning and then destroying his six-string onstage.

It was occasionally mentioned during this book that the late 60s were a period of astronomic change—politically as well as musically—in America. With issues like the Civil Rights Movement, the Watts riots, Vietnam War, the rise of the Black Panthers and several major assassinations, Jimi decided to regroup. He then returned with an all-Black band, featuring old pal Billy Cox on bass and Buddy Miles on drums. They recorded four live shows performed over the course of two days and used the material for a new album called *Band of Gypsys*. It became the only live album officially produced and released by Jimi Hendrix; his Monterey and Woodstock performances were released in bits and pieces.

Jimi Hendrix often played songs by greats like Howlin' Wolf, B.B. King and Bob Dylan, plus he collaborated with Stephen Stills and Buddy Miles. Performing at places like Golden Gate Park and the Whiskey A Go-Go, Jimi opened up for The Monkees, who also happened to be fans. But their fans weren't ready for Hendrix yet, so he hopped off the tour. Nevertheless, he still gained enough exposure after leaving to keep the momentum at full throttle. Unfortunately, Jimi grew tired of all the attention fans gave to his stage antics and his more popular songs, when newer ones he had written deserved to be noticed as well. The second Jimi Hendrix Expereince release became the band's first full-stereo album—it had left/right panning and sound effects, picking up where the previous album left off. Using tricks like detuning his guitar from E to E flat with that new wah-wah pedal, Hendrix was finally becoming a hot ticket in the U.S. market. Within the live arena, Jimi jammed onstage with friends like B.B. King and The Doors' Jim Morrison.

A third release was issued in 1968, a double-album called *Electric Ladyland*. Recorded at the Record Plant in New York with engineers Eddie Kramer and Gary Kellgreen, this was a departure from his earlier work. While producer Chas Chandler started off working with Jimi around the mid-60s, he grew agitated by Jimi's need to be perfect now; along with new characters Jimi permitted to hang out in the recording studio. Chas decided to terminate his association with Hendrix, causing a huge impact on Jimi's artistic direction. Soon, Jimi was playing mix and match with musicians, instruments and sounds used in the making of his new album. As we can imagine, The Jimi Hendrix Experience performed all over Europe. For 1968, Jimi and his group did another Swedish tour, but things took a turn for the worst—after a drunken rampage, he tore up a hotel room, injured his hand, got arrested and paid a hefty fine.

Jimi invested in a new venture—buying Greenwich Village's *Generation Club*. But instead of reopening the club, he decided to make it a recording studio. Ironically, Jimi spent two and half months cutting tracks at the studio as final phases of construction was completed; by 1970, his *Electric Lady Studios* was open for business. This custom-made studio was designed to provide a comfortable, professional environment to record at. To ensure that sessions remained 'on track,' engineer Eddie Kramer was brought in; then he issued a ban on drug use during sessions. After the official grand opening party of Jimi's recording studio, he and Billy Cox left for London to join up with Mitch Mitchell for a show at the Isle of Wight Festival. They kicked off a European tour, but Jimi's mind was still on recording in his new studio.

Jimi Hendrix later headed back to London to rejoin Kathy Etchingham who he was dating, and a year went by before his return to America. A European tour followed and shortly thereafter bassist Noel Redding started his own band, *Fat Mattress*. With this vacancy, Jimi wound up playing bass on new tracks for his upcoming album, and then brought in old friend Billy Cox. Yet, it was plain to see bumpy roads ahead for the band. The final Experience show took place in 1969 at Denver's Mile High Stadium but deterently speaking, police fired tear gas into the audience as the band played *Voodoo Chile*. Jimi and his band barely made it out alive; the following day, Noel Redding officially quit The Jimi Hendrix Experience. Later in 1969, Jimi took a short sabbatical in upstate New York at the suggestion of manager Michael Jeffery, who lived nearby in Woodstock. Eventually, Jimi's drummer Mitch Mitchell began drifting away—this was seen through instances like Jimi's first American TV appearance with Dick Cavett, where Jimi was backed by Cavett's studio orchestra. Later, Jimi and bassman Billy Cox made it to *The Tonight Show*—but Mitch Mitchell was absent once again.

A VIP list of Rock groups got pulled out for the Woodstock Music Festival, scheduled to kickoff in upstate New York from August 15-18, 1969. Easily making the list, Jimi decided to augment his sound by adding a rhythm guitarist and conga players. They rehearsed for almost two weeks, and then it was show time. Unfortunately, Jimi and his band were already up for several days and sleep-deprived, but that didn't stop them from performing. What really slowed them down however, was Jimi's apprehension of large crowds—he heard this one was a record-breaker. To ensure his appearance, promoters shelled out $30,000; this was more than they paid any other act on the bill.

Even though Hendrix was scheduled to go on Sunday at midnight, he decided to close the show—a big mistake. Due to constant rain causing considerable delays, he didn't take the stage until 8:30 Monday morning. While the peak audience had a reported 400,000 people, by Monday morning the number dropped to a meager 30,000-40,000. To add, he abruptly changed the band's name to *Gypsy Sun and Rainbows*, aka *Band of Gypsies*—they played for a record two hours. For fans still in attendance, watching Hendrix play songs like *The Star Spangled Banner*, *Purple Haze* and *Hey Joe* became THE defining moments of 1969.

Many of the remaining fans just caught a snapshot of Hendrix and left during his set. After three days of nonstop partying, festival attendees were starving; and surrounded by mud. Finally completing his set, Jimi was so exhausted that he collapsed. In the post-Woodstock era, Hendrix and his band played two more times, in Harlem and at Greenwich Village. Unfortunately, many people had already left the Harlem show when he arrived, plus his guitar was stolen—strangely enough, it was later returned. After the Greenwich Village show, Jimi and the band hit the studio a few times, then disbanded.

By 1970, Jimi was preparing for a new Experience tour, while the Band of Gypsies did a Madison Square Garden Vietnam-related benefit concert. Like at Woodstock he took the stage late, this time at 3 a.m. After playing just one song, he snapped back at a fan and played a second tune before eventually exiting the stage. A number of speculations followed about the spectacle but at the end of the day, no one could tell what happened that night. Although there were plans to reunite the original members of the Jimi Henrix Experience, Jimi was still using Billy Cox on bass and not Noel Redding. This lineup became known as the *Cry of Love* band, although billing continued as the *Jimi Hendrix Experience*.

For the first part of 1970, Jimi Hendrix worked on his new album and did some shows with Billy Cox and Mitch Mitchell, ending up in Hawaii by August. His German show at the Fenmarn Festival on September 6, 1970 turned out to be his last big one. But the plot thickened: Billy Cox supposedly had a bad drug trip and quit the band, while Jimi landed back in London. He jammed with old friend Eric Burden and his group War; this performance was recorded using the latest technology of the time—a cassette. While bootleg recordings surfaced at random places, the cassette was not remastered until December of 2010.

Known for using drugs like LSD, amphetamines and heroin, Jimi Hendrix was said to get un-manageable when he was drunk; but it didn't slow down his ability to sleep with dozens of bedazzled women. On September 17, 1970, Jimi was hanging out at a late night party and left around 3 AM with his girlfriend, Monika Dannemann. At her place, he got a hold of some sleeping pills; while the average prescribed dose was one tablet, the guitarist supposedly took nine. Coupled with wine he was drinking, Hendrix is said to have died from asphyxiation—the bottom line is, he apparently choked in his sleep while throwing up. What a way to go—it was truly a sad day for the music world when Jimi Hendrix died.

After reading his biography *Hendrix*, I felt regret in learning Jimi was looked at by many folks as a free ride but like my mother often said, "no one knows it but those who feel it." (I hear a Bob Marley tune floating around here, too.) There are some who might argue that Jimi needed protection from the people around him, while others would say he needed protection from himself. Either way, Jimi's bright star was extinguished far too soon. Similar to super-heroes like Batman, Superman and Spiderman, I think Jimi's story is one that deserves an updated appearance on the silver screen, too. Although there was a 2000 depiction starring a great actor named Wood Harris, word on the streets hinted at an early 2012 production starring Outkast's Andre Benjamin, codename *Andre 3000*—however, a July 2012 *Rolling Stones* story bore bad news...

It was announced by Jimi's estate, *Experience Hendrix LLC* (run by Hendrix's sister Janie) that they've "made it known many times in the past that no such film, were it to include original music or copyrights created by Jimi Hendrix, can be undertaken without its full participation." This means the movie would not feature Jimi Henrix songs. Instead, it would use songs written by the Beatles, Muddy Waters, Elmore James, Curtis Knight and the Squires—but way down in the mix, experience tells me there was a money issue floating around somewhere. Since the first time I saw Andre 3000 pop up in Outkast back in the 90s, he was my personal pick hit to play the part of Jimi Hendrix. Maybe it's me but Andre's persona, from his looks to his talents—strikes a connecting chord that always made me think of one of the world's most misunderstood guitarists. For more information on Jimi Hendrix, you can strike up a few interesting chords about this Superhero Rock Star at places like www.jimihendrix.com.

Jimi Hendrix had unabashed raw talent and plenty of it, so that's one reason why he wound up staying in demand. But it took more than raw talent to get new music to the masses—it also took charisma, personality and money back then; and still does now! Coincidentally, there are relatively new public mediums whose timely arrivals came in comparable fashion to a developing superstar. Some would say these mediums could complement the raw potential, charisma and persona of great guitarists like Hendrix. The Internet is a big one, and *Global Positioning System* (GPS) navigation is another.

GPS is not entertainment in its purest form, yet our analysts report the emergence of this mobile-based technology is now poised to make as big an impact as any other broadcasted medium. Just check the dashboard of any new car coming out these days… and it's already in your cellphone. Better yet, ask anyone who seeks to avoid traffic! That's a little food for thought, so now let's ingest a quick data capsule and wash it all down with some cool, refreshing lemonade. It will all help to facilitate and capacitate the answer to Agent "Slick" Nick Pinkerton's earlier issued Superior Intellect Pop Quiz, plus we have a word from our sponsors: "This segment of our traveling road show was sponsored by the *Superior Intellect Society*—they proudly say, *come and get yours.*"

QUIZ ANSWER: Robert Johnson, Brian Jones, Jimi Hendrix, Janis Joplin, Jim Morrison and Kurt Cobain all died at age 27, and it's rumored that 4 of the 6 (Hendrix, Joplin, Morrison, and Cobain) had a white lighter with them at the time of their death, making white lighters "bad luck" in certain crowds. The media was drawn back to The 27 Club in 2011, seventeen years after Kurt Cobain's death—Amy Winehouse passed away at the age of 27. Although the singer mentioned her fear of dying at that age just three years earlier, it's unclear whether a white lighter was ever found in her possession.

Flipping the coin over, a popular refillable windproof lighter has always been the *Zippo*, and I remember some really cool metal-rod lighters that Epic Records made. These 'highly flammable' promotional items were used in a campaign to support singer Kipper Jones and his band Tease—back around the mid-80s, they had a hit called *Firestarter*. An old proverb goes, "persistence pays... for those who stay in the game" (I actually made it up, but it fit). However, that comment was made because I have to tip my hat to any artist from decades past who is still on the battlegrounds today. Kipper Jones still heats things up in the high-paced music game at his own pace, at his own production firm, *Young Legends Recordings*. He also does a stunning show with my other old buddy, keyboard wiz William Green—they blew folks away at a 2014 Centennial Olympic Park *Wednesday Wind Down* performance in Atlanta. Okay budding musicologists, while we contemplate "things that make you go *hmmm*," here's an unusual FAST *"Club 25"* FACT:

Aaliyah (August), Lisa "Left Eye" Lopes (April), James Brown (December) and Michael Jackson (June) all left us on the 25th day of the months they passed on to the realm of eternal music. Don't be surprised if the list has grown by the time you're reading this, and a special thanks go to my "TMH Hall of Famers" "Slick" Nick Pinkerton, Max the "International Mystery Man," Vic the "Ram," Sean "the Connoisseur," that "Beast" Rob McCarthy, Chris "Red Heat" Marcus, Mike "Doc" Berg, Brian "B-Funk" Smith, Mike "The Joker" Furedy and the rest of my old niche gang for providing that great trivia info!

Like Jimi Hendrix, multi-textured Psychedelic Rock was released by acts akin to Pink Floyd, The Grateful Dead and Black Sabbath, who became legendary figures to fans and aspiring artists across multiple continents. Musicians entered the game from all over, even down under. Heavy Metal groups like Australia's AC/DC, plus Britain's Led Zeppelin and U.S. issues from Aerosmith to KISS to Bruce Springsteen picked up cues and proceeded to mine more fertile areas of the industry. No matter where the music came from however, we can be sure that the center of attraction revolved around an electric lead or rhythm guitar, codename AUSS: *Amped Up Six String*. Now let's tune into a new frequency and pick up some pointers on how other players in the music game put their money where 'that big mouth' was.

BROADCASTING'S MOUTH-ALMIGHTY

Time stamp: the 1960s. Enter personality radio. It quickly became the norm on Top 40 radio stations, and spread throughout the industry. Back in the old days, there were a bunch of smooth talkers who schmoozed their way across the airwaves, into record label offices... and straight to the bank: but were bonafide *hustlers*—according to street terms. At Top 40 radio, tracks were shuffled around a list of regularly played songs. This list was called a *playlist*, and many stations had up to 40 songs on it, ergo the term *Top 40*. The format became a primary focus of major label promotion departments and their huge budgets. With additional complexities like unorthodox tactics, more innovative marketing approaches crept into the mix. Let's take a more in-depth look at some not-too-secret methods record companies used in figuring out the path to achieving corporate dominance and maximum airplay for their acts:

- Record labels made it commonplace for artists to ignore legal advice and sign their rights away on the dotted line; this became a classic catch-22 scenario many labels intrepidly took advantage of
- Radio promotions utilized advertising, t-shirts, parties, limousines, vacations and more. *Cross-collateralization* left openings for shady execs to put artists' money into anyone's wallets (including their own), spend tons of corporate cash, and charge it all back to the act
- This technique became a standard that was often enforced by record companies to keep the upper hand on their artists—entertainers always seemed to owe labels for incurred costs spent by labels on behalf of the artist, "for promotional purposes"

It takes a certain personality to be effective in the music *biz*, because this mindset incorporates the mental capacity to think like a record label, manager, producer, and entertainer. It's a methodology that tends to steer artists toward the straightest path for getting airplay, shows, and *paid*—hungry vocalists, producers and musicians tuned in, with tight wallets. Of course, quite a few musicians ended up abandoning their dreams of stardom, if "making it" didn't happen timely enough. Many acts traded in illustrious hopes for other careers, rather than face retirement by fading out of the music *biz "po,' broke and lonely"* (sounds like the name of an Epic Records group I once promoted). *Cross-collateralization* can be a pretty slick trick, but here's some free advice: it's always wise for folks who sign recording contracts to question all expenditures, in order to instill a conservative mindset for managing *how* their money is spent.

ROUND AND ROUND WE GO

For the right price, some records on radio playlists got more airplay than others, because a new way of doing business behind the scenes soon emerged; this new protocol employed the *DJ*, or *Disc Jockey*. DJs acquired the power to pick and play records they—and sometimes radio station personnel, managers, promoters, or record labels—felt could keep listeners calling in to request and listen to on the radio. If the notes all lined up, a listener base would be formed around songs the DJ picked as "hit-bound." And the listeners would keep on tuning in to *his* show.

After television got more traction in the market, radio stations tried to keep up. Stations that played all forms of Rock, R&B, Jazz, Country, Oldies, Gospel and more had personality jocks expounding over the airwaves. Although early DJs were obligated to recite scripted material from monologues, the bulk of their shows consisted of improvised subject matter that required their creative input. In-between monologues, DJs played music by established performers as well as unknown artists with potential mass appeal.

This new radio format turned virtual unknowns into overnight sensations, as influential DJs transformed into A&R or *artist & repertoire* representatives. Alan Freed was one of these guys, and record companies loved him if he played their records. This also means he was probably loathed by those who failed to attract his ear (or wallet) to their music and/or money. Freed is regarded as the first radio DJ to openly admit he took payola money during the early days of the Rock era. Freed admitted he even got undeserving credit as a songwriter on some tracks, in exchange for playing music of certain acts over the air. Many people in the music industry used this tactic to maximize their income in *the entertainment biz*—a shady industry that started off with plenty of loopholes to slip through, walls to scale, and in-your-face deception.

March 21st, 1952, Cleveland, Ohio: That's said to be the exact date and place where Alan Freed's *Moondog Coronation Ball* took place... and where *Rock-n-Roll* was officially born. As a key proponent of the entity, Freed also happens to be the first person inducted into the *Rock-n-Roll Hall of Fame*. Alan Freed moved his show from Cleveland to New York in 1954 and added live performances to the agenda. He's credited with delivering real good music to the masses by helping to launch the careers of Chuck Berry, Buddy Holly, Little Richard and others. Across the 'radio tracks,' men like *Blues Boy* B.B. King, Jack L. Cooper and Jack *The Rapper* Gibson marked their presence as the first Black radio representatives from the urban and rural sectors. By the mid-50s, the market had exploded by broadcasting music like R&B, Jazz, Swing, Big Band and Gospel. These genres became the staple of the music menu that stateside Blacks, and many other cultures consumed.

Before this time, a part of America's music culture was subdued, characterized by what later became known as Adult Contemporary (call it "AC"), Easy Listening and Middle of the Road releases by Paul Anka, Nat "King" Cole, Sammy Davis Jr., Dean Martin, Frank Sinatra and others. Many of these artists brought excitement to the stage, both during and after the war. And then they brought it to Vegas, the new post-war playground of entertainment's movers and shakers. While some artists' careers thrived in Vegas-styled live performances, others double-dipped their fingers in Hollywood's film and television pie, too.

Around then the world of Jazz (including Swing, Bebop and Big Band), carved a niche and had its own self-contained fan base. Collaborations between acts like Frank Sinatra and Count Basie ensured more crossover appeal, but signs of Rock's imminent arrival hovered. Dedicated fans of Adult Contemporary, Easy Listening and Middle-of-the Road sensed Rock-n-Roll's oncoming onslaught and complained it reared an ugly head. Rock-n-Roll subsequently arrived with a bang that drowned out the sweet, innocent sounds of Rosemary Clooney, Pat Boone, Perry Como, Mitch Miller, The Ray Conniff Singers and Lawrence Welk. Opponents of Rock's rebellious sound said "this music will deliver our youth to the depths of Hell." But it worsened for the opposition when they realized that many of Rock-n Roll's ringleaders were Disc Jockeys. So the motto of the story goes: *You can't stop a movement if it pushes with power, and you can't stop the music if a DJ plays it every hour!*

Once a hot record got in the DJ's hands, an uncontrollable music movement tended to 'erupt and engulf' the listening audience. Prior to the 50s, no movement made an impact upon listeners like the one that came during the Rock-n-Roll/R&B transition. What it sparked was the interest of a new, youthful audience that wanted to turn the music up LOUD and DANCE. Musicians that played Rock and R&B helped facilitate that objective perfectly. Many people are aware of New Orleans musician Fats Domino and his contributions to the worlds of Boogie Woogie, Piano Blues, R&B and Rock-n-Roll. But not many know about all the musicians, songwriters, arrangers, producers, studios… and a special writing partner who helped keep the wind blowing under those wide wings. Let's get an INSIDE VIEW of *Dave Bartholomew*.

A #1 Billboard chart topper for Fats Domino was *Ain't That A Shame*, and it wouldn't be stretching things to say that this song is a confirmed "Golden Oldie." While Fats Domino remained out front, his 'silent partner' Dave Bartholomew turned out not to be so silent at all. Dave Bartholomew was born in 1920 and by the 50s he became a top New Orleans arranger, composer and bandleader. This Jazz innovator was a prominent figure in New Orleans' music scene because as a composer-musician, he was a conduit that enabled a smooth transition between styles like Jump Blues and Big Band, to R&B and Rock-n-Roll.

Making a modest start on the tuba, Dave worked his way to the trumpet before moving into the fast lane. As big-boned artists like Chubby Checker and Fats Domino poured fuel into R&B music's gas tank, the dawn of Rock music was opening new lanes for riders who got on board. REWIND: Before tipping the scales of mid-50s Rock-n-Roll, Dave Bartholomew played a healthy balance of New Orleans Jazz, Dixieland, Big Band, Swing and Rhythm and Blues. By 1947, he was recording for the DeLuxe label under the guise of arranger/bandleader/talent scout. Among many musicians he worked with during his heyday are:

Frankie Ford	Terces LaBune	Tommy Ridgley
Samuel Kane	Smiley Lewis	Randy Quinson
Chris Kenner	Robert Parker	Larry Sands
Earl King		Shirley & Lee

Besides his classic hits with Fats Domino, Dave
produced a few other popular tunes:

Lawdy Miss Clawdy - Lloyd Price
Let the Good Times Roll - Shirley & Lee
I Hear You Knocking, One Night (Of Sin) - Smiley Lewis

The Imperial Records years brought successes like Fats Domino and over forty hits. One of his biggest records was a cover version of *Blueberry Hill*. The song was first published in 1940, with music written by Vincent Rose and lyrics by Al Lewis/Larry Stock. Many acts covered the song—it was recorded six times in 1940 alone. Dave Bartholomew got a piece of the action by doing musical arrangements for Fats Domino's version. They 'rode high on the hog' for a number of years but by the mid-60s, Bartholomew was moving between labels. Dave eventually established one and named it after his old neighborhood, *Broadmoor*.

In addition to previously mentioned acts Dave Bartholomew worked with, he wrote a number of songs that were so appealing, they were covered by other acts too. In the 50s, Gale Storm did his *I Hear You Knocking*; Dave Edmunds re-did it in the 70s. Pat Boone, Rick Nelson and even King Elvis covered Dave's songs. And get this one: Chuck Berry's only #1 Billboard hit was a modified cover version of Dave Bartholomew's now-famous *My Ding-a-ling*. All this activity kept the accomplishments of Bartholomew at a high pace—it's easy to see how he wound up being recognized in the *Louisiana Music Hall of Fame* and the *Songwriter's Hall of Fame*. Never failing to keep it moving, Dave Bartholomew could sometimes be found playing at the famous Preservation Hall, and you can still find tons of great information on him, online. The moral of the story boys and girls, ladies and gentlemen: behind every great act… are other great acts!

Here's another example of a great act that followed another great act by recording a cover song and turning it into a hit record. In doing so, he initiated a whole new way people danced. Hank Ballard and the Midnighters released *The Twist* in 1959, a year before Chubby Checker unleashed his version. Although Ballard's original did well, it was Checker's cover that hit #1 on the charts in 1960 and sparked the trend of dancing solo. In fact, *The Twist* spearheaded a complete revolution in how people interacted with music… and partners were no longer required for lone dancers to "work it out" on the dance floor. Over the course of the following year, this song twisted its way across the globe and made Chubby Checker an international star. *The Twist* blasted off to astronomic levels in 1961, after millions of people watched Checker perform it on *American Bandstand* (R.I.P., Dick Clark). Regarding a 50th anniversary celebration of *The Twist*, sources at sites like www.cbsnews.com and www.nola.com/music report how Chubby Checker saw his trend-setting song develop: "the dance popularized couples dancing apart to the beat of the music, a revolutionary idea that's now the norm." As for doing live shows after 50 years, "If you're looking for some guy who's all worn out," … "stay home."

At the 2010 celebration, Chubby Checker performed a free noontime concert that was held at his hometown Philadelphia's City Hall—the slim-n-trim 68-year-old sported a denim jacket with "skintight" jeans. Now codenamed *Slim The Twist Man*, Chubby Checker entertained the crowd with hits from Chuck Berry to Little Richard and The Beatles, plus he performed a few of his own dance-craze-starting hits like *The Fly*, *Pony Time* and *The Hucklebuck*. The latter spawned a once risqué dance with 'somewhat suggestive' hip thrusts. Performing it for the audience, Mr. Checker shook what his mama gave him, to the tee. Bringing dancing fans onstage with him, *the Twist Man* remarked:

"Back in the 60s, you couldn't do the hucklebuck because it was nasty," but times have changed—"It's 2010; everything's nasty, so we're going to do it." Coupled with 90-degree weather, we can best believe like Fats Waller said, "the joint was jumping." This was nostalgia at its best and for more great times, you can check out www.chubbychecker.com or maybe even have a New Orleans-styled experience at sites like www.jointsjumpin.com. While we're speaking of Fats Waller, let's get a closer look at this multi-talented act that became a singer, composer, Jazz pianist, organ player and even a legendary comedian.

THE SKINNY ON FATS WALLER

Born just after the turn of the 20th century, Fats Waller was the youngest of four children. With a Reverend for a father and an organist for a mother, Fats started playing piano at the age of six—as he got groomed to play organ in his dad's church. By the time he was fourteen, Fats was already a skilled organist who played at the Lincoln Theater in Harlem. At fifteen, he was writing original compositions and against his father's wishes, Waller started work in local cabarets and theaters. In 1918, he won a talent contest and began recording in 1922 at the age of eighteen.

Fats Waller mastered the stride piano after studying under 'the greatest,' James P. Johnson. Traveling around America and Europe, Fats popularized songs like 1919's *Squeeze Me*, 1929's *Ain't Misbehavin'* and *Honeysuckle Rose*. Codenamed *"The Black Horowitz"* by his musical peer Oscar Levent, Waller was composing and selling Swing music in the 20s and 30s but unfortunately, when some tunes become hits, others made false claims of ownership without his knowledge or permission. Regardless, many of his standards are still recognized today.

Fats Waller was such an in-demand pianist that we had to open a classified file to reveal a dramatic part of his life. In 1926 after a performance in Chicago, Fats was kidnapped, thrown into a car and taken to the Hawthorne Inn, a property owned by alleged gangster Al Capone. Undercover informants followed Fats inside to find a fully engaged party going on. With a gun poking him forward, he made his way to a piano and was instructed to start playing it. Fats wound up as a headlining act at the event, later identified as a birthday bash for Al Capone. After playing for supposedly three days, Fats came home exhausted and inebriated… with swollen pockets full of tip money. That same year, Fats Waller began recording for the Victor label; he stayed with them for most of his career.

FAST FACT: In the year between 1926 and 1927, Fats Waller made solo pipe organ records on a full sized church organ. This was a major first for him.

Our undercover operatives report that Waller wrote well over 400 tunes; many were collaborated with Andy Razaf. One of their 1929 hits, (What Did I Do To Be So) *Black and Blue* also became a big hit for Ethel Waters and Louis Armstrong. As far back as the 1930s, Fats Waller was well received in faraway places like Ireland and the UK. He was featured in an early BBC broadcast, and even recorded songs for EMI using the Compton Theatre organ of the pre-Beatles *Abbey Road Studios*. Known in certain circles for making recordings in just one take, Waller threw special touches in his records by manipulating dynamics, tension and release: his playing style went from soft to loud, and built musical climaxes that were like roller coaster rides.

Fats Waller made appearances in motion pictures like 1943's *Stormy Weather*. It was released about five months prior to his untimely passing on December 15, 1943 during a cross-country train ride. Waller influenced music greats like Count Basie and Errol Garner; this pair of musicians brought Waller originals like *Ain't Misbehavin'* back to life for a whole new generation to enjoy. Here lies proof that we mustn't rely only on the sound of new music, because older classics have earned their merits time and time again. Upon further investigation, you'll discover a wealth of unforgettably tasty Fats Waller tunes. For a full buffet of music data on this incredible musician who satisfied appetites for great sounds, Google up a search and visit sites like www.fatswaller.org.

Opening the lens wider, we all know about America's dance crazes of the 50s and 60s. English and other music fans across the waters soaked it all in, too. Being un-candid for a moment, let's just say the British Go-Go scene (not to be confused with Go-Go music from Washington, D.C.) was heavily influenced by classic American Rock, R&B and Soul. Please note that Go-Go meant different things to different people, in different countries. Per our friends at Wikipedia, "Go-Go derived from the French expression *à gogo*, meaning *in abundance*, *galore*, which is in turn derived from the ancient French word *la gogue* for *joy* and *happiness*."

1960s-era Go-Go included reference to the British Go-Go scene regarding male and female solo dancers. In addition, women were hired for dancing to songs like *The Twist* on bar, club and discotheque tables—these dancers were featured attractions in nightspots from Thailand to Japan, from New York to San Francisco. Moving forward in time, there were many other descriptions of the Go-Go scene but ours will end here: just know that some of it evolved into tons of non-stop music by a plethora of acts, all supported by knee-high boot-cladden Go-Go dancers with toys or animals clenched in their hands… or draped around their bodies.

Musically speaking, Go-Go entails anything from stripped down guitar sounds to a psychedelic cacophony of distortion, thick bass grooves with punchy horns—or even organs, beach sounds and Pop melodies. Then we've got the Washington, D.C. version; it's heavily abundant with percussion galore. There are a number of D.C.-based Go-Go groups but if you do a search, E.U. may pop up on the radar first. That's due to their smash hit *Da' Butt*, featured on a 1988 "Spike Lee Joint" called *School Daze*. And on G.P. (General Principle) alone, a heartfelt R.I.P. goes out to Chuck Brown, who left us for Go-Go Heaven in mid-2012. But you can find his special blend of Go-Go online at www.windmeupchuck.com. FYI, there'll be more on D.C.'s Go-Go music in an upcoming release, where I talk with the legendary Trouble Funk trumpeter, Charles "CB" Bell.

One important reason for this book's creation was to tell a story of music's evolution, while disseminating little-known facts about the industry and people who helped build it. To me, much of the 'hoopla' surrounding entertainment is over-exaggerated. I think the criteria for stardom depends primarily on the "it" factor—*either you have it, or you don't*. In my opinion, few people are born stars; to garner airplay and TV exposure, contenders require things like personality, training and pure raw talent. They all play important roles in "the big pic," and every contender should see that vision clearly… if they want someone else to see theirs.

The final verdict: professionally speaking, if you're an artist who's determined to break into the *biz*, a safe protocol in gaining public exposure is to follow the straight and narrow with regards to income. Even with a 9-5 job, it still takes plenty of discipline to save money. Refrainfully speaking, 'stashing your cash' could lead to better control over your finances… invest in yourself by taking time to master budget management, no matter how big or small it is. Remember, this is valuable advice because unlike our next music *biz* soldier, you don't have to learn the hard way that a *budget* (or lack thereof) 'definitively dictates' success or failure. At the end of the day, your budget will dictate the level of interaction you have with radio DJs, station managers, nightclubs, recording studios, record companies, publicists and more.

Just like their superstar opposites, starving artists need lots of exposure—they can always try to do the '*come up with a potential solution*' thing by taking chances, but sometimes one just never knows '*what comes with the outcome.*' Let me recant the story of an extraordinary gentleman who followed his own protocol through the crooked and wide, to end up supplying the growing needs of a high-traffic music pipeline. As it expanded, this pipeline needed a higher grade of combustible fuel in order to feed plenty of music power into the 'monolithically explosive' record industry.

ONE KOOL POE KAT

Allow me to introduce a legendary "Kool Kat" who's had the SPOTLIGHT ON him since the early days of Rock-n-Roll. During one of my adventures with CBS Records in mid-80s Atlanta, I had the pleasure of rubbing elbows with Bobby Poe, his wife and their son for the first time—it was at Pop music star Cyndi Lauper's birthday bash. This event happened at a hotel just a hop, skip and jump away from the Atlanta airport, in an area I call *Airport Hotel Alley*. The party was sponsored by CBS distributed Portrait/Epic Records, during a music convention bearing the *Poe* name. Unlike many players in the game, Bobby Poe spent his entire adult life in the music industry. Navigating his way as a 1950s performer and songwriter, Poe went on to become a successful artist manager, record producer, concert promoter and industry trade magazine publisher. During his 50-plus years out on the battlefield, Bobby Poe saw everything from racism and violence… *"Sex, Drugs and Rock-n-Roll!"*

FLASHBACK: As a local hero with the state champion Coffeyville Red Ravens, a young Bobby Poe finished college and chased the American dream. Coffeyville had gotten more civilized by this time but back in the 19th century, things were still a little rough around the edges.

> **BANK FACT:** In the late 1800s, Bobby Poe's hometown of Coffeyville, Kansas was where folklore about the Jesse James Gang and the Dalton Gang circulated. When two Coffeyville banks were robbed simultaneously, citizens got vigilant and killed most of the Dalton Gang's members.

Fast forwarding to modern times, Bobby Poe put "first things first" to support his family—work in the oil well pump industry got the bills paid. Poe figured if Elvis could go from being an average blue-collar worker to the center of entertainment bliss, so could he. And co-workers who heard him sing Elvis songs on the job agreed! Also known as "The Poe Kat," Bobby got his preliminary start in the industry around age 22, after the light turned green for him to proceed forward at a 1955 Christmas party. Accepting a bet to get up and sing with a Black Jazz band, Poe belted out Elvis' *Love-Me Tender* and ended up receiving a standing ovation... plus $20 from the bet. Historically speaking, the nightclub owner offered him a job and just like that, the Poe Kat saga began.

Now officially in "showbiz," Bobby Poe picked up some musicians and started playing at the club, which led to them becoming the first local band to perform Rock-n-Roll there. As their synergy solidified, singer and pianist Big Al Downing signed on to add a new dimension to the group's sound with his renditions of Fats Domino and Little Richard. Mixed in with Poe's Elvis and Jerry Lee Lewis songs, this made for a winning combination. The opportunity was a music promoter's paradise—before all was said and done, they were covering songs from the Everly Brothers on through most of that era's hit makers. Bobby Poe and his Poe Kats were hot!

By 1957, the Poe Kats were receiving praise and requests to perform on TV, but Bobby kept hitting the REWIND button as he mentally struggled with whether he should continue working a 9 to 5 to pay bills, or venture into the industry's abyss. PAUSE: With a wife and kids to support, Bobby Poe made the ultimate sacrifice and chose the latter. As misery loves company, before he could quit Poe was promptly fired for making a judicious decision to pursue his dream. RECORD this: with no more full time job, Bobby Poe 'elevated down' to playing music on weekend gigs in order to feed the family. Times got so rough that even the milkman helped out, by giving the Poes free milk. FAST FORWARD: The bottom fell out for Bobby when he was forced to sell the last of his valuables—a watch and ring—to buy some ham and a loaf of bread. CUE: As one door closed another opened, but the lesson learned here is: plan your work route well, for "if you don't own the business, you can be fired at anytime." STOP: Things haven't changed much, so budding entertainers take heed…

Relentlessly speaking, Bobby Poe and his band floated around 'searching for the searchlight' on sometimes stormy seas. But they kept their *music biz hustle* on by navigating Poe's perpetual *U.S.S. Songship* to ports where 'high seas rollers' like Elvis producer Chet Atkins and agent/manager/promoter Jim Halsey were docked. After debarking the ship's gangplank, Poe struck a round of good luck when his band teamed up for a classified rendezvous—the Poe unit was assigned a 'mission critical.' Their new operation was to back up newly established *Queen of Rockabilly* Wanda Jackson, who many would agree looked just as good as she sounded. The alliance was short-lived, but it gave Poe's troupe additional experience to put forth when their *preparation met opportunity*. The group's final mission together was at a 1958 show on New Year's Eve in Montrose, Colorado with Marty Robbins: he just became a new Pop/Country sensation himself. By the 80s, I found myself marketing his records, along with other Country acts on the Columbia and Epic labels.

In the early days when Wanda Jackson first spread her wings, she was talented enough to attract the attention of the *King of Rock-n-Roll*—Elvis—as movers and shakers like Jim Halsey encouraged Wanda to deliver her trademark Rockabilly sound to the masses. After doing so, she took off on tour with the Poe Kat Band. The entourage quickly found themselves mingling with celebrities and laying tracks down when the RECORD button was pushed. Many not-so-secret sessions were held in impervious studios like the Capitol Records Tower in Hollywood.

> **OAK-AGED FACT:** After introducing the world to Wanda "Queen of Rockabilly" Jackson, Jim Halsey went on to manage a legendary Country music group called *The Oak Ridge Boys*—for over a quarter of a century.

In the late 50s, Rock-n-Roll and R&B each gained popularity, but stagnant racial laws like Jim Crow were still enforced in states like Arkansas and around the south. At one point, the tension led to casualties in a segregated community—among them being *The Little Rock Nine.*" Arkansas' Governor Orval Faubus remained steadfast in his belief that Black kids should not attend the all-White Little Rock Central High School. In September of 1957, "the race ticket" was special delivered to taxpayers, teachers and students alike, when the Governor called in the National Guard to stop nine little kids from getting a quality education. This was obviously a long time before "no child got left behind."

Coincidentally, Bobby Poe and The Poe Kats got booked to do a gig at the University of Arkansas the same night of this embarrassing social travesty. Keep in mind that segregation was in effect at the University too! Nevertheless, Black students gravitated towards Poe's fellow band member, Big Al Downing, like magnets. He "did his thing" and entertained everyone while onstage but offstage, the restroom sign still said *Whites Only*—this was quite a flame-throwing scenario to be found in. Adding to the heat, Bobby Poe perpetuated an act considered as unpopular because they traveled and performed with a sizeable Negro man who was a part of the band. For Poe, Downing was both "a member and a client," as illustrated when Poe used to sneak Big Al into motels out on the road. They utilized an approach I call *incognegro tactics*–Al covered his head and carried the band's equipment straight into the room!

Can anyone see a ray of sunlight from this snapshot girls, boys, ladies and gents? Before September of 1957 was over, President Eisenhower deployed an executive directive—for The Little Rock Nine to become full-fledged students at Little Rock Central High School. Race relations in America continued to be a volatile issue throughout the remaining years of the 50s and right into the 60s, when hippies and musicians alike began echoing early variations of Rodney King's "Can't we all just get along?"

AND QUITE A SET THEY MADE

During the late 50s, Bobby Poe was considered by a few as a "pretty boy" who often traveled with a Black piano player in his band. Anyone familiar with the times would know that this was quite a challenge back in those days. Subsequently, Poe and/or Big Al Downing were targeted for harassment by local "buzzed bad boys." Depending upon where they played results varied, but it wasn't always a pretty scene out on the road. To make it through a night of drunken bullies, Poe would buy rounds of drinks to befriend potential sparring partners before his shows began. This *subduement strategy* showed superior execution of Poe's "pre-show security intelligence." Years later, Poe pointed out how The Rolling Stones security was once handled by a "socially networked" group, codename *The Hell's Angels*: *Extreme Motorcycle Club*!

One day, Bobby got a call from a guy named Jim Lowe after returning from their 1958 West Coast tour with Rockabilly Queen, Wanda Jackson. Although Jim was a Dallas radio DJ, he also had a record label called *White Rock Records*. Jim offered Bobby Poe and Big Al Downing solo record deals, and a series of hits soon followed. Poe's *Rock and Roll Record Girl* and Big Al's *Down On The Farm* topped charts in the Texas region and heightened both of their reputations as true industry contenders destined for greatness. With people like Sam Phillips from Sun Records snooping around, Poe unremittingly tried to lure in music biz heavyweights. Sun's roster included legendary acts: Elvis, Jerry Lee Lewis, Roy Orbison, Johnny Cash, Charlie Rich and Carl Perkins were just a few. As luck would have it, the messenger of misery stepped in to shake things up once again. Right in the midst of Poe's *Rock and Roll Record Girl* rising up the charts, a music publisher stepped in to shut the tune down. He believed Poe's hit sounded too much like a song in his catalog and pulled some strings to make Poe's song a hard-to-find Rockabilly collectible—it ended up getting pulled off the market. This incident is merely one of many setbacks Poe overcame to become the legend he is known as today.

Around January of 1959, Bobby Poe had his sights set on Philadelphia, where Dick Clark and *American Bandstand* were catapulting overnight sensations into music *biz*tory icons, through the magic of television. At this point it was an attainable dream, but before Poe and the gang were slated to wake up in Philly, they took a final wake up call from a proverbial "Wizard Of Oz" back in Kansas... Upon being given a directive of "follow the yellow brick road," the band was off to a meeting with Philadelphia's Music Mayor Dick Clark. Marching out in full battle gear on the "mother of all missions," the Poe Kats headed northbound. Along the way, they executed a return engagement at an Army base in Missouri—not only did Bobby Poe and the Poe Kats break their previous attendance record there, Poe's group surpassed the base's top record: previously set by *Tommy Dorsey and his Orchestra*.

A BIGGER BITE OF THE ACTION

Picking up gigs in places like Boston's *Combat Zone*, Poe and his Kats experienced a taste of "the baseball bat as a weapon" when they were introduced to big city life in the Northeast. Seeing a little dirty work that went on behind the scenes firsthand, Bobby Poe began pursuing other options like managing Big Al's career, which was still on the upswing. Teaming Big Al up with stars like Esther Phillips, Bobby Poe got several songs recorded and released. Out of this effort, *Mr. Hurt* took off in 1963 and had *American Bandstand* written all over it.

Almost every artist out there has experienced taking a step forward and being pushed back by two steps. I can relate through my own rags-to-riches-to rags adventures—the same thing happened to me and other folks I know. In Bobby Poe's case, by the time his *Mr. Hurt* single was taking off, the label backing it folded. This was another painful setback that fueled the fire of success for Poe. Regardless, he still kept it moving:

- Poe was hired to write songs for Fats Domino in 1964
- Although he made a connection with Esther Phillips, Bobby tried to team up Big Al and Aretha Franklin; but it never materialized
- Poe managed and co-produced Big Al Downing and *The Rhythm Rockers* (later called the *The Chartbusters*), featuring former *Poe Kats* lead guitarist/vocalist Vernon Sandusky
- *The Chartbusters* released a track for Mutual Records called *She's The One*—it peaked at #33 on Billboard's Pop chart with 750,000 records sold, landing them onstage at *American Bandstand*

Although things looked good on the outside, if one took an observatory PAUSE, a different scenario could be seen taking place on the inside—it eventually caused a rift to grow between Big Al, the band and the Poe Kat. Bobby Poe often sought advise from friend and mentor Lelan Rogers (older brother of future Country music star Kenny Rogers); Bobby and Lelan formed a long-lasting friendship that spanned over four decades. Utilizing Lelan's advise, Bobby was soon leading the band as manager and producer. He hit the PLAY button and the band collectively decided on a permanent move from Kansas to Pennsylvania, where they'd be closer to Philadelphia, Dick Clark, *American Bandstand*... and the nearby entertainment buzz of New York City. STOP: Like big dreamers such as Quincy Jones, Berry Gordy (and yes, myself even), Bobby Poe had an entertainment conglomerate being built in the dungeon of his mind—and would act on this vision when the time was right.

Even with dissention growing in the camp Big Al Downing, his band and Bobby Poe strategized, executed action, and worked their way through it. Three key players remained as anchors to keep *The Chartbusters* moving: Bobby Poe managed and produced, Mitch Corday (Big Al's drummer) booked the band, while music director - lead guitarist Vernon Sandusky kept the band performing like a finely-tuned machine, out on the road. It was business as usual after they set up an office in Washington, D.C. and Poe signed up additional acts to manage; some had million-selling track records. In true Kool Kat fashion, Poe just happened to be among the first promoters to book West Coast bubble gum poster band, *The Beach Boys*, in the Baltimore/Washington D.C. area.

The Chartbusters continued a meteoric climb to the top of the music food chain and after expanding their personnel list, were now on the same playing field as peers like *The Animals*, *Jan & Dean*, *Johnny Rivers*, *Herman's Hermits* and *The Lovin' Spoonful*. As evidenced by a variety of events, the 60s unfolded musical wonders from all points of the spectrum. To look granularly through the music kaleidescope of this era, let's shift gears and pull out our trusty superior issue micro-binoculars. Conducting top-secret reconnaissance operations on music's interwoven color bars of infrastructure will lead us into deeper infiltration on the industry *biz*tory of that Kool Kat, Bobby Poe. With that said, our Captain indicates it's time to tighten the straps on those thinking caps, as we go to another level of initiating high-level intelligence gathering ops...

-9-
FLIPPING THE SCRIPT

Around 1949, popular music of Afro-Americans dubbed by Billboard magazine as "race music" was renamed *Rhythm and Blues* (R&B). Popular White releases obviously sold more, but hot R&B records could sell in the neighborhood of 5 million units a year, and that was nothing to sneeze at in those times! Jumping to today's fickle music market, some acts would be lucky to sell 500,000 units—even with a moderate hit! Those kinds of figures on the R&B side warranted further investigation, so Pop artists zoomed in for a closer look. During the 60s, acts like The Beach Boys, The Beatles, The Monkees and Rolling Stones dominated the Pop/Rock charts while as a result of being overshadowed, AC/Easy Listening/Middle-of-the-Road music quietly took a back seat.

During the 70s, 80s and 90s, new formats popped up on the radio dial, while older ones got revamped. *Top 40* picked up monikers like *Contemporary Hit Radio* (CHR) and centered on exerting gravity in the Pop music space. AC/Easy Listening/MOR from the 50s and 60s "golden era of hit music" became known as *Oldies*, *Light* or *Soft Rock*. Underground or non-mainstream Rock was tagged as *Modern* or *Alternative Rock*. In the meantime, *Album Oriented Rock* or *AOR* didn't depend upon the latest hit single for programming—like the name implies, this format primarily focused on playing album tracks. There was also *Classic Rock*, which reflected hit-single based mainstream Rock of the 60s, 70s and 80s. Across the railroad tracks, an updated term for new mainstream R&B became *Contemporary Hit Urban Radio*, commonly known in certain circles as the *Churban* format.

And let's not forget *Old School*, a reference to 70s/80s Dance, R&B and Funk. The *Quiet Storm* and *Love* space was reserved for folks who listened to slower tempo, ballad styled compositions. For mostly instrumental music there was *Smooth Jazz*, but please believe it when I say the list doesn't stop there. In case it wasn't mentioned earlier, the term "Pop" is another way of saying "Popular" music and poetically speaking, some good Pop can be found at music icon Bobby Poe Jr's label, *Pop Music Records*—check out www.popmusicrecords.com. This is where you can cash in your own share of music *biz*tory—a big thumbs up goes to Bobby Poe Jr. for providing me with great info on his dad's life story!

211

As the time controlled music choo-choo train chugged its way towards the new millennium, networks of high-energy radio stations got branded as *Dance*, *Foxy*, *Hot*, *Power* and more. If we were to wrap it all up in a nutshell, radio world's market segmentation became a 'latest way' the proverbial powers that be devised for advertisers to classify where to divert ad dollars. Factors like these were essential when record labels sent their legion of promotion men out to fight in the *Chart Domination War*. You see, there was a constant struggle going on for 'power positioning' on radio playlists—but a forced truce was eventually incurred because these days, airplay is automatically tracked. On the other hand, insiders say numbers can still be manipulated; for the right price. While all of that could just be hearsay... what's REALSAY is this: radio airplay is the #1 tool used by advertisers like record companies to generate *ALE*. Nowadays, the expanded music market is capable of selling a million copies of a new release in a single day!

Another popular music type with a bluesy, intimate R&B sound—*Soul*—took root during the 60s. Soul music has elements partial to Gospel and was a secular style that not only appealed to Blacks, but to all creeds, colors and cultures. Lyrical content of the overly expressive Soul style generally surrounds topics of people's most innermost feelings on personal issues relative to love, life, joy and pain. Vocals were often delivered through emotional cries, with high falsetto vocals by males— plus, there was a wide assortment of sighs, whispers, moans; and wails that could send shivers up the spine. Watch out for a listing of popular Soul acts, coming up soon.

GOOD FOLK

During the 60s and 70s, Folk music exploded with artists like:

Joan Baez	Joni Mitchell
The Byrds	Bill Monroe
Bob Dylan	Pete Seeger
Woodie Guthrie	Simon & Garfunkel
Keb' Mo'	James Taylor
The Kingston Trio	Townes Van Zandt
The Mamas and The Papas	Doc Watson

All of these artists and more were part of the momentum that brought Folk and Folk-Rock to the mainstream. Closer ties were made between the worlds of Folk and Folk-Rock with Soft Rock, Adult Contemporary, Easy Listening, and Middle-of-the-Road. Like other established American styles, Folk music subdivided into segments, and then reunited to make up Folk as a whole genre. Because it's usually accompanied by acoustic guitar, Folk music automatically tends to sound different from most other styles. All in all and just for clarification, Folk is basically produced in the studio, performed onstage, promoted and marketed to the masses, much like the previously mentioned genres. Probably the biggest difference between Folk and Pop is in how they are received in the mainstream. For instance, Folk music is often absorbed in smaller doses than Pop and other genres, but it tends to offer a longer shelf life with regard to radio airplay than Pop. This was just fine for record labels—they often invested huge sums of money to tap into the massive but often short-lived radio traffic certain genres produced.

Many Folk artists have come and gone, but the multi-dimensional Bob Dylan is one visionary who knew what the folks wanted! As a huge success with his distinguished Folk style, Bob Dylan altered his peculiar acoustic guitar sound with the electricity of Rock, before moving on to higher ground. Dylan also raised eyebrows in the world of Country music during the 60s, when he wrote hits with the one and only Johnny Cash. A steadfast Columbia Records artist, Bob Dylan transitioned from a Folk hero into a Rock god with his dynamic *"Electric Set"* performance at the renowned 1965 Newport Folk Festival. Professionally speaking, I see nothing wrong with acts that could jump from Folk to Country and Rock, but some artists who switched their style to suit the demands of the industry were called "sellouts." These genre jumpers sometimes made drastic style changes in exchange for a bigger slice of the pie. And then there were those who did it purely for artistic reasons, like our subject Bob Dylan who wrote, sang and played most of his music on the guitar and harmonica—sometimes he did this all at once.

Moving further south, creative acts like Jimmy Buffett and Willie Nelson demonstrated their own specialized brand of 'acoustic-electric guitarism' to become staples in their relative sectors of the industry. These songwriters played a mixture of Bluegrass, Country and Folk, sprinkled with a little Pop and Rock. Artists like Bob Dylan, Johnny Cash, Jimmy Buffett and Willie Nelson rose to stardom by selling large amounts of records and cashing in on widely geographic, sold-out tours.

213

Jimmy Buffett's career set sail as a Country artist from Nashville, Tennessee in the late 60s. It's been said that Buffett became a Nashville renegade who later washed ashore as a street musician on New Orleans' Gulf Coast. Like many musicians there, he was dedicated to generating revenue by performing for tourists in public places. This was known as "busking," a fairly common practice for musicians. Artists like Joan Baez, Bob Dylan and Joni Mitchell were all known for "Café busking" early in their careers. To make a long story short, after taking a busking trip to Key West, Florida with Country singer Jerry Jeff Walker, Jimmy Buffett became a Key West resident—this is where he established his "easy-going beach bum" persona… did someone's parrot say *Mayor of Margaritaville*?

Jimmy Buffett's 1970 debut album *Down to Earth* had a Folk-Rock flair to it, and paved the way for his trademark "Key West-slash-Gulf & Western" sound. Next up was a key word called diversification: Buffett expanded his influence as an author, businessman, film producer, philanthropist… and pilot. With classic songs like *Margaritaville* as the staple for his own brand of gaudy sound, Jimmy's legion of fans followed him to performances and became known as "Parrotheads." Buffett's track record includes sold out concerts with his *Coral Reefer Band*, roles in film and television, various business ventures, charity work and even a bit of legal controversy. To amalgamate your own "information buffet" on Jimmy Buffett, you can visit his South Florida stomping grounds just about any time of the year, or if the wallet won't work well, click on www.margaritaville.com.

BATTLE OF THE 'B'

In my eternal quest of rooting for the independent underdog artist, I've unearthed another special treat from the 'sunshiney' state of Florida, courtesy of my good friend Dominic Medico, Musicology codename *Sous Agent Chef D*. Besides our mutual love for cooking and eating our own *tasty tongue tinglers*, Dom and I enjoy similar flavors of music, all spread out on a huge eye-ear-and-mouth-watering menu. In the background sound palette of my mind, I hear Carly Simon singing her classic 1977 hit; this tune comes from an ultimate secret agent flick, *The Spy Who Loved Me*. With that said, let's just say "nobody does it better" than *Chef D*—not when it comes to describing Alligator Alley; or an old friend named Bryce and his music-gatorish band.

Dominic points out how his pal Bryce Rutkowski had a band called *Boxelder*. Like the previously mentioned *Mayor of Margaritaville* Jimmy Buffett, this group developed a unique form of "easy-going beach bum" sounds that it's safe to call *Surf-n-Skate-n-Rock-n-Roots-n-Reggae*. On that note, our Florida-bound party machine shifts into "overdrive" as we pull that cooking chef out of the kitchen to host a subliminally quick spin to a small grid in the Florida zone.

ALL BOXED IN

Thanks for your musicologistic interruption L.A.—I was just heading over to my custom-built, southside patio bar. That's where I like to stretch out on a hammock and enjoy a few rounds of Florida's *hottest party group!* Just outside our secret compound, an oversized party bus makes its approach; mobile agents confirm it as the *Musicology Machine*—as it pulls up, our security camera will zoom in for a closer look. In the meantime, we've got all kinds of exotic drinks lined up at the patio bar, awaiting 'those who dare to stare.' Due to the searing heat outside, we will quickly execute operation *DDMM* (Disembark Da Musicology Machine) so we can welcome the party bus passengers, grab a few cold ones and head over to my 'hammock galley.' That's where we'll hang out and crank up the sound of this *major-indie* group I've been listening to for many Southern moons now.

REWIND: Back when I was a young Florida operative, Bryce Rutkowski was the voice of Boxelder, so we'll begin this briefing with the early version of our *B-handle*. But before opening door number one, let's pull up www.boxelder.com for a quick quote: Our house drink is brought to you by "*The Boxelder Recipe: 2 shots of Rock and 1 shot of Reggae. Directions: Combine all ingredients together in a large shot glass. Stir and serve.*" This routine is typically followed by opening door number two and coining Sean Penn from his second film *Fast Times at Ridgemont High*—"Hey bud, let's party!" Whether you can walk a straight line or not, the stage is now set for you to follow me through door number three.

It's playtime: as the door opens to reveal the backstage den of our patio bar, we see Boxelder's recipe in action: stretched out on the hammock side of our spacious patio are a few 'concoction casualties.' As we head to the V.I.P. section, please note the hazy colors taking over our immediate surroundings, as the speakers power up to serve up some serious sounds from my old buddy Bryce... and his *Surf-n-Skate-n-Rock-*

n-Roots-n-Reggae band, *Boxelder*. Logging in thousands of music miles with over ten years of non-stop touring, Boxelder racked up no less than five chart-worthy albums on the independent music side. Making their rounds through cities and towns across the country, this group knows how hard life on the road can get. They also know what selling ten thousand copies 'outta the car trunk' feels like, too.

For a while, I knew what it felt like to mimick Agent Superintendent L.A. Jackson, as I ran everywhere with Boxelder's music. I promoted them 24/7 around the tree-laden vicinity of GPS location— *Latitude 26° 54' 51" Longitude -80° 12' 19.163"*—otherwise known as Jupiter, Florida. Even if people see it as a small town, I still compare it to its namesake, which is our fifth and largest planet. Although I've heard people call it *Juniper*, we won't mistake it for the popular tree of that same name: but we will get a little 'tree-some' going, for comparison purposes.

> **TREE-SOME FACT:** Boxelder took its name from a maple tree family member, scientific name *Acer Negundo*.

To add to the equation, my favorite tree is the waving Palm tree (*Cocos Nucifera*) —it makes me think of my hometown in Florida and Boxelder's inviting music, while Agent L.A. takes to the Linden tree (*Tilia Vulgaris*), possibly due its medicine-like qualities: yet another "thing that makes you say hmmmm." It's now time to get back on track and head to the beach with our surfboards and skates in hand. Floating through the air is a familiar sound common to the area. Listening more closely, it seems as if Boxelder managed to slide right into the surfing industry—by getting their music featured on the soundtracks of a few surf films. The group also had tours sponsored by *Smith Optics* and *Surfer Magazine*; even *ESPN2* opened its doors, through their extreme sports programming hookup. To substantiate information I already knew from back in the day, I went online and found the latest communiqué capsule at www.rootsmusic.com: it confirmed the *Surf-n-Skate-n-Rock-n-Roots-n-Reggae* music scene was executing an action identified as *compounded expansion*!

As Boxelder boxed-in a solid fan base through supporters at college and commercial radio, advertising powerhouses like Clear Channel gave a positive head-nod by opening up markets in Jacksonville, Orlando, Tallahassee and West Palm Beach to the band. This garnered not only airplay for their music, but also opening slots at major concerts.

Having releases like *Deep Water Influence* and *Finding A Way* led the way to tours with folks like San Diego's *Slightly Stoopid*, along with Grammy winning *Toots & The Maytals*. The list didn't stop there either friends; Boxelder caught the ears of other top players in the game—like Eric Schilling, codename *Grammy Producer*.

SINGER-B-GOOD

Finding a need to push the limits of creativity, Boxelder's lead vocalist Bryce Rutkowski singlehandedly struck out on his own trek for fame and fortune. He signed a solo recording contract with Contempt Records, and then released an EP that showcased his growth as an artist of great potential. To confirm his musically dynamic abilities, folks like Michael Lyons signed on as a songwriter, after hearing Rutkowski's cutting-edge music. Turns out, Lyons is an old pro at touring with acts like *Black River Circus*; also climbing aboard was Max Fraser, who played bass for *Doorway 27*; this was another group that represented the surfy West Palm Beach Rock-Reggae scene. Officially going by the name *B-Liminal* since 2007, Bryce continued his route through the music *biz* maze, switching labels in 2009. After leaving Contempt Records for Jett Beres (Sister Hazel) and Secret7 Records, he released new albums to keep the B-Liminal market 'exponentially expanding.' Over the years, Bryce kept great company while performing on live shows with:

Arrested Development	Red Jumpsuit Apparatus
Authority Zero	Reel Big Fish
Pato Banton	The Rock Boat
Citizen Cope	Rock Boat X
Fishbone	Rombello 2011
Donavon Frankenreiter	Sister Hazel
Michael Franti	Sixthman
G. Love	Slightly Stoopid
Less Than Jake	Soja
Pennywise	Bunny Wailer
Pepper	Yellowman
Lee "Scratch" Perry	

As B-Liminal builds a growing audience by carving out a new niche in the *biz*, be sure to catch some of that *Surf-n-Skate-n-Rock-n-Roots-n-Reggae* music if you're in the Florida neighborhood, or visit Bryce and his "Bliminal Music" online at places like Facebook, Last-FM, Linked In, Reverbnation, Sonicbuds and more. Well, it's back to the main patio bar to replenish my *exotic Medico elixir* and play another CD from my favorite local group. Then, I might whip up a few more concoctions and "hang" around hammock alley—with the B-Liminal sound on full blast. L.A. Jackson will take it from here and safely get you back to A-Town, where the itinerary predicates a lane change into the heart of Country music land. Thanks for joining me in this flavorful segment of L.A.'s narrative encyclopedia. As you absorb the rest of his intellectual creativity, allow me to flash the sign of the horns and say *"FBB Forever!"*

Thanks for being a good *"Florida Beach Bum,"* Special Sous Agent Dominic Medico, codename *"Chef D."* That was an informative taste of Triple B (Bryce, Boxelder and B-Liminal) so on that note, we'll catch up with you at a Jupiter headquarters debriefing later. Now, I'd like to acknowledge another good friend—he's a former co-worker from my CBS Records/Sony Music days.

MODERN COWBOYS

There's no way I can think of Country music without thinking of Tim Pritchett, codename *That Hillbilly Cat*. In addition to being a top record promoter, Tim was a relatively good-looking Southern gentleman. Always polite yet noble in his own way, Tim had hair down to his shoulders that shielded a pair of earrings; they swung around and moved in rhythm when he walked. This was one cat that always looked cool… and I NEVER heard anyone call him names like *sissy*!

No sooner than I met Tim at the CBS Records branch office in 1984, he started calling me *"Lankon Jackson."* Over the years, your friendly "Jamaicavemon" picked up other monikers from branch members like *"L-Boogie," "Action Jackson," "Young Jack"* and one of my faves, *"Jamaican Jack."* My co-workers at the branch covered every aspect of the record business from the sales, marketing, distribution and promotion sides. Tim promoted Columbia and Epic's vast Country music catalog at radio stations—from I-95 down in Florida, all the way up to Route One in Maine. I remember the good times we had during the mid-to late 80s at the Atlanta operations center, coded as location *EPSERO* (Executive Park Southeast Regional Office). Reason being, co-workers like Tim always made sure I had an invite to the label's Country events.

Tim Pritchett was a great promotion man who also had skills as a musician, recording engineer, producer and historian. One day as we were talking shop, Tim schooled me on a few little-known music facts from the 50s and 60s; one was that we each admired a Turkish entrepreneur who struck gold—make that multi-platinum, on dozens of occasions. Ahmet Ertegun was that man, and he's known for founding Atlantic Records and being a "hands on" kind of guy during the length of a highly successful career. Tim pointed out that this multicultural label was formally formed in New York City in September of 1947, prior to becoming a major part of urban, suburban and rural music scenes not just across America—but around the world.

Sharing his vast music *biz*tory with me, Tim Pritchett reflected that plenty White musicians took to playing Blies and R&B in cities like New York, L.A., Atlanta and Memphis. On the flip side, folks like Johnny Cash played Rock in groups called "The Million Dollar Quartet" out of Memphis before becoming a Country music icon. Related acts include Carl Perkins, Jerry Lee Lewis and *King* Elvis Presley. Elvis is credited with opening doors and helping out quite a few R&B singers, among them Fats Domino. Besides being a big singer, Fats had a big gambling habit in Vegas. Sometimes Fats came up on the short end of the winning table; when he did, Elvis paid his debts and let Fats open up at his shows.

Tim Pritchett gave me a few bits of personal Fats Domino history, too. Being that they ran in the same circle, when Tim went to New Orleans, he stayed at Fats Domino's house. With tons of custom cars all over the place, Tim hinted that he would later continue the tradition of dream car ownership—I'll expound on that a little more in a few minutes. From the stories he told me, Tim's no stranger to crashing at a celebrity's house; let him tell it and he'd say, "I was cool with everybody. Back in 1989 when I went to England, I stayed at rocker Peter Gabriel's house in Bath. You see, I travel the world as codename *That Hillbilly Cat*." And I thought Tim was just another pretty-faced Urban Country Music Cowboy.

After our Sony days ended in the mid-90s, Tim Pritchett offered me a new initiative: through a 'visit-tour' of his Marietta recording studio. To throw in a little *Saturday Night Live*'ish humor, let me just say "*Zee Country museec beez has been beddy, beddy goot to Teem.*" You see, being the modest kind of guy he is, Tim never really showed or told me how good Country music had treated him. To explain quickly, I remember pulling up in front of Tim's studio, and being greeted at the door with his customary "welcome aboard, Lankon." After that, we listened to tons of great music by his guitar-playing son John, as well as from a talented pool of acts Tim was engaged with at the time. While he gave me pointers on how his studio's centerpiece (the mixing console) functioned with its other components, I was already making mental plans to upgrade my home studio in hopes of keeping up with *The Timster*.

Further development of our longtime kinetic energy made me want to continue 'kickin' it with the Pritchett,' so I contemplated a possible integration—the thought of engineering at Tim's studio and helping his son John pick up paid gigs sounded appealing... Tim Pritchett had two sons and like our other officemates with kids at the time: they're all grown up now! Tim's oldest son Jason also got his feet wet in the music game. He spent 7 years at Universal and was the National Director of Artist Development for Island/Def Jam. As a musician, John avoided the uphill battle to get signed *and supported* by a major label, especially with the Internet of the mid-90s looming around, ready to rear its *file-sharing* head. Instead, John opted to remain true to his roots and from what Tim told me, still enjoyed having fun by playing around town with his band.

Another thing I remember is marveling at Tim Pritchett's custom automobile collection. Earlier, I mentioned that he was inspired by Fats Domino's collection, so guess what Tim made plans to do? Tim swore to continue the tradition of dream car ownership, and that's exactly what he did. Due to my old age I can't recall them all, but I DO remember his big, black Cadillac Coupe DeVille; it had a diesel engine and not one, but two batteries! After a while, he picked up a supercharged, custom built Pontiac Fiero that he told me "went 400 miles per hour!" (No wonder his hair was always slicked back...) Tim's collection of what I deem as *limited edition steel horses* was so remarkable that to this day, I still think of Tim "rolling up all duded up" in one of his beefed up rides. It rekindles an anthemic line from a Willie Nelson classic: *Mammas Don't Let Your Babies Grow Up To Be Cowboys*. Being that Tim promoted all the Country music released by Columbia and Epic Records (including Willie Nelson), he quite naturally had incredible sound systems in his cars.

As an Urban Country Cowboy, Tim Pritchett was often heard ending conversations with *"Have a big ol' gud'n or a good ol' big'n, whichever comes first!"* Sadly speaking, Tim lost his battle with a long illness and passed away on December 9, 2013, so he won't get to read this book here on Earth now. But he thoroughly enjoyed *Musicology 2101*, and he also read this section, because I sent it to him during the summer of 2013. In fact, we joked about it quite a bit in the months before he departed so I'm mailing a copy of the book to him, up in Music Heaven. (May God bless Tim's lovely wife Lisa and the rest of his family.) One thing I'll always remember about *That Hillbilly Cat*: if an event had any kind of rhythm in it, Tim usually showed up—driving one of his custom-crafted steel horses. In my heart, this Urban Country Cowboy was, is and forever will be a *good fella*!

Speaking of cowboys, here's the rundown on a music cowboy Tim Pritchett spent a lot of time promoting: Willie Nelson. He's logged in as one of the best Country singer-songwriters in history, and is also a distinguished activist, actor, author and poet. Along the winding road, many Country and Pop artists recorded *Willie the Writer*'s songs. During high school, *Nelson the DJ* went terrestrial at local radio stations like KHBR in Hillsboro, Texas, and KBOP in Pleasanton, Texas, while moonlighting as a honky-tonk singer at night. Willie took some time to serve in the army, but eventually moved from Texas to Nashville in 1960. While there he landed a publishing deal, composed marketable songs and toured with another Country act named Ray Price—Ray went on to raise a few eyebrows in the massive music maze himself.

By 1965, Willie Nelson hooked up with the Grand Ole Opry and released albums produced by the legendary Chet Atkins, codename *Elvis Producer*. Strange as it may sound, I got in where I fit in during the 80s; one way was marketing and promoting records by acts like Chet Atkins and Willie Nelson right next to my good friend, Tim Pritchett. Back in the early days, it was just a part of the 'day-to-day music *biz* process' on my priority plate. I'm proud to have helped push Country music out to the masses, along with the music of other Columbia/Epic/Def Jam acts. Comically speaking, I was just like Flip Wilson's *Geraldine* character running around to record stores as I proclaimed "the devil made me do it." But in retrospect, it was more like the Discovery Channel's Mike Rowe— all I can say is: *it was a dirty job…* but someone had to do it.

During the *Outlaw Country* music movement of the 1970s, Willie Nelson found himself glaring at the SPOTLIGHT more and more. He eventually overshadowed his Country image after moving back home to Texas in 1972. Setting up shop in Austin, he recorded albums that featured genres like Blues, Folk, Jazz, Pop, Rock, Western Swing; even Reggae. Willie released Country music's first million-selling platinum album (*Wanted! The Outlaws*) in 1976—it also featured Waylon Jennings, Jessi Colter and Tompall Glaser. By the mid-80s Nelson, Jennings, Kris Kristofferson and Johnny Cash formed a group I helped promote, *The Highwaymen*. This collabo scaled the charts to levels previously unseen, spawning more albums and tours than ever! Willie pushed the limits of creativity by working with producers like Booker T. Jones and Ray Charles, who we'll be discussing soon with two other legendary acts, Sam Cooke and Nat "King" Cole.

Willie Nelson's success swelled to include ample acting roles in movies and on television. Willie also made extensive charitable contributions to help raise inconceivable sums of money, as shown through 1984's *We Are The World* single. He was also a catalyst for fundraising concerts like 1985's *Farm Aid*, which brought in trendsetting musicians like Bob Dylan, Dave Matthews and Neil Young. Nelson's work with diverse 'Poppers and Rockers' such as Paul Simon, Kid Rock and Phish continues today. Also inclusive in Willie Nelson's ventures were previously unfathomable collaborations with acts like Sinead O'Connor, Wynton Marsalis and Hip-Hop *Don Lion*, Snoop Dogg. From the looks of his dossier, I'd say Willie Nelson had genres jumping straight to *him*, instead of it being the other way around.

As a spokesperson for a slew of positive-thinking organizations, the reality-singing, guitar-toting, Black Belt in Taekwondo known as Willie Nelson was "On The Road" again in 2010. On this particular trip from Los Angeles to Texas on November 26th, Nelson experienced technical difficulties on his tour bus—apparently, the Texas Border Patrol found issues with some marijuana discovered moonlighting onboard as a backup musician. Regardless of all circumstantial evidence, Willie Nelson's many contributions to the Country and Pop music cultures clearly outweigh that $2,500 bail money posted to keep his show on the road. (By the way, it was never confirmed that Willie smoked a joint in the White House, either.) In closing, I know I said it before but I'll say it again: "*Mammas Don't Let Your Babies Grow Up To Be Cowboys*." For more on buzz codename *Free Willie*, visit www.willienelson.com.

OKEY DOKEY

Now let's get a new perspective on homegrown music I classify as Americana, which is comprised of many different flavors. Our next act helped expand music's borders by combining dominant genres into one stereo output, through his voice and his guitar. Oklahoma singer-songwriter John Weldon Cale goes by musician codename *JJ Cale* and is an originator of the Tulsa Sound. This sound mixed Blues, Country, Folk, Jazz and Rockabilly together, with a splash of Spanish or Flamenco guitar thrown in for effect. Our story begins when Cale moved to Nashville, early on in his career. He was hired by the Grand Ole Opry's touring company, but after relocating to places like California and Oklahoma, he returned to Nashville and gained traction by recording a few solo albums.

FLASHBACK: During the mid-60s, Cale got booked to play at a club on the Sunset Strip. Our underground Intel says the club owner dubbed him as "JJ" so he wouldn't get mistaken for another musician named John Cale. This Cale played with Lou Reed in New York's *Velvet Underground* from 1964 through 1973. All that playing live on the road eventually paid off—in 1972, JJ Cale hit the Billboard charts with a Top 25 hit called *Crazy Mama*. But speculation says the song could have gone higher, had Cale made it out to *American Bandstand* to perform the song.

As JJ Cale explained in the 2006 documentary *To Tulsa and Back*, Dick Clark invited him to be a guest on the show, then was informed there would be no band. Cale was supposed to *lip-sync* the song, but lip-syncing was far from his mind. While Milli Vanilli would have jumped at the chance to "non-sing" as some would call it, JJ Cale made a stand: there would be none of that on his watch! Cale's song *Crazy Mama* became a classic that had a fairly good chance at hitting the Top 5 target, but because he passed on performing it in a popular national TV broadcast, the song didn't soar to the top as originally planned. Fortunately, the music world was still good to JJ Cale—he transformed into a cult figure and a wide variety of acts covered his tunes:

The Allman Brothers	Kansas
Chet Atkins	Freddie King
The Band	Lynyrd Skynyrd
Captain Beefheart	Herbie Mann &
Johnny Cash	Cissy Houston
Eric Clapton	Harry Manx
Randy Crawford	Carlos Santana
Jai	Widespread Panic

Mistakenly speaking, when I first heard Eric Clapton's cover versions of JJ Cale's *After Midnight*, *Cocaine* and *I'll Make Love To You Anytime*, I thought Clapton was the original writer. A newer CD, *Clapton*, also features collaborations with JJ Cale, plus, three Cale songs are on an Eric Clapton/Steve Winwood *Live From Madison Square Garden* CD/DVD recorded in 2008. A year later on February 24, 2009, JJ Cale released an acclaimed new album called *Roll On*—in March, *Rolling Stone* magazine interviewed him about it. This was Cale's first new CD in over four years; it followed a Grammy Award-winning gold album with Eric Clapton in 2006, *The Road to Escondido*. Cale also had plans to tour, for the first time since 2004. Each stop on the tour saw a portion of proceeds getting donated to a local animal charity or rescue effort. At the end of the day, lots of hard work led to JJ Cale being nominated for induction into Nashville's Songwriters Hall of Fame, codename NaSHoF.

> **LIGHT FACT:** JJ Cale's *Travelin' Light* was originally featured on his 1976 album *Troubador*; it was covered by Eric Clapton and Widespread Panic.

According to spatial data from NASA spaceflight.com, "STS-132: Final EVA completes battery task." What does *that* mean? On Friday, May 21, 2010, JJ Cale's latest version of his song *Travelin' Light* was played to awaken the crews of the Atlantis Space Shuttle and International Space Station, just before their early morning spacewalk. Back on Earth in February of 2011, Sony Music released a Silvertone Records collection of Cale's compositions from 1989-1992 called *The Silvertone Years*. Songs from albums like *Travel-Log* and *Number 10* were featured, and in a description of his Silvertone releases on Cale's website at www.jjcale.com it says, *"once you hear that guitar or the voice, you immediately know it's JJ Cale."* It doesn't get any Caler than that! We will now from the Tulsa sound to the sound of "Nashville South," through our next artist. Although he brings contemporary Country music to the masses, his music's not from Nashville: it's exported from Nashville's southern neighbor—let's tune in.

SPOTLIGHT ON: Corey Smith

Let's FAST FORWARD to today's out-of-the-box Country singer/songwriter. These days, he resembles someone who goes outside of tradition—outside of Nashville even—to establish an all-encompassing sales base that grew to unheard of proportions. The subject just described is Corey Smith, codename *Jefferson Record Breaker*. Being an hour from Atlanta and about thirty minutes from Athens, Corey Smith's center of operations in Jefferson is a place where he was born, raised and will always call home.

In a self-penned biographical reflection found on his website, Corey Smith compares writing his bio to composing a song, going as far as calling the process "therapeutic." Compressing thirty-three years into just a few paragraphs, Corey acknowledges his wife, two sons, and dainty North Georgia residence. He notes there was a period when he devised a plan to keep things moving from far outside of the city limits; even though Corey knew just about everyone, he felt as if there wasn't a good hometown fit. Comically speaking, he devised *Jet'n Outta Jefferson*, a Southern-flavored, hypothetical version of the film, *Escape From New York*. Although this pseudo-production never left the storyboard, Corey eventually made his way out of Jefferson.

Despite Corey Smith's rugged look today, he professes to not being a jock, geeky superior intellect, redneck or thug, back in his high school years. In an alternate view Smith saw himself as a "nameless face," looking for that feeling of belonging somewhere that he could easily fit in. By his senior year of high school, Corey musically morphed into a slightly inebriated but full-blown, guitar-toting "human jukebox"—and he let everyone know it. But the urge to *get outta Dodge* had already kicked in and it kicked Corey out of Jefferson: to study in Paris. Through a University of Georgia program, scholarship money and student loans, Smith found himself in a new city on the other side of the Atlantic. Although he was interacting with a totally different culture within a matter of weeks, Corey soon longed to be home again. As countless listeners can attest to, music stepped in and saved the day for Corey. Without the familiar sounds of the Allman Brothers or Lynyrd Skynyrd in his CD library to carry him through, Corey may have abandoned his classes in France for a "Midnight Train To Georgia," like Gladys Knight sung in her song.

After Corey Smith graduated from the University of Georgia in Athens he got married, had kids and settled down to work as a high school teacher. With the American dream in hand, Corey's rural lifestyle got reflected through songs he wrote. Music incrementally played a larger role along his travels, and Corey recollects this when he first started off. Initially, he just wanted to be seen—but after a while, music became more therapeautic in helping him get through day-to-day struggles. Later in life, Corey saw his dreams unfold as a result of extreme musicality from within. He had a plan in mind since his teaching days and when the time came to blast off, three rocket boosters were in place; plus an auxiliary. They were all well armed and ready to go—disguised as fully produced albums and cash-paying gigs, all fired up for chartbound deployment.

Selling out the famed *Georgia Theater* on his first try in December of 2005, Corey Smith remembers the Zac Brown Band opening up for him. Suddenly, the heavens parted and Smith was rocketing through a star-studded music universe at the speed of sound. During the course of five years, he logged in over 700 shows with more than 700,000 tickets sold, earning himself a galactic gross figure of $7.5 million. Adding a trio of albums recorded since quitting his day job, Corey had a combined total of six albums and as his manager Marty updated me, was "just shy" of 1,000,000 single sales!

That's pretty unheard of by Nashville standards but it's just right for Corey Smith, who was determined to run his Country music *biz* from home in Jefferson, Georgia. From there, Corey operates fan-based field exercises using tools like file sharing, social networking, word-of-mouth and an evolutionary stage show; he stays booked at venues from Jefferson to Seattle. By refining his live performances as well as writing and producing his own albums, Corey arrived at his latest release, *The Broken Record*. Production-wise, this project offered both old and new songs that were either enhanced or minimized. As a result, listeners get treated to a music mix of the Corey everybody knows—with the Corey no one ever fathomed before. Corey Smith has a long list of accomplishments behind him and remains right on course, as he looks ahead to the future through super-tinted UV solarized binoculars, because it's a bright one… For more on Jefferson, Georgia's own Corey Smith, hit the web at starting point www.coreysmith.com.

A TIP OF THE HAT

With so much focus on the modern-day cowboys just mentioned, it wouldn't be nice to leave out music's cowgirls, so prepare for the 'hot picks' that follow. These women were great singers, and some were also proficient musicians. Here's a partial list of some talented female singers who belt out hot Country tunes:

Alison Kraus	Faith Hill	Michelle Nixon & Drive
Alysha Black-Wimberly	Georgette Jones	Mother Maybelle Carter
	Holly Dunn	Naomi Judd
Amber Leigh	Janie Fricke	Natalie Tidwell
Anne Murray	Joy Lynn White	Norah Jones
Barbara Mandrell	Juice Newton	Pam Tillis
Bonnie Stewart	June Carter Cash	Patsy Cline
Brenda Lee	K.D. Lang	Patti Page
Candi Carpenter	Kimberly Cash	Patty Loveless
Carlene Carter	Laura Lynn	Reba McEntire
Carrie Underwood	Leann Rimes	Rebecca Lynn Howard
	Linda Ronstadt	Shania Twain
Crystal Gayle	Lisa Marie-Presley	Tammy Wynette
Deana Carter	Lisa O'Kane	Tanya Tucker
Dolly Parton	Louise Mandrell	Taylor Swift
Donna Fargo	Lynn Anderson	Trisha Yearwood
Dottie Rambo	Martina McBride	Wanda Jackson
Emmylou Harris	Mavis Staples	Wynonna Judd
	Melody Dunn	

A number of these fabulous ladies also made themselves known on the Pop charts. Some had Pop/Jazz overtones in their music (Nora Jones), while others were known in other genres like R&B/Soul (Mavis Staples). A few even graced the film and television screen (Dolly Parton, Reba McEntire). But there's one more important lady you should know about, so get ready as we turn the…

SPOTLIGHT ON: Dottie Rambo

There are some who might associate Gospel primarily with Black singers and musicians, but my good friend Stephanie codename Agent Apache Wolf, says "open up your lens!" For those who are wondering why she might say that, I'll step to the side and let you get it "straight from the Wolf's mouth." Picking the Native American-powered brain cells of Apache Wolf, we find that she is extremely proud of her Indian heritage, displaying it through the knowledge she shares, clothes she wears… and poems she likes to perform from time to time. But you'll have to come to Atlanta for a glimpse of this rare Wolf in live performance mode! For now, let's acquire some intel this Special Agent secured on Dottie Rambo, Musicology codename *Heavenly Voice*.

Thanks for the introduction, L.A.—I just want to let more people know the Gospel world isn't made up of just one color, but a beautiful mixture of *tonal ambiances*, as I like to call them. Since I consider myself to be colorblind, let's take a colorblind view by opening the lens to reveal a Gospel music world occupied by Blacks, Whites, Reds, Browns and Yellows—any creed that found a calling to share the *Good Word*. That's one thing Dottie Rambo did all too well as a beloved Gospel singer-songwriter. Dottie Rambo won ASCAP, Dove and Grammy Awards; this was a sign that she traveled the high road to success. But she wasn't by herself—along with husband Buck and their daughter Reba, we see a Gospel singing force called *The Rambos*. Just to get a rough idea of how deep Dottie was when it came to songwriting, just look at the numbers: she wrote over 2,500 Christian and Country tunes!

I once told L.A. Jackson about Dottie Rambo being referenced as Elvis Presley's Gospel godmother, and if you need a good example why, just check out a few songs *King Elvis* re-recorded as cover tunes in his early years. She also influenced Music Queens like Barbara Mandrell, Carol Channing, Whitney Houston and Dolly Parton; they've all recorded Dottie Rambo compositions at some point in their careers. In our wide-angle view, a long list of top secular recording acts from A to Z also recorded her songs:

227

Johnny Cash	Alison Krauss	Connie Smith
Barbara Fairchild	Jerry Lee Lewis	Hank Snow
Larry Gatlin	Bill Monroe	Mel Tillis
Crystal Gayle	The Oak Ridge Boys	Rhonda Vincent
Vince Gill	Jeannie C. Riley	Porter Wagoner
Wanda Jackson		Dottie West

Christian/Gospel/Spiritual artists we can add to the list include:

Vanessa Bell-Armstrong	The Florida Boys	Bobby Jones
The Blackwood Brothers	The Happy Goodmans	Ron Kenoly
	Steve Green	Doyle Lawson
The Booth Brothers	Danniebelle Hall	Mark Lowry
Commissioned	Nancy Harmon	Walt Mills
The Crabb Family	Lamelle Harris	Janet Paschal
Andrae Crouch	The Hemphills	Sandi Patty
Jimmie Davis	Jake Hess	Karen Peck
DC Talk	The Hoppers	The Speer Family
Jeff and Sheri Easter	The Isaacs	Albertina Walker
	Aaron Jeoffrey	Karen Wheaton

Adding a twist to the tale, this highly respected Gospel singer actually grew up with an ear for Country music. Let's look at how it all happened by connecting a few dots. When Dottie was a little girl, she grew up as Joyce Reba Luttrell. She enjoyed listening to the Grand Ole Opry on WSM radio so much that she learned how to play guitar; stuff like that happens a lot! Fortunately, this took the bite out of growing up poor, and provided the young singer with a quality source of motivation.

By age eight, Dottie Rambo was composing songs at her favorite 'studio spot,' a creek bank near the young star's Kentucky home. With supportive parents urging her on, the growing ten-year old performed popular Country songs on a nearby radio station. Things got more interesting when she was twelve and got saved; being a born-again Christian meant she would be singing and writing Christian and Gospel—no more Country music. Unbelievably, her father didn't support this decision: it was his way, or the highway. Trusting her inner feelings, Dottie took the latter option. She wound up in Indianapolis, Indiana and started *The Gospel Echoes*, a trio that performed across the South and Midwest. In 1950, the 16-year old met Buck Rambo at a revival event—after the pair got married, they kept the show on the road. Dottie had to be relieved at this point, because she was on the road by herself for years, finding shelter with pastors and their families.

The Gospel Echoes became the *Singing Rambos*, and *The Rambos*. After the *Happy Goodman Family* introduced her to Governor of Louisiana Jimmie Davis, Dottie did a performance for him—he was also a popular Country and Gospel artist. Dottie signed on to Jimmie's publishing company and during that period, found his name listed as "co-writer" on her songs, even though the lawman didn't contribute to their creation. Right now, the Wolf part of me is saying, "a savvy entertainment attorney wasn't on her side when she signed that contract." For Jimmie, this perk crept through the small writing on the contract, and Dottie had to 'chalk it up to the game.'

During the 60s, Dottie Rambo got more well known because of her songwriting skills, live performance capabilities and her part in groups like *The Singing Rambos*. Dottie's compassionate side led her as far away as Vietnam in 1967, where she entertained U.S. troops stationed in war torn jungles; she even found time to minister in local field hospitals. After securing a record deal with Warner Brothers, Dottie Rambo reeled in radio airplay, record sales, and more artists were covering her songs. Dottie's name was already being uttered throughout the industry in 1968, when she was blessed with a Grammy Award for *Best Soul Gospel Performance*. While Dottie's album, *It's The Soul Of Me*, raised industry eyebrows, her group (*The Gospel Echoes*) had poor sales and got dropped from the Warner label. In the aftermath, Warner Brothers offered to keep Dottie as a solo "R&B" act, but she opted to sign on with the Christian based Benson Records.

Keeping her power of collaboration at an all-time high, Dottie Rambo blessed the masses by collaborating with Christian leaders from Billy Graham, to Benny Hinn, to T.D. Jakes, to Oral Roberts and Pat Robertson. Showing her diversity, in 1978 Dottie Rambo released a Christian children's audio book called *Down By The Creekbank*—it was a huge success and went platinum. Then a previously unheard of feat took place, with Whitney Houston revamping Dottie Rambo's *I Go To The Rock* for the movie soundtrack of *The Preacher's Wife*. Whitney and Dottie each won a 1998 GMA Dove Award for that one, and I ran out and bought the DVD as soon as it hit the streets! Once again, this demonstrates how powerful the synergies of people and music can be: Whitney made *I Go To The Rock* Dottie's biggest hit.

Dottie Rambo wrote songs that were covered in the secular and non-secular realms by a vast amount of artists that take up letters from A to Z. In addition, Dottie kept the camera lens on "wide" through appearances on a long list of top shows that aired on Christian and mainstream networks. She even had her own highly rated show on TBN in the 80s, *The Dottie Rambo Magazine*. In the late 80s, her health declined due to serious back ailments, and then came a breakup with her husband in the early 90s. Nevertheless, Dottie still rebounded and during the mid-to-late 90s, she remained visible at churches, on TV and onstage.

After an 18-year hiatus, Dottie Rambo returned to the studio in 2002 for vocal exercises; she came out with another chart-topping hit, *Stand By The River*. Teaming up with Dolly Parton, Dottie showed she still had the magic that brought her to the industry's forefront. A 2004 CD/DVD was released, *We Shall Behold Him: A Tribute to Dottie Rambo*—it ran the full gamut of A-list performers. By 2007, Dottie was doing national tours, including stops at old friend Dolly Parton's *Dollywood* theme park. Before year's end, a new album was recorded and work began on another one. Unfortunately, on the way to a 2008 Texas Mother's Day show, Dottie was fatally injured in a bus accident—just after completing a show at Calvary Life Church in Granite City, Illinois.

Dottie Rambo was taken away from us long before her due date, but she was allotted some 'just enough' time to create many special musical gifts. Fortunately for us, traces of her spirit were left through tons of Country, Christian and Gospel songs—now, a wide fan base easily relates to it. For extended satisfaction, there were several posthumous music releases plus accolades like Christian, Country, Dove, Grammy, Lifetime Achievement, Pioneer and Songwriter of the Century Awards. There was even a collector's edition Anniversary Doll, made by Annalee. Dottie Rambo will always be remembered for many contributions to the entertainment world. She has been the focus of numerous TV specials and more. You can top it all off by doing an online search, where additional information can be found on Miss Rambo's many accomplishments.

Dottie Rambo's induction into the *Christian Music Hall of Fame*, *Georgia Music Hall of Fame* and *Music City's Walk of Fame* will always serve as stark reminders of this heavenly singer and songwriter. She now shares her talents exclusively within the Pearly Gates, for a select audience. Should you feel the spirit taking over, get blessed with more music data at www.dottierambo.net.

In my book, Dottie Rambo was one lady with a true gift from God, the sole holder of unlimited power. Here on Earth, we humans still can't even put that into proper perspective. But I believe Native Americans like the Apache understands how the system works; so do wild canines like the Wolf. There may be those who are unaware that the Apache and the Wolf each possess a sixth sense, and I pull 'equal energy' from both of them when I'm doing deep meditation exercises at home. And when I want to play deeply inspirational spiritual music, there's always a Dottie Rambo CD within reach... plus, my iPhone is all loaded up for when I'm on the go as a high-fashion poet, or as a U.M.O.— *Undercover Music Operative* with Agent Superintendent, L.A. Jackson.

It's a good time to bring him back now because at this point, I've got to go summon the ancient spirits and disseminate this great excursion I had with you all. I hope you see that through Dottie Rambo and others like her, the Gospel world isn't made up of just one color, but a beautiful mixture of tonal ambiances. If you agree, then my mission here is accomplished. As it's said in the Apache language, "*Ka dish day*"—until we meet again. This is "not-so-secret" Agent Apache Wolf signing off; may God watch over you and thanks for having me along!

Well *ahee-ih-yeh* or *thank you*, Agent Apache Wolf—we hope to do an "operation interception" with you again in the future! By now it should be easy to see how Gospel music crossed many boundaries in order to be used by anyone that wants to get closer to God, fans... or the bank. But seriously, singers and musicians who create this music opened up their inner lens to show that our differences should not hinder us, but bind us.

So now that you've heard it "straight from the Wolf's mouth," I hope the knowledge you've gained will be used to help extend hands out to neighbors in fellowship, instead of looking sideways at them. Here's some advice: try not to look down at anyone, unless you are helping to pick him or her up. In other words, we should always strive to find new ways of positive communication— Dottie Rambo and Apache Wolf used their special gifts to unify God's people; Dottie brought to life songs filled with Heavenly insight, while Apache likes sharing deeply insightful poems. If you let them inspire you, then you too will inspire others to seek *Superior Intellect.*

-10-
ALL IN A DAY'S WORK

Some may not realize it, but many acts performed more than one music form in order to collect their ROI (return on investment) for fame and fortune. Back in the early days, Blacks with Gospel music backgrounds used the process I call *genre jumping* to become great R&B performers. Artists like Ray Charles effortlessly crossed the Gospel, R&B, Pop, Rock and Country borders. He was influenced by Blues, Country, Jazz and R&B musicians like Louis Armstrong, Charles Brown, Nat "King" Cole, Louis Jordan and Art Tatum. There are plenty of books about this icon, plus the movie *Ray* did a great job depicting his musical genius. With that said, I'll run through some more key points about him here and later, I might throw in a golden nugget for you to walk with.

- He combined the styles of Barrelhouse, Country Blues and Stride
- While on Atlantic Records in the 50s, he became a Soul music pioneer by mixing R&B, Gospel and Blues
- During the 60s on ABC Records, he blended Country and Pop to achieve much crossover success
- At ABC Records, he was one of the first Black acts given total creative control by a major label
- Frank Sinatra gave Ray Charles big kudos by calling him "the only true genius in show business"
- Billy Joel was quoted saying, "This may sound like sacrilege, but I think Ray Charles was more important than Elvis Presley"
- Ray Charles is #10 on Rolling Stone's "100 Greatest Artists of All Time" and #2 on the "100 Greatest Singers of All Time" list

Ray Charles' DNA kept his legacy moving into the next era through daughter Sheila Raye (more data's coming soon), like Nat "King" Cole did with Natalie. Jumping back to genre jumpers, Nat "King" Cole started off as a Jazz artist before going 'Pop' and ending up with over 100 singles and 24 albums from a 20-year career. Cole was said to be the second most successful Pop singer of his generation... behind Frank Sinatra. Another famous genre jumper was Sam Cooke, who went from Gospel to Soul, R&B and Pop. His first #1 hit single was *You Send Me* and that song still sends me back in time, to when my parents played it on our Grundig sound system. There's a wider scope of Sam somewhere in this book series—please be sure to read it, if you haven't done so yet.

Ray Charles, Nat "King" Cole and Sam Cooke were masters of their craft who unlike most Black performers of their era, controlled the rights to their music. A young Bobby Womack took cues from them and created a long-term career by fusing strong elements of Blues, Soul and Gospel with sounds from guitars, pianos, organs and horns. As usual, all the achievements of these artists can't be documented here, but a wealth of music data is easily obtainable on them. I implore you to look online or in libraries and you'll discover more significant contributions these musicians have made to music *biz*tory. There are many elements that combine to make longlasting careers for talented artists. Being able to genre-jump allows certain acts the flexibility of showing a deep knowledge of their craft. Along with that knowledge comes a sense of ownership, which can't be taken away. A few choice acts were adamant about keeping as much ownership as possible to pass on down the line, through residual income.

As you have seen (or have yet to see), legendary acts like Ray Charles, Nat "King" Cole and Sam Cooke had DNA that was so powerful it fueled more generations of music makers (Sheila Raye Charles, Natalie Cole, Wade Jones) that each possessed an uncanny ability to genre-jump at lightning speed. One of the most important things a true talent must do is GET PAID, and it's no myth: this game is all about survival of the fittest! We're about to take a quick look at some staggering figures, so when you see $300 concert tickets at the box office, try to remember what kind of pipeline it's feeding…

Besides being exceptional singers, many Pop, Rock, Folk, Country, Gospel, Soul and R&B artists wrote their own songs, did their own productions and maintained their own publishing rights. Publishing is another lucrative part of the industry, so here's an example of the kind of income that's generated in the worldwide market:

World revenues from music publishing: 2000 (in $US million)

Public performance revenue

	US	Japan	Germany	France	UK	Other	World Total
Radio	291.8	108.9	50.8	23.0	60.3	179.3	714.1
TV/cable/satellite	317.0	16.1	4.3	122.2	64.4	465.1	1,069.1
Live performance	203.1	158.2	180.9	174.6	126.0	450.4	1,293.2
Sub-total	811.9	283.2	316.0	319.8	250.7	1,094.7	3,076.3

Reproduction revenue

	US	Japan	Germany	France	UK	Other	World Total
Mechanical royalties (record sales)	691.5	311.3	258.7	105.8	195.9	432.1	1,995.3
Synchronization royalties (TV, movies)	156.7	80.5	67.8	50.8	124.6	189.5	669.9
Other	-	16.1	16.0	17.0	-	23.8	72.9
Sub-total	848.2	407.9	342.5	173.5	320.5	645.5	2,738.1

Distribution revenue

	US	Japan	Germany	France	UK	Other	World Total
Sheet music sales	316.1	19.9	140.2	58.3	69.2	125.2	728.9
Rental/lending rights	n.a.	30.9	6.6	-	-	2.4	39.9
Sub-total	316.1	50.7	146.8	58.3	69.2	127.6	768.8
Other	30.4	78.9	28.8	49.7	26.2	80.1	294.1
Grand Total	2,006.5	820.7	834.0	601.2	666.6	1,948.2	6,877.3

Source: National Music Publishers' Association

As you can see, music publishing is the ending result of music that gets broadcast, performed, recorded, sold and/or rented. Opening up the Internet lens, we can add to the picture by noting music performances and sales that generate even more publishing income. Let's keep things moving forward, so we can check out a few memorable guitarists—their instrument of choice makes good music, *and* makes music sound good… "good enough to generate good income for good people."

Through publishing, songwriters can obtain income in a choice of ways; like having other acts perform or record newer versions of their compositions. The ending result of this practice has come to be known as *cover songs*. As White artists clamored to cover Black songs, Black Pop stars like Harry Belafonte jumped on the bandwagon and scored big by mixing covers with original compositions. Incidentally, one of my favorite Harry Belafonte songs has a lyric in it that goes, *"Day-O"*—alternatively known as *The Banana Boat Song*. Harry displays a flawless ability to "hit the high note" in it. Belafonte's immense talent presented itself throughout the course of his extraordinary career and it's one that definitely should be explored—if you hit the search button enough, you'll get the whole point on this incredible Belafonte *mon*.

Augmenting great cover tunes by folks like Ray Charles, Dion, Jack Jones, Lead Belly and Joni Mitchell, Harry Belafonte's Caribbean-flavored songs (also called Calypso music) transposed the West Indian experience for audiences around the world to enjoy. The 60s found this music style in such great demand that far away places like San Francisco had entertainers like Maya Angelou doing Calypso-styled performances! Adding more flavors to his mix, Belafonte had the pleasure to work with heavyweight directors like Robert Altman.

Harry graced the big screen with stars like Bill Cosby, Sidney Poitier, Richard Pryor and Flip Wilson in the 1974 classic, *Uptown Saturday Night*. Belafonte also made his mark as a narrator for many documentaries along a journey that landed him as one key player in a monumental mass recording. It was the U.S.A. for Africa's *We Are the World*, and you may remember mention of this project earlier, in *Musicology 2101*. In the long run, even Harry saw the value of remaking songs written by other folks and he capitalized off it, not to mention songs of his that were covered by other folks. So like I said, if you haven't had a chance to experience "Missa Tally Mon," do yourself a *flavor*…

As cover records became more popular, many White artists who remade songs originally performed by Blacks often placed their photographs in the record's artwork. This approach was copied by many Pop acts, but it wasn't a luxury always afforded to Blacks who sought to enter the mainstream music market. Some artists didn't find out what their single or album artwork looked liked until *after* the record was released. Piling on top of that note, some of them had no idea their record was for sale until they heard it on the radio, were told by friends, or found it as they flipped through the new release section at a record store.

Summing things up, prior to the "digital (r)evolution," the industry philosophy regarding in-store record sales focused on what took place in "brick and mortar" retail stores. Expanding our view, we can see that right along with physical brick and mortar music stores, today's book retailers are also getting tagged as last reps of a dying breed. During the process of 'due diligence research' for this book, it was discovered how closely the book and music industries mirrored each other—authors and artists were found at the tail end of book publishers' and record labels' payment trail. A typical demand-generation salesflow process for the pre-digital music industry model follows:

- Record labels sent out advance copies of potential hits to radio stations and record retailers
- Also included in mailings were key publicity outlets like the press and other print/media sources
- Interviews and shows got set up as the record took on wind with radio airplay
- When airplay was sufficient, buyers began purchasing the music at record stores
- Initiatives were constructed around tours to support local/regional/national activity
- Ample quantities of music product got shipped to the warehouses of chain retailers and regional distributors, destination: consumers!

Just add the Internet and other variables to the cacophony of sales, promotions, media interviews and/or performances taking place during this often unpredictable process, and you could get a whirlwind of well-lubed, music *biz* motion: thus, M-O-N-E-Y ($$) is made. The cash flows back from sources like radio stations to the performance rights organizations (PROs) that monitor everything. PROs also distribute income to publishers and composers, while record store sales generate mechanical sales revenue, which usually comes back to the record label. After a series of lengthy calculations (and some sneaky manipulations), the artist got "net proceeds." I heard it's sometimes best to keep doing live shows "in lieu of…" hence the term, *starving artist*. And I'm willing to bet an all-around entertainer with the initials of B.P. knew exactly what a starving artist looked like, because things weren't always so peachy for him in the early days of Rock-n-Roll. That said, let's bring it back to home base and finish up our version of *Bobby Poe: Music Biz Wizard from Kansas*, because as we all know—there's "no place like home."

POE-ETICALLY SPEAKING

Here are some more music *biz*tory notes based on this Oz-like icon that hosted an annual conference that represented the mainstream Pop, Rock and Country music worlds down south in Atlanta, in our neck of the woods. Because I spent roughly half of the 80s and 90s working at the Atlanta branch of CBS Records/Sony Music, highlights of my career include going to numerous music conferences and conventions.

I 'saw the scenario' as Sidney Miller worked the crowd at his huge *Black Radio Exclusive* New Orleans shindigs, before the *Essence Music Festival* moved in. I also dropped in on *Mello Yello* man Jack "The Rapper" Gibson at the one and only *Atlanta Family Affair*, and there was J.R. Dino's *Million Dollar Record Pool Conference*, where I picked up a nice award for helping them out with merchandising materials over the years. In the college market, my longtime associate Tony Baraka and his lovely wife Rhonda moved to Atlanta from Tuskegee. I used to load them up with music for *Tafrija*, their magazine that focused on music *biz* goings on; just so you know, "Tafrija" is a declassified Swahili codeword for *celebrate*. Tony went on to initiate the *Southeast Urban Music Conference* (SUMC), which is still active today. Back in the late 90s I did production work to create the first SUMC sampler CDs for conference attendees, after Tony received the DAT tapes of various record labels' featured artists.

Before Tony and Rhonda Baraka made their move to *A-Town*, there was an annual event called the *Black College Radio Conference*. It was held by a former WSB-Atlanta television reporter—I fought to make sure that CBS Records, Columbia, Epic and Def Jam acts were well represented. Lo Jelks worked for WSB from 1967 to 1976, and was one of the first African-American faces on a major television station in the South. There was one more annual music event I remember: the *Bobby Poe Pop*

Music Convention and Seminar. Since the Poe Convention represented the Pop, Rock and Country music sides of *the biz*, it was one of *the bizziest* music conventions in Atlanta when I was working for 'the big label.' Similar to music events like Sidney Miller's *Black Radio Exclusive* and Jack The Rapper's Atlanta *Family Affair*, I executed high-profile operational duties at conferences and conventions. Some of my chores included ensuring the proper implementation of Columbia and Epic's point-of-purchase materials in the hotel's hospitality suites and ballrooms. Hence, I tended to find myself running subvertive undercover missions, as well as functioning as set designer, poster police and security… I was at my best when I went to these kinds of functions because I was as my pals in Full Force say, "*in the place to be!*"

Bobby Poe's *Pop Music Convention and Seminar* attracted a crowd comparable to any major conference held in New York or Los Angeles. And in case you wonder why I have so much to say about this visionary, it's because Poe managed to successfully navigate his way through many of the sudden twists and turns that were so willingly offered to him… and also because he was a major player in the music industry of the South. Many are unaware of the incredible contributions of Bobby Poe, or his evolution as an on-and-off starving artist, entrepreneur and family man, complete with a lion's share of music *biz* ups and downs. (Trust me, I can relate to where he's coming from!) During the mid-80s when I worked at CBS Records, there were only a few trailblazers holding their own in the ever-changing "*Sex, Drugs and Rock-n-Roll*" codename "*SD&RR*" climate. Now if you'll excuse me, I'm going to run and check with someone to make sure the "*Sex, Drugs and Rock-n-Roll*" phrase is still politically correct; I don't know, maybe I AM getting old.

SINK OR SWIM

TIME STAMP: the mid-to-late 60s. Now finding himself jumping into parody records, Bobby Poe and radio industry friend Harv Moore produced *Interview of the Fab Four* using sound bites from Beatles songs. A similar tactic was used through 70s songs like *Mr. Jaws*, *The Streak*, *Superfly Meets Shaft* and somewhere along the line, Weird Al Yankovic came up with a weird idea to make his own parodies based on hit songs. Subsequently, life was never the same for me—I found myself promoting them in the 80s. Weird Al was later seen drivng to the bank in custom cars with B wings (Bentley) or RR (Rolls Royce) embellished on the hood.

238

Keeping the wheels spinning, here's a messenger of misery moment—unlike the songs mentioned above, Bobby Poe's *Interview of the Fab Four* was not cleared to use those particular sound bites, and the song was pulled off shelves before a lawsuit ensued. If "the business" had been handled properly, Bobby Poe and his business partner would have been sitting pretty: they had pre-orders of 500,000 copies. It was time to head back to the drawing board to concoct a new hit-making strategy, because sometimes you have to *keep coming back to get what you want out of life*. Poe kept moving forward, even after his ups and downs in the 60s and another deal fell through with the British Walkers Shoe Company—it had the potential to put a cool million into his hands.

The year 1967 saw Bobby Poe change the pace; he and his partners got into the club business. By 1968, they were getting out—sagas of 'alleged allegations' took the drama from bad to worse. A series of unlucky incidents caused Poe and his partners' stint as club owners to STOP, almost as quickly as it began. Misfortunes included being framed for an arson they didn't commit, problems with paying the club's rent, and nearly being arrested for 'stealing' their own property back. If we were to PAUSE and zoom in for a closer look, we'd see they were actually retrieving belongings that were previously held in police custody. FAST FORWARD: The legalities surrounding these mishaps eventually got resolved and led to an arrest of the real perpetrator—Poe's landlord! RECORD: By this time, Bobby Poe had one leg outside the "music business within" door, as lead guitarist/booking agent Vernon Sandusky went off to PLAY some twenty-two years worth of guitar with the ever-inventive Roy Clark: codename *Guitar-Pickin' Music Man*.

New opportunities were presented to Poe, like one at a club called *The Cellar Door*. This 'comeup capability' came through a bartender named Jack Boyle, but Poe passed on the chance to book up-and-coming bands that went on to greatness (like *The Mamas and The Papas*), after all he had just been through. Twenty-five years later in the 90s, that same bartender made millions of dollars by selling his business as *Cellar Door Productions*—it became one of the biggest booking agencies in the country. By 1968, Bobby Poe and Mitch Corday started a triad of music biz trade reports called the *Pop Music Survey*, the *Country Music Survey* and the *Soul Music Survey*.

COVERING THE BASES

Bobby Poe staffed these new ventures by partnering with his old radio buddy Harv Moore to oversee the *Pop Music Survey* (PMS). Not long after, he pulled in a *Cashbox* magazine staffer to manage the *Country Music Survey* (CMS). A top DJ from a Philadelphia R&B station was tapped to run the *Soul Music Survey* (SMS), which became Poe's "cash cow." Soon after, celebrities like Joe Frazier, Jim Brown and Roosevelt Grier each befriended Poe with music projects, and he made their plans a reality. Unfortunately, the fatal shootings of civil rights supporters like John F. Kennedy (1963), Malcolm X (1965), Robert F. Kennedy and Dr. Martin Luther King, Jr. (both in 1968), had driven a stake in the heart of U.S. race relations once again. A massive straw had broken the camel's back, and Blacks in the *biz* were no longer willing to tolerate White control over their music.

Things had gotten sticky in America but by 1969, Bobby Poe had a seminar in the works for Country music radio programmers and record promoters; by 1970 the stage was set for 1973's *Pop Music Seminar*. As things progressed, elements from the underworld made their appearance and Bobby Poe was right in line for "unscrupulous practices" to come his way. He opted to drop a few business units, particularly the *Soul Music Survey*. The irony for Poe is that he was an early proponent of integrated Rock-n-Roll bands, and the *Soul Music Survey* had grown into a genuine, grass chomping, cash-bearing cow. Yet, Poe found himself looking like a casualty in the racism war as he was forced out of the Black music industry through no direct fault of his own. Without the *Soul Music Survey* to subsidize the *Country Music Survey and Seminar*, Bobby Poe would have to shut down the CMS. Luckily, Nashville's music community and Poe's friend Tom McEntee along with Country radio broadcasters took over the Seminar, enabling the CMS to kick off and grow, celebrating its 40th birthday by 2009.

In 1971, Bobby Poe became publisher and editor of the *Pop Music Survey*, due to partner Harv Moore taking a Program Director's position at a radio station and resigning as PMS editor: it was a conflict of interest. This reminds me of how labels signed artists to recording contracts that fell under the protocol for management and publishing contracts, too. This three-point-play strengthened the labels' claim to ownership and thus gave them the right to have complete control over their acts. I later found out that many of these practices were considered as conflicts of interest, even though they were widely executed across the record biz battleground. After a while, I learned it was taboo for the head of a label be intimately involved with an artist from the roster, but by the time my former "Big Boss" Tommy Mattola married Mariah Carey, enforcement of this "conflict of interest" policy had subsided.

Taking in all the action were the inquisitive-minded, armed with a loaded finger pointing in the air, asking questions like *Were certain rules meant to be broken, and who had the power to break them?*" Did things really change that much by the 90s and beyond? I don't know, but I'd bet my last buck that there's a long line of guys who considered breaking a few rules for a shot at the once single, now double-babied Miss Mariah, codename *Butterfly*. Before more babies, chicks or kittens pop up in classic *Sylvester & Tweety* form, let's get back to the Kool Poe Kat.

In 1973 when Bobby Poe was laying out the groundwork for his first *Pop Music Convention and Seminar*, he wanted to make it special with the addition of a celebrity golf tournament. The tournament almost fell through, because Poe didn't have the $1,000 downpayment to secure a full-page ad in *Billboard* magazine; that was until long-time mentor Lelan Rogers introduced Poe to his younger brother. Poe finally got the money he desperately needed from Lelan's sibling, Country music star Kenny Rogers—he 'incidentally' became the first celebrity to sign up for Poe's golf gala. Soon, Kenny was followed by a slew of heavy hitters, including the former head of Buddah Records: the bright and colorful Neil Bogart went on to become Casablanca Records' all-powerful ringleader during the bedazzling Disco era. Neil brought in comedian Robert Klein as Master of Ceremonies, and then Columbia Records' Johnny Nash signed on. Johnny was riding high at the time with a #1 record called *I Can See Clearly Now*. Let's use our mounting superior intellect to figure out how the *Pop Music Seminar* turned out…

Bobby Poe's Pop music conference ran for almost a quarter century, even after he retired in 1996. Around that time, anyone who was someone in the record business would corroborate that if you participated in the Pop-Rock-Country music game, "The Poe" was one *do-not-miss* affair to mark on the calendar. It was during the Poe era that the term "*Sex, Drugs and Rock-n-Roll*" was born, so it wouldn't take a rocket scientist to figure out what was going on before, during, or after the music *biz* discussions took place. Audacious behavior wasn't uncommon at music gatherings—in fact, similar sightings have taken place at all sorts of happenings across the music board. At one such affair, I saw a crowd gathered around an 'engaged' couple having a go at it in the lobby of a major hotel. Based on stories that folks like Al Teller, Don Miller, Ron Herbert and Ray Mariner told me, I can only imagine what other behind-the-scenes activities took place.

POEVOLUTION

With his son as a new partner, 1979 saw Bobby Poe Sr. working hand in hand with Bobby Poe Jr. As they moved into high gear, the Poe convention expanded its scope for inclusion of a "*Ms. Pop Music*" beauty contest, leading to codename OED (Operation Expanded Dimensions). In the meantime, record labels struggled to change the laid-back, yet over-the-top party imagery that had been dispelled across the industry. New mandates were making it through the pipeline, and if certain executives wanted to keep their jobs, they had to comply with top-down governance. This included standards embedded in a revised blueprint of the customary 'corporate environment' model.

I watched the metamorphosis occur during the CBS Records-to-Sony Music Entertainment transition of the late 1980s. More non-traditional industry execs were slipping into custom suits and ties—as new people from professions like accounting, finance, operations or even the medical industry entered the playing field; and the numbers were growing. Before this trend began however, much of the industry's staffing came from sectors like music retail, publishing, recording studios and the tour circuit. Another additive that fueled this personnel shift in the industry was the appearance of more ambitious women yielding absolute power. Signs that new policies finally made their way into the "Good Ol' Boy" etiquette had arrived—and the way of doing all things music biz would never be the same again! The manifestation of this commotion in the industry revealed itself at subsequent Poe conventions that garnered the interest of keynote speakers and special guests like Carol Channing, Dolly Parton and Media Queen, Oprah Winfrey. In addition to super-heavyweights like Michael Jackson, there were many celebrities who made special appearances:

Clive Davis	Howard Cosell	Larry King
Don Imus	James Brown	Elton John
Jimmy Buffett	Eddie Murphy	The Moody Blues
Bruce Hornsby	JohnMellancamp	Crowded House

And there were plenty more, including a fun-loving artist that upon hitting the REWIND button, we'll see was honored at my maiden voyage to the Poe Convention—Cyndi Lauper. FAST FORWARD: After he retired in 1996, Bobby Poe went on to found Grove, Oklahoma's Grand Grove Opry in 1999. On a weekly basis, local and national Country music events were broadcast from this music theater on Vinita, Oklahoma's KITO radio. RECORD: Poe continued to promote Country music concerts there until 2005, even after the Opry building picked up new owners. PLAY: March of 2009 saw Bobby Poe and The Poe Kats inducted into the Kansas Music Hall of Fame. PAUSE: Unfortunately, Poe was diagnosed with throat cancer in 2009. While he overcame the cancer, he grew steadily weaker during recovery. With over fifty years worth of service in the music biz, we can STOP to look back and see how Bobby Poe relished being able to depart from what some would call the big show, on his own terms. Along the way, he acquired over a hundred gold and platinum records, with even more legendary friends and allies—all from a few 'slightly shady' eras in the industry.

What I can say is this: even though it was a shady business, people from all walks of life still didn't think twice about 'trading their souls for a million in cash,' just to be a part of the hoopla. Let me also point out that some folks referred to the machinery of motion in the Pop music *biz* as a *big show* or *circus*, while others simply called it a zoo. Despite what we see on TV and elsewhere, it's still a free country; whatever you choose to call the music industry is strictly up to you. While I often wonder what Bobby Poe retrospectively called it, I'm just happy to have been in the same room with the man at one celestial point in music biz time.

And now we've arrived at somewhat of a twilight zone, where we'll bring into being a cosmic final thought from my man Rod Serling: "There is a fifth dimension, beyond that which is known to man. It is a dimension as vast as space and as timeless as infinity. It is the middle ground between light and shadow, between science and superstition." Please be aware that you have just arrived at secret location TMZ... and no, it's not that *Thirty Mile Zone* celebrity gossip show. It's *The Musicology Zone*—where we deliver tasty music treats for your inner thoughts to contemplate...

Well that was delicious food for our minds to munch on, plus it got topped off with some great multi-dimensional news. Thanks go out to TTZ Chairman Rod Serling, now permanently lodged in the cosmos, still smoking his Oasis cigarettes. However, this is the MU$IC *BIZ*, and sometimes it takes more than gold, platinum, good people and cosmic wisdom from *The Twilight Zone* to navigate through dark rooms, hallways and tunnels cluttered with shady people all around. But one "Kool Kat" did it—somehow, Bobby Poe set up a strategy for success and used his superior intellect to 'cut through the chase' and ride out the course he set forth, sometimes on the fly. And now a moment of silence to take a PAUSE FOR THE CAUSE: during his recovery on January 22, 2011, a regretable report says Bobby Poe suffered a fatal blood clot and his soul sailed off into musical eternity. He's presently logged in at Heaven's Grand Stage, along with all the stars he worked with back in those revolutionary days. Tributarily speaking, I call that point of time the "Monolithic Golden Era of Music *Biz*tory."

Staying abreast of the digital revolution, we can thank the Poes (Senior and Junior) for their online entertainment company *Pop Music Records*. Go ahead and access it to get more info about two men with the same name—Bobby Poe—and a funny Internet comedy show called SVENGALI, plus lots of American (and U.K.) Pop music history. Visit www.popmusicrecords.com for tons of great Pop-n-Poe music, and blog site http://poekat.blogspot.com to get the full, unedited version of THE POE KAT and his multi-dimensionally unique story. Do you remember the actor who plays the Dos Equis *Most Interesting Man in the World*? (I heard it's Jonathan Goldsmith, but for some reason I think of Maximillian Schell)—whoever it really is, "he once had an awkward moment, just to see what it felt like." This leads to my final thought before going birdy: the Poes are some of the most interesting men in the music world that I've had the pleasure to "rub elbows and do a little *biz* with."

CODENAME CMTM: *CHIROPTERA MANUMUS & TURDU MIGRATORIUS*

Through 'the Poe Connection,' I met other most interesting music men, like Ron Herbert and Ray Mariner codenames Batman and Robin. Although their crime-fighting skills are unquestionably unconfirmed, these two super-friends sure did some banking up—as superheroes in the music BU$INE$$. Ron Herbert (Batman) made his mark as a successful artist manager, then as a VP of Operations and National Radio Promotion. He did this by converting dozens of records from the major labels into gold and platinum—after passing them through the 'hitmaking magnification scope' in his hi-tech Buckhead Batcave.

As a professional radio personality, major label promotion exec and a few other interesting things, Ray Mariner (Robin) regulates the airwaves. He holds court as one of Atlanta's "golden voices" at top-rated radio station *Star 94*. Combined, these guys held so much music *biz*tory clout that along with Bobby Poe Jr., they all need motion pictures made about them! To extend the thought, I'd be willing to bet Bobby Poe Sr. would "Pop up" at least 3 times: once for each life he touched between his son Bobby Jr, Ron Herbert and Ray Mariner. And I'd go as far as paying (what is it, $25 these days?) to watch these movies, too.

If not for most interesting guys like these, lots of music would never have made it to the masses because high levels of distribution power are required to keep it all moving. The extensive involvement these extraordinary gentlemen have in the music industry rivals few—their solo efforts, as well as "collective super-hero peership" pretty much covers most of the music *biz* spectrum. Please note: although there'll be a comprehensive rundown on the impact of radio and DJs in a future book, I thought it would be helpful to present a brief scenario for you now. Choosing Ron Herbert and Ray Mariner as lead-ins for this part of our radio and DJ overview was a no-brainer. On that note, I've presented three inside scenarios and you just got your first one, with the Poe legend.

Scenario two takes us to the heart of Buckhead, where the Batman (Ron Herbert) peers down at the city of Atlanta from the balcony of his gold and platinum riddled, hi-rise Batpad. Simply put, this music industry superhero turned singles into monster hits, through the magic of radio promotion. As a result, he's been largely responsible for determining which songs influenced listeners, to the tune of "millions of records" being sold. As a longtime manager and record promoter, Ron stepped up his game in 1996 by assuming the post of VP of Operations with Jeff McClusky & Associates, a mass-market molder of radio hits that was based in Chicago. As a music overlord based in Atlanta, Ron oversaw the nuts and bolts that kept JMA's big machine rolling.

245

With an incredible passion for music and the people who create it, this longtime kid at heart is a big music fan; and quite a big man too, measuring in at six feet and a pair of inches. Cradled in his lookout above the city, the Batman leans onto the balcony rail. From an overhead shot, he seems as if he were ready to swoop down in stealth mode to deliver a fatalistic new hit to radio friends like Ray Mariner (the Boy Wonder), over at Atlanta's *Star 94*. When asked why he chooses such a dangerous role to play, Ron slowly turns, looks into the eye of the camera and says, "*I am the Batman of Music.*" In his eyes, we see the reflection of precious round metal hanging on the walls. The camera pans to the reflected wall and scrolls down, row by row, revealing the names of those he helped to *shape*, *mold* and *make it* in the highly competitive Rock world.

FAST FORWARD: Ron Herbert uses a micro-sensor from his Bat-beltpack to roll back the tape of his exciting life. We arrive at when he was a 19-year old student at U.S.C.—the University of South Carolina—codename *Batschool South*. PLAY: Ron stakes claim to not one or two, but three nightclubs; plus he had a Chinese restaurant on the side. In traditional Bat-style, Ron carried a little secret: he had an appetite for infusing fresh blood into bands and one of them was *Mason*, from Virginia. Let's PAUSE to point out that as a fellow businessman, Bruce Wayne would have been proud of Ron's business savvy; he worked hard to manage a wingful of businesses. I also raise the question of whether Ron the Bat may have at some time feasted on Jamaican blood, with all those jobs he had...

REWIND to the very foggy early-to-mid 70s: Ron Herbert hasn't been landed a good three hours, but he runs right into Peter Grant (Led Zeppelin's manager) at a Los Angeles hotel; yet they were both promoting the band's latest album. Ending up with a VIP room and seated in a limo with the band, Ron says to RECORD this: "At the end of the day, it's not who you know, but who knows *YOU*"—with Ron's blessings, a few recommendations to his friends and a huge hit called Stairway to Heaven, the Led Zeppelin IV album went on to sell over 23 million copies.

From his early aspirations of being the promoter's promoter, Ron Herbert liked saying profound things to people through microphones while introducing them to superstars at sold-out Rock concerts. Besides managing groups like Mason, Ron aka the Batman also spread his wings around groups like, landing them a deal with Curb Records. After the 80s decade kicked in, our nocturnal hero was actively using his superior intellect (with a side of sonar and infrared night vision), for the task of scoping out new terrain to dominate as an overlord. Touching down in Washington D.C. around the mid-80s to exercise operation *Touch and Go*, the Bat attended an intown radio convention; this is where he locked his sights in on new prey to catch. He then snagged the 'keys to the city' from his future boss, record promoter Jeff McClusky. Jeff was on the lookout for an alpha male with 'batty intentions' for the use of those city keys: in running Jeff's big Chicago-based machine down south, on the ATL side.

Shortly thereafter, McClusky and Associates transformed into one of the most successful firms in the country. Promoting records for acts from Mariah Carey to R.E.M. to Tom Petty, Ron managed groups like *Moment of Silence* and *Madfly*; in fact, the Batman had very little time to hang upside down enjoying the view. Taking on a project with a then-unknown artist named Bruce Hornsby, Ron proved his worth by tapping radio station veins in key cities like Atlanta, Charlotte, New Orleans and Savannah. Hornsby's initial bite, *Every Little Kiss*, slowly crept to #70 on the *Billboard* chart, but a well-placed follow-up bite from The Bat instantly drew blood the next time. It also took Hornsby's *The Way It Is* and *Mandolin Rain* on a bypass excursion from the dead music morgue, to life at the top of the charts… and *another few million sold*.

Testing records on the radio from market to market, Ron Herbert found he could gauge the probability of a record's chart-climbing success: or imminent crash to death from a lack of radio bites, as opposed to bat bites. But once The Bat bit, it triggered a contagious condition leading DJs and listeners alike to administer frequent doses of favorite hit songs to stabilize the condition, codename *musicana criticallicus*. Naturally, Batman had the antidote locked up in his Bat-lab of the sky... Ron saw tons of records shoot through the roof and enter the charts, all from repeated doses administered through constant listener-to-DJ interaction.

Rarely giving interviews, Batman explains the process: "As more listeners request a song, it gets increased airplay and exposure, triggering a rise in temperature as it climbs up the playlist. Then a multi-station fire alarm codename ALE, sends a signal of green that there may be a *hot hit* coming through the pipeline; these days, we've got people Tweeting, too!" Once similar symptoms appear in multiple markets and sales kick in all around, the song enters Billboard's charts. As advanced stages of *musicana criticallicus* take effect across different music markets, the "infected" song becomes "hitbound."

In a musical nutshell, Ron *Batman* Herbert exercised major level skills as a barometer for hitbound singles by established acts, while developing newer artists like Salomé Jackson, *codename Sangin' Singer with Swagger* (www.reverbnation.com/salomejackson). She's one diva-to-be that's worthy of a good look up! Getting the inside scoop on a record's popularity weeks—maybe even months in advance, helps Ron to react quickly when positioning a new hit. With the flim-flammy nature of the *biz* it's sometimes *hit or miss*... Ron's Bat-intentions keep him on the winning side. So now we know why he keeps the Boy Wonder nearby; and a 24/7/365 monitor on his web pages. They're parked at places like www.bonusmusic.com, www.moneymarketron.com and www.youtube.com/theronnieh. With that said, let's move on to our next scenario.

BOY WONDERMAN

Scenario three takes us into the heart of the Batcave, where the mild-mannered Batman, Ron Herbert, issues a series of commands through his wireless micro-communications device; the *Bat-Droid*. Finding a secret entrance and stumbling into Ron's Batcave one day while 'driving home from Jamaica,' I stumbled upon Ray *Robin* Mariner in the lab talking to his iPhone's *Siri*. He was conducting his own set of secret experiments—in addition to concocting terrestrial theories and broadcasting bylaws along the way. To my surprise, Ray was rather inviting and upon a hearty welcome, proceeded to show me around as Ron wrapped up his high-power phone call.

As I took in the sights, I discovered quickly that Ray Mariner certainly wasn't bashful. In telling me about his past, we discovered quite a few commonalities; like promoting some of the same Columbia Records artists for Sony Music. By the time we finished name-dropping with each other, I felt right at home. It turned out that Ray knew a few of the promotion guys I worked with during my decade at Sony Music like Don Miller, Jeff Shane, Chris Siciliano and Richie Tardanico—this quartet was among my more colorful co-workers, to put it lightly. Keeping things moving as codename *Robin the Boy Wonder*, Ray has a pretty colorful history under his belt, just like my former co-workers; plus Bobby Poe (both Senior and Junior)! I guess that's what qualified us to run in the same circle at different times.

Originally from the Windy City of Chicago, Ray Mariner's music superhero instincts picked up preliminary Bat-signals that guided him south, where he expanded his superior intellect at Appalachian State University in North Carolina. Another signal directed Ray to the microphone; since then, he was never far away from one. Following low-level, guided impact signals from "beyond the Batcave," Ray plotted a course that took him through radio markets in Charlotte, Cleveland and Orlando. Through these adventures, Ray went from being just another radio DJ to being a 'master air personality.' Then, he jumped to the other side of the fence in the 90s: as a promotion man for Columbia Records! While there, he promoted artists from Aerosmith to Mariah Carey to Bruce Springsteen. Ray's in-depth knowledge of the music biz finally took shape as he jumped back over the fence to radio, tapped into sources from the industry and used his streetwise Robin sense to interact with listeners on the Internet. The Boy Wonder had become a true, multimedia medium through which hot hits would flow—from record labels to his radio show, from clubs to live venues.

With a clear view of *the big picture* from both the radio and record label sides, Ray Mariner observes, "it's important for artists to be prepared when they get to the point of *breaking out* at the radio level because in achieving airplay, it can go either way!" A hot song can become a huge hit virtually overnight, and that's better than "hanging around, waiting for a song that fails to get any traction." He adds: "These days, it's so competitive that artists often have a harder time garnering further interest if they don't come correct the first time around." And not many know it better than Batman's partner in crime and rhyme, *Robin Ray*.

Around 2003, Ray Mariner took his skills to another level by plugging in to a new power source and arising early to "catch the worm" at a major market radio station—Atlanta's *Star 94*. As co-host of the *Cindy & Ray* morning show, Boy Wonder chopped it up and woke folks up to his voice every day. As half of Star 94's winning team, this drive-time host along with show partner Cindy codename *Starbird*, pulled 'topical topics' off their menu with serious issues, as well as humorous ones. Out of the limelight, Ray relaxed by exercising secret missions from the golf course, and sloping down dangerous hills on skis. He could also be found executing extreme sports like bungee jumps, or activating the cruise control on stock racecars at upwards of 150 miles an hour!

Another of Ray's highlights outside many self-proclaimed "Ro-Bat" adventures includes going to Iraq around 2005. He took that trip to talk with troops stationed in Baghdad and served as Atlanta radio's conduit between American soldiers and their stateside families. All I can say is, anyone who can survive a twenty-four hour trip from Atlanta to Baltimore to Spain to Baghdad, gets a duly justified salute from me. But unlike G.I. Ray, I just never developed the curiosity or capacity to find myself surrounded by Kevlar… and tons of live ammunition being fired everywhere, from all kinds of guns. I may not know much, but I do know one thing: "bullets have no names!"

Besides stirring things up like a live-action spoon with limbs, DJ "Robin" Ray Mariner starred in dozens of wild and crazy microphone moments on Star 94. Plus, he was always on active duty—hanging out with the Batman at the Batcave, which happened to be located just down the street from Ray's Top 40 radio station. Here, Robin Ray held court from his perch behind the mic; in a high-profile job, high above the streets of Atlanta. In summarizing the broadcast industry, Ray states "major market radio stations are key vessels that deliver the goods directly to their target: music listeners, aka *the people*." On any given day, a "no name" could mushroom into a "larger than lifer," just from receiving multiple plays of a song fans enjoy hearing. The trick is—it takes MONEY to get heard. Radio station owners, as well as advertisers, like the sound of that. Stations generate revenue by selling time slots to advertisers so they can promote products and services over the air, just before or after a hot song is played.

Stations and their advertisers know what comes next—the sound of cold hard cash; a result of listeners (codename *potential buyers*) tuning in. Breaking things down, radio stations get paid by their amount of accumulated listeners; this is all based on a complex, cumulative rating system. Bottom line is, the more listeners, the higher they're rated, and the more they could charge advertisers: I call it "radio real estate." Advertisers tune in, looking for the "best spot" to market their wares on radio stations' music map, otherwise known as *the playlist*. Even the Robin (Ray Mariner) used one for his morning show with Cindy aka *Starbird*, when conducting business from their prime location—behind the microphone in the WSTR eagle's nest.

To hear Ray Mariner aka Robin speak in what I dub the *Dialect of Intellects*, I tuned in to his morning show on Atlanta's highly rated Star 94—that's 94.1 on the FM dial. If you happen to be out of the ATL's terrestrial reach, you can always log in at www.star94.com to get your own spin on their programming. As far as the winged one known as Ray *Robin* Mariner, in 2011 he got married on the same April weekend as my good friends James Echterhoff and Susan Nesmith. Creeping around in the background was our ultimate covert prankster Michael Furedy, codename *Smiling Wedding Crasher*. Also getting married that weekend was the British Royals, Prince William and Kate Middleton, so CONGRATULATIONS to all the newlyweds!

Like most industry experts, extraordinary gentlemen with names like *Bobby*, *Ron* and *Ray* would agree on one thing about the pre-Internet model of the music industry: radio was the final delivery point before a record exploded and caused millions of energized fans to run out to record stores and BUY, BUY, BUY! But before the music even hit retailers' bins, it had to go through an enormous, somewhat organized system of distribution channels. This task was not an easy one, but someone had to do it. Much like guys such as the Poes, Ron Herbert and Ray Mariner, I'm glad to have gotten a ride on the old Model T version of the "big machine," at semi-stable capacity. After file-sharing, downloads and who knows what else, it's anyone's guess what kind of ride is planned ahead in the Internet age. We are now about to jump through another portal of people, time and places, in order to give you a peep into a part of the mechanism that helped drive the power for this monolithic music machine.

Music *biz* superheroes like the *Poe Force* (Big Bobby and Little Bobby), as well as Batman and Robin (Ron Herbert and Ray Mariner) all saw a major music industry slogan launch itself, through an amalgamation of colorful individuals. And to this day, they'll confirm one thing about *The Good Ol' Golden Days*: there was no greater influence on the planet than the power of "*Sex, Drugs and Rock-n-Roll*." But major music muscle still needed to be exercised—in order to power up, deploy and push tons of music-related products through a huge distribution pipeline for shotgun marketing to the masses, while creating special niche audiences.

The next subject from my inner circle list brought about a new way of target marketing that had never been used before, and still goes out of his way to break barriers in matching music artists with retail products to create a win-win mix at the cash register. Starting off in the 70s making music but ending up in the 90s as a street promotion guru, he helped bridge the gap between the boardroom and the buyer; then rode off into music *biz*tory. Now he's back with hot babes, cold brew and a mean media mix that'll simply make ya say, "hmmm…"

-11-
RUFFING IT UP IN THE "A"

Industry mover and shaker Stephen Stone is a veteran who travels with his antennas up—way up! I've known Stephen for many years, dating back to my days at Sony Music. Achieving early success in Rap and Hip-Hop, he pulled a concept from Country singer Kenny Rogers' song, *The Gambler*: "You got to know when to hold 'em, know when to fold 'em, know when to walk away, and know when to run..." I make this correlation because Stephen knew when it was time to Young MC it and "bust a move" at the dawn of Internet file sharing. Since there's a mountain's worth of Stony information to drill through, some of Stephen's adventures will be disclosed here and then we'll pick up again later—there will be more inside info in an upcoming book that more fittingly covers the evolution of Rap/Hip-Hop music. For you to get an inside view now however, let's take it from "the top of the rock."

As a master promotion man, Stephen Stone's Musicology codename is *Pro Marketing Wizard*; but as a live performer and studio musician based in Philadelphia during the 70s and 80s, he played keyboards for a hefty list of people. At the very least, he had lots of fun creating TV commercial soundtracks for various New York ad agencies—some of his most memorable work includes: Pillsbury - *The Freshest Ideas Are Baking;* TDK - *So Real;* Kodak - *The Times of Your Life;* Kool-Aid - *Kids Love it... So Do Moms* and M&Ms - *They Melt in Your Mouth, Not in Your Hands.* Depending on your age, you might recognize a few—I know I did. During the early 80s, he recorded and toured with artists like Madonna. Simultaneous to working with other acts, Stephen developed his own solo career working at Columbia Records and in-between gigs, studied to earn a Bachelor of Arts degree in music. Even though Stephen might not tell anyone how good he plays keyboards, I saw him work his magic and to say the least, it was a touching experience watching this man tickle the ivory. In fact, Stephen's so good that he had Kathy the Bartender playing the piano as soon as she sat down next to him!

Stephen Stone eventually gained an interest in what happened to songs upon their final 'mix and master.' To get a closer look at the process that formulated in Stephen's mind, let's just say he and his music *biz* partners wound up launching a juggernaut—just to see what the music world thought of acts like Kris Kross, Cypress Hill, The Fugees and Lauryn Hill. You see, producer Jermaine Dupri was no dummy—he got Kris Kross placed on another new startup label and in exchange, was given the green light for his new *So So Def* label, and distribution through Columbia Records. After Kris Kross, the next big act to go through Dupri's conduit was multi-platinum selling R&B singers Xscape, and the rest is music history! But before *So So Def* came along, Stephen Stone was rolling up his sleeves as a strategic partner in "just another new start-up label." Stephen grasped a firm understanding of how finished product by acts like these went through an evolutionary lifecycle: it powered a pipeline that included radio, press and retail, terminating at the cash register. Up for grabs were records, tapes, CDs, plus other merchandise like videos, posters, caps, t-shirts and of course, concert tickets.

To feed the record *biz* pipeline of 1992, Stephen Stone deployed a little-known tactic called "street promotion." These days, almost no song can become a hit without utilizing some form of it, as a standard protocol of today's music industry. Although I never did say the name of Stephen's start-up label, there's a good reason why, and it's coming soon friends! The main lesson here is that Mr. Stone channeled his energy into perfecting one thing: marketing strategy, for without it, a song could die a quick and miserable death. Marketing strategy was directly tied in to street promotions—what you are doing in the streets to maximize visibility of a hot song (or in some cases, a song someone wants to get hot). Fortunately, none of Stephen's records fell into the 'death by non-airplay' abyss, because (drum roll, please) the name of his musical juggernaut of a label was… *Ruffhouse Records*. Ruffhouse was founded in 1989 by Chris Schwartz and Joe Nicolo, in a joint venture with Columbia Records. The label's lifecycle ran for a good 10 years and by 1999 Stone, Schwartz and Nicolo felt a change coming in the wind, then sold the company to Columbia and went their own ways.

Back when I worked at Sony Music, I helped market Kris Kross' early 90s releases by screaming out about their impending arrival while passing out promo copies on the streets. Many people just couldn't understand what was about to hit them over the head; by the time it finally hit them, I had 'conveniently' given away all the promos in my stash. Now they had to BUY the music if they wanted it, because my *musicandy* store was closed. I also took part in marketing and promoting The Fugees. Some of us were flown in to New York, where we saw them perform a high-energy show in support of their debut album. The show had a rough edge to it—putting things lightly, I *ducked and covered* to avoid any possible flying objects as those young Hip-Hoppers pounced all over the stage and into the audience!

It turns out that The Fugees navigated through some pretty adrenalin-filled events just to get where they were, and Stephen Stone filled me in on one: when the group was recording tracks for their first release, they traveled from the New York/New Jersey area to Philadelphia, where the Ruffhouse studios were located. One day, the pre-multi-platinum act arrived early for a session and rung the doorbell. Apparently, no one answered, so they knocked... and knocked and knocked. When Stephen finally showed up, he found the group *assuming the position* lined up on a wall—the police had their guns drawn on them, tagging the Fugees to fit the profile of "urban hoods." Needless to say, the resulting session was filled with adrenalin-laden lyrics to shake off the bad vibes they had just gotten from the police. Thank God the officers weren't 'happy trigger-pullers,' because we would never have been blessed to hear the fruits of The Fugees' labor.

Offsetting the dark drama from above, Stephen Stone shared some great stories with me, and I could tell there were many fun times had at the Ruffhouse studios. Going off the tilt, another tale involved the mischief Stephen and his cohorts pulled on studio clients back in the day. Installing a hidden microphone in the bathroom stall, their plan was to record celebrity clients as they went in and out of the commode. With "very windy" sound bytes captured, they put together a *gaseous* tune and called it *The F@&+ Song*. Stephen said, "it was so funny, we were left laughing on the floor... but we never released it for fear of getting our butts sued off, no pun intended." Even today, Stephen thinks the record would be a far—make that a *chart*-topper, if they had the nerve to "push it out." One day Stephen might just play it for me but he says, "If I identified the individual 'wind chimers,' there would be a long line of lawyers trying to de-wind me in court!" Now, where'd they put the Lysol?

At the beginning of this chapter, I mentioned that Ruffhouse 'super-strategizer' Stephen Stone traveled with his antennas up. He knew when to ride the big wave, and when to get back on solid ground. With the onset of Internet file sharing, many labels in the industry resembled ostriches with their heads stuck in the ground, unable to see any upcoming derailment. To be clear, music downloading was poised to deliver a crippling blow to the industry, and no one would be excluded. With that thought in mind, Stephen and company sold the once tiny little start-up to the Sony conglomerate and kept it moving. The following year, downloading turned the music industry upside down!

Chris Schwartz and new partner Kevon Glickman then opened up a new candy store called RuffNation Records, while Joe "The Butcher" Nicolo expanded his role by mixing in film work with his regular "butcher work"—producing and mixing music. Going back, Joe and his brother Phil were known as *The Butcher Brothers*. They renovated an old butcher shop into a recording haven and proceeded to do tons of production work with an assorted list of artists including:

Anthrax	Bob Dylan	John Lennon
Cypress Hill	Amy Grant	Nine Inch Nails
Dog Eat Dog	Luscious Jackson	Urge Overkill

During the early 2000s, Stephen Stone and his partners dabbled in the movie business, teaming up with Merv Griffin. Next, Stephen got involved with creating the hugely successful *Fantanas* for Coca Cola's Fanta brand. With perfect timing, *The Fantanas* were Coke's answer to Pepsi's Britney Spears advertising campaign. For over ten years since debuting in 2002, *The Fantanas* have remained a hot mainstream ticket. In his spare time, Stephen earned a Juris Doctorate degree and spread his hands out further. During covert operations, Stone set up new alliances with the Universal Music Group and Avalonza, where he has updated his 'Marketing Strategy 101' plan to include *branded entertainment*.

By 2009 Stephen Stone joined forces with marketing partner Bridgette Ewell, and together they tested out a new and strategic marketing initiative. It proved itself to work like nothing else out there... thus their multi-branding concept was born. It was obviously an effective choice, because Stephen's been popping up on the radar screens of everyone from "Madison Avenue to Hollywood Boulevard." It is at this intersection where we make the 'proverbial pit stop,' because the top-secret work Stephen was executing is way too high-level for us to even discuss right now, let alone think about. But in an act of compassion for our readers, the street marketing wizard exclusively released some 'declassified intel' that could only be shared here.

As you should know, being L.A. Jackson qualifies me to function as Agent Superintendent. There are a number of perks that come with the job, so around the end of May 2012, Stephen Stone invited me to an event called "*Party In The Park*." This event he put together was held every Thursday night between 7:00 and 10 p.m. in Atlantic Station's Millennium Gate Park on 17th Street. Atlantic Station is one of the newest neighborhoods in Atlanta, and was on the list to be home of London-based Pop sensation music group, *ANYTHING BUT MONDAY*. The girls in the group thought it would be a good idea to start giving out free beer to everyone in the neighborhood prior to their arrival, so when they actually did arrive and start creating traffic jams, people would be less inclined to be ticked off with them.

There was already plenty of food, shopping, business centers and living space in Atlantic Station—I was sure any remaining spaces would be filled after Anything But Monday's arrival. When I finally made it to the "park under the arch," music was playing and people were gathering to enjoy a show by a wonderful local music group called Sol Star. As it turns out, the group was sponsored by Anything But Monday, Musicology codename *ABM*, along with Mirosa Beer: "a proudly brewed product of Italy." To put it lightly, an ample supply of Mirosa was at hand for everyone in attendance. Topping things off, there was free Mirosa Beer pound cake, made by the Pound Cake Company of Atlanta... and it was out-of-this-world delicious!

The sole reason why all this activity was possible is due to magical qualities found in that deliciously refreshing Italian brew called *Mirosa*. Straight from Mirosa headquarters website is some quick-brewed background info—strangely enough, it sounds like a bedtime story I used to hear as a little boy, somewhere long ago, in a land far beyond... "*Birra Mirosa* originates from the Tarricone brewery, nestled in the breath-taking picturesque, one thousand year-old town of Balvano, Italy. It is a premium light golden Pils-style beer with delicate foam. On the palate, Birra Mirosa offers a subtle texture of bitter and sweet echoes that resonate from the freshest air and most invigoratingly pure water to be found anywhere in existence on this earth. The mountainous streams and springs that supply the water that goes into Birra Mirosa flow from a place where overpopulation and excessive industry do not exist. Each morning a gentle mist settles over the valley of olive and lemon groves, cleansing and rejuvenating all of life. Consequently, Birra Mirosa translates into one of the most pleasant beer experiences ever to be had."

But wait, there's more: "And now the master brewers have just outdone themselves by perfecting Birra Mirosa Lemon, which is by far the quintessential, most refreshing and enlivening beer experience that any beer connoisseur the world over is ever going to know. It is inexplicably a beverage blend that could only have been accomplished through truly authentic southern Italian passion. The Mirosa family of brands are brewed in the style that represents the finest craft beers in the world, by a brewmaster who combines old world brewing techniques, new age technologies and quality ingredients, which all combine to brew us a product with a flavor profile that is original and unequal in today's marketplace." What a touching story—our sources say it'll either make you thirsty for Mirosa; or put you to sleep. Keeping me awake, Stephen Stone tells me there are other fabulous flavors a-brewin' in the vats, so get those taste buds ready for some real refreshing treats on the way to your favorite beverage center…

I came to discover that Mr. Stone's latest music project was the 4 times platinum music group from Britain, Anything But Monday. I also learned that the girls themselves actually owned the Mirosa Beer Company, which was distributed by the distributors of Anhueser Busch. This made them the first female beer company owners in the world! To top things off, I heard Anything But Monday was affiliated with Pitbull's tour. After the girls wrapped up their tour, the plan was for them to move to Atlanta for a double initiative: to release their music for the first time in the United States—and the official launch of their beer company. On a side note, Forbes magazine already courted a story of these amazing "artistic entrepreneurs!"

Apparently, Stephen Stone still had plenty of branding firepower left inside his *big music bag of tricks*. These girls were inseparable from their beer brand, and have actually created a new business model for the entire music industry... a long-overdue adventure! When I asked Stephen for more details, he said, "Anything But Monday will have a debut release that's going to be a beer-drinking party anthem—by 2013, they'll be the hottest new group in America. (As of November 2013, *99 Bottles of Beer* was #1 on the DJ Top 50 Crossover and Dance chart—woo-hoo!) On top of that, when the girls arrive in town, they are going to throw the BIGGEST party in ATL history!!!! There'll be free beer for over 20,000 people and dig this: the event is going to be the pilot for their new reality TV show—about a bunch of girls that run a beer company!" The ABM girls had huge plans in place for this clandestine cacophony of musical liquidity—the party of the century included swimming pools (that's right!) filled with Mirosa Beer, chicken cooked with Mirosa Beer, hot dogs and hamburgers cooked with Mirosa Beer, and an array of Mirosa Beer deserts. Oh yeah, Mirosa beer shampoos was also going to be offered up by "hot, sexy girls and buffed-out guys."

Stephen Stone said that anyone who was a music head in the State of Georgia would be invited; all they needed for access was to show their driver's license, and partygoers would think they died and went to heaven long before the night was over. (To be politically correct Stephen advises, *"Drink, don't drive!"*) The PR firm handling this massive event hinted the party was going to be an inferno, and would be "the sexiest, wildest and most fun night on the face of the earth—one day, folks will brag to their grandchildren that they were there!" To keep things under wraps, the date and location of the party was held top secret because the event was going to be so extravagant that the Anything But Monday girls didn't want to risk it getting shut down before it began. If any more info than that went out, I'd turn up on the missing persons report…

As a slowly retiring connoisseur, I had a chance to try Mirosa's current flavors—and came back for more *Mirosa Lemon*. In a special promotion Stephen Stone hipped me to about a month earlier in April 2012, buyers of Mirosa Beer were entitled to a share of stock in the company. I had to own "my piece of the brew" and purchased a six-pack of the regular flavor to get started; surprisingly, it didn't taste bad at all—it was like Heineken without the aftertaste. In a sense, I came to *Party In The Park* on May 31st for a second opinion; Mirosa passed the test with flying colors! While confirming the flavor, we had some down time—I got filled in on how this extraordinary chain of events got put together, link by link. After Stephen introduced me to some associates, I was drawn in like a fish on a hook. As Stephen expounded, I thought it was pretty gutsy for the music group to make an executive decision through new plans: they would transfer their music assets… by relocating from London to Atlanta.

In-between the conversations and the official move, business got handled. Stephen Stone fills in the blanks by telling how a meeting was set up with Anheuser Busch underboss Peter Busch who, as I discovered at www.billchurchwrites.com, once got a drop of Budweiser from an eyedropper when he was an infant—before his first taste of milk. Plus, Peter once said in an interview that he could ride horses before he could walk. While the eyebrows are up, let me squeeze in that Peter's father August was the long-time chairman and CEO of Anheuser-Busch as well as chairman of the St. Louis Cardinals baseball team. So let's just speculate that Pete's sitting on a ton of old money, okay?

At their meeting with the beer mogul, Stephen Stone and Anything But Monday presented Peter Busch with a taste test: it included a bottle of Mirosa and a bottle of Peter's family beer, *Bud Lime*. Stephen points out that upon the first sip, he saw "a sign of interest" through Busch's facial expression. After a few swallows went down the hatch, the meeting was concluded shortly thereafter—Anything But Monday signed on for a distribution deal through the Anheuser Busch pipeline. The beer giant hadn't brought an outside product onboard for a good decade, but it was sealing a deal with Stephen Stone, Anything But Monday and Mirosa. The writing was on the wall: with a tasty new product to distribute, Anheuser Busch would go from making a cool $10 million a week, to maybe 12 or 13—not a bad deal at all…

N' GET ON DOWN AND PARTAY

If I thought I had fun the last week of May at Stephen Stone's *Party In The Park*, then I was severely understated in comparison to the one on Thursday, June 7, 2012. Although I couldn't stay the whole time on my first go-round, I've been 'shutting it down' since round two. The second *Party In The Park* event I attended was 'twice as nice' because Sol Star, the band that played the previous week made a return engagement; and there was another band called Political Cheesecake. This turned into a real treat because after Sol Star finished their opening set, Political Cheesecake cranked it up; after they did a few songs Sol Star came back up, and then Political Cheesecake returned and closed the set. Although I did the networking thing, a few moments were taken to hear each group hammer out great originals; Political Cheesecake performed great covers by Stevie Wonder, Prince and Michael Jackson.

Upon my arrival, the plan was to get the Mirosa Beer drink-ready, meaning they needed a good icing down. Stephen Stone was already getting everything else in position; then folks started showing up and the place began looking like a festival folks could have paid to get in. As far as drinks were concerned, the only competition Mirosa had was a beverage company that was giving away samples of a watermelon-flavored fruit drink. One by one, friends I invited to this event began arriving, like Josh Golden. Josh is the only person on the planet who believes my story of "chillin' out" with rapper-actor Method Man on his bus when he stopped through town on 2011's *The Smoker's Club* tour—that's because Josh was right there with me! After Golden's arrival, my other friend Kash showed up. We used to work together, but then he got an offer he couldn't refuse and it was "G chat" after that. Kash told a few of his DJ friends about the event, and I looked forward to meeting them so we could talk about getting airplay for Anything But Monday, somewhere down the line. As my fellow music agents made appearances, I introduced them to Stephen Stone—up next was another peer, Carlos Tejeda, who you should remember was our tour guide through *The Music of Mexico*, which kicked off our journey at the beginning of this book. Carlos did a great job explaining styles like *Norteño* and *Narcocorrido*, so I made sure he knew about the *Party In The Park*.

Some of Kash's friends showed up and soon after, Carlos made his appearance. By now, the place had packed up and sub-groups were breaking off into their own respective areas. Meanwhile, my old friend Keith B-Well codenamed *KB* showed up. Keith and I can lose contact for months at a time and then hook up in a heartbeat. That's because we're old neighbors—we go way back to 1970s Park Place in Brooklyn; I lived at 919 and he lived at 959. Although I didn't know it in the 70s, Keith had an older brother named Mike—he was the biggest, baddest guy on the block. KB moved down to Atlanta a few years ago and we reconnected through a 30-year block party reunion I found out about through Facebook. While I was taller than Keith back then, I tilt my head up to look at him now, so that scenario has changed drastically.

The following weeks turned into months, as my relationship with Stephen Stone grew tighter and tighter. I decided to try my hand at getting musicians on the Millennium Gate *Party In The Park* bill—my first act would be none other than Atlanta's *Urban Guitar Legend*, guitarist Elliot Holden. If this worked, I'd pull in other acts I knew, like Peach City Records' affiliated acts Kimosha LeToi, Ade and Onny. The following weeks saw return engagements for Elliot, who did solo sets and sets with his band; he blew the crowd away every time. Needless to say, I heard Mirosa Beer had Elliot on their *national poster boy* list…

Over the course of the next few weeks, I noticed the crowd getting larger and larger—some estimates had the crowd at 500 people, and that's not bad for a small park in the middle of the dense Atlantic Station locale. The following week, Elliot Holden performed with Political Cheesecake then Stephen Stone and his crew went out to promote Mirosa Beer at a *Rave Weekend*—I tagged along. This 3-day event was actually called *The Impulse Music Festival* and was held at Durhamton Plantation's Off-Road Motocross and ATV Park in Union Point, Georgia. That was a turning point for me, as I started seeing more of Stephen Stone's big picture. When I caught up with Team Mirosa in Union Point, I couldn't believe how much ice they had in the truck, to keep all that Mirosa Beer cold. From this moment forward, I began having a whole new relationship with ice that you'll hear more about later. But I'll never forget this three-day event, because when I was waking up around 8 a.m., Stephen and his team were just going to sleep—this was *guerilla niche marketing* at its best!

The following Atlantic Station *Party in the Park* events featured an incredible lineup of local artists, including R&B singer Vedo, Hip-Hop MC A Hustla and more of guitar master Elliot Holden. Elliot really stepped up his game, because he wound up doing more return engagements than any other music act that performed at the weekly event. Elliot performed by himself in an acoustic setup or with his laptop and backup tracks—then he'd bring in his band the next week to blow everyone away as an amped up 'dyno trio.' You don't know how many times Stephen Stone told me "Elliot's incredible!" Incredibly enough, Elliot led his band and other bands in jam sessions where everyone's sound system was blasting out music at the same time. The audience was treated to a barrage of sound coming at them from all angles; perspectively speaking, you would have had to be there to get the full effect.

After a rained-out week, we returned to Atlantic Station's Millennium Gate arch to have what I call "Peach City Records night" at the *Party in the Park*. My business partner Wade Jones and I had been planning to have artists Kimosha LeToi and Onny perform with a band and after a few rehearsals, this week was 'show week.' The night before, I prayed like crazy for there to be no rain, and those prayers were answered. Remembering the rush of emotions I felt at rehearsal, they came back again when the band plugged up and got ready for sound check. Wade brought down a ton of audio gear to ensure the sound was right and as usual, he did a great job! During the performance, singers Kimosha and Onny did their thing and seamlessly covered tunes by John Legend and Earth, Wind & Fire. Led by musical director and bass player extraordinaire Levi Patton, the band held down a tight groove with an R&B/Jazz backdrop.

While "the show went on," in retrospect that was a pretty rough day because the starter on the Mirosa truck went out and we wound up using my car to transport the beer and ice. Luckily my old buddy from the 90s, Walt C, connected me with his friends at *Meehan's Irish Pub* and saved the day. After running around all afternoon getting enough ice to keep the Mirosa Beer cold, I finally gave Kathy the Bartender my last two bags of ice. Then I caught what was left of the *Peach City Revue* beta test and surmised they'd be out on the road soon—this was artist development in the making! There will be a full report on Peach City Records and its *Peach City Revue* down the line, but for now you can get your appetizer on at www.reverbnation.com/label/peachcityrecordsllc. The following week, lifesaver Walt C's curiosity got the best of him—he wanted to know more about the *Party In The Park*, so I invited him down: he brought his wife, kids… and one of his artists to perform.

JOHN WAYNE - WHO???

One day in July of 2012, I was having an email chat with Walt C, codename *Q-Sick*. We were talking general music *biz* stuff and then the Mirosa *Party in the Park* popped up. When I invited Walt to the event earlier, I was secretly inviting him down to meet Team Mirosa (Stephen Stone and Kathy the Bartender). Walt said he was totally aware of who Stephen Stone was; in fact, Walt had acquired his card a year earlier, but just never got a chance to call him. After Walt hooked us up with Meehan's ice to save the day, I invited him down to check out the next event at Atlantic Station; he asked if an artist of his could come along—that was music to my ears!

Logging in time with his own Rock-Rap crew *The Brew*, Walt C and his *Rock-2-Def Music* began working with producers and acts like Sam Sneed, Colt Ford, John Wayne Bailey and Babi Mac. Sam Sneed did a lot of production work with Dr. Dre on Death Row Records, while Country singer/rapper Colt Ford featured RUN-DMC's DMC on his 2010 release, *Chicken and Biscuits*. Along with Colt Ford and DMC, Walt C put John Wayne Bailey in the mix as a featured vocalist on the song, *Ride On...Ride Out*. *Chicken and Biscuits* debuted at #8 on Billboard's Country album chart and #4 on the Rap album charts. Undeniably speaking, over the past few years I've noticed the growth of this new Country-Rap genre; it seems to be uniting people in different ways.

Even *Georgia Music Industry Association* 'Big Boss' Jimmy LeFavour jumped on the bandwagon, by writing an SEC Country-Rap flavored anthem called *Southern Pride* (SEC Style). This was done to support the Southeastern Conference and welcome two new college football teams aboard: Texas A&M and Missouri. You can check out www.secanthem.com for more great info and I'll 'go deep' with that story when we get to an industry profile of the GMIA in our next installment, *Musicology 2103*. Raising my eyebrows upon Walt's description of Babi Mac, I became intrigued to hear more. You see, Babi Mac is a knockout "10+" blonde from Knoxville who raps her fanny off! Walt C. was recently in the studio with her working on a new single called *Tennesee Honey*, the first offering from our newly dubbed "Queen of Tennesee." Anyway, after divulging more info about our *Party In The Park* to Walt, I looked forward to seeing him and his artists paying us a visit.

Zooming in to the highly spiritual John Wayne Bailey, he has a CD out called *Voice For The People*. You can find it streaming online and up for sale at iTunes, as well as at all the usual spots. Guest appearances are made by the likes of DMC (one third of RUN-DMC), Greta Gaines, Selby Bailey and a list of other music *biz* movers and shakers. John Wayne's music is a toss-up of Top 40, Alternative, Hip-Hop and Gospel Rock. His message is one of reflection and it looks into the struggles and thought processes of our daily lives. When we first began talking, John was working on viral videos to be posted throughout the year. The *Voice For The People* CD project was produced by Walt C, who added "Q-Sick" to his name and worked with acts from Culture Shock to the Dogg Pound. The CD was mixed by Jeff Tomei; he engineered and mixed for Jerry Cantrell, Collective Soul, Corrosion of Conformity, Jackyl, Matchbox 20, Edwin McCain, Smashing Pumpkins and many others.

When John Wayne Bailey is asked about his unique vocal style, he says "it's a hybrid of Chris Cornell, Train and Everlast Daughtry, with music speaking on faith, hope, politics, life; and the challenges we see everyday." Keeping his creds up to par, John performed on BET's nationally syndicated program, *The Monique Show*. He also performed at select shows between 2011 and 2012 so naturally, he did a great job at *Party In The Park*—we looked for his return to bless the crowd again. Among John Wayne Bailey's latest projects, he's been secretly working with a totally humanitarian singing group called *Iconic Journey*. Backed by the Martin Luther King family, their first performance was in Washington D.C. at the 50th anniversary of the March on Washington. The group's second performance was at the King birthday celebration—it aired on CNN and Fox. Multi-Grammy nominee Christopher Capehart serves as manager of group, through his company *Awspire*. John Wayne Bailey has been tight-lipped about his work with Iconic Journey but he comes clean right now for one reason:

"We have a contract in the works for an exciting new reality TV show. I'm a free agent in this situation, but I still have other projects and commitments in front of me." Elaborating on aspects of the reality TV show John says, "it focuses on the group's 12 singers of different races and musical styles—I represent the Pop-Rock side." Placed in a plethora of *world humanitarian* situations, John Wayne Bailey and Iconic Journey will be filmed on location wherever God leads them to pray for and encourage people. "We'll also be filmed right in the studio, as we write songs to support our ongoing efforts to lift hearts and spirits... all of these miracles are in the works, so keep your antennas up for God's signals!"

Rounding out his skill set, John Wayne Bailey does music worship with Ministry leaders and churches, plus he gives music and production lessons in his spare time. John Wayne goes way out of his way to help the kids, and that's one thing I really admire about him. While he finalizes new projects with his *On Fire LLC Youth Events* and *Youthfest*, you can check out Rock 2 Def Music's website and www.reverbnation.com/johnwaynebaileyproject to "...Stay plugged in for updates, new music and videos..."

I guess you can say we've been lucky with the artists that came to perform at *Party In The Park*—they were all great! Not only were the acts impressive, but so were the folks who showed up to watch them. One of them was my old pal *DJ Strong*, who let me run my mouth on his world-famous "Life Music Radio" show on WATB enough times for me to fully understand and appreciate the broadcasting process. Now, I have my own show on *Raw Truth Radio* (www.rawtruthradio.net). This station is run by my radio show mentors Michael Garrett Jr. (codename *DJ Mike Gee*) and Vernon (*DJ 12*) House, so big shoutouts to Team WRTR! As a traveling showman, DJ Strong codename *Lyvation Man* happened to have some cool blue lights in his car the day he visit our *Party In The Park* event; he pulled them out to add a new dimension to the Mirosa Beer table—that changed the atmosphere drastically when the sun went down!

Over the next few weeks, we saw more people than ever show up—the pressure was on to keep the party going, so we came up with new ideas. Deciding to buy a gas grill and start selling hot dogs, we let hype man Josh Golden step in as *Chef Global Appeal*. Immediately taking my cue, I found a large jar, filled it with Mirosa Beer and threw hot dogs in it to marinate: the crowd loved it and ate up freshly cooked dogs while a cute little trio called *2 Too Cute* sung and danced like they had a hit record out. The audience moved in for a closer look, while Stephen Stone, Kathy the Bartender, Barry Huff and Team Mirosa took it all in from under a new Team Mirosa tent.

Over time, our ice-acquiring tactics changed. We now needed to get a huge supply to keep all that Mirosa Beer cold and after receiving new orders from the top, *Operation Hotel Raid* took on a new initiative: having L.A. *Da Ice Man* onboard. All coolers, buckets and garbage bags were on deck as we drove from hotel to hotel, identifying and then draining the ice machines of their precious contents. Every week, we paid a visit to a different hotel and rolled out with enough ice to keep the party going all evening—we also kept a case of Mirosa Beer on standby, "in case" anyone had a hindrance, so to speak. Every so often, old friends and assorted agents turned up at the park party—several Musicology Agents made low-profile appearances, like Vic "the Ram" Kash, Max Lee our *International Agent of Mystery*, Carlos Tejeda our *Triple A Agent* from Mexico, Chuck Taylor aka *Agent Ixon*, French Agent Stephan Minyono codename *Tree Tall* and his sidekick, the beautiful *Agent Carol Line*. You'll read more 'secret stories' about these characters throughout this book series, but we've got to close out the story for now.

Although we had a few rainy days, word on Mirosa Beer's *Party In The Park* was spreading like wildfire that couldn't be extinguished by rain—we even had a Jazz artist named Tim Reid fly all the way down from Detroit to perform with his band. One day, my friend from the late 90s, Calvin Jennings appeared. We go back to legendary musician Edsel Robinson's studio compound; Edsel let me put my studio in a house he had a studio setup in—he was in the front and I was at the back. Calvin owned a barber shop down the street and often hung out with us after we did production work. Cal has some great things going on at www.lil-boy.com and www.corp.lilboy.com, and he came down with a young, college-aged kid named Ryan Klos (www.reverbnation.com/ryanklosmusic). It just so happened that they made a Mirosa Beer jingle: I immediately had it thrown into the CD player, so we could play it and see how the crowd responded. It went over well and ever since, Calvin and Ryan have been coming back; they even brought guitarist Matty G to perform the jingle live, along with a few of their original tunes. One week I won't forget was when Kathy the Bartender brought her mom out, and Ryan serenaded her!

Like I said before, the Mirosa Beer *Party In The Park* brought out all kinds of folks; even basketball player Robert "50" Martin came out to enjoy the vibe—I made sure he left with a to-go pack. Opening the lens, Robert's dreams of being a basketball player started off long before he arrived at North Carolina's High Point University. After he left college in 1995, Luxembourg in Europe was next; he played there for 5 years. Known to many people as "50," he also played in the USBL, ABA and IBA. This gentle giant (offcourt, that is) has been playing for the *And1* team since 2001. With moves rivaling the Harlem Globetrotters, codename *International B-Ball Man* jumps a straight 50 inches into the air, and this represents the "50" tag.

Robert "50" Martin loves to travel and meet new people, making him a basketball Ambassador. Playing with *Team And1* has taken Martin to over forty countries including Africa (Angola, Ethiopia, Kenya, Tanzania, Uganda), Australia, China, France, Germany, Japan, Serbia and others. Opening the lens wider, we see "50" on ESPN TV show *Streetball*, plus the *And1 mixtape tour* for 5 years running. He was also a baller on And1's video game, featured in *Slam* and *Vibe* magazines, and even 'played an actor' in the movie *Semi Pro*. Musically speaking, you can watch for him in videos like *So What* by Ciarra, *One Call Away* by Chingy and *Crank It Up* by David Banner.

Besides his commitment to the art of B-Balling, another thing I admire about Robert "50" Martin is his love for music. Carrying a really cool composure, he was only too happy to share his thoughts on music: "Music to me is a motivation and relaxation tool. I listen to music to get hyped up before games. If I want to relax, I would listen to soft Jazz. I like all types of music—as long as it sounds good." Because Robert also likes Mirosa Beer, we had plans to get him on Team Mirosa as our sports spokesman. His undying support kept him coming to Mirosa's *Party In The Park*, and that meant an awful lot!

After taking a photo op with him one day, out of curiosity I asked how he got wind of the beer and he said, "I found out about the *Party In The Park* through music group Anything But Monday. They told me about their new beer, and it was like, *Yo!!* I mentioned that I would love to help promote the product so here I am, looking forward to working with Team Mirosa. This brew tastes so good—I'm Robert "50" Martin and you can trust me on that!" Because of Robert's love for basketball, you can find him scoring big points on the courts and online, you can follow his moves at www.and1live.com.

One week we had a pony ride for the kids, but the animal wouldn't stop chomping on the park grass and the Millennium Gate's management said it had to go. The animal's owner left to get her vehicle to transport the white pony (with pink highlights on the mane and tail) back to the ponderosa, and I soon felt like a dope left holding a rope—attached to this horse. Suddenly, it started raining and I was singing a new song called *"Walking This Horse in the Park in the Rain."* I guess that's better than being stuck in the desert *on a horse with no name*, like 70s Rock group America said in their song. Puppetly speaking, the pony dragged me across the park as it chomped up grass—that's until the Millennium Gate's Donna Whitmire, codename *Super Trooper* came to my rescue.

Donna snatched the rein out of my hand so fast that the horse stopped munching and looked up to see what was going on. Apparently, Donna grew up around horses and even trained them; she took control and led the horse away from the delicious, green grass in order to preserve the Millennium Gate Park's golf course-like appearance. That's when my buddy, "Money" Mike Morrison, seized the moment for a photo op—with his lovely daughter sitting on the pony. A big 'thank you' goes out to Donna for saving the day and relieving me from that 'runaway pony.' And 'thumbs up' to the Millennium Gate's wonderful staff: Gaurave, who we

268

always bugged to let us in at weird hours, plus Ross Faulds, Dick Sharkey and "Captain" Rodney Mims Cook. Simply stated, Mirosa Beer's *Party In The Park* would have been nothing without these special people!

The week of September 6, 2012, more heavy-hitters came out, including *Shakey's Ribs* owner Mr. Cooper codename *Barbeque Master*. He had baby-back rib slabs and whole chickens 'grilling with a purpose' on his mobile grills and served up tasty food for folks all night long! Musically speaking, in the house was King Malachi, "a proud member of the Dungeon Family" which includes:

- Organized Noize: Rico Wade, Sleepy Brown, Ray Murray
- Outkast: André 3000, Big Boi
- Goodie Mob: Big Gipp, T-Mo, Cee-Lo Green, Khujo
- Parental Advisory: Mello, K.P., Big Reese
- Society of Soul: Sleepy Brown, Roni, Big Rube, Ray, Rico Wade
- Joi
- Witchdoctor
- Killer Mike
- Purple Ribbon All Stars: Big Boi, Konkrete, Vonnegutt, Sleepy Brown, Rock D
- Kurupt/Dungeon Family West

There will be a more comprehensive Dungeon Family profile, plus a conversation with my good friend Warren "E-Dub" Bletcher, who did lots of engineering work for the Outkast conglomerate. That's all in an upcoming book on the history of Rap and Hip-Hop, so stand by. On a side note, King Malachi is also the CEO of *Hustlin' Boy Records* and *Malahchee Wear*. This performing artist, singer, rapper, vocal arranger and show promoter is also the winner of Atlanta's Independent Artist of the year award for 2010 and 2011. While at the Mirosa Beer table, King Malachi took a great picture with Kathy the Bartender and it looks so good, I'm thinking about turning it into a poster. Thanks to the flow of Mirosa, I can't recall the name of the last song King Malachi performed; but it was a *banger* and he sure did bring the house down with it!

Another act on the bill that night was my man Bobby Johnny Wesley (www.airbornemusic.com), who had a new CD out called *Tickets Out Of Helen*. That's quite befitting, because he drove all the way down from Helen, Georgia to perform. I've got to salute this music soldier because when he came down to perform a few weeks earlier, it started raining as he was doing the second song. Needless to say, we had to shut down the party—no one wants to see what an electrocuted musician looks like (but you can think of vampires and sunlight to get a rough idea). This time around, the skies were clear and we all got treated to a *double-double*: while Bobby Johnny was warming up, a slightly inebriated fan unexpectedly got up and belted out a few songs with him—they got a standing ovation for that one. Personally speaking, I give Bobby Johnny Wesley a standing ovation because he bought a whopping TWELVE *Musicology 2101* books from me in 2013, putting him in the #1 position on my individual book buyers list!

Later that eve, my good friend Calvin Jennings' artist Ryan Klos came back to perform the Mirosa jingle he wrote, plus he played some new songs from his growing repertoire. Last but not least was my good friend, Americana artist and fellow peer from the Georgia Music Industry Association, Stephie Rae. This gifted singer-songwriter 'showed her stuff' twice: she performed with her guitar in front of the audience then afterwards she deployed her chiropractic skills on me and a few other folks with less-than-perfect backbones. Stephie Rae brings her adjustment bench wherever she goes and this time, the good doctor took a pinch out of my left shoulder… without breaking a sweat!

Another week went by, and a hot band called *Remixx* came out to perform. The group really got down playing classic hits from back in the day, and had everyone singing and dancing to the songs they played. You can get a chunky taste of their style at www.fatbeatsinc.com. One of the best things I liked about Mirosa Beer's *Party In The Park* was the wide range of cultures and nationalities that showed up to take in all the action—it wasn't long before I heard there were plans to turn this event into a great big festival and take it on the road…

All I can say is, he who appeals to multiple cultures wins! Stephen Stone did it at Ruffhouse Records and with the Fantanas; now he's doing it again using the combination of Anything But Monday and Mirosa Beer. On the visual front, I saw Stephen chatting with heavyweight video dudes like Clear Image Studio's Donnell "DC" Chandler, "Toon Troop" Williams and DeWayne Mincy aka "Mr. Green Screen" of Palladium Pictures—that only means one thing to me, reality show speaking…

After Samanda from Anything But Monday and Stephen Stone met with Anheuser Busch in 2011, Mirosa Beer popped up in places like Publix, Kroger, Tower and other package stores that I checked for stock. Now it was up to the PR machine to keep getting the word out; yours truly signed up to help! So did Kathy the Bartender—quoting Stephen Stone, "Kathy the Bartender is God's gift to this campaign. It's been my experience to note that some folks lost focus handling multiple projects, but Kathy locks in to her tasks and doesn't let go until the deed's done."

By the time you read this, we should see Kathy the Bartender's face everywhere Mirosa Beer is (like your local store). We should also have seen a track or two by Anything But Monday rising up the charts! And while worldwide 'track spinners' like DJ Syntronik remixes songs like *99 Bottles of Beer*, just remember that Stephen Stone aka *Pro Marketing Wizard*, Kathy the Bartender and Agent Superintendent L.A. Jackson have been on the loose promoting that hot female group Anything But Monday, with tons of ice cold Mirosa Beer. I can't close things out without giving big shoutouts go out to everyone I've had fun with at Team Mirosa: Joe Bronco, Josh Golden, Barry Huff, DeWayne Mincy, Winnie Pierre, David Robinson, David Siegel, and a few other special agents.

Utilizing the brand placement capability of his company Avalonza, I'm confident Stephen Stone and the team will make Anything But Monday a household... better yet, a *clubhold* name—DJs everywhere LOVE 'em! Keep in mind that all you have to do is type "Anything But Monday," or "Mirosa Beer," into your search engine, exercise some patience, and you'll learn more about the groundbreaking, trend-setting projects on Stephen Stone's calendar. (How does *End of the Millennium Party* grab you?) If we're lucky, there will be more divulged information in the next book, *Musicology 2103*.

A MUSEUM BAR APPETIZER

Just prior to the kickoff of 2012's *Peachtree Village International Film Festival* and Terry Bello's *International Soul Music Summit* August 17–20, my good friend Tony Baraka invited me out as a VIP guest to see some acts perform at Atlanta's *Museum Bar*. The Museum Bar is what I'd classify as an *Upscale Restaurant, Bar & Lounge*. It's one of the newest venues for Atlanta diners-slash-partiers who seek a high-quality *one-stop hotspot* to get an "exclusive night-out experience."

The historical 15,000 square foot structure, located at 181 Ralph David Abernathy Blvd., is right off the Interstate 75/85 connector, just minutes from the state capital; and seconds from Turner Field. With a full-service restaurant, bakery, three lounges and a signature nightclub, the Museum Bar's menu boasts seafood, poultry, salad and pasta offerings from Tuesday through Saturday. I guess that would explain Tony Baraka's expanding waistline. (Just kidding, Tony!) Getting serious again, outgoing diners can also take in food, drink and dance at the Museum Bar's Sunday Brunch and Social. One reason why I go out of my way to talk about this venue is because centuries-old architecture was used to build it: this hotspot was originally constructed in the 1890s and was previously called St. Stephen's Missionary Baptist Church before catering to a secular crowd. It also looks like a smaller version of another church converted into a performance venue: The Tabernacle.

Today, the completely modernized church is loaded with interior stonewalls, gothic columns and thirty-foot ceilings. Zooming in, the Museum Bar is comprised of three levels of entertainment space, all designed by renowned interior designer Jim Weinberg—Jim had a hand in designing distinctive clubs and restaurants from New York to San Francisco. Yielding a full vodka bar and breathtaking skyline views, the Museum Bar is there to satisfy every mood, and they hit the sweet spot through an enticing bakery loaded with delectable cakes, cupcakes and specialty desserts. Hungry for more?

Looking at the Museum Bar's concert size stage, it's easy to see how the venue accommodates live music—magical performances from local, regional and national acts grace the stage on a weekly basis, plus they have a house DJ, VIP entrance and private VIP lounges, too! The story has to move on now, so for more informational morsels, just come on down; if you can't make it, you can still have a VIP cyber-experience at www.atlantamuseumbar.com.

My longtime friend Tony Baraka did a great job picking The Museum Bar—this was going to be a great night of "Soul Sessions." For tonight, there would be a live performance by Berlin, Germany's Kaye-Ree. This vocalist delivered a unique brand of Soul music called *International Soul*, along with her guitarist and a percussive tabla player. Also on the bill was platinum R&B singer KeKe Wyatt, who performed with a guitarist, keyboardist and drummer. Let's re-enact tonight's episode, starting at the top with our opening act, Kaye-Ree. To me, this 'pleasantly proficient' singer from Germany actually looks like she could be from anywhere but Germany. With her hair wrapped up and dressed in typical mid-eastern fashion, Kaye-Ree entertained the audience with smooth, melodic vocal renderings of her songs. Accompanied by a guitarist and a tabla player, the words coming out of her mouth sounded crystal clear. While she was like a breath of fresh air at times, there were periods that brought back memories of an artist I used to market for Portrait/Epic Records, Sade.

Since her 2009 debut, Kaye-Ree attracted the attention of multiple cultures, which should always be a goal for today's artist. Performing in multiple configurations, she and her band delivered a truly unique sound—in acoustic and electrified formats. Over the past few years, Kaye-Ree brought sonic snippets to places like London's Ronnie Scott's Club, Hamburg's Café Beautiful Views, and Munich's Club Muffathalle in her German homebase. She also performed at New York's Soul Bar and in Atlanta's International Soul Music Summit. Always willing to play anywhere, Kaye-Ree also entertained at open-air festivals, including Aschaffenburg's *Africa Festival*, Frankfurt's *Museum Embankment Festival* and at the Weissenhäuser Beach *Baltic Soul Weekender*.

Crossing over into other genres is important for many artists—making sure she was seen in front of Hip-Hop audiences too, Kaye-Ree opened shows for Kurtis Blow and Busta Rhymes. She also performed with Paul Carrack, the SWR Big Band and Stevie Wonder; from that growing list of people, it's a given she'll keep doing big things. Performing at huge events like trade shows, she caught the attention of the International Automobile Exhibition in Frankfurt and was featured in a Mercedes Benz video clip. Humanitarily speaking, Kaye-Ree participated in doing charity events for Haiti's earthquake victims and worked with the Go-for-Ghana Project. Kaye-Ree also captured the attention of large sporting events like the World Cup soccer tournament, where she sang the popular song *Africans* in Cape Town, for thousands of folks.

With a second CD to add with her first one, Kaye-Ree meshes her lyrics and collaborates alongside composer-guitarist Felix Justen. To recreate the energy of her live shows, Kaye-Ree records songs as if she were in concert, relying less on automated, digitized sonic support. She also pulls inspiration from classic divas like Ella Fitzgerald, Billie Holiday and Nina Simone to deliver her own versions of timeless songs. After winning an Afghan tabla in a contest, Kaye-Ree recorded a Persian influenced song; other great songs can be found online at her website, too.

Kaye-Ree's international brand of Global Soul surpasses styles, borders and religions to unite listeners and spiritually draw them closer together. I was pleasantly surprised to make new musical discoveries at www.kaye-ree.com, www.youtube.com/kayeree and at www.facebook.com/kayeree5. I certainly hope you check her out and become a fan, like I did.

Playing the part of *Mr. Good Host*, Tony Baraka kept stopping by my table to make sure I was good. He introduced me to some of his people and kept working the room, all dappered up in a business suit and tie. As I ran my mouth talking about 'who knows what,' a guest seated one table over approached me. Apparently he heard me saying something that caught his attention, because it seemed like he wanted to hear more. But when this guy started talking, I shut up and listened to what *he* had to say—in all actuality, this guy was a walking legend!

Let me clear my throat as I open the lens to expose more: Producer/songwriter/arranger Jimmy Basil Roach hails from the Bedford-Stuyvesant section of Brooklyn, New York. Also called "Bed-Stuy," this neighborhood was right next to mine in Crown Heights, and Fulton Street was our borderline marker that separated Jimmy Roach and I. Headquarters to multi-leveled brownstone homes, Bed-Stuy was the neighborhood where the Chips—*Rubber Biscuits* lived. Jimmy jammed with the group when Sammy Strain was with them, before he left for a group called *The Lyrics*. They did shows on the talent circuit scene, but never made any professional recordings. Going back further in time, we see a young Jimmy Roach taking private piano lessons when he was fourteen; piano lessons were standard ops in his house. Around 1963, Jimmy became a staff writer for Chardon Music and wrote *The Kitty Kat Song*—it was on the B-side of Lee Dorsey's first big hit, *Ride Your Pony*. Jimmy worked with Chardon until 1965, when he joined the military. After Jimmy's return he picked up where he left off, writing compositions bursting with soul. Examples include *I'm By Your Side* for Brenda & the Tabulations, *Too Much Pride* for the Persians, *I Miss You* for The O'Jays, and plenty of others.

In 1969, Jimmy Roach made a move to Detroit and clinched a job as staff writer and arranger with Hitsville, USA. An old writing partner named Rosemary McCoy hooked him up with Pam Sawyer, who collaborated with him on a song David Ruffin recorded, *My Whole World Ended*. This song opened the door for Jimmy's Motown affiliation. Striking up a solid relationship with Jimmy Ruffin (older brother of The

Temptations' David Ruffin), Roach produced an album that ended up sitting in the label's vaults, unreleased. Jimmy went on to arrange for The Four Tops and The Miracles' 1970 Christmas album, and was so dedicated to developing the sound of Detroit that he stayed behind after Motown relocated to Los Angeles.

Connecting with producer Don Davis, Jimmy Roach went on to write *Hit and Run* for Roz Ryan, who picked up gigs as a Broadway actress—she became the Choir Director in a 90s sitcom called *Good News*. Over time The Supremes, The Dramatics, Esther Philips, The Dells, Gloria Gaynor and The Spinners featuring Philippe Wynne also benefited from Jimmy's writing skills. Unfortunately, after producer Thom Bell cherry-picked The Spinners to produce for Atlantic Records, Jimmy found himself cut out of the picture. To fill the void, during the 80s Jimmy managed and promoted Detroit music group *Everlife*, getting them signed to 20th Century Fox Records. The label stalled with moving the group through their pipeline, so it was Jimmy Roach who stepped in and pushed it locally, through a label that used the first two letters from each of his names: *Jibaro Records*. With over 125 BMI affiliated songs in his repertoire, Jimmy went into early retirement in the mid-80s, as the Rap/Hip-Hop phenomena made a targeted approach. Utilizing his entrepreneaur skills, Jimmy got into the retail sector; but the industry kept beckoning him back.

By the time I ran into Jimmy Roach at the Museum Bar, he was preparing to make a comeback. This time, he'd be based in Atlanta with his Jibaro Music Company and new production studio—this was history I had to see! Since we hit it off so well, Jimmy and I made a pact to keep in touch, and exchanged business cards. We made good on that pact and a year later, Jimmy came to my book signing party and got his autographed copy of *Musicology 2101: A Quick Start Guide To Music "Biz" History*. And since he's featured in *Musicology* 2102, I'm sure he's going to end up with a copy of this book too!

The headlining act was about to grace the Museum Bar's stage, so Jimmy and I started making our way back to sit at our respective tables. It would just be a matter of time before the R&B Diva known as Keke Wyatt made her appearance on stage; the band was already cranking out a groove to open her set with. As I glanced over at Jimmy's table, he glanced at me—we exchanged a head nod and two positive thumbs up, then Keke Wyatt's show began.

Ketara "Keke" Wyatt became widely known during the early 2000s, but the real work actually started a long time earlier. Before she exploded on the scene with platinum R&B singer Avant and released her own album of precious metal, Keke Wyatt was getting what I'd call intense training exercises—that's because she was born to a pair of vocalizing musicians! Well-versed in Spiritual music, Keke's family had an open menu when it came to non-Christian music. Singing since the age of two, a young Keke Wyatt was engaging live audiences by the time she was five, singing songs she learned from her parents. By the age of ten, Keke was recording professionally—on a local Midwest label's compilation Gospel album.

> **VOCAL FACT:** Working with assorted Gospel labels on demo songs, Keke Wyatt was paid $1,500 per track to record her captivating voice through the microphone.

Soon, industry heavy-hitters began scouting Keke Wyatt. Throughout her childhood, Keke's parents encouraged the young singer to explore other genres; Keke quickly learned how to write and perform from Gospel to Country, R&B, Pop; even Opera. Raised in Indianapolis, Keke picked up other musical cues when she spent time in places like Kentucky and Texas. With influences like Ella Fitzgerald, Donny Hathaway and Stevie Wonder, she discovered 'the art' of soulful singing by performing with a number of local girl groups. It quickly became obvious to many that Keke's mature style was way ahead of her age group's limitations.

Getting a chance most teenagers don't often run across, Keke learned the ropes from a songwriter/producer named Steve "Stone" Huff. He worked with acts like The Isley Brothers, Joe, Avant and a wide range of artists, so he had "highly credible" stamped all over. Opportunities like these didn't come up often, and doors opened along the way. Along a compelling path to fame and fortune, Keke learned how people can "burn you and leave you," taking all the credit with them. Despite the bumps and bruises, Keke navigated her way to R&B singer Avant and together, they recorded a song called *My First Love* for MCA Records. MCA did a great job promoting it, because I remember hearing it all the time on Atlanta radio, at clubs and at roller skating rinks while hanging out with Arrested Development's 70-something year-old, roller skating elder and spiritual advisor—Baba Oje. Plus, remaking a classic Rene and Angela song never hurts, either!

MCA Records made a calculated decision based off the Top 10 success of Avant's hit. Though it was released some two years after being recorded, the label signed Keke Wyatt to a solo deal. Recording her debut album in a record two weeks, Keke enlisted the aid of powerful players like MCA's Louil Silas, American Idol's Randy Jackson and Quadri El Amin, who managed Boyz II Men. Armed with hits galore, the album had a new single that teamed Keke up with Avant again. After some domestic issues surrounding Keke and her then manager-husband, Keke's *Soul Sista* album made it to platinum status. Now an artist with global appeal, Keke was known in far away places like Europe, Korea and Japan. The year 2004 saw the singer switching from MCA to Cash Money-Universal-Motown. All set for a new release in 2005, Keke's album got postponed until the following year. The first single appeared to be a great potential add at urban radio but after lackluster support, very little chart or airplay action came out of it. This led to a shelved project and a lot of lost time, despite tracks written by folks like Bryan Michael Cox and Tank. It also featured a Rachelle Ferrell remake, as well as special appearances by Avant and Ginuwine.

By late 2006, Keke Wyatt exited from Cash Money and signed on with TVT Records after reuniting with former manager Quadri El Amin. Once again in 2007, Keke got the short end of the deal when her release was pushed back for another year: the really bad news is TVT Records filed for bankruptcy and the album was never released. Showing her resilience, she switched lanes and starred in a theatrical production called *Love Over Board* alongside Avant and cast members like Karen Malina White, Khalil Kain, Carl Payne and comedian Miguel Nunez Jr. Musically speaking, Keke bounced back again with a 2010 single and album called *Who Knew?* This was followed with hints of a duets album with former labelmate Avant.

Combining all of her experiences to deliver a riveting performance, Keke Wyatt ensured all eyes remained on her through a vocally as well as visually compelling stage show. Any great singer knows how to take an onstage break—letting band members 'show their stuff' and engaging with the audience is what it's all about. During their relative sets, I remember Kaye-Ree and Keke constantly checked with the audience to make sure they were in good spirits, while sharing personal stories. Working every inch of the stage, Keke Wyatt sent a message loud and clear, like Gloria Gaynor did in her classic 70s hit, *I Will Survive*. It's a definite that we'll see and hear much more of this 'young veteran' who dishes up a fascinating blend of R&B, Soul, Gospel and more… along her course of delivering acapella performances in perfect pitch. There's more to behold on Keke online at places like www.myspace.com/kekewyatt, so don't miss out on a golden opportunity to know Keke Wyatt!

NOT A WEEK WEEK

The week was shaping up to be a busy one—after my Wednesday night run to the Museum Bar, Thursday beheld another Atlantic Station *Party In The Park*, and Friday came rolling along with a huge V.I.P. party. Once again, the annual Peachtree Village International Film Festival's Friday V.I.P. reception was held at the 'prestigiously distinguished' law offices of Bernard Coleman and Womble Carlysle. In 2011, I tagged along with my old friend Tom Davis aka *Dr. Love.com* but this year, a little more was brought to the table—my Team Mirosa pal Barry Huff arranged for Mirosa Beer to be served up, ice cold! We decided to strategically place Mirosa at each of their two bars: one was in the main reception area, with another in the rear section of the offices near a conference room.

After bringing up Mirosa "coolers 'n cases," we decided to hang around and see who showed up. I heard they were expecting folks like Charles S. Dutton, Ed Gordon, Reginald Hudlin, Vivica Fox, Lisa Wu Hartwell, Omari Hardwick, Marla Gibbs and more for the screening of a new film called *The Obama Effect*. A few unexpected guests I ran into included actress Terri Vaughn, who I bumped into from time to time when I stopped by her Green Room Actor's Lounge on Peachtree Street in L.B. (Lower Buckhead). Besides running into my old pals Full Force, I also ran into Ray Charles' daughter Sheila Raye Charles, Wilson Pickett's daughter Saphan Pickett, Lisa "Left Eye' Lopes' little sister Reigndrop, and Domique Wilkins' brother, John. Let's go back into the memory banks for a multi-layered INSIDE VIEW.

A RAYE OF HOPE

From where I was standing in the main room, I saw Sheila Raye Charles but couldn't see all the celebrities onstage when famed lawman Bernard Coleman delivered his "welcome" speech. After they took a few group photos, everyone slowly dispersed and I wound up talking with a few friendly people I bumped into. Then the search was on for a candid moment with Sheila Raye Charles! A photographer buddy of mine led me straight to her and it was showtime—I introduced myself to her publicist

Angela Moore, codename *Miss Nonstop Projects To Do* (see www.mypublicist.com), the next thing you know, I was telling Sheila Raye how glad I was to meet her. Once again as I 'divested information,' the book you now hold in your hands came up and we were in networking's fast track. We discussed ways to collaborate on ventures we each had in mind: in short, I felt I made a good connection with the incomparable Sheila Raye Charles. Was this a strange occurrence or destiny? The plot thickens, but before we get stuck—let's get to know a bit more about the daughter of music legend Ray Charles.

Sheila Raye Charles had been singing in church since she was little and by the time our gifted vocalist was a teen, the prestigious Allard Academy of Los Angeles accepted her as the youngest student, ever. It wouldn't be long before Sheila Raye was performing for the Jazz ensemble at places like Disneyland, Knott's Berry Farm and at competitions across the state. But the stress of being a child of the late, great Ray Charles had its moments of darkness, as Sheila fought her own set of demons to fully understand her true purpose in life. Sharing her story with me privately, I couldn't help but wonder how many children of celebrities were faced with similar challenges. When Sheila was 19, she went against her father's wishes after being discouraged from pursuing a career in music. Nevertheless, her talent revealed itself and eventually Ray welcomed his daughter and her band into his exclusive studio and produced a number of compositions. This helped to get her further into the music game… under the spotlight of fame.

The 24-hour life has a way of creeping up on some of us and eventually takes a toll on the mind, body, family, relationships, bank account, or all of the above! After Sheila Raye encountered a series of life-changing events, her career took a turn for the worse but today she says those past experiences "give great meaning and countenance to her music." Now traveling the globe delivering her distinct sound to worldwide audiences, Sheila Raye Charles delivers an "intensely inspiring message of hope and love," through acoustic Jazz and R&B. Found in her lyrics are personal accounts of past journeys and memories of her iconic father—he broke down color barriers from just a few tickles of his fingers on a piano keyboard.

Coming full circle, Sheila Raye Charles is making her own mark in the music industry and to prove it, there are releases like 2004's *Introducing Sheila Raye Charles* and 2009's *Behind The Shades*. Like my friend Wade Jones and a select few, I believe music has to go "back to the musicians"—Sheila offers a fulfilling dish for those who come to the table with an appetite. These days, we can find Sheila Raye Charles dishing her talent out to hungry audiences as she engages them with spine-tingling renditions of her father's big hits like *America the Beautiful*, *Hit The Road Jack* and *Georgia*. From a marketing standpoint, I see Sheila Raye capturing many segments of the musical pie because songs like these crossed the color barrier to touch EVERYONE who listened to it: simply put, they changed the world.

There's no telling where Sheila Raye could appear—churches, Jazz festivals, arenas, clubs, or even high-profile 'embassy exclusives.' While performing, Sheila shares stories of her recovery from drug addiction and a spiritual journey that led to her own personal growth and new outlook on life. She now has an eye-opening life story called *Behind the Shades*, which opens the lens on an intensely high-paced career; and a new relationship that she now shares with God. After an experience like the one Sheila Raye had, I'd pay good money to see her show—hopefully that will happen soon, because I could tell from our conversation how passionate about life... and music, Miss Charles is. At the end of the day, Sheila Raye says, "the only thing that matters is whether you remain down on your back—or eventually stand up on your feet to fulfill your destiny." I just admire that positive outlook! To get your own outlook of this phenomenol singer and her legacy, visit sites like www.sheilaraycharles.com, www.rememberingourfather.com, www.myspace.com/sheilarayecharles12, or just do your own cybersearch.

THE DAUGHTER'S SECTION

From my professional observations, publicist Angela Moore aka Pro Agent *Miss Nonstop Projects To Do* was right in the mix. Working on a project called the *Legendary Daughters* tour, she planned to feature divas like Sheila Raye Charles, B.B. King's daughter Claudette King and Wilson Pickett's daughter, Saphan Pickett. Miss Moore told me Saphan Pickett was getting groomed to hit the stage and perform her dad's songs; likeminded divas like Sheila Raye Charles and Claudette King are also doing songs to keep the memory of their fathers alive and kicking. Events such as these appear to be a growing trend, with similar shows like April

2012's *Daughters of Legends* tour—it shined light on the legacies of John Lee Hooker and Van Morrison… through performances by their daughters Zakiya Hooker and Shana Morrison.

Although Claudette King couldn't make it to the reception, sometimes I still can't believe the story that connects us: one summer day in 2011, Peach City Records act Kimosha LeToi rode with Claudette to an out-of-state party for a producer my associate Wade Jones knew, Robin West. Kimosha let Claudette hear some music we recorded earlier in the summer with producer Adam Slawson at his North Atlanta Nutation Recordings studio, where lots of musical goodies are born (www.nutationrecordings.com, 404-82-MUSIC). Claudette heard the saxophone player on one song and inquired who this musician was—it turned out to be PCR's in-house sax man Dante Hawthorne, and he wound up being asked to play in Claudette King's band. More recently, Dante and I ran into each other at a new release party for Xscape's Tosha Scott; he just came back from doing a cruise ship show somewhere in the Caribbean, so there's still a ray of hope that one day, I'll meet Ms. King.

Making correct strategic moves along the way, Angela Moore told me she represented all three legendary ladies. They moved from other cities to be in Atlanta, where they'd gear up for a massive tour through rehearsals and preliminary performances. While at the party, I noticed the PVIFF was promoting several new productions and one of them was about Saphan Pickett's dad—the Wilson Pickett Jr. Legacy planned to present a musical called *In the Midnight Hour: The Music of Wilson Pickett*. This fantastic event was scheduled at the Porter Sanford III Performing Arts Center for September 21-23, 2012. Among the featured stars was NAACP Image Award winner Cassi Davis. This Broadway-styled jukebox musical celebrates the music legacy and life of a musical beacon that helped shape genres like Soul, Rhythm & Blues and Southern Rock: the world reknown Rock-n-Roll Hall of Famer, "Wicked" Wilson Pickett codename *Southern Rock Godfather*.

Just to let you know, the Wilson Pickett Jr. Legacy inspires young people to achieve their greatest dreams through the Wilson Pickett/Brandon Miller Scholarship Fund. In doing so, the WPL stimulates and encourages youth to experience the music of a true Soul, R&B and Rock icon. Founded in 2010, the scholarship fund supports deserving students who need help, like tuition and fee assistance: in Atlanta, scholarships have been awarded to students at Spelman and Morehouse

Colleges. Reports are coming in that the 2012-2013 scholarships were awarded to four high school juniors and seniors. According to the website, one major source of funding for this scholarship program was the production of *In the Midnight Hour: The Music of Wilson Pickett*. The musical was a good reason to make sure Saphan Pickett was in the house at that VIP reception—who could be a better promoter than the man's own daughter? For more information, you can check online at places like www.thewilsonpickett.com and www.atlantatheaterfans.com. Now, let's see who else I ran into at this invitation-only special event...

REIGNDROP'S PRETTY HEAVY

I've often wondered if my music life is a strange occurrence, or destiny. I put that out there because this one is REALLY weird... You see, the first thing I said to TLC's Lisa "Left Eye" Lopes in 1994 when I met her was how interesting her sense of fashion was. Getting a little brain-dead every now and then, I had no idea who this tiny dynamo was at the time; but I found out later.

How ironic that eighteen years later, I'm at a celebrity-studded party hosted by Womble Carlyle's Bernard Coleman, and I see an even shorter version of Lisa "Left Eye" Lopes. I said to myself, "Self, I'll be darned if she doesn't remind me of Left Eye. This little lady was dressed in colorful attire and when we were introduced, I had a momentary lapse of thought. I mentioned how interesting her sense of fashion was... Moments later, when they called the names of celebrities in the house, the smell of déjà vu floated around me through the air. Looking at the picture we took together, there's no mistaking Reigndrop Lopes shares the same DNA as big sister, Lisa "Left Eye" Lopes. Needless to say, it was an enlightening experience to be on the production set for 2013's TLC biographical movie, where the multi-platinum group was portrayed by a trio of great actresses. I bumped into T-Boz (Tionne Watkins) on the set and congratulated her for maintaining creative control in keeping the film as real as possible; I'm sure Left Eye would have approved. With that said, let's open up the lens on her *little sista* for more takes.

After being tagged with codename *Reigndrop* because of her pint-sized body, it stuck. There is no doubt that this young lady will be compared to her big sister—they look like twins! Some folks are asking: will Reigndrop pick up where *big sista* left off? Will she stake out a new path of success down another road? Or will she do a little bit of both?

Reigndrop Lopes plays her part well with strikingly similar looks and high-level output, so clear out a path as Little Miss Reigndrop delivers the goods. She's been leading the life of a Rock star by practically living in the studio, writing new songs for her upcoming release. Describing the music, Reigndrop asserts, "It is definitely a hot, rocked out Hip-Hop." Growing up, Reigndrop listened to the sounds of Aerosmith, Run-DMC, Missy Elliot, Linkin Park, Alanis Morissette, Evanescence and others, so I can see where she's coming from. With an edge that says Hip-Hop and Rock, we can add the subtitle of *"First Lady of Hip-Rock"* to her name. Reigndrop has a repertoire that extends from self-analysis to vividly imaginative; she also captures the lives of her subjects as if she were "walking in another person's shoes."

As an artist, Reigndrop writes songs that include topics like abuse, for those who have been hurt or betrayed in some way. Because her father was in the army, the family traveled often and lived among various cultures. This led to a strong ability to connect with crossover music styles and now, there's no doubt about it: *"The sound is Hip. The sound is Rock. The sound is REIGNDROP!"* Reigndrop's web page says it all, and she backs it up flawlessly because like her big sister Left Eye, she spent years practicing her craft live, as well as in the recording studio. Looking at the big picture, Reigndrop had access to the best studio gear due to her big sis forming UNI studios in 1998 to record projects. After her tragic accident, the family opened it up for business… and for Reign to drop down music slated as *Crossover Classics.*

I said it before and I'll say it again: he, or in this case *she* who appeals to more than one culture—wins. I'm glad to have met Lisa "Left Eye" Lopes and her baby sister Reigndrop, who has the makings of something good to look forward to. You might as well get to know Reigndrop too, because based on what I've seen at sites like www.reigndropmusic.net, this cute little lady's going to be around for awhile! Meeting Reigndrop Lopes was priceless—she must have been a toddler when I met her sister, Lisa "Left Eye" Lopes way back when. Was this a strange occurrence, or destiny? You be the judge.

Switching scenes back to the VIP party, I strolled around the posh offices of Womble Carlyle, noticing all the people getting their networking thing on. Although I didn't feel much like talking, the reverse held true—people wanted to talk to *me*. I made some great connections after folks took a look at the *Georgia Music Industry Association* business cards I handed out (There's some great information on this exciting music organization in my next book). I followed the GMIA card up with a promotional Mirosa Beer card. Trying to locate a good spot to post up and watch the goings-on, I ran into my good friend Josh Golden. I was hanging out with Josh and Wu Tang soldier NLZ one day then ended up chillin' with Method Man on his tour bus… but that's a whole 'nother story. Staying on track, Josh was engaged in a conversation with a big guy who looked like a pro basketball or football player to me. A few of us shorter people contemplated who he was earlier, but didn't get too far. When I got within earshot, Josh introduced the big guy as John Wilkins and as it turns out, John is basketball great Dominique's younger brother.

Quite naturally, his hand swallowed mine when we shook—but before the fear of him crushing my hand sunk in, he released. We got into a conversation that took us back to the early 90s, when Atlanta Hawks Forward Dominique Wilkins' little brother opened a nightclub and put his big brother's name on it. The soft-spoken giant fired one back: he not only helped open the club—he ran the club as General Manager! That was amazing to me, because I remembered an interesting night I had at Dominique's club with an artist I was marketing at the time. I asked John if he was there the night I brought Epic Records artist Victoria Wilson-James through. She was a part of England's hot Soul II Soul crew, and she also had a hit record called *Through*. The local Epic promotion guy was out of town at the time; I was asked to fill in and like a true team player, willingly complied. To my surprise, John Wilkins remembered my story perfectly because he just happened to be working at the club that night.

As mentioned elsewhere, music artists usually did promotional visits through different cities to help stimulate excitement, airplay and sales. For this run through Atlanta, the plan was for Victoria Wilson-James to do a promotional show at the club, and V-103's Ryan Cameron was the MC. There were no dressing rooms in the club, so Victoria and I waited for Ryan in the limousine until he showed up and it was "on with the show" after that! The tall model-esque diva code-lettered *VWJ* rocked the house with songs from her album. After the show, I signalled the limo driver as the star mixed and mingled with her fans. Then, breaking out my secret weapons, I passed out posters and CD singles to distract the crowd around Victoria, as she slipped out the door and into the limo—that old trick worked every time. Working at the club, I bet John Wilkins saw all kinds of late-night tricks getting played.

It's funny, because John Wilkins and I were in the same place at the same time, but never actually met—until twenty-something years later. Besides who he's related to, I discovered John is a big-time music fan, and he had some big-time projects brewing in his vat: for the past few years, he's been promoting an award show. Held annually at the prestigious Fox Theater, "*Salute to the Legend Weekend*" features a must-see Legendary Awards and Celebrity Fashion Show (www.legendaryawards.com). If you're lucky, you can catch a sneak peek at www.wsbtv.com/videos/news/p2p-legendary-awards-dominique-wilkins/vF7Ls/.

Back at the Womble Carlyle offices, several ladies in the room were struggling to get at John and network, so he couldn't talk with us much longer and left with them—but not before we exchanged business cards. I don't know where you'll be in February when John holds his event, but I plan to be sitting front-and-center at the Fox, if not kicking it backstage with an "ALL ACCESS" pass around my neck. For now, it's off to another private *Peachtree Village International Film Festival* party at the W Hotel in Colony Square near "the people's station," *V-103*.

In addition to the public relations people, my associate Barry Huff had been getting Mirosa Beer into some impressive, high-level events. When Barry told me he was doing a Mirosa promotion at the PVIFF's VIP party, memories of the prior year's events flashed through my mind—once again I ran into my Brooklyn homeboys from back in the day, *Full Force*. My partners Josh Golden and Barry Huff were big Full Force fans, so I got talked into taking a picture of Josh and Barry with Bowlegged Lou, Paul Anthony and B-Fine. I'm a little shy in front of cameras but surprisingly that night, I found myself taking pictures with Divas like Sheila Raye Charles and Saphan Pickett, the next generation of Ray Charles and Wilson Pickett. The cake's icing was topped off with a little 'Reigndrop from the Left Eye.' While pictures and videos may decay, memories like these will never fade away.

And as we speak, I continue making new memories; this time with legendary folks like *Diamond D Paris* who spent a few decades at Motown, under the wings of Berry Gordy. Diamond also manages my good friend, GMIA board member and singer-songwriter Stephie Rae Grenier, who plays guitar and also does back adjustments! I'll have plenty more to say in an upcoming installment. Diamond recently introduced me to music All-Star Eric "*Fats*" Gallon, who played drums for acts like:

Regina Bell	LaWanda Page (Sanford & Son)
William Bell	Sly Stone
Mary Davis (S.O.S. Band)	The Chi-Lites
Harold Melvin & The Blue Notes	The Manhattans
Jimmie Bo Horne	The Mighty Dells
Millie Jackson	Sam & Dave
Lattimore	Johnny Taylor
Anthony Lockett (Cameo)	Joe Tex
Gwen McCrae	Wildman Steve
Rudy Ray Moore (Dolemite)	Doug Wimbush (Living Colour)

It took a minute to get a handle on his name, but I did in fact stumble upon another legend with a serious story to tell. On Fats Gallon's own accord, playing *Funky Drums* was the only thing on the menu, and he's proud to have made "Real Music Without Drugs" (also the title of his book and video). With a father and brother who were also entertainers, please join me in the next installment of my Musicology series for the big scoop on Fats. But that's only if you want to pick up more *Superior Intellect* on this "Funky Drummin' Tall Boy" who has done so much to inspire fans worldwide. They say there's six degrees of separation but in a few cases, I'd be inclined to recalculate the math by doing 'short' division.

Another great act we'll get to know is my man Charles "CB" Bell, who played trumpet for a legendary Go-Go group called Trouble Funk. In the next book, CB gives us the *real run-down* on Go-Go's origins… and a super-icon named Chuck Brown. After international man of mystery "Mad" Max Lee introduced me to CB, we went on to develop a relationship that has now crossed us over into Peach City Records territory. I can't spill the beans just yet, but stick around for more juicy info on this "diverse synergy."

Well the buzzer just went off, so that brings us to the end of this portion of our musical journey through people, time and space. The additional data found next will help jog your memory about what was just read, and prepare you for our next adventure in the timeless world of music. I hope you discovered some information in this book to be useful in some way, so thanks for hanging in there: "*May you find eternal knowledge and everything else you search for in the vast, infinite world of music.*" Watch out for Musicology 2103, where I'll continue on as your self-appointed tour guide—until then, don't forget to keep it moving!

FINAL THOUGHTS

If you were lucky enough to read *Musicology 2101: A Quick Start Guide to Music "Biz" History*, you know that we wrapped up our adventure in the Caribbean and Latin America. So it made sense to pick things up here in Book #2 with the music of Mexico and keep working south to Brazil, before bringing our story back to the United States. As always, it was my intention to disclose little-known facts about music history and those who contributed to its growth.

Once again, the task of combining intensive research with professional and personal experience was quite a challenge but the more I learned, the more motivated I became about completing this phase of my grand project. One of the most gratifying rewards I picked up along the way was the inclusion of friends who are originally from countries like Mexico and Brazil. It was also a pleasure to include friends from right here in the States who are near and dear to me. Once again, I'd like to show my personal gratitude to all involved who put forth a hand in helping to get this project completed.

During our adventure, we got familiar with music from other lands, plus we took a candid look at Classical, Folk and Gospel. A recap of how the record industry was born gave light to its spectacular growth by the new millennium. Besides music, the industry also encapsulated genres like spoken word, poetry and comedy. We met a few singers who could act... or actresses who could sing, and observed that a major portion of American music was created by guitars. Details about this adaptable instrument and the musicians who helped push it out front to the centerfield helped shine light on its popularity. We also saw how other forms of entertainment like Comedy, Country and Folk helped expand the industry to levels never seen before.

As "the biz" grew, it picked up its own share of underlying luggage as well. Despite all the ups and downs, the music business still exists and nests comfortably in the growing media world; as a cleverly disguised, stripped-down version of its former self. Once again, allow me to repeat that after writing the Musicology book series, I still find myself listening to music an entirely different way these days. In addition to the lyrics, I absorb the elements of rhythm, melody, harmony and texture—separately and combined—to grasp what I find interesting about each one.

287

These days, I still remain conscious of featured instruments from the percussion, string, wind and electronic families. Although I always felt it, I discovered through close and intense listening, research and documentation, that music is truly one of the most engaging mediums of communication given to mankind for further development. Through the delivery of this book series, my feelings, opinions and suspicions about music's history and essential elements have once again been confirmed.

The music and entertainment industry is saturated with smoke screens as well as true talent, so it constantly demands new ideas to "keep things moving." However, not everyone will be a successful composer, musician, singer, MC or even a loyal fan, so remember—the only group of real importance that you should always try to 'educate and entertain' in this world is God, your family, good friends and yourself. No matter what stresses life brings, God ordained life to be lived to the fullest: and for music to sooth souls. I'll see you on the next Musicology tour through people, places and time!

EPILOGUE

As it grew, the record industry picked up supporting organizations: ASCAP, BMI and the RIAA are among those that became regulatory leaders in a modern generation of music lovers, as continual innovative breakthroughs in technology filtered down to the music. The 'Golden Era' of everything faded, as music styles expanded in leaps and bounds—from Rock to Fusion to Funk. By the late 70s, Disco came along and pulled the rug right out from under everyone's feet. Radio and club playlists; along with record store bins, got clogged with tons of Disco music.

Record companies supported the explosion of new music genres— by releasing as many records as they could, a practice that generated millions. Owned by media giants, record labels expanded their budgets to stay ahead of the next guy. To prevent competitors from dominating radio airplay and radio playlists, bigger budgets were created to basically buy airtime, as labels bid against each other in battles that grew to astronomic proportions. After the damage had already been done, the government stepped in and investigated what became known as 'payola scandals.'

Experimental recordings led their way to the birth, maturity and explosion of the record industry as Blues, Country, Folk, Gospel, Jazz, R&B, Rock, Heavy Metal, Funk, Disco, World, Club/Dance and Rap/Hip-

Hop became the most widely accepted musical forms in America; and ultimately around the world. Suddenly, record companies found their artists becoming trendsetters being followed by more than a few fans. Looking ahead, we'll take an in-depth view at how the industry continued to grow in leaps and bounds, all the way into the digital age. That's all coming up in our next adventure, so get ready!

<u>OUTRO</u>

I would like to acknowledge the many new artists that I have yet to meet and work with (ALWAYS keep your head up), the players and creative people I was blessed to have met or developed friendships with that have been out there *keepin' it movin'* all these years in the Atlanta music-media scene and beyond:

My publicist Lyn K., "Branding Queen" Afrika, Tony "Many Hats" Baraka, Silas "Si-Man Baby" Alexander, Arrested Development (alla y'all!), Angry Black Man, The Atlanta Star Record Pool (Marvin, Lewis Howard and crew), The Atrium soldiers, Pope Arthur of Dognschnautn (just like gentlemen, eh?), Sir Al of Germany, Chopper City's Bam, Los Angeles' own Bambu, Norm "We Go Back To The 90s" Banton, Rose and Ramon Bergout, Big Body, DJ Mike "gots to keep it movin!" Blocker & www.allaroundsound.biz, Bonecrusher, Bow Wow, Randy (Broad 1) Broadus, Bobby (Got My Own Show) Brown, The B.U.R.N.Z. Family, Ryan Cameron, Brian Castle, Caustic Dames, Cecille Leslie (We go way back), Chris "DJ Mirosa," Citty Da Cookie Man, George (Funk Doctor) Clinton, Kevin (Chief Rocker) Crocker, Moses Dailey, the Atlanta Entertainment Association and Hearsay Records–keeping it moving with my man Sinatra, Tom (Dr. Love) Davis, Sirius satellite radio's James 'D-Train' Williams - from Cunningham to Prelude; from Columbia to now–where's my Cordoba!, Jermaine (JD) Dupri, Monica Ewing, Mitch (Biker Boy) Faulkner, Full Force–from The Amplifiers to now is a long time comin'!

My niched *Hall of Famers*: Max Lee, Edna Jones, Sandra, Kimmy, Marcella Ruela, "Queen Mother" Ericka, Chris 'MS Tech' Bennett, Rob 'Beast' McCarthy, Chris 'Red Heat' Marcus, Brian 'B-Funk' Smith, Mike 'Doc' Berg, Victor 'Kash' Ramkissoon, Carlos "Just Listen To Me" Tejeda, Mike 'Trouble' Furedy; Bache 'Mystique Films' Holland, the masters of the mix: DJ Hershey "Stop! Hammer Time!," DJ Jelly (back in the Peppermint days), *breddah* DJ Legacy & The 5 Star Generals, DJ

Nabs - remember *The Piper, Business Doin' Pleasure* singles, and that picture with our homeboy Cheba, (R.I.P.), DJ Red Money, Music Mafia's Flint Fleming, Atlanta's Music Mayor Charles Geer, my Lil Bro Scott 'Lenny Global' Hires, Chip Houston, Keisha (Can't Stop Sangin') Jackson, Kilo, King J, King Z, Kool Ace, Dirty D, Seldom Scene, JaWar (Atlanta Music Industry Connection), Barry "Miami Man" Lehman, Mike "Movin" Jamison, Monroe "Big Bro" Johnson–finish that album… (Cheryl–we'll do lunch).

Janice "Big Momma" Reed, B. Brown (Boom Shaka Laka), Jocelyn "Lady Di" Vickers, Edwin and the Bar-Red Entertainment *Hot Like Fire crew*, Lady X, Lil Jon (holla at your boy - *Okaaay!!!!*), Kris Kross, Angela "Maximum Exposure" Moore, Muffy, my bredren Max "Missa International" Lee, Peter Levy, Patrick Taylor, Rockstone/Wolfpack and L.E.D., MC Shy D (Bronx to Cedar Grove to *Ellenhood*), Michael Mauldin, Universal Studios/Tech Rentals Audiovisual veteran Eric Miller, The Million Dollar Record Pool (J.R. Dino), The Million Mom March and Jacquie Algee–one love! The Original P and J Love, Levi Patton, Allen and Arthur 'EVC' Pope, Professor Griff, Power Born and the 7th Octave, Que, Raheem The Dream, Ludacris & Shaka Zulu, Tod 'Tech II' Rose, Ricky at Mazoos Videography (It's a wrap!)

A special "Thank You" to all the Exposer 3 contributors: my cuz Andrew Bees, Anything But Monday, Kimosha LeToi, Doja, Joe Black, Lyrika Holmes, Terri Carroll, Elliot Holden, Jawan and The Jackson Sisters, Tom 'Dr. Love' Davis, Johnna Jeong, Chyna Nicole, Fitzroy Francis, Yohon Trotter, Baybee Strange, Lion Tafari, Lady X, Kendra King, Warren J. Gallimore, and Onny.

Big Respect to Legendary VIPs like Jack 'The Rapper' Gibson, Jill Bell, Allen 'The Music Specialist' Johnston, Tosha Ford, Tom 'This Guitar Can Talk' Long, Marsha Washington George aka 'Radio Lady,' "Massa Man" Tony Winger, Christopher Baskett, Demetrius Ramsey, Casual Cal, Jay Dixon and crew at iSoulRadio.com, Che Reason, Royalty & Teflon (the next wave is comin'). Thanks Scrapploc (The Educated MC) for the Fela Kuti CD, my bredren Scruface (miss ya mon!), Mack Menace and the Beatxstrodenairs team, Vernon Slaughter, College Park Slymn, Jimi (Truck) Starks, Larry Starks, Arnell (The Don) Starr, Jeremy (Wild Man) Stodghill, Strong & Lyvation Entertainment, 2unes, The Uptown Entertainment Band, Quaanda Ray, Gary Wade, Cameron Wade

& 3 A.M., Wali (The Jumpin' Jack), Jamal (ATL Web Radio), Walt C., Rock-2-Def, The Brew, crew at Dugans on Ponce, B.K. (That's Entertainment) Williams, Xscape, Don 'Golden Child' Yute... the list goes on & on.

And I can never forget my much-talented friends on "Team Audiovisual Elite" who've cheered me on throughout the years – BIG THANKS for the continued motivation and support: Kerry Abbott, "AV Guru" Patrick Adudu-Oke, Allicia Brown and Chaz Cain at All Access, The AVMG crew, Ronn *Brown Bread* Media" Allen, Andre "AV Guy With The Eye," Greg Anderson, Jason "I Got A Pop Up" Ashfield, Jay "Comin' Atchi" Atchison, Mr. Bankz, James "JB" Barlow, Joe "It's Not On My Order" Bart, Jason "Hustlin' Man" Bedford, Will "Silverhook" Berryman, Warren "Outkast" Bletcher, Mike "Speakin-n-Spinnin" Blocker, Bob the "Man Down," Arvine "Always Workin" Bradford, Mike "Mr. CGC" Bruce, Rajiz "Hall of Famer" Bryant, Ricky "Lil Bro" Budd, Brian Byle, Adrian Carter and Pierre "Pole Vault" Castor.

Donnell "DC" Chandler, Marlon "The Main" Character, Elliot Charles, Gary "Producer Man Chizo" Chisolm, Dave "Mr. Freeman PD" Cohn, Coy "The AV Guoy," Calvin Crosby, Mervin "Mr. Weeziana" Crump, Tim "OG" Daniels, Stuart "I'm Plugged In" Danneman, Ryan "Westwood" Darling, Marcus "Audio Dude" Davis, Andrew "Just Got Started" Dixon, Vince "I'm the Big Boss" Dixon, Qui Dotson, Brandon "Scenic Guy" Dunn, Curtis "Party Right Here" Duren, Clint "Breakfast of Champions" Fletcher, Cassandra "Florida Momma" Furco, Keith "History of Jazz" Gantt, Marcus "Mr. GWCC" Garnett, Sean "Tick-TLC Movie Man" Gentry, Arthur "Guitar Guy" Glanville, Perrin "Lenny" Green, Antjuan "Rig King" Grimes, Sheila "Let's Get It 'n Go" Hamilton, Homer "Triple H" Hammonds, Ed "Movie Man" Harlegue, Micah "I Want Your Job" Harris, Mike "The Time Machine" Harris, Dante "Saxman" Hawthorne.

John, Ricky and Wesley "The Hayes Brothers," "Young Gun" Wesley C. Hayes, Bobby "Laid Back" Hill, Amir "Mr. GICC" Jackson, my man "Always Workin" James at the GICC, Brother Man BK Jackson at the GCC, My "Brotha From Anotha Motha" Ranson Jackson, Bredda Dane James, Jay "Where's My Check" Johnson, Monroe "Big Bro" Johnson, Mario "Fabulouso Steel Gloves" Jones (where's my belt?), my Peach City Records Partner In Crime Wade "J-3" Jones, Herman "Size 18" Jones, Ian "Where's the Next Gig" Kelly, Dana "On The Road Again"

291

Kopec, Kozmo, Bryan "Cool Breeze" LaMarr, LaMont "LeEye B," Gett's Larry "Military AV Biker," On Events friends like Russ "I Drive A Convertible" LoPinto, Doug "Light 'Em Up" Luster, Brian "They're All Crazy" McKinney, Bill & Sarah Maier, "DJ-AV Guy" Kobe Marson, and Donrad "Bredren Rentex" Martin.

Bill "I Got An Exotic Dancer" McCollum. Bryce "I Got The Hookup" McElroy, Greg "Mac Man" McMillan, Robert "Sound Wizard" McTigue, Brad McWorthers, Anton "Champ Da DJ" Miller, Nathan "Room With A View" Miller, Stan, Brent and Austin Milner, DeWayne "Mr. Palladium" Mincey, Muhammad, Dave "I Got This" Naglit, Dirk "Sarge of AV" Needham, Rogers Nelson, Chris "Project Master" O'Halleran, Izzy "The Legend" Onuoha, Mark "Corporal" Pentecost, "Queen Pam" at Gett Productions, Rod "Mr. Ellenhood" Pass, Bridgette "Good Peeps" Powell, Marlando "Bredda Bredren" Powell, Darell "The Voice" Pressley, Barney "Buddy" Putnam, Dustin Quintera, Ben "Busy Project Man" Rogers, Jim "I Can Get It Fixed Or Buy You A New One" Reeves.

Rico "Yard Bwoy," Gerel "Video Vixen" Roberts, Manny "Rennaisance Man" Rodriguez, Sonja "Sound Gal" Rubino, Frank "I Need A Break" Rutland, Jeff "Old Sheraton Boss" Sabourin, Tammy Rowe, Jodie "Workin' Out" Rush, Jai Saint & Lance Aquasanta at VTS, Kristen "They're All Crazy" Scales, Chris "I Covers It All" Scriver, Sam "Need To Scan This" Shelton, Eric "McGyver" Sherman, Wil "Artman" Siedel, Kenny "Way Back" Sigler, Lon "Baseball" Slack, Adam "Pro Mix" Slawson, Stuart "Long Distance Driver Man" Smith, Slim, Leo "Catch Me At The Twelve" Soto, Mark "Mr. Maso From Nawlins" Soublet, David "Lego" Stivers, Amie "Breaktime Buddy" Thompson and my new "Breaktime Buddy" Nate Hall Jr.

Bredda Wes Walters, "Mr. Red" Steve Williams, Chuck "Mr. Ixon" Taylor, AV Wiz Kid Tory (Hyatt Regency), Team Sheraton's Andrew, Cole, Matt and Seth, ON Events/Tech Rentals, "Too Tall" Thomas Tucker, Scott "Gotta Dispatch" Tunnell, Ricky "Driva Man" Usher, Mark "Driver Man Chateau" Vaccaro, Anjuli "The Brain" Velazquez, Stephen "I Do Lights" Verner, Rafael "Mi Amigo" Villegas, Ray "Filmin' B-day Bud" Virgin, Hartford "I Get It Done" Walker, Carlton "Biker Man" Williames, Albert Williams, Mark "Jamaican Jaguar" Williams, Gloria "The Eye" Williams, Jonathan "Wise Man" Wisdom, Darrell Witt, Ann "Happy Face" Wright, Ben "Hameen" Wright, Vanessa "The Femme Rigger."

A very special shoutout to Team Wednesday Wind Down at Centennial Olympic Park: Kym "Weld This" Austin, BJ "Lion King," Justin "Mixologist JT" Tolar, Kris "Digital Mix" Owen, Guwayne "G-Man" Gorman, Justin "Music Machine" Melotte, Dane "Yardy" James, Bredda Rico, Paula "Ride To The Garage Woodson," Big Henry the Travelin' Man and Larry "Knowledge Is King" Cook. I can't leave out new friends like the GWCC's Gene "Ops Director" Allen, Greg "Close the Show" Knight, Scott "MC with the Mostest" Baker, or Morris "In The Morning" Baxter at WCLK. Big respect to the many unnamed but unforgotten soldiers out there *still fighting to freelance...* and otherwise keep it moving. Please charge any omissions to old age and a fading memory.

Finally, a big head nod to all the unmentioned friends and peers I've accumulated over the years, so don't believe you're forgotten–my heart can sometimes work better than my brain. Personally speaking, I'll always cherish fond thoughts of the fallen soldiers I've run into, worked with or developed friendships with over the years - these talents have left me with very positive memories and great music: Jimmy Castor, George "Keyboard King" Duke, Sydney Darden (PolyGram), DJ Cosmo (Chit Chat, Club Rio), Cheba (The Piper), Lisa "Left Eye" Lopes, Teena Marie, Rick James, Kevin Parker (Rock -2-Def), LeBaron Taylor (Sony), Richard Tee (Mariah Carey), Luther Terry (PGD), Luther Vandross, Grover Washington, Jr., The Maestro: Barry White and so many others lost in more recent times.

**PEACE, ONE LOVE, and plenty of LYVATION:
THE VIBRATION OF LIFE, THROUGH MUSIC !**

EXERCISES

To jog your memory, try and recall what you have just read in the EXERCISES below.

CHAPTER 1 – MORE SPICES IN THE MIX

1a) What are some popular Mexican music styles? b) At least how many instruments are required to make up a Mariachi band? c) Who is known as the "Queen of Tejano music" and what city was her hometown?

CHAPTER 2 – WHAT HAPPENS IN BRAZIL

2a) What is the largest South American country and name some popular music styles that originate here. b) Name some popular music artists from this country. c) What African music styles influenced music from this country? d) What Fusion styles are popular here?

CHAPTER 3 – A TOUCH OF SPICE

3a) What city is also known as "The City That Care Forgot" and what music style has origins pointing there? b) What Vaudeville entertainer was admired by icons like Michael Jackson? c) Who is famous for performing Black Hillbilly-Mountain music and what year was he inducted into the Country Music Hall of Fame? d) What state did Taj Mahal come from and what style of music did he play? e) Name a few Black singers who performed Classical or Opera music.

CHAPTER 4 – HIGHER GROUND

4a) Name 3 singers who could act… or actresses that could sing. b) What Gospel music label made distribution deals with majors like A&M/RCA and Epic/Sony? c) Name 3 artists that were signed to this label.

CHAPTER 5 – FROM AN INVENTION COMES A MONOLITH

5a) What year did Thomas Edison invent the wax cylinder phonograph? b) What was Emile Berliner famous for and how was it different from the phonograph? c) What 2 record companies were dominant during the 1920s? d) What's the difference between a Jukebox and a Juke Joint? e) What's the difference between the AFM and RIAA? f) Who worked on the Manhattan Project and what radical change did he make to mixing consoles?

CHAPTER 6 – RISE OF THE MODERN AXE

6a) What is the Frying Pan and who was involved in its creation? b) Name 4 musicians who popularized the sound of early electric guitars. c) Name a few popular guitar brands. d) Name some popular guitar sound effects. e) What TV show was Roy Clark affiliated with? f) What 2 brothers founded Chess Records and in what city was it based?

CHAPTER 7 – CHESS & THE FUNNY FARM

7a) What female comedien was listed as "The Funniest Woman in the World" and what record label was she signed to? b) Name 3 popular "old school" comics. c) Name 3 laughter-based TV shows from the 70s. d) What did Slappy White "run away to join"? e) What record label was Eddie Murphy signed to? f) What Rap group was his brother Charlie a member of?

CHAPTER 8 – A GUITAR HEAD GIVES AN INSIDE VIEW

8a) What artist dropped his first name and had a huge hit about *Working In The Coal Mine*? b) Who is listed in Rolling Stone as the world's most popular all-time guitarist? c) Who was the first radio DJ inducted into the Rock-n-Roll Hall of Fame and what was he infamously known for? d) What does A&R stand for? e) Name 2 "big-boned" acts that were popular around the 40s and 50s. f) Who was a successful singer, manager, producer, concert promoter and industry trade magazine publisher?

CHAPTER 9 – FLIPPING THE SCRIPT

9a) Name the following radio formats: AC, AOR, CHR, MOR. b) What term was music made by Blacks referred to as? c) Name an act that switched between Folk, Country and Rock music. d) What is busking and name a few acts who did it. e) What type of music did Tim Pritchett promote and for what record label(s)? f) Name a big hit written by Dottie Rambo and covered by Whitney Houston.

CHAPTER 10 – ALL IN A DAY'S WORK

10a) What is "genre jumping" and name 3 acts that did it. b) What is a PRO and who benefits from their services? c) Name 3 music conferences that were held in Atlanta. d) What was the name of Bobby Poe's band, which 3 publications did he publish, and which one became a "cash cow"? e) Who was "Batman" and "Robin" and what sector of the entertainment industry did they soar in?

CHAPTER 11 – RUFFING IT UP IN THE "A"

11a) What record labels were Stephen Stone affiliated with and name 3 acts he helped make successful. b) What city was Ruffhouse Records based in? c) What turn of events occurred that initiated the sale of Ruffhouse to Sony Music? d) What weekly event did Stephen Stone oversee in Atlanta and what was the affiliated music act he was promoting during this time? e) What music artists are affiliated with Peach City Records? f) Name 3 acts affiliated with Walt C and Rock-2-Def Music. g) What music organization is Jimmy LeFavour associated with? h) What Atlanta-based film event is Bowlegged Lou and Full Force connected to?

ORGANIZATIONS / WEBSITES

AFM	afm.org
AFTRA	aftra.com
Artists Direct	artistdirect.com
ASCAP	ascap.com
BMI	bmi.com
Black America Web	blackamericaweb.com
Central Home	centralhome.com
E-How	ehow.com
Georgia Music Industry Association	gmia.org
Harry Fox agency	harryfox.com
Jazz History	jass.com
Jus' Blues Foundation	jusblues.org
It's Just Us Radio	itsjustusradioshow.com
NAMM	namm.com
NARAS	naras.com
NARIP	narip.com
NARM	narm.com
Nations Online	nationsonline.com
Reverbnation	reverbnation.com
RIAA	riaa.com
SESAC	sesac.com
Sounds of Knowledge	soundsofknowledge.com
You Tube	youtube.com

EXERCISE KEY

CHAPTER 1 – MORE SPICES IN THE MIX

1a) What are some popular Mexican music styles? Jarocho, Bolero, Banda, Narcocorrido, Mariachi, Norteno b) At least how many instruments are required to make up a Mariachi band? 8 c) Who is known as the "Queen of Tejano music" and what city was her hometown? Selena, Corpus Christie

CHAPTER 2 – WHAT HAPPENS IN BRAZIL

2a) What is the largest South American country and name some popular music styles that originate here. Brazil, Samba, Musica Popular Brasileira (MPB), Tropicalia, Clube da Esquina b) Name some popular music artists from this country. Milton Nascimento, Michel Freidenson, Maria Bethânia, Djavan c) What African music styles influenced music from this country? Lundu, Semba d) What Fusion styles are popular here? Bossa Nova , Samba de Roda , Neo-pagode, Samba de breque, Samba-enredo, Samba de Gafieira

CHAPTER 3 – A TOUCH OF SPICE

3a) What city is also known as "The City That Care Forgot" and what music style has origins pointing there? New Orleans, Jazz b) What Vaudeville entertainer was admired by icons like Michael Jackson? John Bubbles c) Who is famous for performing Black Hillbilly-Mountain music and what year was he inducted into the Country Music Hall of Fame? DeFord Bailey, 2005 d) What state did Taj Mahal come from and what style of music did he play? Massechussets, Blues e) Name a few Black singers who performed Classical or Opera music. Paul Robeson, Marian Anderson, Leontyne Price, Roland Hayes

CHAPTER 4 – HIGHER GROUND

4a) Name 3 singers who could act… or actresses that could sing. Pearl Bailey, Dorothy Dandridge, Lena Horne b) What Gospel music label made distribution deals with majors like A&M/RCA and Epic/Sony? Word Records c) Name some artists signed to this label. Al Green, Babbie Mason, Shirley Caesar, Helen Baylor

CHAPTER 5 – FROM AN INVENTION COMES A MONOLITH

5a) What year did Thomas Edison invent the wax cylinder phonograph? 1877 b) What was Emile Berliner famous for and how was it different from the phonograph? Gramophone, it played horizontal discs. c) What 2 record companies were dominant during the 1920s? Columbia, Victor d) What's the difference between a Jukebox and a Juke Joint? *Jukebox* – a machine that played records, *Juke Joint* – a small club where musicians or Jukeboxes could play live or recorded music e) What's the difference between the AFM and RIAA? AFM served musicians, RIAA served record labels f) Who worked on the Manhattan Project and what radical change did he make to mixing consoles? Tom Dowd, made linear faders

CHAPTER 6 – RISE OF THE MODERN AXE
6a) What is the Frying Pan and who was involved in its creation? An early electric guitar, George Beauchamp, Adolph Rickenbacker b) Name 4 musicians who popularized the sound of early electric guitars. Chet Atkins, Chuck Berry, BB King, Les Paul c) Name a few popular guitar brands. Fender, Gibson, Ibanez d) Name some popular guitar sound effects. Distortion, chorus, tremelo e) What TV show was Roy Clark affiliated with? Hee Haw f) What 2 brothers founded Chess Records and in what city was it based? Leonard and Phil Chess, Chicago

CHAPTER 7 – CHESS & THE FUNNY FARM
7a) What female comedian was listed as "The Funniest Woman in the World," what record label was she signed to? Moms Mabley, Chess b) Name 3 "old school" comics who made significant contributions to film or TV. Redd Foxx, Richard Pryor, Flip Wilson c) Name 3 laughter-based TV shows from the 70s. Sanford & Son, Flip Wilson Show, Smothers Brothers, Hee Haw d) What did Slappy White "run away to join"? The circus e) What record label was Eddie Murphy signed to? Columbia f) What Rap group was his brother Charlie a member of? K-9 Posse

CHAPTER 8 – A GUITAR HEAD GIVES AN INSIDE VIEW
8a) What artist dropped his first name and had a huge hit about *Working In The Coal Mine*? Lee Dorsey b) Who is listed in Rolling Stone as the world's most popular all-time guitarist? Jimi Hendrix c) Who was the first radio DJ inducted into the Rock-n-Roll Hall of Fame and what was he infamously known for? Alan Freed, payola d) What does A&R stand for? Artist & Repertoire e) Name 2 "big-boned" acts that were popular around the 40s and 50s. Fats Domino and Chubby Checker. f) Who was a successful singer, manager, producer, concert promoter and industry trade magazine publisher? Bobby Poe, Sr.

CHAPTER 9 – FLIPPING THE SCRIPT

9a) Name the following radio formats: AC, AOR, CHR, MOR. Adult Contemporary, Album Oriented Rock, Contemporary Hit Radio, Middle Of the Road b) What term was music made by Blacks referred to as? Race music. c) Name an act that switched between Folk, Country and Rock music. Bob Dylan. d) What is busking and name a few acts who did it. Playing on the streets for donations, Joan Baez, Bob Dylan, Joni Mitchell, Jimmy Buffett. What type of music did Tim Pritchett promote and for what record label(s)? Country, CBS/Sony/Columbia/Epic f) Name a big hit written by Dottie Rambo and covered by Whitney Houston. *I Go To the Rock.*

CHAPTER 10 – ALL IN A DAY'S WORK

10a) What is "genre jumping" and name 3 acts that did it. Switching from one music genre to another, Sam Cooke, Bob Dylan, Ray Charles b) What is a PRO and who benefits from their services? Performance Rights Organization, songwriters c) Name 3 popular music conferences of the 1980s/1990s held in Atlanta. Jack The Rapper, The Poe Convention, Black College Radio, Million Dollar Convention d) What was the name of Bobby Poe's band, which 3 publications did he publish, and which one became a "cash cow"? The Poe Kats, The Pop Music Survey, The Country Music Survey, The R&B Survey, The R&B Survey e) Who was "Batman" and "Robin" and what sector of the entertainment industry did they soar in? Promoter Ron Herbert, Disc Jockey Ray Mariner, radio

CHAPTER 11 – RUFFING IT UP IN THE "A"

11a) What record labels were Stephen Stone affiliated with and name 3 acts he helped make successful. Ruffhouse, Columbia, Kris Kross, Cypress Hill, The Fugees, Anything But Monday. b) What city was Ruffhouse Records based in? Philadelphia c) What turn of events occurred that initiated the sale of Ruffhouse to Sony Music? The Internet and file sharing/downloading d) What weekly event did Stephen Stone oversee in Atlanta and what was the affiliated music act he was promoting during this time? Party In The Park, Anything But Monday e) What music artists are affiliated with Peach City Records? Kimosha LeToi, Onny f) Name 3 acts affiliated with Walt C and Rock-2-Def Music. John Wayne Bailey, Babi Mac, Colt Ford, Sam Sneed, The Brew, DMC. g) What music organization is Chairman Jimmy LeFavour associated with? The Georgia Music Industry Association h) What Atlanta-based film event is Bowlegged Lou and Full Force connected to? Peachtree Village International Film Festival

REFERENCES

1 – More Spices In the Mix
wikipedia.com, Carlos Tejeda, selenaforever.com, Hispanic Business, Bernard Percy books: How to Grow A Child: A Child's Advice to Parents, Recapturing Technology For Education, Moments of Astonishment, Help Your Child In School, The Power of Creative Writing. New York Times, People magazine, People en Espanol, Bowlegged Lou/Full Force/forcefulworld.com, You Tube.

2 – What Happens In Brazil
Regina Cnossen, Silvia Camargo, princesslatremenda.com, reverbnation.com/princesslatremenda, facebook.com/tremendamusic, instagram/princesslatremenda#, or twitter.com/princesslat, michelfreidenson.com, mariabethania.com, You Tube, last.fm.com, allmusic.com, almirsaterbrasil.com.br, Google, Natan Reiter, Andrea Gomes, Guinness Book of World Records, birramirosa.com, ivetesangalo.com, djavan.com

3 – A Touch of Spice
jamaica-gleaner.com, democraticunderground.com, Spike Lee film – *When The Levees Broke*, bfitforlife.org, pbs.org, Eric Miller, jusblues.org, Keith Gantt/thehistoryofjazzmusic.com, Tom Davis/dr-love.com, usps.com, Inc. magazine (October 2009), blackbanjo.com, Charles K. Wolfe - *Hillbilly Fever: The Lost Tradition of Black String Bands*, David C. Morton/Charles K. Wolfe – *DeFord Bailey: A Black Star in Early Country Music*, Eileen Southern – *The Music of Black Americans*, *Martin Scorsese Presents The Blues*, tajblues.com, pinecone.org, Molefi Kete Asante – *100 Greatest African Americans*, mariananderson.org, wikianswers.com, Marva Griffin Carter – *Black Perspective in Music*, Christian Science Monitor, Rudolph Elie – Boston Herald, mayaangelou.com, rawtruthradio.net

4 – Higher Ground
mahaliajackson.us, mstcog.org, Alicia Myers - bet.com/video/.../monique2150-alicia-s1.html, myspace.com/aliciamyers07, www.facebook.com/AliciaMyersFanPage?sk=info, algreenmusic.com, helenbaylor.com, babbie.com, shirleycaesar.com, Terri Carroll - www.reverbnation.com/terricarroll, http://www.facebook.com/terricaroll1, lena-horne.com

5 – From An Invention Comes a Monolith
crave.cnet.com.uk, criteriastudios.com, tomdowd.com, riaa.org, ifpi.org

6 – Rise of the Modern Axe
misterguitar.us, blog.pandora.com, Rolling Stone magazine, kokotaylor.com, amberyholeata.com, You Tube

7- Chess & The Funny Farm
Nash Information Services

8 – A Guitar Head Gives An Inside View
Rolling Stone (July 2012), Hendrix by Chris Welch, jimihendrix.com, cbsnews.com, nola.com, chubbychecker.com, jointsjumpin.com, fatswaller.org, windmeupchuck.com, Bobby Poe Jr.

9 – Flipping The Script
Billboard magazine, popmusicrecords.com, margaritaville.com, reverbnation.com, rootsmusic.com, willienelson.com, ericclapton.com, NASAspaceflight.com, jjcale.com, coreysmith.com, dottierambo.net

10 – All In A Day's Work
Bobby Poe Jr., poekat.blogspot.com, popmusicrecords.com, National Music Publisher's Association, The Twilight Zone, Ron Herbert, Ray Mariner, bonusmusic.com, moneymarketron.com, reverbnation.com, You Tube

11 - Ruffing It Up In the "A"
Stephen Stone, Millenium Gate Museum, birramirosa.com, billchurchwrites.com, elliotholden.com, lyvationentertainment.com, reverbnation.com, lil-boy.com, corp.lilboy.com, ryan klos music, and1live.com, airbornemusic.com, gmia.org, Peachtree Village International Film Festival, International Soul Music Summit, atlantamuseumbar.com, kaye-ree.com, myspace.com/kekewyatt, Angela Moore/mypublicist.com, sheilarayecharles.com, thewilsonpickett.com, reigndropmusic.net, legendaryawards.com, wsbtv.com, forcefulworld.com

GLOSSARY

A

A&R – artist and repertoire, the meshing of songs with an artist
A-List – the cream of the crop, the best of the best
acclaim – to give honor to someone
accolades – credits or rewards for achieving a task
accordian – a keyboard instrument that makes sound by using air
acoustics – having to do with sound
adaptation – the making of an alternate version of something

AFM – American Federation of Musicians, an organization that protects the interests of member musicians
album – a collection of songs by an artist or artists
amalgamation – a mixture or combination of different things
amass – to collect a quantity of something
anomaly – outside of the norm
anthem – a phrase or short song about something cherished, like love for one's country
anti-establishment – being in an adversary or opposing position than those who make the rules
arrangement – in music, this is the order of how different parts are played, and the specific way they are performed
ASCAP – a performing rights organization that collects airplay income for its members
audacious – daring, bold
audio – related to sound
audio book – a book that is read by someone and recorded onto a medium such as CD
audio engineer – a sound technician that understands how to produce and process sounds
audiovisual – the combination of sounds with visuals like pictures or videos and lighting
augment – to extend
autograph – when a celebrity signs an object that is owned by a fan

B

backstage – the space behind a performance area where artists, guests and technical personnel interact before, during and after performances

ballad – a slow song that usually centers on themes of love

ban – not to allow a person or thing access to a public audience

barrage – a steady onslaught, bombardment

beach bum – a person who often frequents beaches and other places of leisure

bio – shortened term for biography

*biz*tory – the history of the music industry

black box – an electronic device used in sound/video production

BMI – Broadcast Music Incorporated, an organization that collects airplay income for its members

bootleg – not an original copy but a copy of a copy that is sold to unsuspecting buyers

brick and mortar store – a physical store that you walk into and make purchases from

broadcast – to transmit audio/video signals across a geographic area

broadcaster – one who transmits audio/video signals across a geographic area

busking – when artists perform for tourists in public places; they often lay hats or other items on the ground for people to put money in

C

Cabaret – a form of entertainment that includes singing, dancing and often takes place in theaters

cacophony – a bunch of dissonance caused by sounds that do not blend

Capitol/EMI Records – one of the original major labels based in Los Angeles

capitalistic – cash generation based on the theory of free enterprise

Caribbean music – multicultural music derived from the Caribbean region

Carnival – a huge celebration where people often wear colorful outfits, masks and headgear while dancing to live music

cash cow – anything that generates steady streams of income

catalog – archived materials such as books, music, magazines

catalyst – a medium used to channel something through

CGP – Certified Guitar Player, such as the term's originator, Chet Atkins

chain retailer – a retailer with multiple stores throughout a specific region

characteristic – a partial component of the total body

chartbound – about to make it to the charts

Churban – a format which plays a combination of all Contemporary Hit Urban music

collaboration – when several people get together to create something

College Rep – a student who represents a company while learning how to deploy its practices on a professional level

college market – the audience of a college community

compilation – a group of songs by the same or different artists

component – a small part that works with other parts of a bigger mechanism

composition – a song, what something is made up of

composure – poise, the way someone carries themselves in public

conflict of interest

connoisseur – someone who specializes in doing something

correlation – going along the lines of a concept

corroborate – to agree with

cover song – a new version of a pre-existing song

credo – philosophy

crossover – to expand a listener base outside of the core audience

crossover music – music that expands an acts fan base outside of the core audience, music that encompasses multiple genres

cue – a signal, to mark something in preparation for showing, telling, playing

cultureful – someone or something that attracts multiple creeds of people

cumulative – collective

cyberworld – activities taking place on the Internet, the realm of computers

D

déjà vu – the feeling of being somewhere before or knowing someone from another time

derivative – an offshoot from an original, being similar to something

digital device – an electronic unit that operates through binary data (0's and 1's)

direct-to-disc recording – a process where sounds are recorded and mixed straight to a disk in one step , instead of being recorded and then mixed over the course of two steps

discotheque – a nightclub where people go to dance, drink and socialize, mostly popular during the 60s and 70s

distortion – twisting or warping a sound or object

distribution – massive quantities of a product that a manufacturer puts into a pipeline of purchasers who then resell the product

distributor – gets large quantities of products from manufacturers and sells to purchasers who then resell the product

diurnal – taking place in the daytime hours

diversification –multiple streams of financials, products, services

divinity – spirituality

DJ (Disc Jockey) – an individual who plays recorded music for an audience

dominant – strong, more robust than what an object is around

dossier – a profile or detailed report

double-album – a group of songs spread across 2 CDs, tapes or vinyl discs

download – acquiring a file from another computer through the Internet

drive-time – the period of day where broadcasters have the most listeners, usually in the morning and afternoon when people are on the way to or from work

due diligence – taking the time to perform a task properly and by the rules

dynamics – the highs and lows between sounds in a piece of music

E

emancipation – setting free

emulate – to be similar to something or someone else

enamor – to charm or captivate

enlightenment – the establishment of higher awareness of a thought or concept

entree – a main dish on a menu

entrepreneur – one who seeks to generate an independent form of revenue as opposed to working for someone else

ESPY Awards

ethnomusicology

excel – to surpass expectations of an outcome

F

45 rpm – 45 revolutions per minute, a standard speed for vinyl records

fader – the linear part of a mixing console the adjusts the volume of an individual track or channel

falsetto – a high-pitched male voice

fan base – a group of supporters that listen and/or purchase the products of an artist

Ferrari – an expensive, high precision car most noted in the racing circuit

fiesta – a party

file sharing – to exchange data, video or music files between 2 or more people

finale – the last part of a show or performance

flamboyant – colorful or over the top, easy to be noticed

G

gaudy – flashy or extravagant

gazillion – immeasurable, an extremely high number

genre jumping – going from one music style to another

GPS – a satellite-based system used to track moving objects against global coordinates

guerilla marketing – an aggressive strategy used to drive attention towards an artist or product

Guinness Book of World Records – a book that lists people, places or things that supercedes the magnitude of all others in that class

guru – a master of a specialized skill or group of skills

H

hit-bound – a song or act that is on the way to rising up the charts

hoopla – commotion, a happening that focuses on a key object

hyped up – charged up, full of energy

I

i-sub – identified subject

immigrant – a settler from a foreign country

imminent – something that will definitely happen

independent label – a record company that is not owned by a large corporation

independent music – music produced and performed by local artists

independent retailer – a store usually owned by sole proprietors

indigenous – being of native origin to the land where different cultures, animals or plants thrive

induction – being placed into a certain category or group

infinite - unending

inimitable – not able to be imitated, unique

innovation – of original quality, new or improved

integrate – to mix or combine

interpretation – to analyze or explain

J

jingle – a short, catchy tune usually created to promote a product or service

joint venture – a partnership where multiple organizations produce something together

jukebox – a machine that plays pre-recorded music inexchange for money

K

Kaleidescope – having multiple textures and/or colors

L

lip-sync – to sing or perform a song/songs
lucrative – profitable, well-paid
lyrics – the written words to a song

M

mainstream – appealing to a wide audience
major label – a large, corporate-level record company, usually owned by a larger corporation
manipulate – to change an object in some way or another
manifestation – the coming about of something, becoming reality
Mariachi – a style of Mexican music from Jalisco
market segmentation – a market that is made up of a variety of sources
master CD – the disc from which commercial copies are made
master recording – the final recording from which copies are made from
mechanical royalties - money paid to writers for sales of their music
merchandising materials
metamorphosis – to change or transform from one state into a different one
microphone – an electronic device used to turn the sound of a voice or sound into an electronic signal that can be reproduced, transmitted, recorded or mixed
million seller – a product that is purchased by a million or more buyers
Mirosa Beer – an Italian lager beer owned by quadruple-platinum female act Anything But Monday
mixing console – an electronic device that combines sounds from multiple inputs into a unified mix, in mono or stereo (left/right)
MP3 – a music file which is compressed for space on devices and ease of use over the Internet
momentum – drive or force of an object while in motion
mono – a single channel of audio
monologue – a speech given by a host, usually not accompanied by music
monumental – of major importance, not to be forgotten
movie soundtrack – a release made up of music featured in a film
multifaceted – able to perform multiple tasks in different areas
multilingual – of multiple languages
multimedia – the combination of audio, video, lights, photography and art

multitrack – the use of more than one track for multiple channels of simultaneous live or recorded sound

musicana criticallicus – a condition where DJs and listeners play or listen to heavy doses of specific hit songs

N

national radio promotion – promoting a song across multiple channels in multiple cities across the country

Native American – an Indigenous group of people that evolved across the western hemisphere

nemesis – opponent

New Jack Swing – a music R&B/dance style popular during the late 80s to early 90s

new millennium – the period of time that marks the beginning of a new century

nocturnal – taking place in the night-time hours

non-secular – music relative to praise and worship

nostalgia – popular, being of a classic nature from a prior era

novelty – not being mainstream, popularized by people with more eccentric tastes

O

oeuvre – a creative piece of work

Old School – music from the 70s, 80s and 90s

osmosis – changing from one substance to another

overdrive – to push to the limit

P

parody records – humorous records that made fun of something or someone

parameter – a section or part of something

payola – unaccounted for cash that went from record labels/promoters to radio DJs in exchange for playing particular songs to generate chart action and sales

performing rights organization

perpetuate – bring about, enable

philanthropy – having care or generous compassion for others

phonograph – turntable, a vinyl record player

phonautograph

phonautogram – a recording made by the phonautograph

photogenic – a person, place or thing that's pleasurable to look at and take photos, film or video footage of

plateau – reaching of a certain level

platinum – sales in excess of one million units

playlist – a list used by radio stations to determine the top tracks they use

plethora – a wide variety

posthumous – after death

prestigious – being influential

Program Director – the person who makes decisions on what gets aired

prodigious – extraordinary

programming – the order of content as played on a radio station over 24 hour periods

promotional visit – when a celebrity comes to a city to promote their latest project

protocol – a system used to esatblish order in operations

publicity – exposing a person, idea or thing to a wider audience

publishing rights – owning the claim to copyright, meaning no one can copy or sell it without permission

Q

quantify – to expand or multiply

Quiet Storm – a programming format that plays what can be coined as Easy Listening R&B

Quintessential – to represent the best in class

R

radio personality – a radio announcer who plays recorded music while providing commentary and shared opinions of news, health, political or controversial subject matter

radio playlist – a list of 10, 20, 40 or more songs that are played during certain programming timeframes

radio promotion – the way a record label delivers new music to radio stations in order to generate airplay for artists signed to its roster

record store – now a thing of the past due to the Internet, record stores housed music (vinyl, tape, CDs, posters, etc.) for sale to customers

recording studio – one or more rooms specifically designed for music and sound recording

regional distributor – a company that buys from manufacturers and sells to retailers/customers in a specific region

regional radio promotion – promoting a song across multiple channels in multiple cities across a specific geographic areas rendition – a different version of something that was previously created

repertoire – an archive or catalog

reproduction – to duplicate something

resurgance – a cycle that makes certain styles popular over a periodic timetable

retrospective – a linear look at the accomplishments of a person, group or organization

revenue – a stream of income generated from sale of products, services, property, etc.

RIAA – Recording Industry Association of America, an organization that protects the rights of its members

robust – full of zest, strong enough to endure significant stress

royalty – a revenue stream based off airplay, sales of a product or idea

S

satellite radio – a method of radio broadcast that uses satellites to send signals across wide geographic areas

secular – non-spiritual music

show tune – a song made specifically to be performed in a theatrical production

simultaneous– taking place at the same time, in unison

singlewomanly – the accomplishments of a woman all by herself

Smooth Jazz – a relaxing style of Jazz

sonic – having to do with sound

sound bite – a small snippet of sound that offers a sample of what the entire piece sounds like

sound check – the process of testing all microphones and audio lines to ensure that all connections are intact and the performer(s) has quality sound

sound design – technical mapping out and structure of all components that will be used to achieve a specific audio requirement

sound effects

sound reinforcement - when aspects of the sound are enhanced or changed after the primary recording was made

Spaniard – a person who originates from Spain

standing-room-only – a venue where no additional seating is possible; the best way to see an event here is by standing up

starving artist – an artist that struggles to survive through creations of their own making

stereo – being stereophonic as in having two channels, left & right audio

stereotypical – clichéd, taking an pre-judgmental perspective streaming – the broadcast or playback of an audio or video program over the Internet

street promotion – the act of promoting a song, act or product at a grass-roots level

streetwise – aware of how to maneuver in the streets among shady as well as legitimate people

studio musician – a musician that primarily earns a living by playing his instrument in recording studios

subsidize

SUMC – the *Southeast Urban Music Conference*, founded by Tony Baraka during the mid-90s, this conference discusses issues in the music industry and promotes new acts

Superior Intellect – a high degree of mental energy relative to increased knowledge

supernatural – beyond the limits of normal human understanding

synchronization royalties

T

tandem – together with, in alignment with each other

tempo – a steady pulse or beat

terrestrial – geographic areas of the world and the airspace above it

the digital age – present day, the part of history where digital devices became a dominant part of society

the Nashville Sound – a smooth Country music sound that primarily includes sliding, acoustic and electric guitars, drums, fiddles, keyboards

the recording process – a series of production techniques that allow for creation of songs

the underworld – a part of society that functions outside of traditional customs and laws

Top 40 Radio – a format that utilizes a playlist of 40 songs to keep listeners tuned in

trajectory – the angle of a climb or descent

transform – to change from one physical ---- to another

transition – to move from one location or form to another

turntable – a device used to play back sound/music embedded in records

U

ukelele – a small guitar often used to define the Hawaiian and Folk sound

unison – taking place at the same time

unsub – unidentified subject

V

Vaudeville – a variety show that features singers, actors, poets, musicians, comics, etc.

vinyl disc – also called a record, has grooves with music embedded, played back by a turntable using a needle to reproduce the sound in the grooves

virtuoso – someone who is good at what they do

W

wholesaler – an entity that buys directly from manufacturers for sale to retailers or the general public

win-win – a situation where different parties involved each benefit

wireless – using air and not cables or wires to transmit data

World Music – music made with a multicultural fan base in mind

INDEX

ABOUT THE AUTHOR

A valedictorian and contributing author to nationally published Bernard Percy books during elementary and junior high schools, L.A. Jackson finished high school at James Madison in Brooklyn. He then shipped off to Los Angeles City College, transferred and graduated from Georgia State University in Atlanta, before the writing bug really hit. An internship led to a 10 year career with CBS Records/Sony Music, where he worked with most acts on the label, implemented dozens of sales/marketing/promotion campaigns, received gold/platinum albums, numerous awards, and traveled across the U.S., Canada and Jamaica attending industry events.

L.A. became a recording studio owner, audiovisual technician and manager for a global AV company (TAVS), and presently owns media company MKM Multimedia Works. In 2001, he was an executive-producer on the Million Mom March's *Atlanta Artists Against Gun Violence* compilation CD; it featured top Atlanta-based recording acts. In 2002, L.A. secured an international commercial with The GAP for Grammy Award winning Arrested Development's elder and spiritual advisor, Baba Oje. More projects and music-related books are underway as L.A. initiates his '6 books in 5 years' plan, starting with MUSICOLOGY 2101: A QUICK START GUIDE TO MUSIC "BIZ" HISTORY (now available online at places like Createspace, www.createspace.com/4142047 plus Amazon, http://www.amazon.com/MUSICOLOGY-2101-HISTORY-SERIES-ebook/dp/B00B0YI37W and Google Play, http://books.google.com/books/about/Musicology_2101.html?id=qlMTJO-dGlwC).

CREDENTIALS

Founder MKM Multimedia Works LLC, Musicology book series, Executive Producer—Exposer compilation series, Columbia/Epic/Def Jam/CBS Records/Sony Music (1984-1994), Bar-Red Entertainment, Baba Oje Management Board, Million Mom March Foundation, National Association of Record Industry Professionals (NARIP.com), International Gaming Developers Association (IGDA.org), Georgia Entertainment Association (GEA.org), Jus' Blues Foundation (jusblues.org), Georgia Music Industry Association (GMIA.org), Peach City Records, Georgia State University, Commercial Music & Recording, Business concentration (graduated 1987, B.A.), Los Angeles City College, Computer Technology, Electronic Music, Broadcasting (1980)

$19.99
ISBN 978-0-578-15469-5
51999>
9 780578 154695

www.ingramcontent.com/pod-product-compliance
Lightning Source LLC
Chambersburg PA
CBHW062035090426
42740CB00016B/2914